iPhone SDK Application Development

Bill,
Don't hock this on eBay.

Other resources from O'Reilly

Related titles
Android Application
   Development
iPhone Forensics
iPhone Hacks™
iPhone: The Missing Manual

iPhone Open Application
   Development
Learning Cocoa with
   Objective-C

oreilly.com
oreilly.com is more than a complete catalog of O'Reilly books. You'll also find links to news, events, articles, weblogs, sample chapters, and code examples.

oreillynet.com is the essential portal for developers interested in open and emerging technologies, including new platforms, programming languages, and operating systems.

Conferences
O'Reilly brings diverse innovators together to nurture the ideas that spark revolutionary industries. We specialize in documenting the latest tools and systems, translating the innovator's knowledge into useful skills for those in the trenches. Visit *conferences.oreilly.com* for our upcoming events.

Safari Bookshelf (*safari.oreilly.com*) is the premier online reference library for programmers and IT professionals. Conduct searches across more than 1,000 books. Subscribers can zero in on answers to time-critical questions in a matter of seconds. Read the books on your Bookshelf from cover to cover or simply flip to the page you need. Try it today for free.

iPhone SDK Application Development

Jonathan Zdziarski

O'REILLY®

Beijing · Cambridge · Farnham · Köln · Sebastopol · Taipei · Tokyo

iPhone SDK Application Development
by Jonathan Zdziarski

Copyright © 2009 Jonathan Zdziarski. All rights reserved.
Printed in the United States of America.

Published by O'Reilly Media, Inc., 1005 Gravenstein Highway North, Sebastopol, CA 95472.

O'Reilly books may be purchased for educational, business, or sales promotional use. Online editions are also available for most titles (*http://safari.oreilly.com*). For more information, contact our corporate/institutional sales department: (800) 998-9938 or *corporate@oreilly.com*.

Editor: Andy Oram
Production Editor: Sumita Mukherji
Proofreader: Amy Thomson

Indexer: Joe Wizda
Cover Designer: Karen Montgomery
Interior Designer: David Futato
Illustrator: Jessamyn Read

Printing History:

January 2009:   First Edition.

RepKover.
This book uses RepKover™, a durable and flexible lay-flat binding.

ISBN: 978-0-596-15405-9

[M]

1231944724

Table of Contents

Foreword

As a longtime participant in the iPhone hacking community, I have often been asked just what I think about the iPhone SDK. I'll take a moment to reward those of you who have purchased this book with an answer. In short, Apple's iPhone SDK adds some very nice high-level functionality to clean up an otherwise hideous mess. Deep underneath the SDK's comfy pillows rests a very disorganized and poorly designed set of frameworks, but some of that ugly was also very functional in areas where the SDK is not. The SDK is certainly good enough to write a high-quality, functional application for the AppStore (if it weren't, I wouldn't be writing about it). The interfaces provided by the SDK are written well enough for most good developers to design good software, but most people are unaware of the functionality that *isn't* available to them. For those who cut their teeth in the open source world, the iPhone SDK is still a point of contention.

If you're unfamiliar with the politics surrounding the SDK, there are two sets of developer interfaces: those provided by the SDK, and those that Apple uses. While there is some overlap between the two, I wrote about many classes and frameworks you've never heard of in my book *iPhone Open Application Development* (O'Reilly). You've never heard of them because they are not available in the SDK. Many of us in the early iPhone hacking community discovered them by breaking into the iPhone's operating system directly. Throughout many weeks of dumping symbol tables, classes, and experimenting by trial and error, we mapped out the genome for the iPhone's user interface kit as well as many other frameworks, including many that are now private. It is these low-level APIs that developers use when building iPhone software with the open source tool chain, and the same low-level APIs that we found many of Apple's applications taking advantage of to do things the SDK didn't quite allow for.

These low-level APIs are what give open tool chain developers an edge over SDK developers, and in my opinion, offer a better development framework than Apple's SDK. Many of the frameworks on the device have been quietly privatized, making their functionality unavailable to AppStore developers. Not coincidentally, much of this functionality appears to be what is crucial for building applications that Apple might consider to be competitive with their own preloaded software. Of these, the greatest offenses include restricting the Core Surface framework, which would have given SDK developers the ability to render raw pixels directly to a screen layer and incorporate the use of graphics accelerators. Without this framework available, you'll have a difficult time squeezing performance out of applications that require 2D rendering, such as custom movie players, video recorders, or high performance 2D games like my free Nintendo emulator. This is also a key framework needed in order to write applications such as Flash or Java™ with any degree of performance. Another set of APIs you'll find missing is the ability to interface with iTunes music. This is why the SDK version of Nate True's *Tap Tap Revolution* no longer picks songs from your iTunes library, and why you'll only find cool music applications like *SynchStep* (which plays music to the rhythm of your steps) in a third-party repository. Even simple functionality, such as the ability to run in the background or display status bar icons, exists only when using APIs that are restricted from the AppStore. Needless to say, the open source iPhone compiler lets you do many things that the SDK cannot, which some would speculate is designed to ensure Apple will forever have the competitive edge in the iPhone software market.

On the other side of things, the SDK offers something that open source was never much good at accruing: large wads of cash. Developers seem to be able to swallow their distaste for Apple's policies after considering the obscene amount of money there is to be had from an audience as large as that of iTunes. The AppStore financially rewards innovators who are willing to drink the Kool-Aid. The potential for revenue provided by the AppStore gives developers a significant advantage over the open development community, even if your application does turn out slightly crippled.

From a solely technical perspective, the open source compiler can build applications using either the SDK interfaces or the low-level "private" interfaces, depending on which set of headers you care to use. The same is true of Xcode: the private, undocumented interfaces can be easily imported into your project by simply pointing the SDK at the right headers. This gives you four possible combinations for developing applications.

What it really comes down to is this: if you are looking to deploy applications in the AppStore, you must play by Apple's rules. Apple will not accept an application that uses private interfaces or frameworks. Apple has reportedly even rejected flashlight applications that overstepped their bounds and had the nerve to try to adjust the display's brightness on their own. If you're a commercial developer or designing software to deploy on your enterprise, there really is only one viable path for you, and that's to use the sanctioned APIs documented in this book. If, however, you're reading this book as an open source enthusiast, and consider your code to be more of an art form, you may be more interested in writing software as it was intended to be written—without shackles and sandboxes. In this case, I recommend you consider using not only the APIs you'll find in this book, but to further expand your knowledge into the many undocumented APIs and frameworks available. The open source community was the first to build a public compiler and over-the-air, online community software repository for the iPhone, and it welcomes beautiful, full-featured applications.

The iPhone development world is currently suffering from a split personality. Both camps are growing, but polarizing. Many developers have become disillusioned by the number of restrictions placed on the SDK, and argue that it is incompatible with popular open source licenses (such as the GPL), or frequently rant that there would be no need for hacking the iPhone if Apple only opened up their wonderful device.

My desire is for Apple to truly open up the iPhone's operating system, rather than continuing to impose such suspicious and seemingly monopolistic restrictions on the SDK. While the iPhone is by and large the most revolutionary mobile device in history, Apple runs the risk of letting a strong desire to control the market harm both developers and consumers. The mere fact that I can purchase multiple handguns with less hassle than I can an iPhone speaks volumes to Apple's fascination with control. This same obstinate attitude has troubled many developers trying to design for this amazing platform.

It is my opinion that the creativity and innovation of intelligent developers should not be subject to the whims of device manufacturers. Code is a form of expression for many, and to impose censorship on the freedom of expression only seeks to punish innovation when it does not originate from within Apple's campus.

In spite of this, I continue to be awed by the spectacular nature of Apple's products, and I applaud their innovation. Not only is the SDK very well thought out, but Apple's latest version of Objective-C is one of the most elegant and developer-centric languages I've seen to date. Apple is capable of creating beautiful things, and nearly everything about the iPhone is quite beautiful. My only hope is that Apple continues in its success by being the most creative, and not by squelching innovation out elsewhere.

—Jonathan Zdziarski
January 2009

Preface

Enterprise developers everywhere cheered when Apple announced its official SDK in March 2008. The long-awaited development environment finally allowed developers to design commercial applications for the iPhone, and provided a distribution channel capable of reaching every single iPhone user. This book covers the officially sanctioned Apple SDK and subsequent APIs used to develop applications specifically tailored to the AppStore.

The Apple SDK represented great progress in mobile software development, and provided a fantastic open door for the quintessential "overnight millionaire" to walk through. As an SDK developer, you have a direct channel to millions of end users who have the opportunity to instantly purchase your product. The long-awaited removal of Apple's NDA further helped to culminate a significant enthusiasm for this fantastic device and business model. There is no doubt a great opportunity for innovation and profit with the iPhone SDK.

This enthusiasm must be tempered with realistic expectations, however. As an iPhone developer, you'll be designing on a platform that is still considered by and large a closed device. Your applications will run in a restrictive sandbox to prevent certain types of access, and Apple has restricted you from using many private APIs that can access more powerful resources on the device. You'll need to be aware of your environment's limitations so you don't burn hours on code with incorrect assumptions about what you can do.

While many see a pair of fuzzy handcuffs restraining the SDK, it is clearly a powerful enough platform to write good quality games and applications. The SDK introduces easy-to-use objects that are overlaid on the iPhone's more complex low-level frameworks. This makes coding things like user interfaces, global positioning queries, and even settings bundles a much less time-consuming task than with other development environments. Because of this, developers can focus on the more important aspects of a project. With just a few lines, you can create many different types of user interfaces, work with 3D animations, and mix audio sound. This book introduces you to the iPhone development paradigm and walks you through the frameworks that are key to designing full-featured software on the iPhone.

Audience for This Book

This book is geared toward novice and experienced developers writing applications for the iPhone. You'll need some prior knowledge of coding to find this book useful. The iPhone development environment uses Objective-C, which you'll be introduced to immediately. The good news is that you can also use C and C++ in your applications, so anyone with preexisting knowledge should be able to pick up Objective-C pretty quickly. This book isn't a full introduction to Objective-C, but it will help you get your feet wet with a mini primer and countless complete code examples.

As you read this, consider that there is another side to the device that is not covered in this book. Many low-level objects and frameworks are off-limits to the SDK, but have been taken advantage of by the iPhone hacking community. You won't find any of these unsanctioned APIs in this book, with the exception of a few clearly marked examples, so as not to confuse you about what you can and can't use. If you're using the SDK to write applications that you will use internally, or if you'd like to get a better understanding of how the iPhone's plumbing works on a lower level, you may wish to complement this book with a copy of *iPhone Open Application Development*, Second Edition (O'Reilly). The two books combined will not only give you an understanding of what you can do, but also what you can't, as well as the kinds of functionality that you will inevitably compete with in the applications written by the hacking community.

Organization of the Material

Chapter 1, *Getting Started with the iPhone SDK*, explains how to get up and running with the iPhone SDK, and how to build and install sample applications.

Chapter 2, *Interface Builder: Xcode's GUI for GUIs*, introduces you to the Interface Builder, a WYSIWYG tool used to design proprietary iPhone user interfaces.

Chapter 3, *Introduction to UI Kit*, introduces you to the UI Kit framework and teaches you how to design basic user interface elements.

Chapter 4, *Multi-Touch Events and Geometry*, explains event handling and basic geometric structures.

Chapter 5, *Layer Programming with Quartz Core*, shows you how to create and manage layers and transformations using Core Graphics and Quartz Core.

Chapter 6, *Making a Racket: Audio Toolbox and AVFoundation*, shows you how to mix and play sound files using AVFoundation and how to record and play back digital sound streams using the Audio Toolbox framework.

Chapter 7, *Network Programming with CFNetwork*, illustrates network programming with the CFNetwork framework.

Chapter 8, *Getting a Fix: Core Location*, introduces you to the Core Location framework and shows you how to interact with the iPhone's GPS.

Chapter 9, *Address Book Frameworks*, explains the Address Book APIs and how to query and display contacts.

Chapter 10, *Advanced UI Kit Design*, covers the more advanced classes of UI Kit.

Chapter 11, *Application Settings*, explains how to read and write application preferences and work with property lists.

Chapter 12, *Cover Flow*, explains how to construct a Cover Flow style album flipper.

Chapter 13, *Page Flicking*, illustrates page flicking and how to flip between multiple views like pages in a book.

Chapter 14, *Media Player Framework*, explains how to add movie players to your application.

Conventions Used in This Book

The following typographical conventions are used in this book:

Plain text
> Used for menu titles, menu options, menu buttons, and keyboard accelerators.

Italic
> Indicates new terms, URLs, filenames, Unix utilities, and command-line options.

`Constant width`
> Indicates the contents of files, the output from commands, variables, types, classes, namespaces, methods, values, objects, and generally anything found in programs.

`Constant width bold`
> Shows commands or other text that should be typed literally by the user, and parts of code or files highlighted to stand out for discussion.

`Constant width italic`
> Shows text that should be replaced with user-supplied values.

 This icon signifies a tip, suggestion, or general note.

 This icon indicates a warning or caution.

Using Code Examples

This book is here to help you get your job done. In general, you may use the code in this book in your programs and documentation. You do not need to contact us for permission unless you're reproducing a significant portion of the code. For example, writing a program that uses several chunks of code from this book does not require permission. Selling or distributing a CD-ROM of examples from O'Reilly books *does* require permission. Answering a question by citing this book and quoting example code does not require permission. Incorporating a significant amount of example code from this book into your product's documentation *does* require permission.

We appreciate, but do not require, attribution. An attribution usually includes the title, author, publisher, and ISBN. For example: "*iPhone SDK Application Development* by Jonathan Zdziarski. Copyright 2009 Jonathan Zdziarski, 978-0-596-15405-9."

If you feel your use of code examples falls outside fair use or the permission given above, feel free to contact us at *permissions@oreilly.com*.

The code examples in this book have been written and verified with Apple's iPhone SDK versions 2.1 and 2.2. As newer versions are released by Apple, minor changes to APIs could possibly be introduced. Be sure to consult any release notes included with newer versions of Apple's SDK, and consult Apple's *iPhone OS Programming Guide* for any new developments.

Legal Disclaimer

The technologies discussed in this publication, the limitations on these technologies that the technology and content owners seek to impose, and the laws actually limiting the use of these technologies are constantly changing. Thus, some of the projects and instructions described in this publication may not work, may cause unintended harm to equipment or systems on which they are used, or may be inconsistent with applicable law or user agreements. Your use of these projects is at your own risk, and O'Reilly Media, Inc. disclaims responsibility for any damage or expense resulting from their use. In any event, you should take care that your use of these projects does not violate any applicable laws, including copyright laws.

Safari® Books Online

 When you see a Safari® Books Online icon on the cover of your favorite technology book, that means the book is available online through the O'Reilly Network Safari Bookshelf.

Safari offers a solution that's better than e-books. It's a virtual library that lets you easily search thousands of top tech books, cut and paste code samples, download chapters, and find quick answers when you need the most accurate, current information. Try it for free at *http://safari.oreilly.com*.

We'd Like to Hear from You

Please address comments and questions concerning this book to the publisher:

O'Reilly Media, Inc.
1005 Gravenstein Highway North
Sebastopol, CA 95472
800-998-9938 (in the United States or Canada)
707-829-0515 (international or local)
707-829-0104 (fax)

We have a web page for this book, where we list errata, examples, and any additional information. You can access this page at:

http://www.oreilly.com/catalog/9780596154059

To comment or ask technical questions about this book, send email to:

bookquestions@oreilly.com

For more information about our books, conferences, Resource Centers, and the O'Reilly Network, see our website at:

http://www.oreilly.com

Acknowledgments

Special thanks to Layton Duncan, Brian Whitman, and others who have shared their nifty discoveries with me. Thanks also to Jonathan Hohle, Dallas Brown, Brad O'Hearne, and John Draper for their technical reviews of this book and suggestions to help make it even better. Finally, thanks to my wife for not murdering me in my sleep as I obsessed about this book.

CHAPTER 1

Getting Started with the iPhone SDK

If you're new to the Macintosh world, you might be surprised to find that applications don't come in the form of *.exe* files. The excellent design for which Apple is known in its hardware and graphics extends to its software architecture as well, and includes the way applications are laid out in the file system. The same strategy used in Apple desktop systems has been carried over into the iPhone.

Apple has adopted the practice of creating modular, self-contained applications with their own internal file resources. As a result, installing an application is as easy as simply dragging it into your applications folder; deleting it as easy as dragging it into the trash. In this chapter, we'll look at the structure of iPhone applications. You'll also get up and running with the iPhone SDK, explore the Apple IDE known as Xcode, and learn how to install applications on your iPhone. Finally, we'll introduce you to the Objective-C language and enough of its idiosyncrasies to make an easy transition from C or C++.

Anatomy of an Application

Apple came up with an elegant way to contain applications in their operating system. As OS X is a Unix-based platform, Apple wanted to make it adhere to basic Unix file conventions, and so the resource forks of olde were no longer sufficient (or efficient, for that matter). The challenge was to design a structure that would allow an application to remain self-contained while surviving on a file system that didn't believe in cheapening its architecture with proprietary workarounds. The answer came from an older ancestor of Mac OS X named NeXT, which treated an application as a *bundle* represented within a *directory*. The bundle concept introduces an approach to group application resources, binaries, and other related files.

If you look at any Mac application, you'll find that the *.app* extension denotes not a file, but a directory. This is the application's *program directory*. Inside it is an organized structure containing resources the application needs to run, property lists containing information about the application, and the application's executable binaries. The iPhone SDK builds the binary executable for your program and deposits files it needs into this program directory structure. So to build a complete application, it's up to the developer to tell the Xcode IDE which supporting files should be installed. Applications are executed from within a *sandbox* on the iPhone. A sandbox is a restricted environment that prevents applications from accessing unauthorized resources. One of its functions is to prohibit any read or write operations outside of the application's designated home directory. Everything your application needs to run must be self-contained within this directory structure. In addition to this, your application won't know where it is installed, as a unique identifier is added to your application's path at each installation. You'll only be able to find your path by using functions like `NSHomeDirectory` and classes like `NSBundle`, which you'll learn about in the coming chapters.

Each iPhone application has its own home directory containing *Library* and *Documents* folders, and a *tmp* directory for storing temporary files. The program directory for an iPhone application is much less structured than desktop Mac applications, and all of the application's resources are stored in the root of the *.app* program folder. The following is an example of a single application's complete home directory, as it might appear on the iPhone's file system:

```
drwxr-xr-x     mobile  mobile   Documents/
drwxr-xr-x     mobile  mobile   Library/
drwxr-xr-x         mobile  mobile    Preferences/
drwxr-xr-x     mobile  mobile   MyApp.app/
    drw-r--r--     mobile  mobile    _CodeSignature
    -rw-r--r--     mobile  mobile    Default.png
    -rw-r--r--     mobile  mobile    icon.png
    -rw-r--r--     mobile  mobile    Info.plist
    -rwxr-xr-x     mobile  mobile    MyApp
    -rw-r--r--     mobile  mobile    pie.png
    -rw-r--r--     mobile  mobile    PkgInfo
    -rw-r--r--     mobile  mobile    ResourceRules.plist
drwxr-xr-x     mobile  mobile    tmp/
```

This list reflects a very basic simple iPhone application named *MyApp*:

Documents
> A special folder in which your application may store documents created by the user. It will not be shared with any other applications' documents.

Library
> A folder in which your application may store settings and other resources created after installation. Inside this folder is another folder named *Preferences*, which will store your application's preferences. You'll learn how to access them in Chapter 11.

MyApp.app
> The application folder, this represents the actual application. This directory will contain your executable binary and all supporting resources your application relies on.

_CodeSignature

A directory containing code signatures for each file bundled with your application. These ensure that the application has not been modified from its original form. All applications must be signed in order to run on the iPhone.

Default.png

A PNG (*portable network graphics*) image file containing the application's default title screen. When the user runs your application, the iPhone animates it to give the appearance that it's zooming to the front of the screen. The application's *Default.png* file is loaded and scaled up until it fills the entire screen. This 320×480 image zooms to the front and remains on the screen until the application finishes launching. Applications generally use a solid black or white background, a logo, or a background resembling the title screen that an application will display after initializing.

icon.png

A PNG image containing the application's icon. The icon is displayed on the iPhone's home screen. Apple recommends that icons be 57×57 pixels. This file can be named anything you like, as long as it's specified in the *Info.plist* manifest, explained below. Icons are automatically given a "shine" when displayed, so you won't need to worry about drawing rounded edges or lighting effects on your icon.

Info.plist

A property list containing information about the application. This includes the name of its binary executable and a bundle identifier, which is read when the application is launched. You'll see an example property list later in this chapter.

MyApp

The actual binary executable that is called when the application is launched. This is what Xcode outputs when it builds your application. Xcode will automatically place the binary in the application folder when performing a *Build and Go*.

pie.png

An example image resource used by this sample application. The iPhone framework provides many methods to fetch resources, so you don't need to access them directly by path. This is consistent with Apple's effort to keep applications self-contained. The Xcode IDE will take any files you've dragged into your project's *Resources* folder (on the desktop) and will place them into the application's program folder (on the iPhone) when the project is installed.

PkgInfo

This file contains the eight-byte filetype descriptor for the application. The first four bytes should read APPL, followed by the bundle signature identifier. This is explained in the next section.

Underneath Xcode

Before delving into the many great benefits provided to you by Xcode, it would be healthy to understand the basics of how an application is assembled. In the old world of iPhone hacking, this meant rolling your own application by hand. In Xcode, this is done for you. Here's what's going on behind the scenes.

If you were building an application by hand, you'd put together a skeleton *.app* directory to contain it. The skeleton provides all of the information necessary for the iPhone to acknowledge the existence of your application as a bundle so it can be run from the iPhone's home screen.

This book presents many fully functional code examples whose skeleton is built automatically by Xcode. After compiling the example, Xcode creates the example's directory structure inside the project's *build* directory and places its binary and resources into the application folder. If you were doing this by hand, creating the directory would be easy enough:

```
$ mkdir MyExample.app
```

Next, Xcode copies a property list into the application folder to describe the application and how to launch it. The *Info.plist* file expresses this information in XML format and looks like this:

```
<?xml version="1.0" encoding="UTF-8"?>
<!DOCTYPE plist PUBLIC "-//Apple//DTD PLIST 1.0//EN" "http://www.apple.com
/DTDs/PropertyList-1.0.dtd">
<plist version="1.0">
<dict>
        <key>CFBundleDevelopmentRegion</key>
        <string>en</string>
        <key>CFBundleDisplayName</key>
        <string>${PRODUCT_NAME}</string>
        <key>CFBundleExecutable</key>
        <string>${EXECUTABLE_NAME}</string>
        <key>CFBundleIconFile</key>
        <string>icon.png</string>
        <key>CFBundleIdentifier</key>
        <string>com.yourcompany.${PRODUCT_NAME:identifier}</string>
        <key>CFBundleInfoDictionaryVersion</key>
        <string>6.0</string>
        <key>CFBundleName</key>
        <string>${PRODUCT_NAME}</string>
        <key>CFBundlePackageType</key>
        <string>APPL</string>
        <key>CFBundleResourceSpecification</key>
        <string>ResourceRules.plist</string>
        <key>CFBundleSignature</key>
        <string>????</string>
        <key>CFBundleVersion</key>
        <string>1.0</string>
        <key>LSRequiresIPhoneOS</key>
        <true/>
```

```
    </dict>
    </plist>
```

The most important keys are CFBundleDisplayName, CFBundleExecutable, CFBundleIcon File, CFBundleIdentifier, and CFBundleName. The CFBundleExecutable property is of particular importance, as it specifies the filename of the binary executable within the folder. This is the file that is executed when your application is launched—the output from your compiler. Xcode normally sets this automatically, but you can override this behavior.

The iPhone's home screen runs as an application, called Springboard, which is similar to the Finder on a Mac desktop. The Springboard application, as well as much of the iPhone's application layer, likes to refer to applications using a special identifier instead of its display name; for example *com.yourcompany.tictactoe*. The value assigned to the CFBundleIdentifier key specifies the unique identifier you'd like to give to your application. Whenever your application is launched, it will be referenced using this identifier. Because the name must be unique among all other applications on the iPhone, it's common practice to incorporate the URL of your website.

The application's *icon.png* and *Default.png* files are also copied into the program folder, if they exist. If you leave these out, the iPhone will use the worst-looking images possible to serve as default images for both. Make sure to create and include images with these names when you publish your own applications to make them look professional.

Were this application signed by Xcode, it would be good enough to run. In the next section, you'll install the iPhone SDK on your desktop, which will perform all of these steps for you when you build an application—and sign the build with your developer key.

You'll get started compiling example applications as early as Chapter 3. In the coming chapters, you'll build many examples. The examples provided in this book generally do not need any additional resources, however a few will use your Internet connection to download sample images or other files.

 You can download the code examples in this book from the book's online repository at *http://www.oreilly.com/catalog/9780596154059*.

Installing the iPhone SDK

The iPhone began life as a closed platform. Preceding the release of Apple's iPhone SDK, the open source community successfully hacked into the device and wrote a home-brew compiler to build applications. Later, Apple hired some of the developers of this open source tool chain to design the iPhone SDK. As a result, the two behave in a similar fashion: as cross-compilers. A *cross-compiler* is a compiler that builds executables for a different architecture than the one it's running on. Here, the iPhone SDK compiler runs on a Mac OS X desktop machine, but builds executables for the iPhone's ARM architecture.

 The open source iPhone tool chain can run on many different platforms, including natively right on the iPhone, but is not supported by Apple. You'll need to use the SDK to design applications suitable for distribution on the AppStore, which means your developers will all needs Macs.

The commands and pathnames provided throughout this book assume that you've used the procedures from this chapter to install the iPhone SDK in the recommended way. Apple releases new versions of the SDK periodically, so its setup can sometimes change. Newer versions are available on the Apple Developer Connection website at *http://developer.apple.com/iphone*.

What You'll Need

The iPhone SDK requires an Intel-based Mac running Mac OS X Leopard. Each version of the SDK has its own particular operating system version requirements. You'll need about 3.5GB of disk space for the SDK, along with extra disk space for your projects.

While the following aren't required, they will certainly make developing iPhone applications easier.

Apple developer key

You use Apple developer keys to sign applications so that you can install them on development iPhones. Apple gives developer keys to those accepted into Apple's developer program. To sign up, visit the Apple Developer Connection website at *http://developer.apple.com/iphone*. Apple offers two tracks for developers: a standard track and an enterprise track. The standard track provides a basic developer key, allowing you to install applications on your iPhone from Xcode. As a developer, you'll be able to submit your applications for distribution in the AppStore. The enterprise track, which is more expensive, is designed for enterprises that will be using applications internally or with selected partners instead of distributing them through the AppStore. This track includes additional provisioning keys for large enterprises.

An iPhone

You will need an iPhone, of course, if you want to test applications on an actual iPhone device, as opposed to using the iPhone simulator platform. This is strongly recommended. The iPhone needs to be running a version of firmware supported by your particular version of the SDK.

The iPhone Simulator

Without an Apple developer key or an iPhone, you'll have to test your applications using the iPhone simulator. The iPhone simulator is a target platform that you can use to deploy and test iPhone applications on the desktop. The simulator provides an iPhone-like environment with menu options to simulate locks, screen rotations, and other basic iPhone events. It is greatly limited, however, because your desktop machine lacks the necessary hardware to perform certain tasks. Using the simulator, you will get a general "feel" for how your application might function, but you will also miss some important functionality:

- The Core Location API will not be able to provide your GPS coordinates, but may provide you with sample data or broad location-based information, as available for your network.
- The accelerometer API will not be available to the application.
- The simulator is limited to only some gestures, such as pinch, and will not support more than two fingers or indiscriminate multi-touch.
- The application may not initiate phone calls.
- The EDGE/3G network will be inaccessible, but network queries will use your Internet connection as available.
- The camera and microphone APIs may not function. If your application enables these features, it may suffer from a fatal exception.
- Only certain preloaded iPhone applications will be available. These include Contacts, Safari, Photos, and Settings applications.
- You won't be able to see whether any parts of your application might tax the iPhone's CPU or memory, because your desktop machine will have greater resources to run your application. Slow graphics or other issues might not be noticed until it is tested on an actual iPhone.

Downloading and Installing the iPhone SDK

Download the iPhone SDK from the Apple Developer Connection website at *http://developer.apple.com/iphone*. You will be required to create an account if you don't already have one. This is free. The entire distribution runs about 2 GB, so you will want to download it over a high speed Internet connection. The SDK itself comes in the form of a disk image file, which will be placed in your *Downloads* folder by default.

Double-click the disk image to mount it. You should now see the volume *iPhone SDK* mounted. This will appear on both the sidebar of your Finder and on the desktop. Open the volume and a window will appear.

Inside this window, you will see a package labeled *iPhone SDK*. Double-click this package to begin the installation process. After agreeing to the various licensing provisions, you will be presented with the installation screen shown in Figure 1-1.

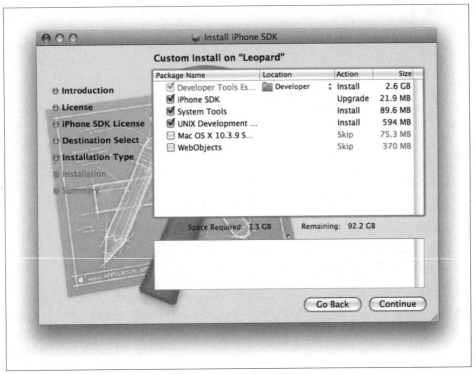

Figure 1-1. The iPhone SDK installer

Ensure that the iPhone SDK option is checked and click Continue. The installer will then install Xcode and the iPhone SDK into */Developer* on your desktop machine.

That's it! You've now installed the SDK for iPhone and are ready to start compiling iPhone applications. We'll explain how to use it in the next section.

Provisioning an iPhone

If you want to install your applications on the iPhone, you'll need a developer certificate and a mobile provisioning profile from Apple. You can create these through the iPhone Developer Program portal. You'll need to pay a fee to join one of the program tracks before you can create a profile. You may sign up by registering at *http://developer.apple .com*. Once you've been accepted into the developer program, you'll be provided instructions to access the developer's portal.

To get set up, you'll perform the following basic steps. Because the program portal's interface is subject to change, use the following only as a guide and be sure to follow the portal's online instructions:

- Log into the program portal. The first thing to do is create a developer certificate. Xcode uses this certificate to sign your applications. Click the Certificates tab and follow the instructions to add a new certificate. Once created, download the certificate and the WWDR Intermediate Certificate as instructed. The WWDR Intermediate Certificate is Apple's key, which you'll also need. Once downloaded, double-click each of these certificates to add them to your keychain.

- Now register your iPhone in the portal by clicking the Devices tab. Registering your iPhone is necessary because you can only install your test applications on registered devices. You'll need your iPhone's unique device ID, which you can obtain from Xcode's device organizer. Launch Xcode, then go to the Windows menu and select Organizer. This will cause a window, shown in Figure 1-2, to appear with a list of devices. Connect your iPhone, and you will be prompted to use the device for development. Click the device in the left pane of the organizer. An information window will appear containing the device ID of the iPhone. Use this to register your iPhone in the program portal.

- Next, click the App IDs tab to create an application bundle identifier. This identifies the application (or group of applications) you'll be developing. This identifier can be wildcarded, allowing you to install any application using a given bundle prefix. To run this book's examples on your iPhone, create a wildcard using *com.yourcompany.** as a bundle identifier. You can name the application "Examples," or whatever you like.

- Next, create a provisioning profile for your mobile device. The provisioning profile allows you to install applications compiled with the identifier you've just created on your iPhone. Select the application ID to associate with the profile, as well as the developer certificates and devices to use with the profile. After you've created the profile, download it to your desktop.

- To add the provisioning profile to your iPhone, click the plus sign (+) in the organizer underneath the box labeled Provisioning and navigate to your provisioning certificate. Once installed, you'll be able to install applications onto this device from Xcode.

The organizer window also allows you to view the console and crash logs from your device, and take screenshots.

Building and Installing Applications

Now that you've installed the iPhone SDK, the next step is to learn how to use it. The iPhone SDK functions as a component of the Xcode IDE. To launch Xcode, navigate to the newly created */Developer* directory on your hard drive. Open a finder window and then click the disk icon in the sidebar. Now double-click the *Developer* folder,

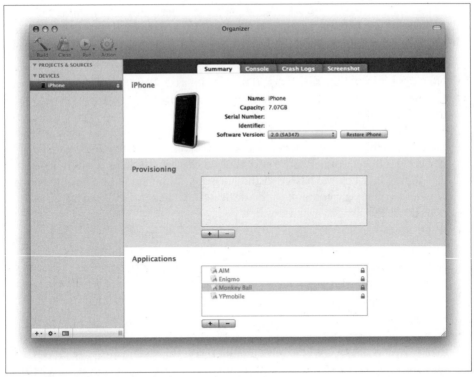

Figure 1-2. Xcode Organizer window

followed by *Applications*. Drag the Xcode application onto your dock to make launching it easier.

> The */Developer/Applications* folder is separate from Mac OS's default *Applications* folder. You can drag the folder onto the dock as a stack to have all developer applications easily accessible, or drag it onto the sidebar to click through to it using the Finder. You'll be accessing this folder a lot as you continue to develop software, so you'll want to make it easy to get to.

After launching Xcode, select New Project from the File menu. A window will appear, prompting you to select a template for your new project. Underneath the iPhone OS heading, click the Application category. You'll see several different types of application templates to choose from, as shown in Figure 1-3.

Model-View-Controller

Software development on the iPhone follows the model-view-controller (MVC) paradigm. The goal of this architecture is to abstract business logic, such as your

Figure 1-3. Available iPhone application templates

application's data and the rules that govern it, from the user interface (UI) components displayed to the end user. Three key pieces are needed to implement MVC. The *model* represents the data and business logic for your application. The *view* represents the UI elements that present the data to the user and allow them to act on it. The *controller* provides the interaction between the UI elements and the data, such as responding to multi-touch gestures, interaction events, and transitioning between different portions of the logic.

You'll see these concepts reflected in the names given to many iPhone classes. In many cases, controllers will also encapsulate a view, making it easy to control the view without having to write very much code to connect them.

Application Templates

Xcode provides several skeletons for implementing the MVC architecture in your application. The following templates are most commonly used:

View-based application

Applications using only one view should use this template. A simple view controller manages the application's primary view, using an interface-builder template for layout (although we'll show you how to remove this and build your own if you like). Simple applications without any navigation should use this template. If your application requires navigation through multiple views, consider using the navigation-based template.

Navigation-based application

The navigation-based template is ideal for applications that traverse multiple views and require a means of navigation between them. If you can envision your application having screens with "Back" buttons in them, chances are you should use this template. A navigation controller handles all of the internal work in setting up navigation buttons and transitioning between "stacks" of views. This template provides a basic navigation controller and a root (base-tier) view controller to display information.

Utility application

Ideal for widget-type applications, where an application has a main view that you can "flip" around like a widget in Leopard. You may also be familiar with these from Konfabulator (the third-party predecessor to Apple's Dashboard). The iPhone's Weather and Stocks applications are good examples of utility applications. This template also includes an information button that causes the view to flip around to display the application's flipside, which is commonly used to change settings or the information displayed.

OpenGL ES application

If you're creating 3D games or graphics, use this template. It creates a view configured to render a GL scene and provides a sample timer to animate it. OpenGL programming is not covered in this book.

Tab bar application

Provides a special controller displaying a button bar along the bottom of the screen. This template is ideal for applications such as the iPod or Mobile Phone applications, where a row of tabs along the bottom provides a series of shortcuts to the core functionality of the application.

Window-based application

If none of the other five templates suits your needs, this very basic template provides a simple application with a window. This is the bare minimum framework you'll need in order to start your own application.

Xcode Project Layout

After creating a new project, its contents will be laid out in a self-contained window like Figure 1-4. The project encapsulates the sources, frameworks, and resources for the application.

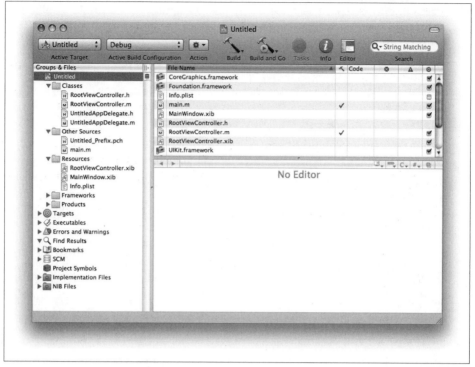

Figure 1-4. A newly created iPhone project

The following groups can help organize your project:

Classes

> The files containing the Objective-C classes that your applications use. These include the application delegate object, view controllers, and other objects you create. As you add new class files to your application, they will appear in this group.

Other sources

> Other sources compiled into your application. By default, this includes precompiled headers and your application's `main` function, which instantiates the Cocoa application object. If your application incorporates additional C functions or C++ classes, add the files here.

Resources

> Application resources that are not compiled in with your application's source code, but are copied into the program folder when the application is built. These can include images or sounds, game levels, or other important files.

Frameworks

> The frameworks that your application links with. These are shared libraries linked at build time to add functionality. For example, a 3D game will link with the OpenGLES framework, which contains the routines to render 3G graphics.

Sound-intensive applications will likely take advantage of the Audio Toolbox or AVFoundation frameworks, which contain routines for playing and mixing different types of sound.

Products

The build target for your application.

Prototypes

Throughout this book, you'll be given a list of prototypes to check out at the end of most sections. Prototypes are header files that contain a list of all supported methods and properties that are available to you as a developer. While this book covers a majority of the methods and properties available, reading the prototypes on your own might reveal additional, and sometimes obscure interfaces that may have either gone undocumented or been added since this book's release. They'll also show you what arguments a method expects, and what data types will be returned.

You can find header files within a framework folder's *Headers* subfolder. Because there are different versions of the SDK, the exact path these can be found differs slightly. The standard format for the path to these prototypes is:

*/Developer/Platforms/**PLATFORM**/Developer/SDKs/**VERSION**/System/Library/Frameworks/*

The full path relies on two variables, **PLATFORM** and **VERSION**. There are two primary platforms in the SDK: *iPhoneOS.platform* and *iPhoneSimulator.platform*. You use the former when building an application for an iPhone or iPod Touch device, and the simulator platform when you build an application for the iPhone simulator. Each platform contains its own set of frameworks, shared libraries, and prototypes.

The **VERSION** variable refers to the version of the iPhone SDK for that platform. The version is prefixed by the platform name and suffixed with an *.sdk* extension.

The full path for an iPhone platform running the version 2.2 SDK would look like the example below:

*/Developer/Platforms/**iPhoneOS.platform**/Developer/SDKs/**iPhoneOS2.2.sdk**/System/Library/Frameworks/*

To make it easy to find this directory, add the following to your *.profile* script, so that the SDK environment variable is set every time a new shell is created:

```
export PLATFORM=iPhoneOS
export VERSION=2.2
export SDK=/Developer/Platforms/${PLATFORM}.platform/Developer/SDKs\
/${PLATFORM}${VERSION}.sdk/System/Library/Frameworks
```

You'll then be able to change directory using the environment variable SDK:

```
$ cd ${SDK}
```

Within the folder at this path, you will find the individual frameworks available in the SDK, each with a *Headers* directory containing the prototypes for that framework. Be sure to check these out when prompted, as they contain a great wealth of verbose information about what's available to developers. The general rule of thumb is this: if you find a class, property, or method in the SDK headers, it should be sanctioned for use in your application.

> While a framework's headers will tell you which APIs you can use, they will not necessarily tell you in what way they can be used. Apple maintains a set of human interface guidelines and other policies that govern AppStore software. You'll need to be sure your application doesn't violate any of Apple's nontechnical restrictions, such as duplicating functionality of an existing preloaded application. Consult the latest version of your SDK agreement and other supporting documents from Apple to learn about design restrictions.

Adding Frameworks

For a given type of functionality, all of the classes and methods needed to provide it are grouped into a framework. For example, the Core Location framework provides all of the functionality needed to perform global positioning. The UI Kit framework provides all of the functionality needed to implement user interfaces. You'll need to *link* to a framework in order to use the functionality it provides. This design logically separates the different pieces of the iPhone's operating system for developers, and allows your application to link only to the components it needs.

> When you link a framework with your application, its classes, functions, and symbols are made available to your application as if you wrote them yourself. *Static* linking compiles the objects directly into your application. *Dynamic* linking loads the objects at runtime. Adding a framework in the following fashion uses the dynamic method of linking.

Throughout this book, you may be prompted to add one or two frameworks to your example in order to add support for a particular type of functionality. To do this, Right-click the *Frameworks* folder in your Xcode project and select Add→Existing Frameworks, as shown in Figure 1-5. Navigate to the iPhone SDK's *Frameworks* directory and choose the correct framework folder. Upon clicking the Add button, you should see the new framework appear in the *Frameworks* folder of your project. This will link the framework with your application.

> It may be necessary to navigate to the *Frameworks* folder within your SDK. Use the pathnames you've just learned about for prototypes to find them.

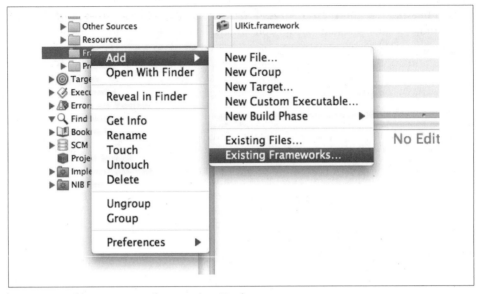

Figure 1-5. Adding an existing framework in Xcode

Setting the Active SDK

Xcode allows you to build your application for either a physical iPhone device or for the integrated iPhone simulator. Different versions of the SDK may also be used to accommodate a specific version of the iPhone firmware. To switch between device and simulator builds, or to change the SDK version, click the Project menu in Xcode. Scroll down to the menu item labeled Set Active SDK and choose the SDK you want to build for. You can also choose whether to build with or without debugging support by choosing from the menu labeled Set Active Build Configuration. Building for the Debug configuration will allow you to trace your application's program execution to identify potential problems.

Building an Application

There are two ways to build an application using Xcode: the GUI and the command line. The easiest way, of course, is to simply click the Build button at the top of the project window or to click Build and Go to build and run the application. This will invoke the compiler and output the results of the build into the status bar. If the build fails or has warnings, you'll be able to click the appropriate icons on the status bar to get more information.

If you come from a Unix background, or just have an affinity for pain, you may be more comfortable building on the command line, especially if you use a command-line text editor in lieu of the Xcode IDE. To build from the command line, use the **xcodebuild** command:

```
$ xcodebuild -target Project_Name
```

Installing an Application

Once you have built an application, you can install it on your iPhone directly through Xcode. As mentioned earlier, this requires a valid developer key from Apple. When the application is installed, it will immediately appear on the iPhone's home screen, then be launched by the debugger.

To install from within Xcode, use the Build and Go toolbar button. This will recompile any changes made since the last build and install it onto the iPhone. If you don't have a developer key, and are building for the iPhone simulator platform, the application will be installed in the iPhone simulator and then run.

To install from the command line, use the `xcodebuild` command with the `install` build option:

```
$ xcodebuild install -target Project_Name
```

Transitioning to Objective-C

Objective-C was written by scientist and software engineer Brad Cox in the early 1980s. It was designed as a way of introducing the capabilities of the Smalltalk language into a C programming environment. A majority of the iPhone's framework libraries are written in Objective-C, but because the language was designed to accommodate the C language, you can use both C and C++ in your application as well. Objective-C is used primarily on Mac OS X and GNUstep (a free OpenStep environment). Many languages, such as Java and C#, have borrowed from the Objective-C language. The Cocoa framework makes heavy use of Objective-C on the Mac desktop, which also carried over onto the iPhone.

If you've developed on the Mac OS X desktop before, you're already familiar with Objective-C, but if the iPhone is your first Apple platform, you may be transitioning from C, C++, or another similar language. This section will cover some of the more significant differences between these languages. If you have a prior background in C or C++, this should be enough to get you up and writing code using the examples in this book as a guide.

Messaging

The first thing you'll notice in Objective-C is the heavy use of brackets. In Objective-C, methods are not *called* in a traditional sense; their objects are sent *messages*. Likewise, a method doesn't *return*, but rather *responds* to the message.

Much of this can be chalked up to semantics, however, at least in terms of what the developer experiences. Your application's program flow is nothing alien to a C or C++ program: when you invoke a method, your program waits for a response before continuing, allowing you to assign the return value or invoke methods as part of conditional statements.

Unlike C, where function calls must be predefined, Objective-C's messaging style allows the developer to dynamically create new methods and messages at runtime, or test to see whether an object responds to a particular message. The downside to this is that it's entirely possible to send an object a message to which it isn't programmed to respond, causing an exception and likely program termination. For example, you can compile code that will send the following message to an object:

```
[ myObject heyWhatsUpHowYouDoin ];
```

At runtime, the application will raise an exception unless a method exists named heyWhatsUpHowYouDoin to respond to the message. Of course, the advantage to this is that a method might exist for the object, but be undocumented in the class's prototypes. We'll show you just a few examples of undocumented methods like this in Chapter 3.

Given an object named myWidget, a message can be sent to its powerOn method this way:

```
returnValue = [ myWidget powerOn ];
```

The C++ equivalent of this might look like the following:

```
returnValue = myWidget->powerOn();
```

The C equivalent might declare a function inside of its flat namespace:

```
returnValue = widget_powerOn(myWidget);
```

Arguments can also be passed with messages, provided that an object can receive them. The following example invokes a method named setSpeed and passes two arguments:

```
returnValue = [ myWidget setSpeed: 10.0 withMass: 33.0 ];
```

Notice the second argument is explicitly named in the message. This allows multiple methods with the same name *and* argument data types to be declared—polymorphism on steroids:

```
returnValue = [ myWidget setSpeed: 10.0 withMass: 33.0 ];
returnValue = [ myWidget setSpeed: 10.0 withGyroscope: 10.0 ];
```

Class and Method Declarations

While you can define C++ classes in Objective-C, the whole point of using the language is to take advantage of Objective-C's own objects and features. This extends to its use of interfaces. In standard C++, classes are structures, and their variables and methods are contained inside the structure. Objective-C, on the other hand, keeps its variables in one part of the class and methods in another. The language also requires that you specifically declare the interface declaration in its own code block (called @interface) separate from the block containing the implementation (called @implementation). You construct and name methods in a Smalltalk-esque fashion, and they somewhat resemble regular C functions.

The interface for our widget example might look like Example 1-1, which is a file named *MyWidget.h*.

Example 1-1. Sample interface (MyWidget.h)

```
#import <Foundation/Foundation.h>

@interface MyWidget : BaseWidget
{
    BOOL isPoweredOn;
    @private float speed;
    @protected float mass;
    @protected float gyroscope;
}
+ (id)alloc;
+ (BOOL)needsBatteries;
- (BOOL)powerOn;
- (void)setSpeed:(float)_speed;
- (void)setSpeed:(float)_speed withMass:(float)_mass;
- (void)setSpeed:(float)_speed withGyroscope:(float)_gyroscope;
@end
```

The important semantic elements in this file are explained in the following sections.

The "id" data type

In the example just shown, the id data type is defined as the return type by the alloc method. This data type is a generic type used to reference any arbitrary object. Think of the id data type as the Objective-C version of a void pointer. Wherever specified, any object can be used. You'll see this data type used throughout the book, especially in cases where a delegate is assigned to an object to receive special notifications of events.

Imports

The preprocessor directive #import replaces the traditional #include directive (although #include may still be used). One advantage to using #import is that it has built-in logic to ensure that the same resource is never included more than once. This replaces the roundabout use of macro flags found routinely in C code:

```
#ifndef _MYWIDGET_H
#define _MYWIDGET_H
...
#endif
```

Interface declaration

The interface for a class is declared with the @interface statement followed by the interface's name and the base class (if any) it is derived from. At the end of your class declaration, you'll end the block with the @end statement. Within this block, you'll declare all class variables and methods for the class.

Methods

Methods should be declared outside of the braces structure. A plus sign (+) identifies the method as a static method, while a minus sign (–) declares the method as an instance method. Static methods don't need to be invoked for any particular object; they are methods that represent the entire class in general—for example, "the Widget class". Instance methods are invoked for a named instance of a class—for example, "my Widget" and "his Widget".

The alloc method is a good example of a static method. It is responsible for allocating and returning a new instance of the given class. In your code, you'll call this method whenever you create a new object by referencing the class directly, for example MyWidget. Instance methods that are specific to an instance of the MyWidget class, such as setSpeed and powerOn, should be invoked by referencing the named object. Many Cocoa classes provide static and instance methods for initializing objects.

Every declared parameter for a method specifies a data type, a local variable name, and an optional external variable name. Examples of external variable names in Example 1-2 are withMass and withGyroscope. The notifier (calling method) that invokes the method refers to method's external (public) variable names, but inside the method the arguments are referenced using their local variable names. Thus, the setSpeed method uses the local _mass variable to retrieve the value passed as withMass.

If no external variable name is supplied in the declaration, the variable is referenced only with a colon, for example :10.0.

Implementation

The suffix for an Objective-C source code file is .m. A skeleton implementation of the widget class from the last section might look like Example 1-2, which is named MyWidget.m.

Example 1-2. Sample implementation (MyWidget.m)

```
#import "MyWidget.h"

@implementation MyWidget

+ (BOOL)needsBatteries {
    return YES;
}
```

```
- (BOOL)powerOn {
    isPoweredOn = YES;
    return YES;
}

- (void)setSpeed:(float)_speed {
    speed = _speed;
}

- (void)setSpeed:(float)_speed withMass:(float)_mass {
    speed = _speed;
    mass = _mass;
}

- (void)setSpeed:(float)_speed withGyroscope:(float)_gyroscope {
    speed = _speed;
    gyroscope = _gyroscope;
}
@end
```

Just as the interface was contained within a single code block, the implementation begins with an @implementation statement and ends with @end.

In C++, it is common practice to prefix member variables so that public methods can accept the actual name of the variable. This makes it easy to reuse someone else's code because you can deduce a variable's purpose by its name. Since Objective-C allows you to use both an internal and external variable name, a method is able to provide a sensible name for the developer to use, while internally using some proprietary name. The true name can then be referenced as a parameter of the method, while the method's local variable name is prefixed with an underscore; e.g., _speed.

Consider the example setSpeed method just shown. When invoked, its external argument name, withMass, is used:

```
[ myWidget setSpeed: 1.0 withMass: 2.0 ];
```

Inside the method's code block, the internal variable name, _mass, is used:

```
- (void)setSpeed:(float)_speed withMass:(float)_mass {
    speed = _speed;
    mass = _mass;
}
```

Properties

Objective-C 2.0 introduced the concept of properties. Properties are an intermediary between instance variables and methods; they add a syntactic convenience by allowing the developer to address variables directly, rather than through separate setter/getter methods. Properties are similar to public variables, but allow the behavior of their access to be defined. Additionally, properties invoke methods that can be overridden when the property is read from or written to.

To work with an instance variable in earlier versions of Objective-C, you would typically write two methods—one to read the variable (a getter) and one to write (a setter):

```
BOOL myVariable = [ myClass variable ];      /* getter */
[ myClass.setVariable ] = YES;        /* setter */
```

Properties allow the developer to change his syntax to address the property's name for both operations. This changes the code to look more "C-ish":

```
BOOL myVariable = myClass.variable;
myClass.variable = YES;
```

You can define properties with a number of different storage semantics. These include assign, retain, and copy. You can also define properties as readonly. Define a property for a variable named size in the class definition as follows:

```
@interface MyClass : BaseClass
{
    int size;
}
@property(copy) int size;
```

In the class's implementation, use the @synthesize statement to implement the property:

```
@implementation MyClass
@synthesize size;
...
@end
```

When the @synthesize statement is used, a getter and setter method are automatically generated internally if they don't exist in your code. These methods are transparently called whenever the property is accessed:

```
myClass.size = 3;
```

You can also define custom setter and getter methods without using @synthesize:

```
-(int)myGetter;
-(void)setSize:(int)size;

@property(copy,getter=myGetter) int size;
```

Many methods you may have seen in previous versions of Objective-C code have been replaced with properties in the iPhone SDK.

Protocols

A protocol is a set of methods that an object agrees to implement in order to communicate with another object. You'll use many protocols throughout this book known as *delegate protocols*. Delegate protocols are protocols that notify an object about events occurring in another object. To implement a protocol, your interface declaration simply declares that it supports the given protocol. This way, other classes requiring a certain protocol can expect that your class will respond to the methods used in the protocol.

A class can implement any number of protocols. You'll receive a compiler warning if your implementation is incomplete.

As an example, presume that a `BaseWidgetDelegate` protocol is a protocol you've designed to alert an object of events occurring within a given widget, such as a powering on event or the event of its power settings changing.

Use the `protocol` statement to define the methods used in the protocol. You can specify the methods that are mandatory to implement the protocol using the `required` statement:

```
@protocol BaseWidgetDelegate

- (void)baseWidgetDidChangePowerSettings:(float)newPowerLevel;

@required
- (void)baseWidgetDidGetTurnedOn:(id)widget; /* This method is required */

@end
```

A class looking to send these types of notifications might define a variable containing the pointer to an object to receive notifications:

```
@interface MyWidget : BaseWidget {
    id delegate;
}
```

They can define a property for its delegate and require that the object assigned to it implement the `BaseWidgetDelegate` protocol:

```
@property(assign) id<BaseWidgetDelegate> delegate;
```

The class desiring to receive notifications must now implement the `BaseWidget Delegate` protocol to be assigned as the widget's delegate. The example to follow declares a `WidgetManager` class and specifies the protocol be implemented within the class:

```
@protocol BaseWidgetDelegate;
@interface WidgetManager : NSObject <BaseWidgetDelegate>
...
@end
```

The only thing remaining is to implement the actual protocol methods in the class's implementation.

Once implemented, your application code can assign the widget manager class to the widget's `delegate` property without generating a compiler warning, because it implements the `BaseWidgetDelegate` protocol:

```
myWidget.delegate = myWidgetManager;
```

Categories

Objective-C adds a new element to object oriented programming called *categories*. Categories were designed to solve the problem where base classes are treated as fragile to prevent seemingly innocuous changes from breaking the more complex derived classes. When a program grows to a certain size, the developer can often become afraid to touch a smaller base class because it's too difficult by then to determine which changes are safe without auditing the entire application. Categories provide a mechanism to add functionality to smaller classes without exposing your changes to legacy code.

You can place a category class "on top" of a smaller class, adding to or replacing methods within the base class. This can be done without recompiling or even having access to the base class' source code. Categories allow you to expand base classes within a limited scope so that any objects using the base class (and not the category) will continue to see the original version. From a development perspective, this makes it much easier to improve on a class written by a different developer. At runtime, portions of code using the category will see the new version of the class, and legacy code using the base class directly will see only the original version.

You might be thinking about inheritance as an equally viable solution. The difference between categories and inheritance is the difference between performance-tuning your car versus dressing it up as a parade float. When you tune up your sports car, you add new components to the internals of the vehicle, which cause it to perform differently. You may even pull out some components and replace them with new ones. The act of adding a new component to the engine, such as a turbo, affects the function of the entire vehicle. This is how inheritance works.

Categories, on the other hand, are more like a parade float in that the vehicle remains completely intact, but cardboard cutouts and papier-mâché are affixed to the outside of the vehicle so that it only appears different. In the context of a parade, the vehicle is a completely different animal to spectators, but when you take it to the mechanic, it's the same old stock car you've been driving around.

As an example, the widget factory is coming out with a new type of widget that can fly through space, but is concerned that making changes to the base class might break existing applications. By building a category, the developers ensure that applications using the MyWidget base class will continue to see the original class, while the newer space applications will use a category instead. The following example builds a new category named MySpaceWidget on top of the existing MyWidget base class. Because we need the ability to blow things up in space, a method named selfDestruct is added. This category also replaces the existing powerOn method with its own. Contrast the use of parentheses here to hold the MySpaceWidget contained class with the use of a colon in Example 1-1 to carry out inheritance:

```
#import "MyWidget.h"

@interface MyWidget (MySpaceWidget)
- (void)selfDestruct;
- (BOOL)powerOn;
@end
```

A complete source file implementing the category is shown in Example 1-3.

Example 1-3. Sample category (MySpaceWidget.m)

```
#import "MySpaceWidget.h"

@implementation MyWidget (MySpaceWidget)

- (void)selfDestruct {
    isPoweredOn = 0;
    speed = 1000.0;
    mass = 0;
}

- (BOOL)powerOn {
    if (speed == 0) {
        isPoweredOn = YES;
        return YES;
    }

    /* Don't power on if the spaceship is moving */
    return NO;
}
@end
```

Posing

In Objective-C, a subclass can *pose* as one of its super-classes, virtually replacing it as the recipient of all messages. This is similar to overriding; only an entire class is being overridden instead of a single method. A posing class is not permitted to declare any new variables, although it may override or replace existing methods. Posing is similar to categories in that it allows a developer to augment an existing class at runtime.

In past examples, you created some mechanical widget classes. Well, at some point after designing all of these widgets, you developed a need to perform advanced diagnostics. Rather than rip out functions in the original class, you've decided to create a new subclass named `MyDiagnosticsWidget`. See Examples 1-4 and 1-5.

Example 1-4. Sample interface for posing (MyDiagnosticsWidget.h)

```
#import <Foundation/Foundation.h>
#import "MyWidget.h"

@interface MyDiagnosticsWidget : MyWidget
{

}

- (void)debug;
@end
```

Example 1-5. Sample implementation for posing (MyDiagnosticsWidget.m)

```
#import "MyDiagnosticsWidget.h"

@implementation MyDiagnosticsWidget

- (void)debug {
    /* Generate debugging information */
}
@end
```

Instead of changing all of the existing code to use this class, the autonomous class can simply pose as the widget class. The `class_poseAs` method is called from the main program or another high-level method to invoke this behavior:

```
MyDiagnosticsWidget *myDiagWidget = [ MyDiagnosticsWidget alloc ];
    MyWidget *myWidget = [ MyWidget alloc ];
    class_poseAs(myDiagWidget, myWidget);
```

Now, any other methods you've replaced in the posing class would pose as if they were from the original base class.

Additional Resources

As you read many examples in this book, you'll see references to objects used in Apple's Cocoa environment. Most of these objects will begin with the prefix `NS`, such as `NSError` or `NSString`. The Cocoa environment provides a number of standard objects like this to handle arrays, strings, and other such objects; many are available both with the iPhone and the Mac OS X desktop environments. We'll show you how to work with some of these objects in relation to the example at hand, however entire books have been written just to document Cocoa classes. If you run into a class you're not familiar with, Apple's online documentation can provide you with a complete explanation. The Apple Developer Connection website hosts a Cocoa reference available at *http://developer.apple.com/reference/Cocoa/*. From here, you can read a reference for a particular topic or enter the class's name into the search window to be taken directly to the class's documentation.

To learn more about Cocoa and Objective-C programming, you may also check out the following great resources from O'Reilly:

Learning Cocoa with Objective-C, Second Edition, by James Duncan Davidson and Apple Computer, Inc.[*]
    http://www.oreilly.com/catalog/learncocoa2/

Objective-C Pocket Reference by Andrew M. Duncan
    http://www.oreilly.com/catalog/objectcpr/

---

[*] *Learning Cocoa 3.0 with Objective-C*, by Greg Winton and Michael Beam, will be available from O'Reilly in the summer of 2009.

CHAPTER 2

Interface Builder: Xcode's GUI for GUIs

One of the most time-consuming steps in writing an application can be designing the UI. The iPhone has a UI that's unmistakable from any other mobile device—a feature-rich, high-resolution form factor designed to accommodate navigation without a stylus (it's fat finger-friendly). Old school hackers who have written UIs by hand will tell you that they require a lot of code and more time than a developer wants to spend on them. The good news is that Apple went to great lengths to make it simple for SDK developers to implement a standard set of UIs. The iPhone SDK includes a utility named Interface Builder, which gives the designer a WYSIWYG drag-and-drop environment for creating and editing windows, creating views, and placing controls on the screen with little effort. The user can store the screen layout as a template file, which your application can read and synthesize as an object in your application. This allows you to create a user interface in minutes and make future changes with little or no code changes. Desktop developers might remember this approach from resource forks of the past.

The Interface Builder application can be found in the */Developer* applications folder on your desktop machine. If you followed our advice in Chapter 1, you've already dragged this folder onto your dock, and you can launch it by opening the dock stack and selecting the *Interface Builder* application. If you haven't heeded our sage advice, you'll need to navigate to your hard drive in the Finder and launch Interface Builder from the */Developer/Applications* folder.

While using Interface Builder doesn't preclude you from creating your own UI objects in Objective-C, many developers like to forego Interface Builder completely and define all UI components within their code. You'll learn how to do this at the end of the chapter.

Synthesizing is the term Apple uses to describe the dynamic creation of linkage between a variable and the object it is connected with. When a class synthesizes an object from an Interface Builder template, the object is assigned to a variable within your class. View controllers, windows, and other types of Interface Builder objects can all be synthesized, allowing you to access them as variables without your application directly creating them.

Windows, Views, and View Controllers

Windows and views are the base classes for creating any type of user interface. A window represents a geometric space on a screen, while a view acts like a canvas for objects. Smaller UI components, such as buttons and text boxes, are all attached to a view, and that view is anchored to a window. Think of a window as the frame of a painting and the view as the actual canvas. A window is designed to host only view classes, but views can contain controls, images, and even host subviews such as tables and pickers. You'll learn about the different types of UI components in Chapters 3 and 10.

A view controller is a special kind of view object that manages how its views are displayed on the screen. View controllers can encapsulate one or more view objects and come with the plumbing to automatically handle screen rotations and transitions to other views when the user presses a button or flips the page. The view controller is designed as an intermediary between the view it is displaying and your underlying data and business logic.

Different types of controllers exist to provide different ways to display your data to the user. The iPod application employs a series of tabs along the bottom, allowing you to flip between artist and song lists, videos, and other information. The tab bar itself is available in one kind of view controller class (a tab bar controller), which is always visible on the screen regardless of which page the user is looking at. Other types of view controllers include table view controllers (which display your data in table form), image pickers (allowing the user to select an image from a library), and picker controllers (which solicit input using a series of scroll wheels).

A well-written application will consist of one window, at least one view controller, and at least one view encapsulated within the controller.

Existing Templates

By default, every sample application created with Xcode uses a template created by Interface Builder. This template serves as the major source of information about your application's main screen layout and subsequent window hierarchy. It establishes the key window that users see when your application starts, but also allows you to define which actions trigger transitions to different views. Xcode can build a hierarchy for your UI without having to write a single line of code!

To get started on your UI, use Xcode to create a new *window-based application* named *Example*. This will create a directory named *Example* containing the skeleton of your application.

Each sample application is created with a *MainWindow* template. This template represents the main window object that is loaded and displayed when the application is started. The template name is assigned to your application from the *Info.plist* file, found in the *Resources* section of your Xcode project. The *MainWindow* template is specified as a filename, but without the *.xib* extension, as shown below:

```
<key>NSMainNibFile</key>
        <string>MainWindow</string>
```

Click the *Resources* folder within your project. You'll then see a file named *MainWindow.xib*. This is the Interface Builder template file. Double-click the file to open it in interface builder.

New Templates

To create a new Interface Builder project from a template, select New from the File menu. A window will prompt you to choose the type of template you want to create, as shown in Figure 2-1. Interface Builder templates will be created for you automatically and placed in your project directory.

The *Cocoa Touch* class of templates is specifically geared for iPhone applications. After you select it, the following types of templates will be available:

Application
> Builds an application template, including a primary application delegate and a main window. The application delegate will receive notifications when the application is launched, suspended, or terminated. The main window provides a primary view port to display a view on the screen. Use this template if your application will have just a single screen. You will need to build a view to layer on top of the window, which will be explained next.

View
> Builds a single view within an application. Use this if you're creating a single view screen for an application window, or for each view within an application having many views.

Window
> Template for building windows only. Use this if you'll be manually laying out your views on a single screen. Windows cannot hold individual controls, so if you plan on using them, you'll need to first create a view.

Empty
> An empty template, allowing you to create anything you like from scratch.

Figure 2-1. Interface Builder template selection window

User Interface Elements

Upon opening an Interface Builder template, you'll be presented with a window resembling the iPhone's screen, a smaller document window representing the logical class properties and relationships to different objects, and a library of different UI elements available on the iPhone. From here, use the library window to drag graphical elements directly onto the iPhone window. You'll be able to design the view you'd like to build by dragging and resizing elements. You can change their sizes and adjust their placements with the mouse. Descriptions for each UI element are provided, as shown in Figure 2-2.

The library is arranged according to element category, and different types of elements can be applied only to certain objects. The types of categories follow.

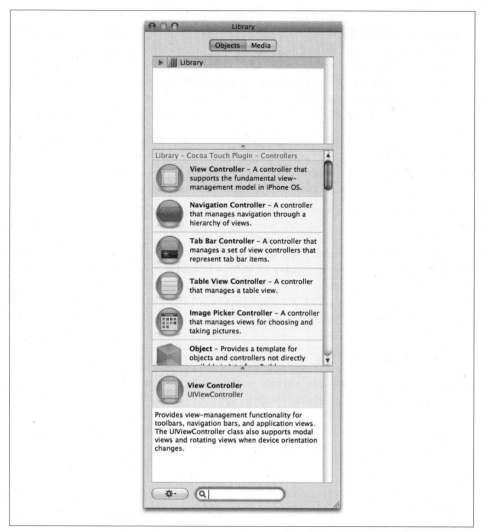

Figure 2-2. Interface Builder library

Controllers

Controller objects are view controller classes that manage data view objects (described next). You can create different view controllers in Interface Builder to manage navigation, individual data views, tab bars, tables, or other elements. A view controller cannot be part of an existing view, so to create these types of objects, drag the element into your document window (that's the smaller window containing the File's Owner and First Responder properties). This will create a new window for the controller where you can drag additional UI elements.

Data Views

Data views are individual view classes that display information to the user. These include text views, image viewers, web views, and many other types of objects. A data view is managed by its view controller, which can render multiple data views and link the view it is displaying with your underlying data. You can add as many data views as you like to an existing view, using the guides to position and size them to your liking. Data views can also contain controls and navigation items.

Any objects added to a data view will appear only in that view. For example, a navigation bar added to the view controller will remain visible as the user transitions between views belonging to the view controller, but a navigation bar added to the data view will be visible only when that specific view is displayed.

Inputs and Values

Whenever a user needs to provide some type of input, an input object is used. These are commonly referred to as controls (not to be confused with the controllers mentioned earlier), and include switches, text boxes, segmented controls, and other objects you'll learn about in Chapter 10. You can add a control to any view, and that view will generally handle the events generated when the control is used.

Windows, Views, and Bars

In addition to controllers and data views, you can add additional window, view, and bar objects to an existing view. For example, to add a search bar so that it is visible exclusively within a given view, drag it onto your standard view class instead of a controlling view. You'll learn how to interact with search bars and similar objects in Chapter 10.

The Inspector

Interface Builder includes an inspector tool, which is used to customize the behavior of objects you create. The inspector tool allows you to change an object's attributes, the connections it has to other resources and files, the size of objects, and most importantly, the actions it takes in response to events such as user input. To display the inspector, choose Inspector from the Tools menu.

Designing a UI

There are two good reasons to build your first UI from scratch. The first is to get a feel for how Interface Builder works. The second is to visualize how the different components of a user interface fit together. There are windows, view controllers, data views, input controls, and a host of relationships that tie them all together. In this section, you'll build a simple interface from scratch and install it into a sample application.

Launch Interface Builder and edit the *MainWindow* template created with your window-based application. Your document window will contain a barebones template with only a window object.

The Window

The *window* object is the primary surface to which you'll attach your view controller. The window represents space on the iPhone's physical screen.

Select the Window icon in the document window and open the inspector by either pressing Command-1 or selecting Inspector from the Tools menu. The inspector will present you with options to change the color of the status bar within your application, the window transparency, the background color, and other window properties. If your application will use multi-touch gestures, they can be enabled here as well.

The View Controller

Drag a *Tab Bar Controller* into the document window. The Tab Bar Controller is a type of view controller that provides a series of tabs across the bottom of the window. The user can then click different tabs to display the various views your application supports. After dragging the controller into your document window, you will see a corresponding icon added to your template. Double-click the icon and a new window will appear containing two tabs and a gray window with the text `View` appearing in the middle. The buttons represent your tab bar, while the gray window represents the first page of your application's view.

If you hover over the name of a tab, you can click to rename the tab. Alternatively, you can select from a list of preset tabs by clicking a button tab and opening the inspector. From within the inspector, you'll be able to set the identifier of the button tab, such as Recents, History, etc. You can also define your own identifier. The identifier will identify the tab so that your code can reference it. You can also add a custom image to the button and adjust its size. Use the inspector to set up both button tabs.

 Many of the properties you're able to set using Interface Builder are reproducible in code. Think of Interface Builder as a GUI for code. While Interface Builder supports many of the same characteristics you can set up in code, it does not support all. You'll start learning about the code side of these objects in Chapter 3.

You're finished with the controller view and window objects for now. Save the template with the name *MainWindow*. You'll come back to it later to make some final changes.

Views

So far you've set up the button tabs in your controlling view, and you are now ready to create the two individual views to coincide with each button. To keep your interfaces modular, we suggest that you create a separate view class to correspond to each tab, and use a different Interface Builder file to describe each. You'll store the actual Interface Builder template for the view in a separate file, and it will be automatically loaded when the user switches tabs.

Create a new *Cocoa Touch View* template. Unlike the application template, this template includes a view class object rather than a window object. This view represents what is displayed to the user when he clicks the first tab.

In the library window, scroll down to the Data Views section and drag a Table View object onto your view. Ensure it is centered at the top of the window and sized to use the entire screen. Click the table and open the inspector. Here, you'll be able to change many different properties pertaining to the look and behavior of the table. When you are satisfied, save this file with the name *Recents*.

Create a second Cocoa Touch View project and, this time, drag a text view into the window. After customizing the text view's properties in the inspector, save this file with the name *History*.

Connecting the Views

You've now created a window, a controlling view, and two data views to display data in. Now all that's left is to connect the controlling view to the individual data views so that each will be displayed appropriately whenever the user taps the corresponding button.

Open your *MainWindow* template. Click the first tab to make it the active tab. Now click the grayed portion of the window labeled View. Open the inspector and enter the filename *Recents* in the field titled NIB Name, without an extension. The gray view window should now read "(Loaded from *Recents.nib*)." Now click the second tab and do the same thing, using the filename *History*. Your resulting template should look similar to the example in Figure 2-3.

Adding Linkage to Code

Once you've finished editing, you'll need to add the two newly created files, *Recents.xib* and *History.xib*, to the Xcode project. Drag them into the *Resources* folder in your project and follow the prompts to add them as resources.

If you take a look at prototype for a project's application delegate class, you'll find a series of properties using the IBOutlet directive. This directive alerts Interface Builder

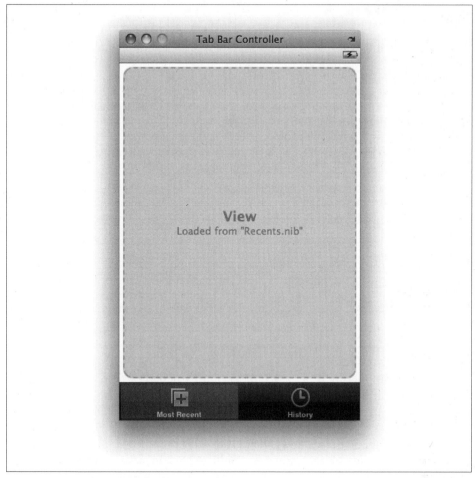

Figure 2-3. A configured tab bar view controller

to the presence of outlets in your code, so it can link the Interface Builder objects with the variable names specified in your code—in this case, `window` and `viewController`:

```
@property (nonatomic, retain) IBOutlet UIWindow *window;
@property (nonatomic, retain) IBOutlet RootViewController *viewController;
```

Inside your delegate class, the window, view controller, and any other objects you've created with Interface Builder are synthesized from the templates you've assigned in your NIB file:

```
@synthesize window;
@synthesize viewController;
```

The `synthesize` directive builds the necessary linkage from Interface Builder into the properties representing the objects in your code, and can be accessed as variables in your class. Internally, they are treated as if they were variables you created yourself:

```
[ window addSubview: viewController.view ];
[ window makeKeyAndVisible ];
```

Externally, any other class containing a pointer to the class can reference them:

```
MyAppDelegate *appDelegate;
[ appDelegate.window addSubview: appDelegate.viewController.view ];
```

The objects from the main template will be loaded in this fashion when the application launches, but you can also instantiate some objects directly from within your code. To create a new view controller object, for example, include a template named *MyController.xib* by adding it to your project's *Resources* folder. Instantiate the class using the `UIViewController` class's `initWithNibName` method:

```
MyApplicationViewController *myViewController = [
    [ MyViewController alloc ]
    initWithNibName: @"MyController"
    bundle: nil
];
```

You'll be able to access the variable in the same fashion as your synthesized objects:

```
[ window addSubview: myViewController.view ];
```

You'll learn more about creating and working with view controller classes in Chapter 3.

Removing Interface Builder from a Project

If you don't plan on using Interface Builder in a particular project, you can remove support for it entirely from the project. Instructions to accomplish this follow. After following these steps, your project will no longer use Interface Builder NIB files to obtain any of its information about the default layout of your UIs. This means you'll need to code in support for windows, views, and other objects yourself. The next chapter will guide you through these objects. You'll still be able to instantiate views from NIB files using the NIB-specific initialization methods you'll learn.

 Interface Builder is a matter of personal preference. Many developers like it because it allows them to create UIs in a WYSIWYG environment. Others find it cumbersome, and prefer having all of their UI objects clearly defined in their source code. Some aspects of Interface Builder have been reportedly buggy, so you'll want to know how to create certain objects if you run into problems.

1. Open your new window-based application and expand the *Resources* folder in the project. You'll then see one or more files with an *.xib* extension, such as *MainWindow.xib*. Right-click each file and select Delete from the pop-up menu. This will delete all Interface Builder templates from the project.

2. Within the *Resources* folder, you'll also see a file named *Info.plist*. Click this file to open it. A property list window will open containing information about your application. At the bottom, you'll see a property key named *Main nib file base name*. Click on this property and press the delete key to delete it from your project, then save your changes. This causes your application to load without requiring an Interface Builder file.

3. Now that you've detached Interface Builder from your application, you'll need to manually specify the name of the application delegate class. This is the class whose `applicationDidFinishLaunching` method will be notified when your application starts up, and is where your UI code will begin. You can find the name of your project's delegate class underneath the *Classes* folder in your project. Its name will be the name of your project suffixed with *AppDelegate*. For example, if you named your project *Wizbang*, the name of your delegate class should be *WizbangAppDelegate*. Expand the *Other Sources* folder in your project and edit the file named *main.m*. Edit the line calling `UIApplicationMain` to reflect the name of your delegate class. An example follows:

```
int retVal = UIApplicationMain(argc, argv, nil, @"WizbangAppDelegate");
```

You can also remove the `property` and `synthesize` directives from your classes. We left them in our examples in case you'd like to make them work with Interface Builder templates.

CHAPTER 3

Introduction to UI Kit

UI Kit is the largest iPhone framework in terms of file size, and rightly so—it's responsible for all user interface functions, from creating windows and text boxes to reading multi-touch gestures and hardware sensors. All of the graphical pleasantries that make the iPhone seem easy to use rely on the UI Kit framework to deliver a polished and unified interface. The same UI Kit APIs are available to all iPhone applications, and understanding how to use this framework will allow you to take advantage of some of the tools and effects that make Apple's own stock apps spectacular.

UI Kit is more than a mere user interface kit; it is also the runtime foundation for iPhone GUI applications. When you launch an application, its `main` function instantiates a `UIApplication` object within UI Kit. This class is the base class for all applications having a user interface on the iPhone, and it provides the application access to the iPhone's higher-level functions. In addition to this, common application-level services such as resigning control to other applications and becoming active again are functions of the `UIApplication` class.

All iPhone applications created in Xcode are linked to the UI Kit framework by default, so you won't need to do anything special to connect it to your application. To create the skeleton for the UI Kit application examples used in this chapter, you'll be instructed to use Xcode to create a new *window-based application*, *view-based application*, or *navigation-based application*. Each uses a slightly different set of files, which we'll provide the code for.

While there are several UI Kit components that you can create using Interface Builder, many developers choose to create UI objects directly within their code. What's more, your application might end up as a hybrid between the standard objects created with Interface Builder and more proprietary view classes. This chapter covers the basic UI Kit objects (that is, the most foundational to most applications) and helps you to choose which to code directly and which to design with Interface Builder. Even if you use Interface Builder to design your entire UI, this chapter will show you how to interact with the objects you create.

Basic User Interface Elements

This chapter is designed to get you comfortable building with the basic user interface components of UI Kit. The more advanced components will be covered in Chapter 10. The basic components include the following:

Windows, views, and view controllers

Windows and views are the most basic classes for creating any type of user interface. A window represents a geometric space on a screen, while a view class fills that void with its own functionality. Smaller UI components, such as navigation bars, buttons, and text boxes are all attached to view classes, and a view is anchored to a window.

A *view controller* is a type of controller class that encapsulates and controls a view. The controller manages the view and how it's rendered on the screen. This augments the view with additional functionality such as built-in support for screen rotations, transitions, and other screen events.

Text views

Text views are specialized view classes for presenting editor windows to view or edit text. The Notepad application is a good example of a simple text view. They are considered humble and are rarely used in light of UI Kit's repertoire of more spectacular classes, but are a great start to get you accustomed to UI Kit.

Navigation bars and controllers

The iPhone UI treats different screens as if they are "pages" in a book. Navigation bars are frequently used to provide a visual prompt to allow the user to return "back" to a previous view, supply buttons to modify elements on the current screen page, and display a number of controls such as segmented controls and toolbars. Navigation bars are found in nearly all preloaded iPhone applications.

A *navigation controller* can manage the navigation for multiple view controllers in such a way that view controllers can be pushed and popped from a view stack, leaving all the work of changing the navigation bar to the controller. Each view controller hosts its own set of navigation bar properties that are displayed by the navigation controller when the view becomes active.

Transitions

Consistent with the spirit of Apple's user-friendly interfaces, window transitions were introduced with the iPhone to allow the user to perceive navigation through the application's screens like pages in a book. Animations are used to make this visual transition from one view to another, rather than simply flashing to the next screen.

Alert views and action sheets

The iPhone equivalents to pop-up alert windows are alert views and action sheets. These appear as modal windows that can pop or slide to the forefront of the screen when an operation requires the user's attention. These are frequently seen on preloaded iPhone applications when a user receives an alert (such as a text message), or attempts to delete certain items (such as voicemail). You can program action sheets to ask the user any question and present a number of different buttons for the response. They prove useful in parts of an application needing immediate attention.

Table views and controllers

Table views are lists that you can use to display files, messages, or other types of collections. They are used for the selection of one or more items in a list-like fashion. The table objects are very flexible and allow the developer to define how a table cell should look and behave. You can tailor tables to display simple lists, grouped preferences, and rolodex-like section lists. This chapter will cover simple tables, and you'll learn about the more advanced uses for tables in Chapter 10.

A *table view controller* manages a table view object and can incorporate the added support of a view controller to a table view. Table view controllers provide automatic handling of screen rotations and other events, and you can push the view controller onto a navigation stack for easy navigation, just like other view controllers. Table view controllers can also act as the data source for propagating a table with information to display.

Status bar manipulation

The status bar is the small bar appearing at the top of the iPhone screen, and displays the time, battery life, and signal strength. You can customize the status bar's style, opacity, and other properties.

Application badges

Applications needing to notify the user of time-sensitive information have the ability to display badges on the iPhone's home screen (the springboard). This alerts the user that your application needs attention and unread messages or other new information is waiting to be viewed. These are used heavily by applications using EDGE or 3G networks to deliver messages.

Application services

When an application resigns its active status, resumes, or is terminated, different methods are notified for an application to handle immediate cleanup or save state. These are sent to the application's delegate, which can then respond by cleaning up or saving important information.

Windows and Views

The most basic user interface component is a `UIWindow` object. A window provides the backing for displaying information within your application. It acts as a picture frame to which you can anchor content. While windows that you create on the desktop appear with title bars, frames, and buttons, the iPhone's `UIWindow` object has no visual features—it is essentially a view port. You will generally create only a single `UIWindow` object to use throughout the life of your application, and anchor one or more objects derived from UIView to it.

The UIView class is a base class designed to accommodate the drawing of objects in windows. If the UIWindow were a picture frame, think of the UIView class as the canvas. Many classes are derived from UIView to create visual objects that render text boxes, tables, and web pages. The base class represents a generic level of functionality that provides basic gestures, drawing routines, and responders. You'll be able to create your own custom classes based on UIView to render your own types of objects, or anchor other UI components to a UIView object to display them.

If you're using Interface Builder in your project, the window and view may be automatically generated for you when the application starts. The instructions for doing this are located in the Interface Builder NIB file, which acts as a sort of resource fork for your user interface. If you're not using Interface Builder, you'll create these objects directly within your code.

Creating a Window and View

Before you can display anything on the iPhone screen, you must create a window to hold content. To build a window, you need a *frame*. A frame is a rectangular region on the screen where your content should be displayed. The underlying structure containing this information is a CGRect structure. A CGRect structure contains two elements: the coordinates for the upper-left corner of the window (the origin) and the window's width and height (the size). Every object that can display itself on the screen has a frame defining its display region, although many higher-level classes automatically calculate this for you. Others are set automatically when a view object is initialized, by means of an initialization method named initWithFrame.

When creating the main window, you'll create a frame whose coordinates are offset to the screen itself. Subsequent objects, however, are offset to the object they are anchored to. For example, the frame of a view anchored to the window will be offset to the coordinates of the window, and not the screen. The objects anchored to the view will be offset to the coordinates of the view, and so on.

An application uses the entire iPhone screen when it is displayed, so you should assign the window a set of coordinates reflecting the region of the entire screen. Two methods exist inside a class named UIScreen to determine this.

The bounds method returns the entire screen's boundaries, including the space used by the status bar:

```
CGRect screenBounds = [ [ UIScreen mainScreen ] bounds ];
```

The applicationFrame method returns the displayable portion of the screen in which your application will be displayed. This space does not include the status bar:

```
CGRect screenBounds = [ [ UIScreen mainScreen ] applicationFrame ];
```

This region, assigned to the CGRect structure `screenBounds`, is then used to create and initialize a new `UIWindow` object:

```
self.window = [ [ UIWindow alloc ] initWithFrame: screenBounds ];
```

The window frame is now created, but contains nothing and has not been instructed to display anything—it is simply an invisible object sitting on the screen. You now require an object that can render content inside the frame, and therefore you'll need an object based on the `UIView` class to fill the window.

As you've just learned, the window's offset is relative to the screen. A view's offset, however, is relative to the window it's attached to. While the window's offset on the screen begins at the pixel underneath the status bar (0×20), the view's offset within the window begins at 0×0, specifying the upper-left corner of the window. To accomplish this, you'll obtain the `applicationFrame` bounds and adjust the vertical offset so that it is zeroed with the window:

```
CGRect viewBounds = [ [ UIScreen mainScreen ] applicationFrame ];
viewBounds.origin.y = 0.0;
```

You'll now use `viewBounds` to specify the offset and dimensions of the view class:

```
UIView *myView = [ [ UIView alloc ] initWithFrame: viewBounds ];
```

 This will change slightly as you learn more about view controllers. When using view controllers, the window will use the bounds of the entire screen, including the status bar, and the view will use the application's frame as is. This allows the view controller to correctly handle screen rotations.

Displaying the View

You've created the window and view pair, but neither has been displayed on the screen. To do this, anchor the view to the window as a subview:

```
[ window addSubview: myView ];
```

Now bring the window to the front and display it using the `UIWindow` class's `makeKeyAndVisible` method:

```
[ window makeKeyAndVisible ];
```

HelloView: Most Useless Application Ever

Before you even get to "Hello, World!" you'll experiment with an even more useless application, "Hello, View!" This application does nothing more than create a window and view pair. In fact, because the `UIView` class is just a base class, it can't even display any text for you. All you'll see is a black screen. What this application does do is serve as the first lines of code any GUI application on the iPhone will use.

You can compile this application, shown in Examples 3-1, 3-2, and 3-3, with the SDK by creating a *window-based application* project named *HelloView*. As with most examples in this chapter, you may wish to remove Interface Builder from the project to get a feel for how each object is individually created in code.

Example 3-1. HelloView application delegate prototypes (HelloViewAppDelegate.h)

```
#import <UIKit/UIKit.h>

@interface HelloViewAppDelegate : NSObject <UIApplicationDelegate> {
    /* The one and only window in your application */
    UIWindow *window;

    /* The view class you'll be displaying in the window */
    UIView *myView;
}

@property (nonatomic, retain) IBOutlet UIWindow *window;

@end
```

Example 3-2. HelloView application delegate (HelloViewAppDelegate.m)

```
#import "HelloViewAppDelegate.h"

@implementation HelloViewAppDelegate

@synthesize window;

- (void)applicationDidFinishLaunching:(UIApplication *)application {
    CGRect screenBounds = [ [ UIScreen mainScreen ] applicationFrame ];
    CGRect windowBounds = screenBounds;
    windowBounds.origin.y = 0.0;

    /* Initialize the window */
    self.window = [ [ UIWindow alloc ] initWithFrame: screenBounds ];

    /* Initialize the view */
    myView = [ [ UIView alloc] initWithFrame: windowBounds ];

    /* Anchor the view to the window */
    [ window addSubview: myView ];

    /* Make the window key and visible */
    [ window makeKeyAndVisible ];
}

- (void)dealloc {
    [ myView release ];
    [ window release ];
    [ super dealloc ];
}

@end
```

Example 3-3. HelloView main (main.m)

```
#import <UIKit/UIKit.h>

int main(int argc, char *argv[]) {

    NSAutoreleasePool * pool = [[NSAutoreleasePool alloc] init];

    /* Call with the name of our application delegate class */
    int retVal = UIApplicationMain(argc, argv, nil, @"HelloViewAppDelegate");
    [pool release];
    return retVal;
}
```

What's Going On

The *HelloView* application doesn't visibly seem to do much, but its internal clockwork functions as follows:

1. When the application starts, its `main` function is invoked, just as in a regular C program. This hooks into Objective-C land and instantiates an application. The application then notifies its delegate, `HelloViewAppDelegate`, which is specified in the call to `UIApplicationMain`. The `main` function is also responsible for initializing an auto-release pool. Auto-release pools are used extensively throughout Apple's Cocoa framework to dispose of objects that have been designated as `autorelease` when they were created. This tells the application to simply throw them away when it's done with them, and they are deallocated later on.

2. The underlying framework calls the `HelloViewAppDelegate` class's `applicationDidFinishLaunching` method once the object has initialized. This is where the Objective-C portion of the application begins life.

3. The system calls the `UIScreen` class's `applicationFrame` method to return the coordinates and size of the application's display window. This will create a new window where the application's main view will reside. Keep in mind that you'll later change this to use the entire screen region as your applications become more advanced in nature.

4. The application creates the main view class, using a display region beginning at 0×0 (the upper-left corner of the window). It then sets the view as the window's content.

5. The application delegate finally instructs the window to come to the front and display itself. This displays the view, which presently has no content.

Deriving from UIView

The *HelloView* example shows the very minimal code needed to construct and display a window/view pair. Because the `UIView` class itself is merely a base class, it didn't actually display anything. To create a useful application, you'll need to either anchor a more useful object to the `UIView` or derive a new `UIView` class to add more functionality. The iPhone SDK provides many subclasses of the `UIView` class that offer differing types of functionality. You can also create your own subclass to build a custom view.

To derive a subclass from `UIView`, write a new interface and implementation declaring the subclass. The following snippet creates a class named `MainView` as a subclass of the `UIView` class:

```
@interface MainView : UIView
{

}
- (id)initWithFrame:(CGRect)rect;
- (void)dealloc;

@end
```

The `MainView` class inherits from the `UIView` class, so at the moment it does the equivalent of the `UIView` class—nothing. In order to make this class useful, you'll add new functionality. Below is a new version of the above snippet, adding variable storage for a text box class named `UITextView`. In reality, you could easily attach a `UITextView` object to the window itself, because it is derived from the `UIView` class. For now, you'll incorporate it into your custom class:

```
#import <UIKit/UITextView.h>

@interface MainView : UIView
{
    UITextView *textView;
}
- (id)initWithFrame:(CGRect) rect;
- (void)dealloc;

@end
```

You'll notice two methods above, `initWithFrame` and `dealloc`. These methods are the default initializer and destructor methods, and will be overridden in your subclass, `MainView`, to expand the functionality of the `UIView` class.

 Classes use a common constructor method named `alloc`, but you shouldn't override these methods. Your own custom initialization code belongs in initializer methods such as `init` and `initWithFrame`.

As you've seen, the `initWithFrame` method is called when the view is first instantiated and is used to initialize the class. A frame is passed to it in order to define its display region. You should place any code that initializes variables or other objects inside this method. The second method, `dealloc`, is called when the object is disposed of. You must release any resources previously allocated within your class here, so that they will be deallocated when the object is destroyed. Both methods invoke their superclass methods to allow the UIView class to handle its own internal functions.

Here are the templates for these two important methods:

```
@implementation MainView
- (id)initWithFrame:(CGRect)rect {

    /* Call the super class's initWithFrame method first,
     * to initialize the UIView object */
    self = [ super initWithFrame: rect ];

    /* If the object has already been initialized, self will be nil */

    if (self != nil) {

        /* Initialize your class's variables here */

        /* Allocate your class's initial resources here */
    }

    return self;
}

- (void)dealloc
{
    /* Deallocate your class's resources here */

    /* Call the super class's dealloc method,
     * to deallocate any resources held by UIView */

    [ super dealloc ];
}
@end
```

HelloWorld: The Traditionally Useless Application

Now that you've learned how to derive a UIView class, you've got everything you need to write an application that does something—albeit a mostly useless something. In the tradition of our respected legends Kernighan and Ritchie, we now present the official useless "Hello, World!" application for the iPhone SDK.

You can compile this application, shown in Examples 3-4, 3-5, and 3-6, with the SDK by creating a *window-based application* project named *HelloWorld*. You'll want to remove Interface Builder from the project to see how all objects are created.

Example 3-4. HelloWorld application delegate prototypes (HelloWorldAppDelegate.h)

```
#import <UIKit/UIKit.h>

@interface MainView : UIView
{
    UITextView *textView;
}
```

```
@end

@interface HelloWorldAppDelegate : NSObject <UIApplicationDelegate,
 UITextViewDelegate> {
    UIWindow *window;
    MainView *myMainView;
}

@property (nonatomic, retain) IBOutlet UIWindow *window;

@end
```

Example 3-5. HelloWorld application delegate (HelloWorldAppDelegate.m)

```
#import <UIKit/UITextView.h>
#import <UIKit/UIColor.h>
#import <UIKit/UIFont.h>
#import "HelloWorldAppDelegate.h"

@implementation MainView

- (id)initWithFrame:(CGRect) rect {
    self = [ super initWithFrame: rect ];

    if (self != nil) {
        textView = [ [ UITextView alloc] initWithFrame: rect ];
        textView.text = @"Hello, World!";

        [ self addSubview: textView ];
    }

    return self;
}

- (void)dealloc {
    [ textView release ];
    [ super dealloc ];
}
@end

@implementation HelloWorldAppDelegate

@synthesize window;

- (void)applicationDidFinishLaunching:(UIApplication *)application {
    CGRect screenBounds = [ [ UIScreen mainScreen ] applicationFrame ];
    CGRect windowBounds = screenBounds;
    windowBounds.origin.y = 0.0;

    self.window = [ [ [ UIWindow alloc ] initWithFrame: screenBounds ]
        autorelease
    ];

    myMainView = [ [ MainView alloc ] initWithFrame: windowBounds ];
```

```
    [ window addSubview: myMainView ];
    [ window makeKeyAndVisible ];
}

- (void)dealloc {
    [myMainView release];
    [window release];
    [super dealloc];
}

@end
```

Example 3-6. HelloWorld main (main.m)

```
#import <UIKit/UIKit.h>

int main(int argc, char *argv[]) {

    NSAutoreleasePool * pool = [[NSAutoreleasePool alloc] init];
    int retVal = UIApplicationMain(argc, argv, nil, @"HelloWorldAppDelegate");
    [pool release];
    return retVal;
}
```

What's Going On

The *HelloWorld* example contains everything you've seen so far, with the addition of a subclass of UIView, MainView, which can display text:

1. The application instantiates in the same way as before; by calling the program's main function, which invokes the UIApplicationMain function and subsequent notifications to the HelloWorldAppDelegate delegate class.

2. Instead of creating a generic UIView class, the application instantiates its own class named MainView, which is derived from the UIView class.

3. The MainView class's initWithFrame method is called, which in turn calls its superclass (UIView) and its own initWithFrame method to let UIView do the work of creating itself.

4. A UITextView class, which you'll learn more about in the next section, is instantiated and attached to the MainView object. This text view is instructed to display the text, "Hello, World!" The UITextView object is added as a subview to the MainView object, and the MainView object is in turn added as a subview to the UIWindow object.

5. The window is instructed to become visible, displaying the MainView object, which displays the UITextView object attached to it.

View Controllers

In the previous example, you created a custom view class named MainView, which took on all of the functionality of a UIView class, and also controlled a UITextView class, capable of displaying text. Imagine now that your application has many different screens, and needs to change between them. Or perhaps your application needs to provide landscape mode rotations. In such cases, you would find yourself in a time-consuming situation to roll your own custom class to control how the UITextView was displayed, or how to transition different text views onto the screen. While you could roll your own, the iPhone SDK provides a view controller class designed to handle all of this work for you.

The UIViewController class provides the low-level functionality needed to create and display one or more views, just like the example MainView class controlled UITextView from the previous example. Apple's view controller also adds built-in support for orientation changes, low memory notifications, and smooth transitions, all of which you'll learn about in this chapter.

In addition to the functionality provided by the UIViewController class, many other controller-type classes exist to make your life as a developer easier. You'll learn about these throughout this book. These controller classes require that you also use the UIViewController class to contain your views, so now is a good time to start using them in your code.

Creating a View Controller

A view controller acts much like the MainView object you created earlier. You'll create a subclass of UIViewController, which will inherit the functionality of its parent class. A prototype for the view controller version of MainView might look like the following example:

```
#import <UIKit/UIKit.h>
#import <UIKit/UITextView.h>

@interface MainViewController : UIViewController {
    UITextView *textView;
}
- (id)init;
- (void)dealloc;
- (void)loadView;
@end
```

Just like MainView, the variables used in the view are stored within the controller class. In this example, a UITextView object is stored in the controller for later display.

When a view controller is initialized, a simple method named init is invoked by the object's creator, instead of the initWithFrame method you used with UIView. A view controller is designed to accommodate orientation changes, so you will need to

---

reconfigure its underlying views to new screen boundaries for events like orientation changes and when the views are initially created. In portrait mode, the screen resolution will be 320×480, but in landscape mode, the resolution will be 480×320.

When a view controller is created, a call to a method named `loadView` is made. You'll be responsible for coding this method to build the underlying `UIView` class and to anchor this view to the controller.

By default, a `UIViewController` class creates a `UIView` object when it is initialized. This object is displayed as the controller's view by default, and can be accessed by addressing `self.view`. When you add your own custom view classes to a controller, you have two options: you can anchor your custom view classes to the existing `UIView` object or replace the view object entirely.

To anchor a custom view class to the existing view, create the custom view in your `loadView` method, and then use the `addSubview` method to add it to the view's display layer. This can be particularly useful if you're displaying multiple views together, such as a table and a picker view. In the example below, two text views are created and displayed vertically:

```
- (void)loadView {

    CGRect bounds = [ [ UIScreen mainScreen ] applicationFrame ];

    textView1 = [ [ UITextView alloc ] initWithFrame:
        CGRectMake(0, 0, bounds.size.width, bounds.size.height / 2)
    ];

    textView2 = [ [ UITextView alloc ] initWithFrame:
        CGRectMake(0, bounds.size.height / 2,
            bounds.size.width,
            bounds.size.height / 2)
    ];

    textView1.text = @"Hello, World!";
    textView2.text = @"Hello again!";
    [ self.view addSubview: textView1 ];
    [ self.view addSubview: textView2 ];
}
```

If you'll only be displaying a single view at a time, or if you have written a standalone custom view class that can display many objects on its own, you may wish to replace the default `UIView` object entirely. You can do this by assigning your own view object to `self.view`. An example of this follows:

```
- (void)loadView {

    [ super loadView ];
    CGRect bounds = [ [ UIScreen mainScreen ] applicationFrame ];

    textView = [ [ UITextView alloc ] initWithFrame: bounds ];
    textView.text = @"Hello, World! ";
```

```
        self.view = textView;
    }
```

 Notice here that it is no longer necessary to set the screen origin to be zero-offset to the window. This is because a window can now be created using the entire screen's bounds, so that the application can control the status bar portion of the screen.

The `loadView` method is generally only called only once, unless the controller's underlying view has been flushed. The controller will flush a view if it's not presently being displayed and memory is short. When this happens, a method within the controller, named `didReceiveMemoryWarning`, is notified, allowing you to perform any cleanup of your own resources. If the view needs to be displayed again, `loadView` will be reinvoked.

Loading from Interface Builder

On top of creating your own objects, you can instantiate view controllers from Interface Builder templates. This allows you to store the UI properties for the view class in an Interface Builder template and fuse it with your custom view controller class. To create a new view controller object, include your *.xib* file by adding it to your project's *Re sources* folder. You can then instantiate the class using the `UIViewController` class's `initWithNibName` method:

```
MainViewController *myViewController = [
    [ MainViewController alloc ]
    initWithNibName: @"MainViewController"
    bundle: nil
];
```

Orientation Changes

When an orientation change occurs, the view controller will check with your object to see if it should change to the specified orientation. The default method provided by Xcode disables all nonportrait orientation changes:

```
-(BOOL)shouldAutorotateToInterfaceOrientation:
(UIInterfaceOrientation)interfaceOrientation
{
    return (interfaceOrientation == UIDeviceOrientationPortrait);
}
```

To support all valid orientations, return a `YES` value. To support only specific orientations, compare the input argument with one or more of the following enumerated values:

UIDeviceOrientationUnknown
    Catchall for errors or hardware failures

`UIDeviceOrientationPortrait`
Oriented upright vertically in portrait mode

`UIDeviceOrientationPortraitUpsideDown`
Oriented upside-down vertically in portrait mode

`UIDeviceOrientationLandscapeLeft`
Device is rotated counter-clockwise in landscape mode

`UIDeviceOrientationLandscapeRight`
Device is rotated clockwise in landscape mode

`UIDeviceOrientationFaceUp`
Device is laying flat, face up, such as on a table

`UIDeviceOrientationFaceDown`
Device is laying flat, face down, such as on a table

After an orientation change, a method named `didRotateFromInterfaceOrientation` is invoked from within the view controller. You can use this to make any application-specific adjustments to accommodate an orientation change:

```
- (void)didRotateFromInterfaceOrientation:
        (UIInterfaceOrientation)fromInterfaceOrientation
{
    /* Add post-orientation change code here */
}
```

Disposing of a View Controller

Finally, when the view controller is disposed of, its `dealloc` method is called. This method cleans up any objects that are local to the controller, and then calls its superclass's `dealloc` method:

```
- (void)dealloc {

    [ super dealloc ];
}
```

Your version of the `dealloc` method will override the class's own version, which is why its superclass's `dealloc` method is subsequently called. Any objects you've allocated within your subclass should be released in the `dealloc` method, which will free them when your view controller is released:

```
- (void)dealloc {
    [ textView release ];
    [ super dealloc ];
}
```

ControllerDemo: Hello World, View Controller Style

This example builds on the previous one by implementing the proper use of a view controller to take the place of `MainView`. As you'll see, the view controller encapsulates the text view in much the same way as the `MainView` class did, but instantly expands the functionality of your application by allowing for full rotation (along with other things you'll learn about later). This example shows the correct use of a view controller's `init`, `loadView`, and `dealloc` methods to build an underlying view, as well as some example routines to accommodate orientation changes.

You can compile this application, shown in Examples 3-7 through 3-11, with the SDK by creating a *view-based application* project named *ControllerDemo*. Be sure to pull out the Interface Builder code if you'd like to see how these objects are created from scratch.

Example 3-7. ControllerDemo application delegate prototypes (ControllerDemoAppDelegate.h)

```
#import <UIKit/UIKit.h>

@class ControllerDemoViewController;

@interface ControllerDemoAppDelegate : NSObject <UIApplicationDelegate> {
    UIWindow *window;
    ControllerDemoViewController *viewController;
}

@property (nonatomic, retain) IBOutlet UIWindow *window;
@property (nonatomic, retain) IBOutlet ControllerDemoViewController *viewController;

@end
```

Example 3-8. ControllerDemo application delegate (ControllerDemoAppDelegate.m)

```
#import "ControllerDemoAppDelegate.h"
#import "ControllerDemoViewController.h"

@implementation ControllerDemoAppDelegate

@synthesize window;
@synthesize viewController;

- (void)applicationDidFinishLaunching:(UIApplication *)application {
    CGRect screenBounds = [ [ UIScreen mainScreen ] bounds ];

    self.window = [ [ [ UIWindow alloc ] initWithFrame: screenBounds ]
        autorelease
    ];

    viewController = [ [ ControllerDemoViewController alloc ] init ];

    [ window addSubview:viewController.view ];
    [ window makeKeyAndVisible ];
}


- (void)dealloc {
    [viewController release];
    [window release];
    [super dealloc];
```

```
}


@end
```

Example 3-9. ControllerDemo view controller prototype (ControllerDemoViewController.h)

```objc
#import <UIKit/UIKit.h>
#import <UIKit/UITextView.h>

@interface ControllerDemoViewController : UIViewController {
    NSString *helloWorld, *woahDizzy;
    UITextView *textView;
}

@end
```

Example 3-10. ControllerDemo view controller (ControllerDemoViewController.m)

```objc
#import "ControllerDemoViewController.h"

@implementation ControllerDemoViewController

- (id)init {

    self = [ super init ];

    if (self != nil) {
        /* Illustrate allocating some objects, even if we don't need to */
        helloWorld = [ [ NSString alloc ] initWithString: @"Hello, World!" ];
        woahDizzy = [ [ NSString alloc ] initWithString: @"Woah, I'm Dizzy!" ];
    }

    return self;
}

- (void)loadView {

    [ super loadView ];

    textView = [ [ UITextView alloc ] initWithFrame:
        [ [ UIScreen mainScreen ] applicationFrame ]
    ];

    textView.text = helloWorld;
    self.view = textView;
}

-(BOOL)shouldAutorotateToInterfaceOrientation:
(UIInterfaceOrientation)interfaceOrientation
{
    return YES;
}

-   (void)didRotateFromInterfaceOrientation:
(UIInterfaceOrientation)fromInterfaceOrientation
```

```
{
    textView.text = woahDizzy;
}

- (void)viewDidLoad {
    [ super viewDidLoad ];

    /* Add custom post-load code here */
}

- (void)didReceiveMemoryWarning {
    [ super didReceiveMemoryWarning ];

    /* Add custom low-memory code here */
}

- (void)dealloc {
    /* Here, the objects we've allocated are released */

    [ helloWorld release ];
    [ woahDizzy release ];

    [ textView release ];
    [ super dealloc ];
}

@end
```

Example 3-11. ControllerDemo main (main.m)

```
#import <UIKit/UIKit.h>

int main(int argc, char *argv[]) {

    NSAutoreleasePool * pool = [[NSAutoreleasePool alloc] init];
    int retVal = UIApplicationMain(argc, argv, nil, @"ControllerDemoAppDelegate");
    [pool release];
    return retVal;
}
```

What's Going On

The *ControllerDemo* example contains everything you've seen so far, but replaces the MainView class with a view controller named ControllerDemoViewController:

1. The application instantiates by calling the program's main function, which causes the ControllerDemoAppDelegate class's applicationDidFinishLaunching method to be notified when the application has launched.

2. A window is created using the entire bounds of the screen. This is needed in order for screen rotation to work correctly.

3. A view controller is created and its init method is invoked. When the view is displayed, the controller's loadView method is notified, which creates a

UITextView object and assigns it the application's viewable region using the UIScreen class's `applicationFrame` method. The text view is then assigned as the view controller's active view by means of setting `self.view`.

4. The view controller's active view is added as a subview of the window and the window is instructed to display. This in turn displays the text view.

5. When the device is rotated, the view controller's `shouldAutorotate ToInterfaceOrientation` method is consulted to see if it should change orientation. The example returns `YES`, and the view controller's internal methods handle all of the work.

6. When the screen has finished rotating, the view controller's `didRotateFromInter faceOrientation` method is called, which changes the contents of the text view.

Further Study

Now that you have a skeleton for any view application, play around with it for a little while before proceeding:

• Try changing the origins and size of the frame used by the view controller and window. What happens to the window and its child? How about when changing the display origin of `textView`?

• Check out the following prototypes in your SDK's header files: *UIWindow.h*, *UIView.h*, and *UIViewController.h*. You'll find these deep within */Developer/ Platforms/iPhoneOS.platform*, inside the UI Kit framework's *Headers* directory.

Text Views

The `UITextView` class is indirectly based on the `UIView` class, with its functionality extended to present and allow the editing of text, provide scrolling, and render various styling options, such as font and color. Text views are practical for text-based portions of an application, such as an electronic book, the notes section of a program, or an informational page to present unstructured information for editing. Structured information is best displayed in other UI Kit objects, which you'll learn about in this chapter and in Chapter 10. You've already used the `UITextView` class in some of the previous examples. In this section, you'll learn how to customize its behavior.

A `UITextView` object inherits from a class named `UIScrollView`, which is a general-purpose scrollable view class. The text view class inherits all of the scrolling functionality of `UIScrollView`, so the developer can focus on presenting content rather than programming scroll bars. The `UIScrollView` class inherits from the base `UIView` class, which, as discussed in the previous section, is the base for all view classes. The following is an illustration of the class hierarchy:

- UITextView adds functionality and inherits the functionality of...
  - UIScrollView adds functionality and inherits the functionality of...
    - UIView is the base class for all view classes, inherits the functionality of...
      - UIResponder is the foundation class for all objects that respond.

Creating a Text View

Because UITextView is ultimately derived from UIView, it is created in the same fashion as other view objects were created in the previous section—using an initWithFrame method. If your text view were attached to a view controller's loadView method, you'd use the UIScreen class's applicationFrame method to determine the view's display region:

```
- (void) loadView {
    [ super loadView ];
    CGRect bounds = [ [ UIScreen mainScreen ] applicationFrame ];
    textView = [ [ UITextView alloc ] initWithFrame: bounds ];
    self.view = textView;
}
```

Alternatively, you can define a custom size for the text view if you are attaching it to an existing view object, such as the controller's default view. The following example creates a 320×200 text view with a vertical offset of 100 pixels down, and then attaches it to the view controller's default view:

```
- (void) loadView {
    [ super loadView ];
    CGRect viewRect = CGRectMake(0.0, 100.0, 320.0, 200.0);
    UITextView *textView = [ [ UITextView alloc ]
        initWithFrame: viewRect ];
    [ self.view addSubview: textView ];
}
```

Once you have created the text view, you can set a number of different properties.

Editing

By default, a text view is editable by the user. If the user taps within the text view, the iPhone will automatically pop up a keyboard and resize the text view to accommodate typing. For read-only text views, set the editable property to NO:

```
textView.editable = NO;
```

Alignment

By default, text is left-aligned in the window. You can change this using the text view's textAlignment property:

```
textView.textAlignment = UITextAlignmentLeft;
```

Use the following values to change text alignment:

`UITextAlignmentLeft`
> Text will be left-aligned (default)

`UITextAlignmentRight`
> Text will be right-aligned

`UITextAlignmentCenter`
> Text will be centered

Font and size

The text font (typeface) and point size can be set by assigning a `UIFont` object to the text view's `font` property. To create a `UIFont` object, use a static method named `fontWithName`:

```
UIFont *myFont = [ UIFont fontWithName: @"Arial" size: 18.0 ];
textView.font = myFont;
```

Additionally, three other static methods exist for easily creating system fonts:

```
UIFont *mySystemFont = [ UIFont systemFontOfSize: 12.0 ];
UIFont *myBoldSystemFont = [ UIFont boldSystemFontOfSize: 12.0 ];
UIFont *myItalicSystemFont = [ UIFont italicSystemFontOfSize: 12.0 ];
```

The following fonts come preinstalled on the iPhone and can be referenced by name:

> American Typewriter
> Apple Gothic
> Arial
> Arial Rounded MT Bold
> Courier
> Courier New
> Georgia
> Helvetica
> Helvetica Neue
> Marker Felt
> Times
> Times New Roman
> Trebuchet MS
> Verdana
> Zapfino

Font selection determines the display font for all text within the text view. A text view does not support rich text.

Text color

You can define text color using a `UIColor` object. The `UIColor` class provides many different methods for easily mixing any color. You can use static methods to create colors, which are released when no longer needed. Colors can be created as white levels, using hue, or as an RGB composite. To create a simple RGB color, specify a set of four floating-point values for red, green, blue, and alpha (opacity) with values between 0.0 and 1.0. These represent values ranging from 0% (0.0) to 100% (1.0):

```
UIColor *myWhiteTransparentColor = [ UIColor colorWithWhite: 1.0 alpha: 0.50 ];

UIColor *myColorHue = [ UIColor colorWithHue: 120.0 / 360.0
    saturation: 0.75
    brightness: 0.50
    alpha: 1.0
];

UIColor *myColorRGB = [ UIColor colorWithRed: 0.75
    green: 1.0
    blue: 0.75
    alpha: 1.0
];
```

If you plan on reusing many different UIColor objects, you may also create instances of them:

```
UIColor *myWhiteTransparentColor = [ [ UIColor alloc ]
    initWithWhite: 1.0 alpha: 0.50
];

UIColor *myColorHue = [ [ UIColor alloc ]
    initWithHue: 120.0 / 360.0
    saturation: 0.75
    brightness: 0.50
    alpha: 1.0
];

UIColor *myColorRGB = [ [ UIColor alloc ] initWithRed: 0.75
    green: 1.0
    blue: 0.75
    alpha: 1.0
];
```

The UIColor class also supports many static methods to create system colors, which are calibrated by the iPhone as closely as possible. These methods include the following, from *UIColor.h*:

```
+ (UIColor *)blackColor;       // 0.0 white
+ (UIColor *)darkGrayColor;    // 0.333 white
+ (UIColor *)lightGrayColor;   // 0.667 white
+ (UIColor *)whiteColor;       // 1.0 white
+ (UIColor *)grayColor;        // 0.5 white
+ (UIColor *)redColor;         // 1.0, 0.0, 0.0 RGB
+ (UIColor *)greenColor;       // 0.0, 1.0, 0.0 RGB
+ (UIColor *)blueColor;        // 0.0, 0.0, 1.0 RGB
+ (UIColor *)cyanColor;        // 0.0, 1.0, 1.0 RGB
+ (UIColor *)yellowColor;      // 1.0, 1.0, 0.0 RGB
+ (UIColor *)magentaColor;     // 1.0, 0.0, 1.0 RGB
+ (UIColor *)orangeColor;      // 1.0, 0.5, 0.0 RGB
```

```
+ (UIColor *)purpleColor;      // 0.5, 0.0, 0.5 RGB
+ (UIColor *)brownColor;       // 0.6, 0.4, 0.2 RGB
+ (UIColor *)clearColor;       // 0.0 white, 0.0 alpha
```

Once you have created a UIColor object, assign it to the text view's color property:

```
textView.textColor = myColorHue;
```

Because a text view doesn't directly support rich text, the color selection affects all of the text within the view.

Colors from Core Graphics

The Core Graphics framework is used widely on the Mac OS X desktop for two-dimensional rendering and transformations. We'll cover some of its pieces in this book, but Core Graphics programming is a topic for an entirely dedicated book in itself. If you're already using the Core Graphics framework for graphics programming, you can apply much of your knowledge to the iPhone.

The Core Graphics equivalent of a UIColor object is CGColor. You can convert a CGColorRef (Core Graphics color reference) to a UIColor object using the colorWithCG Color method:

```
CGColorSpaceRef colorSpace =
    CGColorSpaceCreateWithName(kCGColorSpaceGenericRGB);
float opaqueRed[4] = { 1.0, 0.0, 0.0, 1.0 };
CGColorRef red = CGColorCreate(colorSpace, opaqueRed);
UIColor *myRed = [ UIColor colorWithCGColor: red ];
textView.textColor = myRed;
```

Assigning Content

The text of the view can be set with a property named text. This property accepts an NSString argument. An easy way to set static text follows:

```
textView.text = @"Hello, world!";
```

You can also use the NSString class's many string creation methods to create custom string objects:

```
int nBottles = 100;
NSString *myFormattedString = [ [ NSString alloc ]
    initWithFormat: @"%d bottles of beer on the wall", nBottles
];

textView.text = myFormattedString;
```

You can also create NSString objects from C-style character arrays:

```
char myBottles[] = "100 bottles of beer on the wall";
NSString *myCString = [ NSString stringWithCString: myBottles ];
textView.text = myCString;
```

To access a file in your home directory, use the `NSHomeDirectory` function to obtain the unique path to your application's sandbox. This is the path to the directory hierarchy you learned about in Chapter 1:

```
NSString *myFile = [ NSHomeDirectory()
    stringByAppendingPathComponent: @"Documents/file.txt"
];

NSString *myFileString = [ NSString stringWithContentsOfFile: myFile ];
textView.text = myFileString;
```

The same also exist as instance methods using the `initWith` prefix instead of `stringWith`:

```
NSString *myFile = [ [ NSString alloc ] initWithFormat: @"%@/Documents/file.txt",
    NSHomeDirectory()
];

NSString *myFileString = [ [ NSString alloc ] initWithContentsOfFile: myFile ];
textView.text = myFileString;
```

Displaying HTML

An undocumented API exists to display HTML content inside a text view. Because it's undocumented, Apple likely wants you to use the `UIWebView` class instead, which you'll learn about in Chapter 10. For fun, we'll show you the private method call to do this below, which can be useful for debugging:

```
[ textView setContentToHTMLString:
    @"<HTML><BODY><B>Hello, World!</B></BODY></HTML>" ];
```

 This undocumented API is subject to change at any time. Your application could also potentially be rejected from listing in the iTunes store if you use undocumented APIs.

SourceReader: Web Page Source Code Reader

If you've ever tried to learn HTML, chances are you've used your browser's View Source feature at least a few times. This example uses the foundation library's `NSURL` and `NSString` objects to load the front page from *http://www.oreilly.com* and display it in a text window using a `UITextView`. You'll also see `UIColor` and `UIFont` objects in action, and other text view properties used. This example will build on top of the previous view controller example, adding functionality to the controller's `loadView` method. Because the functionality of performing HTTP requests has been incorporated into the `NSString` class, you won't see any code for loading web page content. The web page content will be automatically loaded after invoking the `NSString` class's `stringWith ContentsOfURL` method. See Figure 3-1.

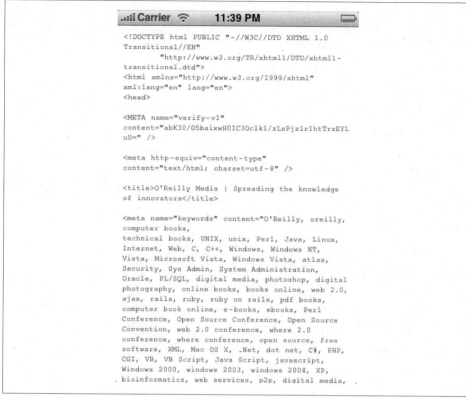

Figure 3-1. SourceReader example

You can compile this application, shown in Examples 3-12 through 3-16, with the SDK by creating a *view-based application* project named *SourceReader*. Be sure to pull out the Interface Builder code if you'd like to see how these objects are created from scratch.

Example 3-12. SourceReader application delegate prototypes (SourceReaderAppDelegate.h)

```
#import <UIKit/UIKit.h>

@class SourceReaderViewController;

@interface SourceReaderAppDelegate : NSObject <UIApplicationDelegate> {
    UIWindow *window;
    SourceReaderViewController *viewController;
}

@property (nonatomic, retain) IBOutlet UIWindow *window;
@property (nonatomic, retain) IBOutlet SourceReaderViewController *viewController;

@end
```

Example 3-13. SourceReader application delegate (SourceReaderAppDelegate.m)

```
#import "SourceReaderAppDelegate.h"
#impo rt "SourceReaderViewController.h"

@implementation SourceReaderAppDelegate

@synthesize window;
@synthesize viewController;

- (void)applicationDidFinishLaunching:(UIApplication *)application {
    CGRect screenBounds = [ [ UIScreen mainScreen ] bounds ];

    self.window = [ [ [ UIWindow alloc ] initWithFrame: screenBounds ]
        autorelease
    ];

    viewController = [ [ SourceReaderViewController alloc ] init ];

    [ window addSubview: viewController.view ];
    [ window makeKeyAndVisible ];
}


- (void)dealloc {
    [viewController release];
    [window release];
    [super dealloc];
}

@end
```

Example 3-14. SourceReader view controller prototype (SourceReaderViewController.h)

```
#import <UIKit/UIKit.h>

@interface SourceReaderViewController : UIViewController {
    UITextView *textView;
}

@end
```

Example 3-15. SourceReader view controller (SourceReaderViewController.m)

```
#import <UIKit/UIColor.h>
#import <UIKit/UIFont.h>
#import "SourceReaderViewController.h"

@implementation SourceReaderViewController

- (id)init {
    self = [ super init ];
    if (self != nil) {
        /* Additional initialization code */
    }
    return self;
```

```
}

- (void)loadView {
    CGRect bounds = [ [ UIScreen mainScreen ] applicationFrame ];

    [ super loadView ];

    textView = [ [ UITextView alloc ] initWithFrame: bounds ];

    UIColor *myBlue = [ UIColor colorWithRed: 0.0
        green: 0.0 blue: 1.0 alpha: 1.0 ];
    textView.textColor = myBlue;

    UIFont *myFixed = [ UIFont fontWithName: @"Courier New" size: 10.0 ];
    textView.font = myFixed;

    textView.editable = NO;

    NSURL *url = [ NSURL URLWithString: @"http://www.oreilly.com" ];
    NSString *pageData = [ NSString stringWithContentsOfURL: url ];
    textView.text = pageData;

    self.view = textView;
}

-(BOOL)shouldAutorotateToInterfaceOrientation:
(UIInterfaceOrientation)interfaceOrientation
{
    return (interfaceOrientation == UIDeviceOrientationPortrait);
}

- (void)viewDidLoad {
    [ super viewDidLoad ];
}


- (void)dealloc {
    [ textView dealloc ];
    [ super dealloc ];
}

@end
```

Example 3-16. SourceReader main (main.m)

```
#import <UIKit/UIKit.h>

int main(int argc, char *argv[]) {

    NSAutoreleasePool * pool = [[NSAutoreleasePool alloc] init];
    int retVal = UIApplicationMain(argc, argv, nil, @"SourceReaderAppDelegate");
    [pool release];
    return retVal;
}
```

What's Going On

The *SourceReader* example contains the core of everything you've seen so far and adds a functional text view containing the contents of the O'Reilly website:

1. The application begins within its `main` function, which invokes the `SourceReader AppDelegate` class's `applicationDidFinishLaunching` method.

2. A window is created using the entire bounds of the screen. A view controller is then created and its `init` method is invoked. The runtime then calls the controller's `loadView` method, which creates the `UITextView` object and assigns it the application's viewable region using `UIScreen`'s `applicationFrame` method.

3. After the text view is created, an `NSURL` object is created using the URL *http://www .oreilly.com*. This is used to create an `NSString` object containing the contents of the web page, which the `NSString` class loads automatically. The contents of the page are then assigned to the text view and the view controller's active view is replaced by means of setting `self.view`.

4. The view controller's active view is added as a subview of the window and the window is instructed to display. This in turn displays the text view.

Further Study

Play around with the text view for a little while before proceeding:

- Using the undocumented API, modify this project so that the actual HTML is displayed rather than the source text. What kind of compiler warnings do you receive and why?

- Check out the following prototypes in your SDK's header files: *UITextView.h*, *UIColor.h*, and *UIFont.h*. You'll find these under */Developer/Platforms/ iPhoneOS.platform*, inside the UI Kit framework's *Headers* directory.

Navigation Bars and Controllers

The iPhone doesn't support toolbars in the traditional desktop sense of a clutter of icons across the top of a window. Since each screen of an application is considered a page in a book, Apple has made its version of the toolbar for iPhone to appear more book-like and clean. In contrast to cluttered toolbars, navigation bars include a page title, directional buttons, and text buttons for context-sensitive functions such as turning on a speakerphone or clearing a list of items. Navigation bars also support controls to add tabbed buttons (called segmented controls) such as the "All" and "Missed" call buttons when viewing recent calls. If you miss the cluttered look, you can create toolbars containing custom buttons too. A small library of standard system buttons also exists.

Navigation controllers "wrap" one or more view controllers, allowing you to add a navigation bar to an existing view controller-based application without worrying about handling window dimension changes or orientation. Navigation controls allow you to stack individual view controllers onto it, automatically managing the navigation between them. This provides smoother navigation and handles the work of updating the navigation bar to adjust to each view's navigation properties.

The properties of a navigation bar—the types of buttons and controls to display—are properties of each view controller, not the navigation controller. This allows each view to define its own navigation bar configuration, which the navigation controller loads automatically when a user navigates to the view. If your view controller says, "I have a speakerphone button," the navigation controller will draw a speakerphone button when the view is displayed.

Creating a Navigation Controller

You can create a navigation controller right after you create at least one view controller, and initialize it with a pointer to the top-level view; that is, the authoritative root view for the application. The navigation controller refers to this as the *root view controller*. The root view controller is the view controller representing the very bottom of your navigation path: the main view for your application that will offer no Back button, and from which other views will originate.

To create a navigation controller, first create the view class that will serve as the root view controller. Then, instantiate the navigation controller using its `initWithRootView Controller` method, as shown below:

```
viewController = [ [ MyViewController alloc ] init ];

navigationController = [ [ UINavigationController alloc ]
    initWithRootViewController: viewController ];
```

When using a navigation controller, attach the navigation controller's view to the window. The view controller is anchored to the navigation controller when the navigation controller is created, and so it too will be displayed when the navigation controller is added to the window:

```
[ window addSubview: [ nagivationController view ] ];
```

The navigation controller will automatically render both it and the active view controller, which will default to the root view controller. When a new view is pushed onto the navigation controller's stack, the new view is displayed until the user presses the Back button or navigates elsewhere. To push another view onto the navigation controller, use the `pushViewController` method. An example follows:

```
[ navigationController pushViewController: myOtherViewController
        animated: YES
];
```

A Back button will automatically be added to the navigation bar when the view is pushed. The title of the Back button will match the title of the previous view controller on the stack. When the user presses the Back button, the view controller will be peeled off the stack and the previous view underneath will be transitioned back onto the screen.

Navigation Controller Properties

The view controller class shown earlier in this chapter can host its own navigation bar properties. This lets you define a different navigation bar layout for each view controller you create. Up until now, you've only dealt with a single view controller in an application, but in a functional application, you will have one view controller for each navigation screen, each with its own properties determining what the navigation bar should look like.

Navigation bar properties are normally set when the view controller's `init` method is invoked:

```
- (void)init {

    self = [ super init ];

    if (self != nil) {

        /* Navigation bar properties */

        self.title = @"My Title";
        ...
    }

    return self;
}
```

You can change the properties set in the view controller after the navigation controller is displayed—the controller will change its navigation bar to accommodate the view controller's latest settings. All changes to the navigation bar are made through the view controller's properties.

Anything visible in a navigation bar is part of a `UINavigationItem` object. The `UINavigationItem` class is the base class for anything that natively attaches to a navigation bar, including buttons and other objects. Apple has made this class private, so you can't access it directly. When each item—such as the title created in the following section—is added to the navigation bar, its `UINavigationItem` object is pushed onto it like an object on a stack.

Setting the title

The navigation title appears as large white text centered in the middle of the navigation bar. The title is frequently used to convey to the end-user what sort of information is being displayed, for example, "Saved Messages." The title also determines the title of the back button, if the view controller is not at the root of the stack:

```
self.title = @"Inbox";
```

Buttons, styles, and actions

You can add buttons to the left and/or right sides of a navigation bar. Because space is limited, the only buttons that you should add are those for functions specific to navigation or to the page being displayed.

The navigation controller automatically creates a new `UINavigationItem` object whenever its `navigationItem` property is accessed. This allows you to assign new objects to the navigation bar without worrying about placement, or even about what the `UINavigationItem` class looks like.

To create a new navigation button, create an instance of the `UIBarButtonItem` class. This class allows you to define a button title, style, and action to be invoked when the user presses it:

```
UIBarButtonItem *myButton = [ [ [ UIBarButtonItem alloc ]
    initWithTitle: @"Do it!"
    style: UIBarButtonItemStylePlain
    target: self
    action: @selector(doit)
] autorelease ];
```

The following properties are used to initialize the button:

initWithTitle

> Sets the title of the button. This argument accepts an `NSString`, which you've already learned about. If the button is a text button, it will be displayed with this text inside the button.

style

> Defines the style of the button. The following styles are available:

UIBarButtonItemStylePlain

> Default button style; displays a glow when pressed.

UIBarButtonItemStyleBordered

> Same as `UIBarButtonItemStylePlain`, but displays a bordered button.

UIBarButtonItemStyleDone

> Displays a blue button signifying that the user should tap it when he has finished editing.

target

> Specifies the delegate for the action. This is the object that will receive notification when the user presses the button. Using `self` will notify the view controller object, presuming you create the button in the view controller.

action

> Specifies the method to invoke when the user presses the button. This notifies the given method name in your target object so it can take the appropriate action.

Once you have created the button, you can add it as the navigation bar's left or right button, at which point it will be displayed immediately:

```
self.navigationItem.leftBarButtonItem = myButton;
self.navigationItem.rightBarButtonItem = myButton;
```

To create a button with a left arrow (a Back button), assign the button to the backBar ButtonItem property. The Back button will only be displayed if the view controller is not the root view controller:

```
self.navigationItem.backBarButtonItem = myButton;
```

When the button is pressed, the selector will be notified on the target object. You'll need to code a method to handle this button press action. The example above specifies the selector doit. Add a method with this same name to your delegate class:

```
- (void)doit {
    /* Place your action code here */
}
```

If, at any point, you would like to disable an existing navigation bar button, you have two options. To make the button disappear entirely, use the button properties you read about earlier to set the button to nil:

```
self.navigationItem.leftBarButtonItem = nil;
```

To leave the button visible, but grayed out, disable the button by setting its enabled property to NO:

```
myButton.enabled = NO;
```

Navigation bar style

The navigation controller itself can be displayed in one of a few different styles. The default style is the standard gray appearance. Three different styles are presently supported.

Style	Description
UIBarStyleDefault	Default style; gray background with white text
UIBarStyleBlackOpaque	Solid black background with white text
UIBarStyleBlackTranslucent	Transparent black background with white text

The style is set using the barStyle property. This property belongs to the navigation controller, and not the view controller, so that it remains consistent throughout the navigation of all views:

```
self.navigationController.navigationBar.barStyle = UIBarStyleBlackTranslucent;
```

Adding a Segmented Control

Controls are small, self-contained UI components that can be used by various UI Kit classes. They can be glued to many different types of objects, allowing the developer to add additional functionality to a window. One common control found in the navigation bars of Apple's preloaded applications is the segmented control.

You'll notice in many preloaded applications that Apple has added buttons to further categorize the information displayed. For example, the navigation bar in the iTunes WiFi Store application displays "New Releases," "What's Hot," and "Genres" buttons at the top. These further separate the user's music selection choice. Segmented controls are useful for any situation where an overabundance of similar data would best be categorized using two or three buttons.

An example of provisioning a control to display "All" and "Missed" calls follows:

```
UISegmentedControl *segmentedControl = [ [ UISegmentedControl alloc ]
    initWithItems: nil ];
segmentedControl.segmentedControlStyle = UISegmentedControlStyleBar;
[ segmentedControl insertSegmentWithTitle: @"All" atIndex: 0 animated: NO ];
[ segmentedControl insertSegmentWithTitle: @"Missed" atIndex: 1 animated: NO ];
```

Once you have created the segmented control, it can be displayed by assigning it to a view controller's `titleView` navigation property. This causes the standard title text to be replaced with your custom view:

```
self.navigationItem.titleView = segmentedControl;
```

You'll also want the class to be notified whenever the user selects a new segment so that it can change to display the new information. To do this, use the `UIControl` class's `addTarget` method to assign a method whenever the control value is changed:

```
[ segmentedControl addTarget: self
    action: @selector(controlPressed:)
    forControlEvents: UIControlEventValueChanged
];
```

In this example, a selector named `controllerPressed` was specified as the method that should be notified in the target `self`. Code this routine into your target class to handle value changes:

```
- (void) controllerPressed:(id)sender {
    int selectedIndex = [ segmentedControl selectedSegmentIndex ];

    /* Additional code to handle value change */
}
```

Each button in a segmented control is referred to as a segment. Access the selected segment with a call to the `selectedSegment` method of the control itself:

```
- (void) controllerPressed:(id)sender {
    int selectedSegment = segmentedControl.selectedSegmentIndex;
    NSLog(@"Segment %d selected\n", selectedSegment);
}
```

Chapter 10 explains the UIControl class's event chain and the segmented control in full detail.

Adding a Toolbar

A navigation style (style property) bar can host a number of different types of objects. You've just learned how to attach a segmented control as the navigation bar's title view to present the user with a series of subcategories. Another popular UI component found on the navigation bar is a UIToolbar object. Toolbars can host a custom set of buttons, including standard system buttons such as Bookmarks and Search buttons. Many preloaded iPhone applications, such as Safari and Mail, use toolbars to extend the functionality of the navigation bar.

Before a toolbar can be displayed, you must first create the buttons you intend to display on it. You'll add each button to an array created using Cocoa's NSMutableArray class:

```
NSMutableArray *buttons = [ [ NSMutableArray alloc ] init ];
```

Image and text buttons

The most common types of buttons are those represented as either images or standard text. Both types of buttons are created as UIBarButtonItem objects, however you will use a different initializer to provision each. Initialize image buttons using the initWithImage method, and initialize standard text buttons using the initWithTitle method:

```
UIBarButtonItem *buttonImage = [ [ UIBarButtonItem alloc ] initWithImage:
    [ UIImage imageNamed: @"button.png" ]
    style: UIBarButtonItemStylePlain
    target: self
    action: @selector(mySelector:)
];

UIBarButtonItem *buttonText = [ [ UIBarButtonItem alloc ] initWithTitle:
    @"Button"
    style: UIBarButtonItemStyleBordered
    target: self
    action: @selector(mySelector:)
];
```

System buttons

In addition to image and text buttons, a small library of system buttons exists to create the standardized, predefined buttons you see in many different applications. You also create system buttons as UIBarButtonItem objects, using the class's initWithBarButton SystemItem method. An example follows:

```
UIBarButtonItem *myBookmarks = [ [ UIBarButtonItem alloc ]
    initWithBarButtonSystemItem: UIBarButtonSystemItemBookmarks
    target: self
```

```
    action: @selector(mySelector:)
];
```

The following system buttons are presently supported, and can be found in the
UIBarButtonItem.h header file.

Button identifier	Description
UIBarButtonSystemItemDone	A blue text button labeled "Done"
UIBarButtonSystemItemCancel	A text button labeled "Cancel"
UIBarButtonSystemItemEdit	A text button labeled "Edit"
UIBarButtonSystemItemSave	A blue text button labeled "Save"
UIBarButtonSystemItemAdd	An image button of a plus (+) sign
UIBarButtonSystemItemFlexibleSpace	An empty, flexible space
UIBarButtonSystemItemFixedSpace	An empty spacer
UIBarButtonSystemItemCompose	An image button of a pen and paper
UIBarButtonSystemItemReply	An image button of a reply arrow
UIBarButtonSystemItemAction	An image button of an action arrow
UIBarButtonSystemItemOrganize	An image button of a folder with a down arrow
UIBarButtonSystemItemBookmarks	An image button of the bookmarks icon
UIBarButtonSystemItemSearch	An image button of the spotlight icon
UIBarButtonSystemItemRefresh	An image button of a circular refresh arrow
UIBarButtonSystemItemStop	An image button of a stop X
UIBarButtonSystemItemCamera	An image button of a camera
UIBarButtonSystemItemTrash	An image button of a trash can
UIBarButtonSystemItemPlay	An image button of a scrubber play icon
UIBarButtonSystemItemPause	An image button of a scrubber pause icon
UIBarButtonSystemItemRewind	An image button of a scrubber rewind icon
UIBarButtonSystemItemFastForward	An image button of a scrubber f-forward icon

Custom view buttons

Like navigation bars, a button can also be rendered as a custom view class, which allows
you to display any other kind of view object as a button:

```
UIBarButtonItem *customButton = [ [ UIBarButtonItem alloc ]
    initWithCustomView: myView ];
```

Creating the toolbar

Add each button you'd like to display to the buttons array you've created:

```
[ buttons addObject: buttonImage ];
[ buttons addObject: buttonText ];
[ buttons addObject: myBookmarks ];
```

Next, create a `UIToolbar` object and assign your array of buttons as the toolbar's list of items:

```
UIToolbar *toolbar = [ [ UIToolbar alloc ] init ];
[ toolbar setItems: buttons animated: YES ];
```

Finally, replace the title view of your navigation bar with your newly created toolbar, just like you did with the segmented control:

```
self.navigationItem.titleView = toolbar;
```

When the navigation bar is displayed, the toolbar will appear in the center.

Sizing

The toolbar uses the default size for the buttons added to it. If you'd like to size the toolbar to fit the navigation bar more snugly, use the `sizeToFit` method:

```
[ toolbar sizeToFit ];
```

Toolbar style

As with many view-based objects, the `UIToolbar` includes a style property named `bar Style`. This can be used to match the toolbar style to the style you've defined for the navigation bar:

```
toolbar.barStyle = UIBarStyleDefault;
```

You can set the bar style to one of three standard style themes used by most other types of bar objects.

Style	Description
UIBarStyleDefault	Default style; gray background with white text
UIBarStyleBlackOpaque	Solid black background with white text
UIBarStyleBlackTranslucent	Transparent black background with white text

PageDemo: Page Navigation Exercise

In this example, you'll build a navigation controller on top of an existing view controller. The root view controller's navigation properties add a Credits button that, when pressed, pushes another view controller onto the navigation controller's stack. When the credits are displayed, pressing the Back button will pop the view controller off the stack, navigating back to the root view. A segmented control has also been added to the root view, allowing the user to choose between displaying text about bunnies versus text about ponies. The behavior is illustrated in Figure 3-2.

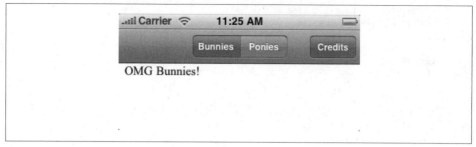

Figure 3-2. PageDemo example

You can compile this application, shown in Examples 3-17 through 3-21, with the SDK by creating a *navigation-based application* project named *PageDemo*. Be sure to pull out the Interface Builder code if you'd like to see how these objects are created from scratch.

Example 3-17. PageDemo application delegate prototypes (PageDemoAppDelegate.h)

```
#import <UIKit/UIKit.h>
#import "RootViewController.h"

@interface PageDemoAppDelegate : NSObject <UIApplicationDelegate> {
    UIWindow *window;
    RootViewController *viewController;
    CreditsViewController *creditsViewController;
    UINavigationController *navigationController;
}

@property (nonatomic, retain) IBOutlet UIWindow *window;
@property (nonatomic, retain) IBOutlet RootViewController *viewController;
@property (nonatomic, retain) IBOutlet CreditsViewController *creditsViewController;
@property (nonatomic, retain) IBOutlet UINavigationController *navigationController;

@end
```

Example 3-18. PageDemo application delegate (PageDemoAppDelegate.m)

```
#import "PageDemoAppDelegate.h"
#import "RootViewController.h"

@implementation PageDemoAppDelegate

@synthesize window;
@synthesize viewController;
@synthesize navigationController;
@synthesize creditsViewController;

- (void)applicationDidFinishLaunching:(UIApplication *)application {

    window = [ [ UIWindow alloc ] initWithFrame: [
        [ UIScreen mainScreen ] bounds ]
    ];

    viewController = [ [ RootViewController alloc ] initWithAppDelegate: self ];
```

```
    creditsViewController = [ [ CreditsViewController alloc ]
        initWithAppDelegate: self
    ];

    navigationController = [ [ UINavigationController alloc ]
        initWithRootViewController: viewController
    ];

    [ window addSubview: [ navigationController view ] ];
    [ window makeKeyAndVisible ];
}

- (void)dealloc {
    [ navigationController release ];
    [ viewController release ];
    [ creditsViewController release ];
    [ window release ];
    [ super dealloc ];
}

- (void)credits {
    [ navigationController pushViewController: creditsViewController
        animated: YES
    ];
}

- (void)back {
    [ navigationController popViewControllerAnimated: YES ];
}

@end
```

Example 3-19. PageDemo view controller prototypes (RootViewController.h)

```
#import <UIKit/UIKit.h>
#import <UIKit/UITextView.h>

@interface RootViewController : UIViewController {
    UITextView *textView;
    UIBarButtonItem *credits;
    UISegmentedControl *segmentedControl;
    UINavigationController *navigationController;
    int page;
}
- (void)setPage;
- (id)initWithAppDelegate:(id)appDelegate;

@end

@interface CreditsViewController : UIViewController {
    UITextView *textView;
    UINavigationController *navigationController;
}
- (id)initWithAppDelegate:(id)appDelegate;

@end
```

Example 3-20. PageDemo view controllers (RootViewController.m)

```objc
#import "RootViewController.h"
#import "PageDemoAppDelegate.h"

@implementation RootViewController

- (id)initWithAppDelegate:(id)appDelegate {
    self = [ super init ];
    if (self != nil) {

        /* Initialize Navigation Buttons */
        credits = [ [ [ UIBarButtonItem alloc ]
                    initWithTitle:@"Credits"
                    style: UIBarButtonItemStylePlain
                    target: appDelegate
                    action:@selector(credits) ]
                  autorelease ];
        self.navigationItem.rightBarButtonItem = credits;

        segmentedControl = [ [ UISegmentedControl alloc ] initWithItems: nil ];
        segmentedControl.segmentedControlStyle = UISegmentedControlStyleBar;

        [ segmentedControl insertSegmentWithTitle: @"Bunnies" atIndex: 0
            animated: NO
         ];
        [ segmentedControl insertSegmentWithTitle: @"Ponies" atIndex: 1
            animated: NO
         ];

        [ segmentedControl addTarget: self action: @selector(controlPressed:)
            forControlEvents:UIControlEventValueChanged
         ];

        self.navigationItem.titleView = segmentedControl;
        segmentedControl.selectedSegmentIndex = 0;
    }
    return self;
}

- (void)controlPressed:(id) sender {
    [ self setPage ];
}

- (void)setPage {
    int index = segmentedControl.selectedSegmentIndex;

    if (index == 0) {
        textView.text = @"OMG Bunnies!";
    } else {
        textView.text = @"OMG Ponies";
    }
}

- (void)loadView {
    CGRect bounds = [ [ UIScreen mainScreen ] applicationFrame ];
```

```
    [ super loadView ];

    textView = [ [ UITextView alloc ] initWithFrame: bounds ];
    textView.editable = NO;

    [ self setPage ];
    self.view = textView;
}

- (void)dealloc {
    [ textView release ];
    [ super dealloc ];
}

@end

@implementation CreditsViewController

- (id)initWithAppDelegate:(id)appDelegate {

    self = [ super init ];
    if (self != nil) {

        /* Initialize Navigation Buttons */
        UIBarButtonItem *back = [ [ [ UIBarButtonItem alloc ]
                initWithTitle:@"Back"
                style: UIBarButtonItemStylePlain
                target: appDelegate
                action: @selector(back) ]
            autorelease ];
        self.navigationItem.backBarButtonItem = back;
    }
    return self;
}

- (void)loadView {
    [ super loadView ];

    textView = [ [ UITextView alloc ] initWithFrame: [
        [ UIScreen mainScreen ] applicationFrame ] ];
    textView.editable = NO;
    textView.text = @"iPhone SDK Application Development\n"
                    "Copyright (c) 2008, O'Reilly Media.";

    self.view = textView;
}

- (void)dealloc {
    [ textView release ];
    [ super dealloc ];
}

@end
```

Example 3-21. PageDemo main (main.m)

```
#import <UIKit/UIKit.h>

int main(int argc, char *argv[]) {

    NSAutoreleasePool * pool = [[NSAutoreleasePool alloc] init];
    int retVal = UIApplicationMain(argc, argv, nil, @"PageDemoAppDelegate");
    [pool release];
    return retVal;
}
```

What's Going On

The *PageDemo* example contains everything you've seen so far, and adds a navigation bar controller for an existing view controller to manage navigation between it and another view controller:

1. The application is instantiated and the program's `main` function is called, which invokes the `PageDemoAppDelegate` class's `applicationDidFinishLaunching` method.

2. The application delegate creates an instance of the root view controller and the credits view controller. A custom initialization method named `initWithApp` `Delegate` is used to initialize the view controller and pass a pointer to the application delegate object, which will handle the actions for each button. A segmented control is also added.

3. After the view controllers have finished initializing, the application delegate continues by instantiating a navigation controller object, attaching a view controller as its root. The navigation bar controller is then attached to the window as a subview, where it displays itself and the view controller it is wrapping.

4. When a user taps the Credits button on the navigation bar, the button's action invokes the `credits` method in the application delegate class. This pushes the `creditsViewController` object onto the navigation controller, automatically transitioning the screen to the new view. When the user presses the Back button, the button's action invokes the `back` method in the application delegate class. This pops the controller off the stack, returning the iPhone's screen to the previous view controller.

5. When the user taps a button on the segmented control, the selector method invokes the `setPage` method. The text that is assigned to the text view depends on whether the user selects "bunnies" or "ponies" in the segmented control.

Further Study

With the code from this section and the previous examples, try having a little fun with this example:

- Try changing this code to add a third segment, "Hax" to the segmented control. If the user selects this segment, the text "OMG Hax!" should be displayed.

- Take the UITextView code from previous examples and add two buttons, one for HTML and one for Text. Tapping each button should change the text view to display the file in the corresponding format.

- Replace the segmented control with a toolbar. Add a UIBarButtonSystemItemAdd system button that, when tapped, makes the text view editable, and a UIBarButton SystemItemDone button that, when tapped, makes the text view read-only again.

- Add a third view controller displaying an HTML view of the text. Push this onto your navigation stack, and add the appropriate buttons to navigate back.

- Check out the following prototypes in your SDK's header files: *UINavigation Controller.h*, *UINavigationBar.h*, and *UIBarButtonItem.h*. You'll find these under */Developer/Platforms/iPhoneOS.platform*, inside the UI Kit framework's *Headers* directory.

Transition Animations

If there's one thing Apple is well known for, it's a devotion to aesthetics in their user interfaces. The effect of sliding pages left and right gives the user a sense of the flow of data through an application, or a sense of "forward" and "back." Even applications lacking a book type of structure can provide the smooth slide and fade transitions offered by UI Kit. Transitions are animation objects that are attached to an existing view so that when the view is changed, the animation is executed.

Fortunately, most of the work of transitions is done automatically for you when using navigation controllers. There may, however, be some occasions when directly applying a transition can be useful. A framework we haven't yet introduced, named Quartz Core, handles the animation for transitions. Quartz Core performs a number of animations and transformations used to create a number of different effects. Use Quartz Core's animation engine to create a transition animation and apply it to your view. Quartz Core spawns a new thread to take over all of the graphics processing during the transition. The developer needs only to add the desired transition to enhance an existing application.

In order to implement transitions in your application, you'll need to add the Quartz Core framework to your project. Right-click the *Frameworks* folder in your project, and then choose Add Framework. Navigate to the *QuartzCore.framework* folder, and then click Add.

Creating a Transition

You'll create transitions as `CATransition` objects, which are objects belonging to Quartz Core's Core Animation suite of functions. An animation contains properties such as timing function, animation type, and duration. To create an animation, call the class's `animation` method. An example follows:

```
#import <QuartzCore/CAAnimation.h>

CATransition *myTransition = [ CATransition animation ];
```

Timing function

The timing function determines how smooth a transition will execute from start to finish. The same animation can be executed at different speeds during the animation. For example, a page flipping animation might begin slow and gain speed at the end of the animation, or vice versa. The following timing functions are available for your animation.

Timing	Description
UIViewAnimationCurveEaseInOut	Slow at beginning and end of animation
UIViewAnimationCurveEaseIn	Slow at beginning, then speeds up
UIViewAnimationCurveEaseOut	Animation slows at end of animation
UIViewAnimationCurveLinear	Uniform speed throughout duration

Set the timing function by assigning the transition's `timingFunction` property:

```
myTransition.timingFunction = UIViewAnimationCurveEaseInOut;
```

Animation types

The animation type defines the type of animation to render. Each animation has both a type and a subtype. The animation's type defines the overall behavior of the transition, while the subtype defines details such as the direction of the transition.

Apple has limited developers' access in the SDK to the animations available, so you can't necessarily add everything you see in Apple's preloaded applications to your own code. The SDK supports the following animation types.

Animation type	Description
kCATransitionFade	Fade from one view to the next
kCATransitionMoveIn	Move the new view in over the old
kCATransitionPush	Push the old view out, bring the new view in
kCATransitionReveal	Move the old view out revealing the new

The following animation subtypes are supported.

Animation subtype	Description
kCATransitionFromRight	New view slides from right
kCATransitionFromLeft	New view slides from left
kCATransitionFromTop	New view slides from top
kCATransitionFromBottom	New view slides from bottom

Set the type and subtype by assigning the transition's **type** and **subtype** properties:

```
myTransition.type = kCATransitionPush;
myTransition.subtype = kCATransitionFromLeft;
```

Duration

By default, a standard duration is set for the animation, causing it to run at normal speed. This is generally **0.3** seconds for most animations. If you wish to speed up or slow down the animation, you can manually set the duration time by adjusting the transition's **duration** property:

```
myTransition.duration = 0.3;
```

Attaching a Transition

To effect a transition, add the animation to the view layer to which your animated view is anchored. For example, if you are transitioning between two view controllers, add the animation to the window's layer:

```
[ [ self.view.superview.layer ] addAnimation: myTransition forKey: nil ];
```

If you are transitioning from one child view to another within a single view controller, add the animation to the view controller's layer. Alternatively, you might use the internal view object within the view controller instead, and manage your child views as sublayers of the main view:

```
[ self.view.layer addAnimation: myTransition forKey: nil ];
[ self.view addSubview: newView ];
[ oldView removeFromSuperview ];
```

If you're using a navigation controller, such as in the PageDemo example, you can add the animation to the navigation controller's view layer to effect a transition between two view controllers:

```
[ navigationController.view.layer addAnimation: myTransition forKey: nil ];
```

As the switch is made between views, the animation layer will automatically execute, showing the transition between the two.

FlipDemo: Page-Flipping Transitions

This example works in a similar fashion to the *PageDemo* example you've already seen. In this example, you'll build a navigation controller on top of an existing view controller. This example displays a left and right navigation bar item, allowing the user to flip between ten pages of text within a single view controller. When this occurs, a new animation is created and added to the parent view to display this transition to the user. A generic `UIView` object has also been added to act as a parent view within the view controller, so instead of `self.view` pointing to an individual text view, all ten text views will be created when the class is initialized. The corresponding pages will then be added and removed as sublayers of the generic view whenever a transition occurs.

You can compile this application, shown in Examples 3-22 through 3-26, with the SDK by creating a *navigation-based application* project named *FlipDemo*. Be sure to pull out the Interface Builder code if you'd like to see how these objects are created from scratch.

 Be sure to add the Quartz Core framework to this project before attempting to build it.

Example 3-22. FlipDemo application delegate prototypes (FlipDemoAppDelegate.h)

```
#import <UIKit/UIKit.h>
#import "RootViewController.h"

@interface FlipDemoAppDelegate : NSObject <UIApplicationDelegate> {
    UIWindow *window;
    RootViewController *viewController;
    UINavigationController *navigationController;
}

@property (nonatomic, retain) IBOutlet UIWindow *window;
@property (nonatomic, retain) IBOutlet RootViewController *viewController;
@property (nonatomic, retain) IBOutlet UINavigationController *navigationController;

@end
```

Example 3-23. FlipDemo application delegate (FlipDemoAppDelegate.m)

```
#import "FlipDemoAppDelegate.h"
#import "RootViewController.h"


@implementation FlipDemoAppDelegate

@synthesize window;
@synthesize viewController;
@synthesize navigationController;

- (void)applicationDidFinishLaunching:(UIApplication *)application {
```

```
    window = [ [ UIWindow alloc ] initWithFrame: [ [ UIScreen mainScreen ] bounds ] ];
    viewController = [ [ RootViewController alloc ] init ];
    navigationController = [ [ UINavigationController alloc ]
        initWithRootViewController: viewController ];

    [ window addSubview: [ navigationController view ] ];
    [ window makeKeyAndVisible ];
}

- (void)dealloc {
    [ navigationController release ];
    [ window release ];
    [ super dealloc ];
}

@end
```

Example 3-24. FlipDemo view controller prototype (RootViewController.h)

```
#import <UIKit/UIKit.h>
#import <UIKit/UITextView.h>

@interface RootViewController : UIViewController {
    UITextView *textView[10];
    UIView *view;
    UIBarButtonItem *prev, *next;
    int page, lastViewed;
}
- (void)setPage;

@end
```

Example 3-25. FlipDemo view controller (RootViewController.m)

```
#import <QuartzCore/CAAnimation.h>
#import "RootViewController.h"
#import "FlipDemoAppDelegate.h"

@implementation RootViewController

- (id)init {
    self = [ super init ];
    if (self != nil) {

        /* Default Page */
        page = lastViewed = 5;

        /* Initialize Navigation Buttons */
        prev = [ [ [ UIBarButtonItem alloc ]
                initWithTitle:@"Prev"
                style: UIBarButtonItemStylePlain
                target: self
                action:@selector(prevpage) ]
            autorelease ];
        self.navigationItem.leftBarButtonItem = prev;
```

```objc
        next = [ [ [ UIBarButtonItem alloc ]
                    initWithTitle:@"Next"
                    style: UIBarButtonItemStylePlain
                    target: self
                    action:@selector(nextpage) ]
                  autorelease ];

        self.navigationItem.rightBarButtonItem = next;

    }
    return self;
}

- (void)controlPressed:(id) sender {
    [ self setPage ];
}

- (void)setPage {

    /* Create a new animation */
    CATransition *myTransition = [ CATransition animation ];
    myTransition.timingFunction = UIViewAnimationCurveEaseInOut;
    myTransition.type = kCATransitionPush;
    if (page > lastViewed) {
        myTransition.subtype = kCATransitionFromRight;
    } else {
        myTransition.subtype = kCATransitionFromLeft;
    }

    /* Add the animation to the top view layer */

    [ self.view.layer addAnimation: myTransition forKey: nil ];
    [ self.view insertSubview: textView[page-1] atIndex: 0 ];
    [ textView[lastViewed-1] removeFromSuperview ];

    lastViewed = page;

    if (page == 1)
        prev.enabled = NO;
    else
        prev.enabled = YES;

    if (page == 10)
        next.enabled = NO;
    else
        next.enabled = YES;
}

- (void)prevpage {
    page--;
    [ self setPage ];
}

- (void)nextpage {
    page++;
```

```
        [ self setPage ];
}

- (void)loadView {
    CGRect bounds = [ [ UIScreen mainScreen ] applicationFrame ];
    [ super loadView ];

    view = [ [ UIView alloc ] initWithFrame: bounds ];
    bounds.origin.y = 0;

    for(int i = 0;i < 10; i++) {
        textView[i] = [ [ UITextView alloc ] initWithFrame: bounds ];
        textView[i].editable = NO;
        textView[i].text = [ NSString stringWithFormat: @"Page %d", i+1 ];
    }

    self.view = view;
    [ self.view addSubview: textView[4] ];

}

- (void)dealloc {
    for(int i = 0; i < 10; i++) {
        [ textView[i] dealloc ];
    }
    [ next dealloc ];
    [ prev dealloc ];
    [ super dealloc ];
}

@end
```

Example 3-26. FlipDemo main (main.m)

```
#import <UIKit/UIKit.h>

int main(int argc, char *argv[]) {

    NSAutoreleasePool * pool = [[NSAutoreleasePool alloc] init];
    int retVal = UIApplicationMain(argc, argv, nil, @"FlipDemoAppDelegate");
    [pool release];
    return retVal;
}
```

What's Going On

The *FlipDemo* example contains everything you've seen so far, and adds an animation to a parent view:

1. The application instantiates and calls the program's main function, which invokes the FlipDemoAppDelegate class's applicationDidFinishLaunching method.

2. The application delegate creates an instance of the view controller. The view controller's `init` method is overridden to define the navigation bar properties to use when displayed, namely, two navigation bar buttons and a segmented control.

3. The view controller creates ten different `UITextView` objects, each containing text. A generic `UIView` object is also created and assigned as the key view for the controller. After the view controller has finished initializing, the application delegate continues by instantiating a navigation controller object, using the view controller as its root controller. The navigation bar controller is then attached to the window as a subview, where it displays itself and the view controller it is wrapping.

4. When the user taps a button on the navigation bar, the button's action is invoked. The selector adjusts the page number and then notifies the `setPage` method. This method then creates an animation and attaches it to the controller's key view. Depending on the direction of the page flip, the animation flips either to the left or the right.

5. The view of the next (or previous) page is added to the key view, and the old page is removed. The animation is automatically executed when this occurs, showing the two pages sliding.

Further Study

Explore transition animations a bit more before moving on:

- Try creating other types of page transitions using the transition types outlined earlier in this section.

- Take the `UITextView` code from previous examples and add two buttons, one for HTML and one for Text. Tapping each button should change the text view to display the file in the corresponding format. Transition from top to bottom and vice-versa when switching between the two views.

- Check out the following prototypes in your SDK's header files: *CAAnimation.h*, *CAMediaTimingFunction.h*, and *CALayer.h*. You'll find these under */Developer/ Platforms/iPhoneOS.platform*, inside the QuartzCore framework's *Headers* directory.

Action Sheets and Alerts

The iPhone is a relatively small device with limited screen space and no stylus. This means users are going to fumble with their fingers and tap buttons by accident. When this happens, a well-written application prompts the user for confirmation before destroying important data. On a desktop computer, applications pop up windows when they need attention. On the iPhone, a modal alert sheet slides up from the bottom, graying out the rest of the screen until the user chooses an option. The term "sheet" continues the page metaphor that Apple uses for the iPhone. The iPhone does, in fact, also support pop-up windows in the form of alerts. These typically convey information, although they occasionally retrieve input as well.

Alerts

Alert views are the simplest of alerts supported by the iPhone. An alert view, represented by the UIAlertView class, is a small pop-up window appearing over an application window. Until the alert is dismissed, the rest of the application cannot be accessed:

```
UIAlertView *myAlert = [ [ UIAlertView alloc ]
    initWithTitle:@"Alert"
    message:@"This is an alert."
    delegate:self
    cancelButtonTitle: nil
    otherButtonTitles: @"OK", nil];
```

When the user presses a button in an alert window, the alert view notifies its delegate by invoking a method named clickedButtonAtIndex. This method belongs to the UIAlertViewDelegate protocol, which the delegate class must implement. To set the delegate class that will receive this notification, set the alert view's **delegate** property:

```
myAlert.delegate = self;
```

You'll then need to add this special method to your delegate class in order to handle the button press. An example follows:

```
- (void)alertView:(UIAlertView *)alertView clickedButtonAtIndex:(NSInteger)buttonIndex
{
    NSLog(@"Button %d pressed", buttonIndex);
    [ alertView release ];
}
```

The clickedButtonAtIndex method is provided with a pointer to the UIAlertView object and a button index. The pointer can be compared with existing objects to determine in which alert view a button was pressed, allowing you to use a single delegate to handle multiple alerts. The buttonIndex parameter provides a zero-indexed button number corresponding to a button in the alert.

When you're ready to display the alert, use the UIAlertView class's **show** method:

```
[ myAlert show ];
```

Action Sheets

Action sheets are larger types of alerts that appear as "slide-up" pages over an existing view. A single view can host a number of different alert sheets, and handles them using the same type of delegate facilities as alert views. A basic alert sheet consists of a title, message, and whatever choices the user should be presented with. It is instantiated in the same way as an alert view:

```
UIActionSheet *mySheet = [ [ UIActionSheet alloc ]
    initWithTitle: @"Please Select"
```

```
    delegate: self
    cancelButtonTitle: @"Cancel"
    destructiveButtonTitle: @"Delete"
    otherButtonTitles: @"Move", @"Rename", nil ];
```

When the user presses a button, the delegate is notified by invoking its `clicked` `ButtonAtIndex` method. For action sheets, this method belongs to the `UIActionSheet` `Delegate` protocol:

```
- (void)actionSheet:(UIActionSheet *)actionSheet
    clickedButtonAtIndex:(NSInteger)buttonIndex
{
    /* Handle action sheet here */
}
```

Action sheets support a type of button known as a *destructive button*. A destructive button is presented in an action sheet to denote a permanently destructive action, such as deleting a message or clearing a log. If you specify a destructive button, it is highlighted in red to alert the user to its dangerous nature:

```
mySheet.destructiveButtonIndex = 1;
```

Like navigation bars and toolbars, action sheets can support one of three different styles.

Style	Description
UIActionSheetStyleDefault	Default style: gray gradient background with white text
UIActionSheetStyleBlackTranslucent	Transparent black background with white text
UIActionSheetStyleBlackOpaque	Solid black background with white text

You can set the style by assigning a value to the action sheet's `actionSheetStyle` property:

```
mySheet.actionSheetStyle = UIActionSheetStyleDefault;
```

One of three methods may be used to display the action sheet. If you will be presenting the action sheet from within a view, use the `showInView` method to slide the sheet up from the bottom of the view:

```
[ mySheet showInView: self ];
```

To align an action sheet with the edge of a toolbar or tab bar, use the `showFromTool` `Bar` or `showFromTabBar` methods:

```
[ mySheet showFromToolBar: toolbar ];
[ mySheet showFromTabBar: tabbar ];
```

Figure 3-3. EndWorld example

Dismissing an Action Sheet

After processing a button press, the alert sheet should vanish—unless, of course, the application has a reason for the user to press more than one button. Use the `dismiss` method to make the sheet go away:

```
[ mySheet dismissWithClickedButtonIndex: 1 animated: YES ];
```

EndWorld: Ending the World (with Confirmation)

The government thought it would be more convenient for the President to carry an iPhone around instead of a suitcase with a big red button. One of the chief programmers conveniently wrote *EndWorld.app*, with a button the President can press at any time to launch nukes and end the world (or at least start a pie fight). The problem, however, is that he's almost pressed it accidentally many times when he thought he was just social networking. In this example, assume that you've been contracted to add a confirmation alert to the EndWorld application—just in case the President didn't really mean to end the world (see Figure 3-3).

The *EndWorld* application displays a navigation bar with an End World button and a convenient text window for typing in any last words. When the President presses the End World button, the application will first confirm by using an alert view.

You can compile this application, shown in Examples 3-27 through 3-31, with the SDK by creating a *navigation-based application* project named *EndWorld*. Be sure to pull out the Interface Builder code if you'd like to see how these objects are created from scratch.

Example 3-27. EndWorld application delegate prototypes (EndWorldAppDelegate.h)

```
#import <UIKit/UIKit.h>
#import "RootViewController.h"

@interface EndWorldAppDelegate : NSObject <UIApplicationDelegate> {
    UIWindow *window;
    RootViewController *viewController;
    UINavigationController *navigationController;
}

@property (nonatomic, retain) IBOutlet UIWindow *window;
@property (nonatomic, retain) IBOutlet RootViewController *viewController;
@property (nonatomic, retain) IBOutlet UINavigationController *navigationController;

@end
```

Example 3-28. EndWorld application delegate (EndWorldAppDelegate.m)

```
#import "EndWorldAppDelegate.h"
#import "RootViewController.h"


@implementation EndWorldAppDelegate

@synthesize window;
@synthesize viewController;
@synthesize navigationController;

- (void)applicationDidFinishLaunching:(UIApplication *)application {

    window = [ [ UIWindow alloc ] initWithFrame:
        [ [ UIScreen mainScreen ] bounds ] ];
    viewController = [ [ RootViewController alloc ] init ];
    navigationController = [ [ UINavigationController alloc ]
        initWithRootViewController: viewController ];

    [ window addSubview: [ navigationController view ] ];
    [ window makeKeyAndVisible ];
}

- (void)dealloc {
    [ navigationController release ];
    [ viewController release ];
    [ window release ];
    [ super dealloc ];
}
```

```
@end
```

Example 3-29. EndWorld view controller prototype (RootViewController.h)

```objc
#import <UIKit/UIKit.h>
#import <UIKit/UITextView.h>

@interface RootViewController : UIViewController {
    UITextView *textView;
    UIBarButtonItem *endWorld;
    UIAlertView *endWorldAlert;
}
- (id)init;
- (void) endWorld;

@end
```

Example 3-30. EndWorld view controller (RootViewController.m)

```objc
#import "RootViewController.h"
#import "EndWorldAppDelegate.h"

@implementation RootViewController

- (id)init {

    self = [ super init ];
    if (self != nil) {

        /* Initialize Navigation Buttons */
        endWorld = [ [ [ UIBarButtonItem alloc ]
                initWithTitle:@"End World"
                style: UIBarButtonItemStyleDone
                target: self
                action:@selector(endWorld) ]
            autorelease ];
        self.navigationItem.rightBarButtonItem = endWorld;
    }

    return self;
}

- (void)loadView {
    CGRect bounds = [ [ UIScreen mainScreen ] applicationFrame ];
    [ super loadView ];

    textView = [ [ UITextView alloc ] initWithFrame: bounds ];
    textView.editable = YES;
    textView.text = @"Enter any last words here, then press End World.";

    self.view = textView;
}

- (void)endWorld {
    endWorldAlert = [ [ UIAlertView alloc ]
```

```
            initWithTitle:@"End The World"
            message:@"Warning: You are about to end the world."
            delegate:self
            cancelButtonTitle: @"My Bad"
            otherButtonTitles: @"OK", nil];

    endWorldAlert.delegate = self;
    [ endWorldAlert show ];

}

- (void)alertView:(UIAlertView *)alertView clickedButtonAtIndex:(NSInteger)buttonIndex
{
    if (alertView == endWorldAlert) {
        NSLog(@"Button %d pressed", buttonIndex);

        UIAlertView *myAlert = [ [ UIAlertView alloc ]
            initWithTitle:@"End The World"
            message: nil
            delegate:self
            cancelButtonTitle: nil
            otherButtonTitles: @"OK", nil ];

        if (buttonIndex == 0) {
            myAlert.message = @"Be more careful next time!";
        } else if (buttonIndex == 1) {
            myAlert.message = @"You must be connected to a WiFi network
 to end the world.";
        } else {
            myAlert.message = @"Invalid Button.";
        }

        [ myAlert show ];
    }

    [ alertView release ];
}


- (void)dealloc {
    [ textView dealloc ];
    [ endWorld dealloc ];
    [ super dealloc ];
}

@end
```

Example 3-31. EndWorld main (main.m)

```
#import <UIKit/UIKit.h>

int main(int argc, char *argv[]) {

    NSAutoreleasePool * pool = [[NSAutoreleasePool alloc] init];
    int retVal = UIApplicationMain(argc, argv, nil, @"EndWorldAppDelegate");
    [pool release];
```

```
    return retVal;
}
```

What's Going On

The *EndWorld* example illustrates the flow of control when using a delegate:

1. The application instantiates as all other examples thus far have and invokes the program's `main` function, which invokes the `EndWOrldAppDelegate` class's `applicationDidFinishLaunching` method, and builds the appropriate window, view controller, and navigation controller classes.

2. The view controller's `init` method is overridden to add a navigation bar button named End World. When tapped, the button's selector, `endWorld`, is notified.

3. The selector creates a new `UIAlertView` object and presents it to the user. When the user clicks one of the buttons, the alert's delegate (currently the view controller) is notified by invoking its `clickedButtonAtIndex` method.

4. The `clickedButtonAtIndex` method determines which button was tapped and constructs a new `UIAlertView` to inform the user of the result of his selection. Oops, not only do you need to be on a WiFi network to use the iTunes store, but also to end the world. Who knew?

Further Study

Play around with alert views and action sheets for a bit to get a feel for how they work:

- Convert the action view in this example to an action sheet. Experiment with adding different buttons. How many buttons will fit on the screen? How much text can they hold? How does the sheet resize itself to accommodate your design?

- Create an alert view with no buttons—one that informs the user a file is loading. Use an `NSTimer` to wait 10 seconds and then dismiss the view without using the `buttonClicked` method.

- Check out the following prototypes in your SDK's header files: *UIAlert.h* and *UITextField.h*. You'll find these under */Developer/Platforms/iPhoneOS.platform*, inside the UI Kit framework's *Headers* directory.

Table Views and Controllers

Tables are the foundation for most types of selectable lists on the iPhone. Voicemail, recent calls, and even email all use the feature-rich `UITableView` class to display their lists of items. In addition to being a basic list selector, the `UITableView` class includes built-in functionality to handle swipe-to-delete, add disclosure accessories, animations, labels, and even images. A special subclass of view controller exists specifically for tables. The `UITableViewController` class encapsulates a single `UITableView` object and provides the plumbing to handle your business logic, screen rotations, navigation bar properties, and all of the other benefits that come with using view controllers.

Creating the Table

A table has three primary components: the table itself, table sections (or groupings), and table cells (the individual rows in a table). The table's data is queried from a table's *data source*. A data source is an object that provides information to the table about which data to display, such as filenames, email messages, etc. The data source must implement the UITableViewDataSource protocol, and respond to a specific subset of methods for providing this information to the table.

When you create the table, you'll provide a pointer to the object that will act as a data source. The data source will be called whenever the table is reloaded or new cells are scrolled into view, so that the table can receive instruction about which sections and rows to display, and provide the data for each.

Subclassing UITableViewController

For most specialized uses, the table view controller can serve as the data source for its underlying table. This allows the table class and the table's data to be wrapped cleanly into a single controller class. In fact, the UITableViewController class is already designed to implement the UITableViewDataSource protocol.

Create a subclass of the UITableViewController object. In the following example, a subclass named MyTableViewController is created. The base class methods used to initialize and destroy the object are overridden to integrate the table portion of the class:

```
@interface MyTableViewController : UITableViewController
{

}
-(id)init;
-(void)dealloc;
```

To add the data source portion of the class, you need to write three methods that answer the data binding's request for data: numberOfSectionsInTableView, numberOfRowsIn Section and cellForRowAtIndexPath. Because the table controller is acting as the data source, you'll write these methods into your controller's subclass.

Use the numberOfSectionsInTableView method to create a set of unique groups within the table. These are most commonly found when creating grouped preferences tables or section lists. You'll learn more about these in Chapter 10. A standard table consists of only one section, so hardcode this for now:

```
- (NSInteger)numberOfSectionsInTableView:(UITableView *)tableView {
    return 1;
}
```

The `numberOfRowsInSection` method should return the number of rows in each section of the table. Since a standard table only includes one section, the value returned should equal the total number of rows in the table. You'll tie this value in with your actual data:

```
- (NSInteger)tableView:(UITableView *)tableView numberOf
RowsInSection:(NSInteger)section
{
    return nRecords;
}
```

Finally, the method named `cellForRowAtIndexPath` returns a `UITableViewCell` object containing the display information for the given table cell. The `UITableViewCell` class is a versatile class supporting text and images, and includes editing and delete confirmation functionality.

Each cell is cached in memory when it is created, so if it's been created before, you'll be able to find it in the table's queue. This allows the table to scroll without needing to recreate the same cells as they fall in and out of view. It also allows a table to internally jettison unused cells when memory is low, recreating them later if necessary. For this reason, your data binding should be prepared to service the same cell multiple times:

```
- (UITableViewCell *)tableView:(UITableView *)tableView
    cellForRowAtIndexPath:(NSIndexPath *)indexPath
{
    NSString *CellIdentifier = [ [ NSString alloc ] initWithFormat:
        @"Cell %d", [ indexPath indexAtPosition: 1 ] ];

    /* Look up cell in the table queue */
    UITableViewCell *cell =
        [ tableView dequeueReusableCellWithIdentifier: CellIdentifier ];

    /* Not found in queue, create a new cell object */
    if (cell == nil) {
        cell = [ [ [ UITableViewCell alloc ]
            initWithFrame: CGRectZero reuseIdentifier: CellIdentifier ]
        autorelease ];
    }

    /* Set some text for the cell */
    cell.text = CellIdentifier;
    return cell;
}
```

The index path used in this example refers to a foundation object named `NSIndexPath`. This object allows not just one index, but several, to be specified within a single object. When referencing the index within a table, the `NSIndexPath` object contains a section number and a cell number. You can query each position of the index using the `indexAtPosition` method. The first position (position 0) always references the *section number* of the cell, and the second position (position 1) always references the *row number* of the cell within the given section. For simple tables, you'll only have a single section, so the section number will always resolve to 0.

You'll look at these methods in more detail later in this chapter.

Table Cells

A table references every record as a table cell object. Instead of thinking as a table cell as just text, think of a table cell as a miniature canvas. The UITableViewCell class provides the functionality to tailor a table cell to accommodate a custom look and feel. Cells can include images, text, labels, and a variety of styles. As you've seen, table cells are queued by the table, and so you'll only need to create cells the first time they're used, or again only if they've been purged from memory.

Each cell is assigned a *reuse identifier* when created. This is used to identify the cell within the table's queue. In the previous example, you incorporated the cell number into the identifier, but you can set any unique value you like:

```
NSString *CellIdentifier = [ [ NSString alloc ] initWithString: @"Frank" ];
UITableViewCell *cell = [ [ [ UITableViewCell alloc ]
            initWithFrame: CGRectZero
            reuseIdentifier: CellIdentifier
    ] autorelease
];
```

After creating a table cell, you can assign a number of different styling options to it.

Display text

To add display text to the cell, use the cell's **text** property:

```
cell.text = @"Frank's Table Cell";
```

Alignment

Adjust the cell's text alignment by setting the **textAlignment** property. You used similar properties when working with text views:

```
cell.textAlignment = UITextAlignmentLeft;
```

The default text alignment is left-aligned, but you may use any of the following values. These are the same values you learned about earlier, used with the **UITextView** class:

UITextAlignmentLeft
    Text will be left-aligned (default)

UITextAlignmentRight
    Text will be right-aligned

UITextAlignmentCenter
    Text will be centered

Font and size

To set the text font and point size for the cell, assign a `UIFont` object to the text view's `font` property. This functions in the same way as setting a `UITextView` object's font. To create a `UIFont` object, import UI Kit's *UIFont.h* header:

```
#import <UIKit/UIFont.h>
```

You can use a static method named `fontWithName` to easily instantiate new fonts:

```
UIFont *myFont = [ UIFont fontWithName: @"Arial" size: 18.0 ];
cell.font = myFont;
```

Additionally, three other static methods exist for easily creating system fonts:

```
UIFont *mySystemFont = [ UIFont systemFontOfSize: 12.0 ];
UIFont *myBoldSystemFont = [ UIFont boldSystemFontOfSize: 12.0 ];
UIFont *myItalicSystemFont = [ UIFont italicSystemFontOfSize: 12.0 ];
```

Font selection determines the display font for all text within the cell only. A table cell does not directly support rich text.

Text color

You can define the cell's text color by assigning a `UIColor` object to the cell's `text Color` property. To create a `UIColor` object, import UI Kit's *UIColor.h* header:

```
#import <UIKit/UIColor.h>
```

You can use static methods to create color objects, which are autoreleased when no longer needed. Colors can be created as white levels, using hue, or as an RGB composite. You've already learned about colors earlier in this chapter.

Once you have created a `UIColor` object, assign it to the cell's `textColor` property:

```
cell.textColor = [ UIColor redColor ];
```

You can also set the color of the text for a highlighted (selected) cell, using the `selectedTextColor` property:

```
cell.selectedTextColor = [ UIColor blueColor ];
```

Because a cell doesn't directly support rich text, the color selection affects all of the text within the cell.

Images

To add an image to a cell, assign a `UIImage` object to the cell's `image` property:

```
cell.image = [ UIImage imageNamed: @"cell.png" ];
```

You can also set the image to be displayed when the cell is in its selected state:

```
cell.selectedImage = [ UIImage imageNamed: @"selected_cell.png" ];
```

The `UIImage` class's `imageNamed` method will retrieve an image from your application folder. All of the images used in your table should have roughly the same dimensions so that your table looks uniform. Depending on the height of your image, you may need to adjust the row height of the table. You can set a standard row height for the entire table by overriding the table viewcontroller's `init` method to set the table's `rowHeight` property:

```
- (id)init {
    self = [ super init ];
    if (self != nil) {
        self.tableView.rowHeight = 65;
    }

    return self;
}
```

Alternatively, if you wish to have variable row height cells, you can define a different height for each cell individually by overriding the `heightForRowAtIndexPath` method within the data source:

```
- (CGFloat)tableView:(UITableView *)tableView
    heightForRowAtIndexPath:(NSIndexPath *)indexPath
{
    if ([ indexPath indexAtPosition: 1 ] == 0)
        return 65.0;
    else
        return 40.0;
}
```

Selection style

By changing the cell's `selectionStyle` property, you can customize the color used when a cell is highlighted:

```
cell.selectionStyle = UITableViewCellSelectionStyleBlue;
```

The default is to highlight the cell in blue; however, the following options are available:

`UITableViewCellSelectionStyleBlue`
Highlight selected cells in blue

`UITableViewCellSelectionStyleGray`
Highlight selected cells in gray

`UITableViewCellSelectionStyleNone`
Do not highlight selected cells

Labels

Labels are miniature view classes that you can add to table cells to further augment the cell with decorated text. Labels are used to add peripheral text to a cell, such as the day, subject, and preview displayed in Apple's Mail application.

A label is initialized with a display region offset to the cell. The following example creates a label that is offset 100×0 within the table cell, and is 50×50 in size:

```
UILabel *label = [ [ UILabel alloc ] initWithFrame:
    CGRectMake(100.0, 0.0, 50.0, 50.0)
];
```

Set the label text using the label's **text** property:

```
label.text = @"Label Text";
```

A label shares many of the same text properties as a cell or a text view. These include text alignment, color, and font:

```
label.textAlignment = UITextAlignmentLeft;
label.textColor = [ UIColor redColor ];
label.font = [ UIFont fontWithName: @"Arial" size: 10.0 ];
```

A label also allows you to use text shadowing. You can even define an offset for the shadow by passing a `CGSize` structure to the label's **shadowOffset** property:

```
label.shadowColor = [ UIColor grayColor ];
label.shadowOffset = CGSizeMake(0, -1);
```

Labels also allow you to define the text color to be used when the cell is highlighted:

```
label.highlightedTextColor = [ UIColor blackColor ];
```

If you really want to uglify your label, you can even set a background color. The background color will only be displayed within the label's display region. This can be useful for debugging when manually laying out labels, or to scare your customers away:

```
label.backgroundColor = [ UIColor blueColor ];
```

Once you have created the label, attach it to the cell as a subview:

```
[ cell addSubview: label ];
```

Disclosures

Disclosures, also known as accessories, are icons appearing at the right side of a table cell to disclose that there is another level of information to be displayed when the cell is selected. These are commonly used on desktop interfaces such as iTunes, where the user first selects a genre, then artist, and finally a song.

In addition to arrows, a checkbox can be displayed to indicate cells that have been selected in tables allowing multiple selections.

Any given cell can display an accessory by setting the cell's **accessoryType** property:

```
cell.accessoryType = UITableViewCellAccessoryDisclosureIndicator;
```

The following accessory styles are available.

Style	Description
UITableViewCellAccessoryNone	No accessory
UITableViewCellAccessoryDisclosureIndicator	Black right-arrow chevron
UITableViewCellAccessoryDetailDisclosureButton	Blue disclosure button

Style	Description
UITableViewCellAccessoryCheckmark	Checkmark, for selection

Implementing Multiple Select

As you've learned, a table cell can display a checkbox accessory via the **accessory Type** property. When the user selects a cell, the table delegate's **didSelectRowAtIndex Path** method is invoked. This method is part of the **UITableViewDelegate** protocol. Adding this method to your delegate will allow you to add multiple selection support to your table by controlling which cells are set with a checkbox accessory:

```
- (void)tableView:(UITableView *)tableView
    didSelectRowAtIndexPath:(NSIndexPath *)indexPath
{
    NSLog(@"Selected section %d, cell %d",
        [ indexPath indexAtPosition: 0 ], [ indexPath indexAtPosition: 1 ]);

    /* Get a pointer to the selected table cell */
    UITableViewCell *cell = [ self.tableView cellForRowAtIndexPath: indexPath ];

    /* Toggle the accessory type */
    if (cell.accessoryType == UITableViewCellAccessoryNone)
        cell.accessoryType = UITableViewCellAccessoryCheckmark;
    else
        cell.accessoryType = UITableViewCellAccessoryNone;
}
```

Editing and Swipe-to-Delete

To allow the user to delete objects in a table, enable the table's editing feature. This will cause each cell in the table to display a red deletion icon to the left. Each table cell will be indented automatically during editing:

```
[ self.tableView setEditing:YES animated:YES ];
```

This action should be triggered by a navigation bar button action, such as a button labeled Edit, or by some similar action. Use the same method to allow the user to leave editing mode when finished editing:

```
[ self.tableView setEditing: NO animated: YES ];
```

During the editing process, a user may delete a record from the table. The user will be presented with a delete confirmation. After confirming, the data source's **commitEditingStyle** method is notified to inform your application that a delete was requested. This too is a method belonging to the **UITableViewDataSource** protocol. It's up to you to service this request by deleting the underlying data from your data source. You'll also instruct the table view to delete the row:

```
- (void)tableView:(UITableView *)tableView
    commitEditingStyle:(UITableViewCellEditingStyle) editingStyle
    forRowAtIndexPath:(NSIndexPath *) indexPath
```

```
    {
        if (editingStyle == UITableViewCellEditingStyleDelete) {
            NSLog(@"Deleted section %d, cell %d",
                [ indexPath indexAtPosition: 0 ], [ indexPath indexAtPosition: 1 ]);

            /* Additional code to delete the cell from your data */

            /* Delete cell from the table */

            NSMutableArray *array = [ [ NSMutableArray alloc ] init ];
            [ array addObject: indexPath ];
            [ self.tableView deleteRowsAtIndexPaths: array
                withRowAnimation: UITableViewRowAnimationFade
            ];
        }
    }
```

 If this method exists in your delegate class, swipe-to-delete functionality
will automatically be made active.

The deleteRowsAtIndexPaths method allows you to delete one or more rows from a
table by passing an array of index paths. You can also specify one of a few predefined
animations you'd like to use to delete the cells. The following animations are supported.

Animation	Description
UITableViewRowAnimationFade	Cell fades out
UITableViewRowAnimationRight	Cell slides out from right
UITableViewRowAnimationLeft	Cell slides out from left
UITableViewRowAnimationTop	Cell slides out to top of adjacent cell
UITableViewRowAnimationBottom	Cell slides out to bottom of adjacent cell

Reloading Tables

If the data within your table has changed, reload the table by invoking the table
view's reloadData method. The data source will be queried again, and whatever changes
you've made to your underlying data will propagate to the table:

```
    [ self.tableView reloadData ];
```

This is only preferred if the table data has changed since the user last interacted with
it, and is not recommended for reloading the table after a cell has been deleted. When
the table is reloaded, the entire table structure is broken down and rebuilt, so you'll
want to be conservative in its use. For the deletion of single cells, use the
deleteRowsAtIndexPaths method to animate the deletion of one or more cells.

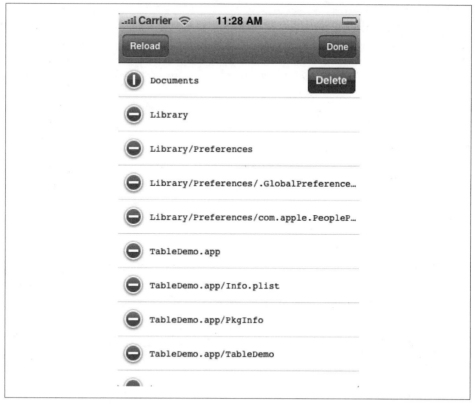

Figure 3-4. TableDemo example

TableDemo: Simple File Browser

The *TableDemo* example displays a table containing a list of files and directories present in your application's home directory on the iPhone, as shown in Figure 3-4. The example makes use of a table view controller, attached to a navigation bar controller to present user editing buttons and a reload button. The user will be able to press the Edit button to delete items from the list (don't worry, it won't actually delete any files). Swipe functionality is also active, allowing the user to swipe to delete a cell.

You can compile this application, shown in Examples 3-32 through 3-36, with the SDK by creating a *view-based application* project named *TableDemo*. Be sure to pull out the Interface Builder code if you'd like to see how these objects are created from scratch.

Example 3-32. TableDemo application delegate prototypes (TableDemoAppDelegate.h)

```
#import <UIKit/UIKit.h>

@class TableDemoViewController;

@interface TableDemoAppDelegate : NSObject <UIApplicationDelegate> {
    UIWindow *window;
```

```
    TableDemoViewController *viewController;
    UINavigationController *navigationController;
}

@property (nonatomic, retain) IBOutlet UIWindow *window;
@property (nonatomic, retain) IBOutlet TableDemoViewController *viewController;

@end
```

Example 3-33. TableDemo application delegate (TableDemoAppDelegate.m)

```
#import "TableDemoAppDelegate.h"
#import "TableDemoViewController.h"

@implementation TableDemoAppDelegate

@synthesize window;
@synthesize viewController;


- (void)applicationDidFinishLaunching:(UIApplication *)application {
    CGRect screenBounds = [ [ UIScreen mainScreen ] bounds ];

    self.window = [ [ [ UIWindow alloc ] initWithFrame: screenBounds ] autorelease ];
    viewController = [ [ TableDemoViewController alloc ] init ];
    navigationController = [ [ UINavigationController alloc ] init
WithRootViewController: viewController ];

    [ window addSubview: [ navigationController view ] ];
    [ window makeKeyAndVisible ];
}


- (void)dealloc {
    [viewController release];
    [window release];
    [super dealloc];
}

@end
```

Example 3-34. TableDemo view controller prototype (TableDemoViewController.h)

```
#import <UIKit/UIKit.h>

@interface TableDemoViewController : UITableViewController {
    NSMutableArray *fileList;
}

- (void) startEditing;
- (void) stopEditing;
- (void) reload;

@end
```

Example 3-35. TableDemo view controller (TableDemoViewController.m)

```objectivec
#import "TableDemoViewController.h"

@implementation TableDemoViewController

- (id)init {
    self = [ super init ];

    if (self != nil) {

        /* Build a list of files */
        [ self reload ];

        /* Initialize navigation bar buttons */

        self.navigationItem.rightBarButtonItem
        = [ [ [ UIBarButtonItem alloc ]
            initWithBarButtonSystemItem: UIBarButtonSystemItemEdit
            target: self
            action: @selector(startEditing) ] autorelease ];

        self.navigationItem.leftBarButtonItem
        = [ [ [ UIBarButtonItem alloc ]
            initWithTitle:@"Reload"
            style: UIBarButtonItemStylePlain
            target: self
            action:@selector(reload) ]
            autorelease ];
    }

    return self;
}

- (void) startEditing {
    [ self.tableView setEditing: YES animated: YES ];

    self.navigationItem.rightBarButtonItem
    = [ [ [ UIBarButtonItem alloc ]
        initWithBarButtonSystemItem: UIBarButtonSystemItemDone
        target: self
        action: @selector(stopEditing) ] autorelease ];
}

- (void) stopEditing {
    [ self.tableView setEditing: NO animated: YES ];

    self.navigationItem.rightBarButtonItem
    = [ [ [ UIBarButtonItem alloc ]
        initWithBarButtonSystemItem: UIBarButtonSystemItemEdit
        target: self
        action: @selector(startEditing) ] autorelease ];
}

- (void) reload {
    NSDirectoryEnumerator *dirEnum;
```

```
    NSString *file;

    fileList = [ [ NSMutableArray alloc ] init ];
    dirEnum = [ [ NSFileManager defaultManager ] enumeratorAtPath:
        NSHomeDirectory()
    ];

    while ((file = [ dirEnum nextObject ])) {
        [ fileList addObject: file ];
    }

    [ self.tableView reloadData ];
}

- (NSInteger)numberOfSectionsInTableView:(UITableView *)tableView {
    return 1;
}


- (NSInteger)tableView:(UITableView *)tableView numberOfRowsIn
Section:(NSInteger)section {

    return [ fileList count ];
}

- (UITableViewCell *)tableView:(UITableView *)tableView cellForRow
AtIndexPath:(NSIndexPath *)indexPath {

    NSString *CellIdentifier = [ fileList objectAtIndex:
        [ indexPath indexAtPosition: 1 ]
    ];

    UITableViewCell *cell = [ tableView
        dequeueReusableCellWithIdentifier: CellIdentifier
    ];

    if (cell == nil) {
        cell = [ [ [ UITableViewCell alloc ] initWithFrame:
            CGRectZero reuseIdentifier: CellIdentifier ] autorelease
        ];
        cell.text = CellIdentifier;

        UIFont *font = [ UIFont fontWithName: @"Courier" size: 12.0 ];
        cell.font = font;
    }

    return cell;
}

- (void)tableView:(UITableView *)tableView
    commitEditingStyle:(UITableViewCellEditingStyle) editingStyle
    forRowAtIndexPath:(NSIndexPath *) indexPath
{
    if (editingStyle == UITableViewCellEditingStyleDelete) {
```

```
        /* Delete cell from data source */

        UITableViewCell *cell = [ self.tableView cellForRowAtIndexPath:
            indexPath ];

        for(int i = 0; i < [ fileList count ]; i++) {
            if ([ cell.text isEqualToString: [ fileList objectAtIndex: i ] ]) {
                [ fileList removeObjectAtIndex: i ];
            }
        }

        /* Delete cell from table */

        NSMutableArray *array = [ [ NSMutableArray alloc ] init ];
        [ array addObject: indexPath ];
        [ self.tableView deleteRowsAtIndexPaths: array
            withRowAnimation: UITableViewRowAnimationTop
        ];

    }
}

- (void)tableView:(UITableView *)tableView didSelectRowAt
IndexPath:(NSIndexPath *)indexPath {

    UITableViewCell *cell = [ self.tableView cellForRowAtIndexPath: indexPath ];

    UIAlertView *alert = [ [ UIAlertView alloc ] initWithTitle: @"File Selected"
        message: [ NSString stringWithFormat: @"You selected the file '%@'",
                      cell.text ]
        delegate: nil
        cancelButtonTitle: nil
        otherButtonTitles: @"OK", nil
    ];

    [ alert show ];
}

- (void)loadView {
    [ super loadView ];
}

- (BOOL)shouldAutorotateToInterfaceOrientation:(UIInterface
Orientation)interfaceOrientation {
    return YES;
}


- (void)didReceiveMemoryWarning {
    [ super didReceiveMemoryWarning ];

}

- (void)dealloc {
    [ fileList release ];
```

```
    [ super dealloc ];
}

@end
```

Example 3-36. TableDemo main (main.m)

```
#import <UIKit/UIKit.h>

int main(int argc, char *argv[]) {

    NSAutoreleasePool * pool = [[NSAutoreleasePool alloc] init];
    int retVal = UIApplicationMain(argc, argv, nil, @"TableDemoAppDelegate");
    [pool release];
    return retVal;
}
```

What's Going On

The *TableDemo* example works as follows:

1. The application instantiates as all other examples thus far have, and the program's `main` function is called, which invokes the `TableDemoAppDelegate` class's `applicationDidFinishLaunching` method, and builds the appropriate window, view controller, and navigation controller classes.

2. The view controller is created as an instance of `UITableViewController`. The controller's `init` method is overridden to load a list of files into an array named `fileList`. It also adds two navigation bar buttons: a system Edit button and a Reload button.

3. When the table is rendered, the controller's data source methods are automatically queried. The `numberOfRowsInSection` method returns the number of rows in the file list. The `cellForRowAtIndexPath` creates a new cell using the filename as the cell title.

4. If the user taps the Edit button, the button's designated selector, `startEditing`, is notified. This replaces the button with a Done button and enables editing of the table. The table automatically indents each cell and adds a delete icon.

5. If the user deletes a row either by editing or swiping, he will be asked for confirmation. Once the user confirms, the delete request will cause the `commitEditingStyle` method to be notified of the request. The method checks to ensure the request is a delete request and deletes the object from the file list and the table.

6. If the user presses the Reload button, the file list is reread and the table is refreshed.

Further Study

See if you can take what you've previously learned and apply it to this example:

- Use `NSDirectoryEnumerator` class's `fileAttributes` method to identify which files are directories. Add a disclosure arrow for cells that reference directories, and push a new table view controller on the stack when the user taps one. The child view controller should have a Back button and display only files that are present in the selected directory.

- Add a new view controller that displays the contents of a file in a UITextView. If the file is binary, display a hexadecimal readout. When the user taps on a file, a new view controller should be pushed on the navigation controller's stack that displays the contents of the file. The new view controller should have a Back button.

- Check out the following prototypes in your SDK's header files: *UITableView.h*, *UITableViewCell.h*, *UILabel.h*, and *UITableViewController.h*. You'll find these under */Developer/Platforms/iPhoneOS.platform*, inside the UI Kit framework's *Headers* directory.

Status Bar Manipulation

The status bar's appearance can be customized to meet the look and feel of your application, or you can remove it entirely if you need the extra screen real estate. The changes you make to the status bar will only affect your application; the standard status bar will bounce back when you press the Home button.

You can change many properties of the status bar using methods from the UIApplication class. The UIApplication class represents your running application. To gain access to this object, use the class's static sharedApplication method:

```
UIApplication *myApp = [ UIApplication sharedApplication ];
```

Hiding the Status Bar

To hide the status bar entirely, use the setStatusBarHidden method:

```
[ myApp setStatusBarHidden: YES animated: YES];
```

If you're going to do this, be sure to hide the status bar before creating any windows or views. Otherwise, the application frame will not include the space taken up by the status bar, and you'll have to reset any affected view classes using the setFrame method:

```
[ viewController.view setFrame: [ [ UIScreen mainScreen ] applicationFrame ] ];

[ [ navigationController view ]
    setFrame: [ [ UIScreen mainScreen ] applicationFrame ]
];
```

Status Bar Style

The status bar style determines its color and opacity. The status bar style sets the overall appearance of the bar:

```
[ myApp setStatusBarStyle: UIStatusBarStyleBlackOpaque ];
```

The following styles are supported.

Style	Description
UIStatusBarStyleDefault	Default; white status bar with black text
UIStatusBarStyleBlackTranslucent	Black transparent status bar with white text
UIStatusBarStyleBlackOpaque	Black opaque status bar with white text

Status Bar Orientation

Normally, the orientation of the status bar is changed automatically when using view controllers. To force the orientation of the status bar, use the UIApplication class's setStatusBarOrientation method:

```
[ myApp setStatusBarOrientation: UIInterfaceOrientationLandscapeRight
    animated: NO
];
```

The following orientations are available on the device.

UIDeviceOrientationPortrait
    Oriented upright vertically in portrait mode

UIDeviceOrientationPortraitUpsideDown
    Oriented upside-down vertically in portrait mode

UIDeviceOrientationLandscapeLeft
    Device is rotated counter-clockwise in landscape mode

UIDeviceOrientationLandscapeRight
    Device is rotated clockwise in landscape mode

UIDeviceOrientationFaceUp
    Device is laying flat, face up, such as on a table

UIDeviceOrientationFaceDown
    Device is laying flat, face down, such as on a table

Application Badges

With the iPhone's numerous different connections—3G/EDGE, WiFi, and Bluetooth—lots of things can happen while you've got that little device stuck in your pocket. Without some notification to the user that there are pending notifications, he's likely to miss everything that's happened while he was busy having a real life. As new features appear in iPhone firmware, such as push notification, your application may receive new information when it is not in the foreground. In addition to this, application badges can serve as a reminder to a user who has run the application but did not finish viewing all messages, notifications, or other data. Application badges are small message bubbles that appear on the program's home screen icon. Application badges are used heavily by Apple's preloaded applications to alert the user to missed calls, voicemail, text messages, and email.

One of the nice features about these types of badges is that the application doesn't necessarily need to be running for the badge to display on the springboard. This is useful in serving as a reminder to the user even after he has exited the application. This also means you'll need to clean up any lingering badges when your program exits.

Displaying an Application Badge

Application badges are one of the easier features to take advantage of, requiring only one call to the UIApplication class:

```
[ UIApplication sharedApplication ].applicationIconBadgeNumber = 42;
```

The applicationIconBadgeNumber property takes an NSInteger object, so you can only set numeric integer values with it, but this is often enough to convey the message that a certain number of new items are waiting.

Removing an Application Badge

An application badge should be removed when the user has clicked to the page with the important events he was being notified about. Removing the application badge is also an easy task. The badge is erased when its value is set to zero. A good place to put such code is after transitioning to the controlling view displaying the new events:

```
[ UIApplication sharedApplication ].applicationIconBadgeNumber = 0;
```

An application badge will continue to hang around even after an application has terminated. This can be useful, but is not always what you want. If an application badge should be removed when the program exits, set this property inside the application delegate's applicationWillTerminate method:

```
- (void)applicationWillTerminate {
    /* We are about to exit, so remove the application badge */

    [ UIApplication sharedApplication ].applicationIconBadgeNumber = 0;
}
```

Further Study

Before going on to learn some of the situations in which application badges can help improve your application's response to state changes, do a little exploration:

- Experiment and determine the maximum number of digits that can be added to an application badge. What happens when you exceed this limit?

- Check out the *UIApplication.h* prototype in your SDK's header files. You'll find these under */Developer/Platforms/iPhoneOS.platform*, inside the UI Kit framework's *Headers* directory.

Application Services

The state of an application is more important on the iPhone than it is on the desktop. Many events on the iPhone can cause an application to suspend or terminate. These different states occur when the user presses the Home button, locks the screen, or receives a phone call. It's important for an application to know when its state is about to change in order to save any settings, halt threads, or perform other actions. While there's nothing the application can generally do about the state it's about to enter, it can at least take whatever actions are appropriate to prepare for it.

Application services are provided by notifying the application's delegate class to events about to occur. All of the methods listed in this section belong to the `UIApplicationDelegate` protocol. The application delegate is specified when you first instantiate the Objective-C portion of the application by calling `UIApplicationMain` in your *main.m* file. If you supplied a NIB file, you define the application's delegate inside the Interface Builder template.

Suspending and Resuming

When the device is locked or a phone call comes in, SDK applications are suspended. When this occurs, the delegate's `applicationWillResignActive` method is notified. This method can be overridden to prepare the application for being suspended, such as closing network connections or saving data:

```
- (void)applicationWillResignActive:(UIApplication *) application {
    NSLog(@"About to be suspended");

    /* Code to prepare for suspend */
}
```

While your application is suspended, it will *not run in the background*. When the application resumes, another method named `applicationDidBecomeActive` is notified. Here, you can add code to resume where your application left off:

```
- (void)applicationDidBecomeActive:(UIApplication *) application {
    NSLog(@"Became active");

    /* Code to prepare for resume */
}
```

 When an application is started, its `applicationDidBecomeActive` method is also notified after its `applicationDidFinishLaunching` method. Be sure your code can tell the difference between resuming and starting.

Program Termination

A program is terminated when the user presses the Home button or the iPhone is shut down. The `applicationWillTerminate` method is called whenever an application is

---

about to be cleanly terminated. It is *not* called when an application is force-quit by holding down the Home button. This method should perform any remaining cleanup of resources, such as making sure all connections are properly closed and performing any other necessary tasks before the program exits:

```
- (void)applicationWillTerminate:(UIApplication *)application {

    /* Cleanup and shutdown code here */
}
```

Invoking Safari

Occasionally, it may be appropriate to call Safari to bring up a web page for your application; for example, when the user presses a Donate or Home Page button in your application's credits page. The UIApplication class supports an openURL method that can seamlessly launch Safari and load a web page in a new window.

To use this, your application needs to create an NSURL object. You were introduced to the NSURL earlier in this chapter. The NSURL object is passed to the application's openURL method, where the application framework processes and launches the appropriate handler application:

```
NSURL *url = [ [ NSURL alloc ] initWithString: @"http://www.oreilly.com/" ];
[ [ UIApplication sharedApplication ] openURL: url ];
```

Initiating Phone Calls

As was just demonstrated, the openURL method calls Safari to launch website URLs. What's actually going on is this: each protocol is associated with a specific handler application. URLs beginning with http:// and https:// are associated with Safari and cause it to open whenever openURL is called using those protocol prefixes. Just as openURL can be used to open websites in Safari, it can also be used to place phone calls. To do this, use the protocol prefix of tel:.

```
NSURL *url = [ [ NSURL alloc ]
    initWithString: @"tel:212-555-1234" ];
[ [ UIApplication sharedApplication ] openURL: url ];
```

When the openURL method is used on a URL beginning with tel:, the phone application will be launched and the call will be automatically placed. Do try and ensure that your application doesn't have any bugs that cause it to accidentally place expensive overseas calls or make prank calls to the White House.

CHAPTER 4

Multi-Touch Events and Geometry

In Chapter 3, you were introduced to some of the iPhone's basic user interface elements. Many objects support high-level events to notify the application of certain actions taken by the user. These actions rely on lower-level mouse events provided by the `UIView` class and a base class underneath it: `UIResponder`. The `UIResponder` class provides methods to recognize and handle the mouse events that occur when the user taps or drags on the iPhone's screen. Higher-level objects, such as tables and action sheets, take these low-level events and wrap them into even higher-level ones to handle button clicks, swipes, row selections, and other types of behavior. Apple has provided a multi-touch API capable of intercepting finger gestures in order to make the same use of finger movements in your UI. The *touches* API tells the application exactly what has occurred on the screen and provides the information the application needs to interact with the user.

Introduction to Geometric Structures

Before diving into events management, you'll need a basic understanding of some geometric structures commonly used on the iPhone. You've already seen some of these in Chapter 3. The Core Graphics framework provides many general structures to handle graphics-related functions. Among these structures are points, window sizes, and window regions. Core Graphics also provides many C-based functions for creating and comparing these structures.

CGPoint

A `CGPoint` is the simplest CoreGraphics structure, and contains two floating-point values corresponding to horizontal (x) and vertical (y) coordinates on a display. To create a `CGPoint`, use the `CGPointMake` method:

```
CGPoint point = CGPointMake (320.0, 480.0);
```

The first value represents x, the horizontal pixel value, and the second represents y, the vertical pixel value. You can also access these values directly:

```
float x = point.x;
float y = point.y;
```

The iPhone's display resolution is 320×480 pixels. The upper-left corner of the screen is referenced at 0×0, and the lower-right at 319×479 (pixel offsets are zero-indexed).

Being a general-purpose structure, a `CGPoint` can refer equally well to a coordinate on the screen or within a window. For example, if a window is drawn at 0×240 (halfway down the screen), a `CGPoint` with values (0, 0) could address either the upper-left corner of the screen or the upper-left corner of the window (0×240). Which one it means is determined by the context where the structure is being used in the program.

You can compare two `CGPoint` structures using the `CGPointEqualToPoint` function:

```
BOOL isEqual = CGPointEqualToPoint(point1, point2);
```

CGSize

A `CGSize` structure represents the size of a rectangle. It encapsulates the width and height of an object and is primarily found in the iPhone APIs to dictate the size of screen objects—namely windows. To create a `CGSize` object, use `CGSizeMake`:

```
CGSize size = CGSizeMake(320.0, 480.0);
```

The values provided to `CGSizeMake` indicate the width and height of the element being described. You can directly access values using the structure's `width` and `height` variable names:

```
float width = size.width;
float height = size.height;
```

You can compare two `CGSize` structures using the `CGSizeEqualToSize` function:

```
BOOL isEqual = CGSizeEqualToSize(size1, size2);
```

CGRect

The `CGRect` structure combines both a `CGPoint` and `CGSize` structure to describe the frame of a window on the screen. The frame includes an **origin**, which represents the location of the upper-left corner of the window, and the **size** of the window. To create a `CGRect`, use the `CGRectMake` function:

```
CGRect rect = CGRectMake(0.0, 200.0, 320.0, 240.0);
```

This example describes a 320×240 window whose upper-left corner is located at coordinates 0×200. As with the `CGPoint` structure, these coordinates could reference a point on the screen itself or offsets within an existing window; it depends on where and how the `CGRect` structure is used.

You can also access the components of the `CGRect` structure directly:

```
CGPoint windowOrigin = rect.origin;
float x = rect.origin.x;
float y = rect.origin.y;

CGSize windowSize = rect.size;
float width = rect.size.width;
float height = rect.size.height;
```

Containment and intersection

Two `CGRect` structures can be compared using the `CGRectEqualToRect` function:

```
BOOL isEqual = CGRectEqualToRect(rect1, rect2);
```

To determine whether a given point is contained inside a `CGRect`, use the `CGRectContainsPoint` method. This is particularly useful when determining whether a user has tapped inside a particular region. The point is represented as a `CGPoint` structure:

```
BOOL containsPoint = CGRectContainsPoint(rect, point);
```

You can use a similar function to determine whether one `CGRect` structure contains another `CGRect` structure. This is useful when testing whether certain objects overlap:

```
BOOL containsRect = CGRectContainsRect(rect1, rect2);
```

For one structure to contain another, all the pixels in one structure must also be in the other. In contrast, two structures intersect as long as they share at least one pixel. To determine whether two `CGRect` structures intersect, use the `CGRectIntersectsRect` function:

```
BOOL doesIntersect = CGRectIntersectsRect(rect1, rect2);
```

Edge and center detection

The following functions can be used to determine the various edges of a rectangle and calculate the coordinates of the rectangle's center. All of these functions accept a `CGRect` structure as their only argument and return a `float` value:

CGRectGetMinX
> Returns the coordinate of the left edge of the rectangle.

CGRectGetMinY
> Returns the coordinate of the bottom edge of the rectangle.

CGRectGetMidX
> Returns the center x coordinate of the rectangle.

CGRectGetMidY
> Returns the center y coordinate of the rectangle.

CGRectGetMaxX
> Returns the coordinate of the right edge of the rectangle.

```
CGRectGetMaxY
```
Returns the coordinate of the upper edge of the rectangle.

Multi-Touch Events Handling

The multi-touch support on the iPhone provides a series of touch events consisting of smaller, individual parts of a single multi-touch gesture. For example, placing your finger on the screen generates one event, placing a second finger on the screen generates another, and moving either finger generates yet another. All of these are handled through the `UITouch` and `UIEvent` APIs. These objects provide information about which gesture events have been made and the screen coordinates where they occur. The location of the touch is consistent with a particular window and view, so you'll also learn how to tell in which object a touch occurred.

Because events are relative to the object in which they occur, the coordinates returned will not actually be screen coordinates, but rather relative coordinates. For example, if a view window is drawn halfway down the screen, at 0×240, and your user touches the upper-left corner of that view, the coordinates reported to your application will be 0×0, not 0×240. The 0×0 coordinates represent the upper-left corner of the view object that the user tapped.

UITouch Notifications

`UITouch` is the class used to convey a single action within a series of gestures. A `UITouch` object might include notifications for one or more fingers down, a finger that has moved, or the termination of a gesture. Several `UITouch` notifications can occur over the period of a single gesture.

The `UITouch` object includes various properties that identify an event:

`timestamp`
Provides a timestamp relative to a previous event using the foundation class `NSTimeInterval`.

`phase`
The type of touch event occurring. This informs the application about what the user is actually doing with his finger, and can be one of the following enumerated values:

`UITouchPhaseBegan`
Sent when one or more fingers touch the screen surface.

`UITouchPhaseMoved`
Sent when a finger is moved along the screen. If the user is making a gesture or dragging an item, this type of notification will be sent several times, updating the application with the coordinates of the move.

UITouchPhaseEnded
> Sent when a finger is removed from the screen.

UITouchPhaseStationary
> Sent when a finger is touching the screen, but hasn't moved since the previous notification.

UIPhaseCancelled
> Sent when the system cancels the gesture. This can happen during events that would cause your application to be suspended, such as an incoming phone call, or if there is little enough contact on the screen surface that the iPhone doesn't believe a finger gesture is being made any longer, and is thus cancelled. Apple humorously gives the example of sticking the iPhone on your face to generate this notification, which may be useful if you're writing a "stick an iPhone on your face" application to complement your flashlight application.

tapCount
> Identifies the number of taps (including the current tap). For example, the second tap of a double tap would have this property set to 2.

window
> A pointer to the UIWindow object in which this touch event occurred.

view
> A pointer to the UIView object in which this event occurred.

In addition to its properties, the UITouch class contains the following methods that you can use to identify the screen coordinates at which the event took place. Remember, these coordinates are going to be relative to the view objects in which they occurred, and do not represent actual screen coordinates:

locationInView

```
- (CGPoint) locationInView: (UIView *) view;
```

Returns a CGPoint structure containing the coordinates (relative to the UIView object) at which this event occurred.

previousLocationInView

```
- (CGPoint) previousLocationInView: (UIView *) view;
```

Returns a CGPoint structure containing the coordinates (relative to the UIView object) from which this event originated. For example, if this event described a UITouchPhaseMoved event, it will return the coordinates from which the finger was moved.

UIEvent

A UIEvent object aggregates a series of UITouch objects into a single, portable object that you can manage easily. A UIEvent provides methods to look up the touches that have occurred in a single window, view, or even across the entire application.

Event objects are sent as a gesture is made, containing all of the events for that gesture. The foundation class NSSet is used to deliver the collection of subsequent UITouch events. Each of the UITouch events included in the set includes the specific timestamp, phase, and location of each event, while the UIEvent object includes its own timestamp property as well.

The UIEvent object supports the following methods:

allTouches

        - (NSSet *) allTouches;

 Returns a set of all touches occurring within the application.

touchesForWindow

        - (NSSet *) touchesForWindow: (UIWindow *) window;

 Returns a set of all touches occurring only within the specified UIWindow object.

touchesForView

        - (NSSet *) touchesForView: (UIView *) view;

 Returns a set of all touches occurring only within the specified UIView object.

Events Handling

When the user makes a gesture, the application notifies the key window and supplies the UIEvent structure containing the events that are occurring. The key window will relay this information to the first responder for the window. This is typically the view in which the actual event occurred. Once a gesture has been associated with a given view, all subsequent events related to the gesture will be reported to that view. The UIApplication and UIWindow objects contain a method named sendEvent:

        - (void) sendEvent: (UIEvent *)event;

This method is called as part of the event dispatch process. These methods are responsible for receiving and dispatching events to their correct destinations. In general, you won't need to override these methods unless you want to monitor all incoming events.

When the key window receives an event, it polls each of the view classes it presides over to determine in which one the event originated, and then dispatches the event to it. The object's responder will then dispatch the event to its view controller, if the view is assigned to one, and then to the view's own super class. It will then make its way back up the responder chain to its window, and finally to the application.

To receive multi-touch events, you must override one or more of the event-handler methods below in your UIView–derived object. Your UIWindow and UIApplication classes may also override these methods to receive events, but there is rarely a need to do so. Apple has specified the following prototypes to receive multi-touch events. Each of the methods used is associated with one of the touch phases described in the previous section:

```
- (void)touchesBegan:(NSSet *)touches withEvent:(UIEvent *)event;
- (void)touchesMoved:(NSSet *)touches withEvent:(UIEvent *)event;
- (void)touchesEnded:(NSSet *)touches withEvent:(UIEvent *)event;
- (void)touchesCancelled:(NSSet *)touches withEvent:(UIEvent *)event;
```

Two arguments are provided for each method. The NSSet provided contains a set consisting only of new touches that have occurred since the last event. A UIEvent is also provided, serving two purposes: it allows you to filter the individual touch events for only a particular view or window, and it provides a means of accessing previous touches as they pertain to the current gesture.

You'll only need to implement the notification methods for events you're interested in. If you're interested only in receiving taps as "mouse clicks," you'll need to use only the touchesBegan and touchesEnded methods. If you're using dragging, such as in a slider control, you'll need the touchesMoved method. The touchesCancelled method is optional, but Apple recommends using it to clean up objects in persistent classes.

Example: Tap Counter

In this example, you'll override the touchesBegan method to detect single, double, and triple taps. For our purposes here, we'll send output to the console only, but in your own application, you'll relay this information to its UI components.

To build this example, create a sample *view-based application* in Xcode named *TouchDemo*, and add the code below to your *TouchDemoViewController.m* class:

```
- (void) touchesBegan:(NSSet *)touches withEvent:(UIEvent *)event
{
    UITouch *touch = [ touches anyObject ];
    CGPoint location = [ touch locationInView: self.view ];
    NSUInteger taps = [ touch tapCount ];

    NSLog(@"%s tap at %f, %f tap count: %d",
        (taps == 1) ? "Single" :
            (taps == 2) ? "Double" : "Triple+",
        location.x, location.y, taps);
}
```

Compile the application and run it in the simulator. In Xcode, choose Console from the Run menu to open the display console. Now experiment with single, double, and triple taps on the simulator's screen. You should see output similar to the output below:

```
Untitled[4229:20b] Single tap at 161.000000, 113.953613 taps count: 1
Untitled[4229:20b] Double tap at 161.000000, 113.953613 taps count: 2
Untitled[4229:20b] Triple+ tap at 161.000000, 113.953613 taps count: 3
Untitled[4229:20b] Triple+ tap at 161.000000, 113.953613 taps count: 4
```

 The tap count will continue to increase indefinitely, meaning you could technically track quadruple taps and even higher tap counts.

Example: Tap and Drag

To track objects being dragged, you'll need to override three methods: touchesBegan, touchesMoved, and touchesEnded. The touchesMoved method will be called frequently as the mouse is dragged across the screen. When the user releases her finger, the touchesEnded method will notify you of this.

To build this example, create a sample *view-based application* in Xcode named *Drag Demo*, and add the code below to your *DragDemoViewController.m* class:

```
- (void) touchesBegan:(NSSet *)touches withEvent:(UIEvent *)event
{
    UITouch *touch = [ touches anyObject ];
    CGPoint location = [ touch locationInView: self.view ];
    NSUInteger taps = [ touch tapCount ];

    [ super touchesBegan: touches withEvent: event ];

    NSLog(@"Tap BEGIN at %f, %f Tap count: %d", location.x, location.y, taps);
}

- (void) touchesMoved:(NSSet *)touches withEvent:(UIEvent *)event
{
    UITouch *touch = [ touches anyObject ];
    CGPoint oldLocation = [ touch previousLocationInView: self.view ];
    CGPoint location = [ touch locationInView: self.view ];

    [ super touchesMoved: touches withEvent: event ];
    NSLog(@"Finger MOVED from %f, %f to %f, %f",
        oldLocation.x, oldLocation.y, location.x, location.y);
}

- (void) touchesEnded:(NSSet *)touches withEvent:(UIEvent *)event
{
    UITouch *touch = [ touches anyObject ];
    CGPoint location = [ touch locationInView: self.view ];

    [ super touchesEnded: touches withEvent: event ];
    NSLog(@"Tap ENDED at %f, %f", location.x, location.y);
}
```

When you run this application, you'll get notifications whenever the user places his finger down or lifts it up, and you'll also receive many more as the user moves his finger across the screen:

```
BEGIN at 101.000000, 117.953613 Tap count: 1
Finger MOVED from 101.000000, 117.953613 to 102.000000, 117.953613
Finger MOVED from 102.000000, 117.953613 to 104.000000, 117.953613
Finger MOVED from 104.000000, 117.953613 to 105.000000, 117.953613
Finger MOVED from 105.000000, 117.953613 to 107.000000, 117.953613
Finger MOVED from 107.000000, 117.953613 to 109.000000, 116.953613
Finger MOVED from 109.000000, 116.953613 to 113.000000, 115.953613
Finger MOVED from 113.000000, 115.953613 to 116.000000, 115.953613
Finger MOVED from 116.000000, 115.953613 to 120.000000, 114.953613
Finger MOVED from 120.000000, 114.953613 to 122.000000, 114.953613
...
Tap ENDED at 126.000000, 144.953613
```

Because you'll receive several different notifications when the user's finger moves, it's important to make sure your application doesn't perform any resource-intensive functions until after the user's finger is released, or at externally timed intervals. For example, if your application is a game application, the touchesMoved method may not be the ideal place to write character movements. Instead, use this method to queue up the movement, and use a separate mechanism, such as an NSTimer, to execute the actual movements. Otherwise, larger mouse movements will slow your application down because it will be trying to handle so many events in a short period of time.

Processing Multi-Touch

By default, a view is configured only to receive single fingering events. To enable a view to process multi-touch gestures, set the multipleTouchEnabled method. In the previous example, overriding the view controller's viewDidLoad method, as shown below, would do this:

```
- (void)viewDidLoad {
    self.view.multipleTouchEnabled = YES;
    [ super viewDidLoad ];
}
```

Once enabled, both single-finger events and multiple-finger gestures will be sent to the touch notification methods. You can determine the number of touches on the screen by looking at the number of UITouch events provided in the NSSet from the first argument. During a gesture, each of the touch methods will be provided with two UITouch events, one for each finger. You can determined this by performing a simple count on the NSSet object provided:

```
int fingerCount = [ touches count ];
```

To determine the number of fingers used in the gesture as a whole, query the UIEvent. This allows you to determine when the last finger in a gesture has been lifted:

```
    int fingersInGesture = [ [ event touchesForView: self.view ] count ];
    if (fingerCount == fingersInGesture) {
        NSLog(@"All fingers present in the event");
    }
```

PinchMe: Pinch Tracking

This example is similar to the previous examples in this chapter, but instead of tracking a single finger movement, both fingers are tracked to determine a scaling factor for a pinch operation. You can then easily apply the scaling factor to resize an image or perform other similar operations using a pinch. You'll override three methods in your view controller, as before: touchesBegan, touchesMoved, and touchedEnded. You'll also override the viewDidLoad method to enable multi-touch gestures. The touchesMoved method will be called frequently as the mouse is dragged across the screen, where the scaling factor will be calculated. When the user releases her finger, the touchesEnded method will notify you of this.

To build this example, create a sample *view-based application* in Xcode named *PinchMe*, and add the code from Example 4-1 to your *PinchMeViewController.m* class.

Example 4-1. Code supplement for PinchMeViewController.m

```
- (void)viewDidLoad {
    [super viewDidLoad];
    [ self.view setMultipleTouchEnabled: YES ];
}

- (void) touchesBegan:(NSSet *)touches withEvent:(UIEvent *)event
{
    UITouch *touch = [ touches anyObject ];
    CGPoint location = [ touch locationInView: self.view ];
    NSUInteger taps = [ touch tapCount ];

    [ super touchesBegan: touches withEvent: event ];

    NSLog(@"Tap BEGIN at %f, %f Tap count: %d", location.x, location.y, taps);
}

- (void) touchesMoved:(NSSet *)touches withEvent:(UIEvent *)event
{
    int finger = 0;
    NSEnumerator *enumerator = [ touches objectEnumerator ];
    UITouch *touch;
    CGPoint location[2];
    while ((touch = [ enumerator nextObject ]) && finger < 2)
    {
        location[finger] = [ touch locationInView: self.view ];
        NSLog(@"Finger %d moved: %fx%f",
        finger+1, location[finger].x, location[finger].y);
        finger++;
    }
```

```
    if (finger == 2) {
        CGPoint scale;
        scale.x = fabs(location[0].x - location[1].x);
        scale.y = fabs(location[0].y - location[1].y);
        NSLog(@"Scaling: %.0f x %.0f", scale.x, scale.y);
    }
    [ super touchesMoved: touches withEvent: event ];
}

- (void) touchesEnded:(NSSet *)touches withEvent:(UIEvent *)event
{
    UITouch *touch = [ touches anyObject ];
    CGPoint location = [ touch locationInView: self.view ];

    [ super touchesEnded: touches withEvent: event ];
    NSLog(@"Tap ENDED at %f, %f", location.x, location.y);
}
```

Open up a console while you run the application. Holding in the option key, you'll be able to simulate multi-touch pinch gestures in the iPhone Simulator. As you move the mouse around, you'll see reports of both finger coordinates and of the x, y delta between the two:

```
Untitled[5039:20b] Finger 1 moved: 110.000000x293.046387
Untitled[5039:20b] Finger 2 moved: 210.000000x146.953613
Untitled[5039:20b] Scaling: 100 × 146
Untitled[5039:20b] Finger 1 moved: 111.000000x289.046387
Untitled[5039:20b] Finger 2 moved: 209.000000x150.953613
Untitled[5039:20b] Scaling: 98 × 138
Untitled[5039:20b] Finger 1 moved: 112.000000x285.046387
Untitled[5039:20b] Finger 2 moved: 208.000000x154.953613
Untitled[5039:20b] Scaling: 96 × 130
Untitled[5039:20b] Finger 1 moved: 113.000000x282.046387
Untitled[5039:20b] Finger 2 moved: 207.000000x157.953613
Untitled[5039:20b] Scaling: 94 × 124
Untitled[5039:20b] Finger 1 moved: 113.000000x281.046387
Untitled[5039:20b] Finger 2 moved: 207.000000x158.953613
Untitled[5039:20b] Scaling: 94 × 122
```

TouchDemo: Multi-Touch Icon Tracking

For a fuller example of the touches API, TouchDemo illustrates how you can use the touches API to track individual finger movements on the screen. Four demo images are downloaded automatically from a website and displayed on the screen. The user may use one or more fingers to simultaneously drag the icons to a new position. The example tracks each touch individually; it repositions each icon as the user drags. See Figure 4-1.

You can compile this application, shown in Examples 4-2 through 4-6, with the SDK by creating a *view-based application* project named *TouchDemo*. Be sure to pull out the Interface Builder code so you can see how these objects are created from scratch.

Figure 4-1. TouchDemo example

Example 4-2. TouchDemo application delegate prototypes (TouchDemoAppDelegate.h)

```
#import <UIKit/UIKit.h>

@class TouchDemoViewController;

@interface TouchDemoAppDelegate : NSObject <UIApplicationDelegate> {
    UIWindow *window;
    TouchDemoViewController *viewController;
}

@property (nonatomic, retain) IBOutlet UIWindow *window;
@property (nonatomic, retain) IBOutlet TouchDemoViewController *viewController;

@end
```

Example 4-3. TouchDemo application delegate (TouchDemoAppDelegate.m)

```
#import "TouchDemoAppDelegate.h"
#import "TouchDemoViewController.h"

@implementation TouchDemoAppDelegate
```

```
@synthesize window;
@synthesize viewController;

- (void)applicationDidFinishLaunching:(UIApplication *)application {
    CGRect screenBounds = [ [ UIScreen mainScreen ] applicationFrame ];

    self.window = [ [ [ UIWindow alloc ] initWithFrame: screenBounds ]
        autorelease
    ];

    viewController = [ [ TouchDemoViewController alloc ] init ];

    [ window addSubview: viewController.view ];
    [ window makeKeyAndVisible ];
}

- (void)dealloc {
    [ viewController release ];
    [ window release ];
    [ super dealloc ];
}


@end
```

Example 4-4. TouchDemo view controller prototypes (TouchDemoViewController.h)

```
#import <UIKit/UIKit.h>

@interface TouchView : UIView {
    UIImage *images[4];
    CGPoint offsets[4];
    int tracking[4];
}

@end

@interface TouchDemoViewController : UIViewController {
    TouchView *touchView;
}

@end
```

Example 4-5. TouchDemo view controller (TouchDemoViewController.m)

```
#import "TouchDemoViewController.h"

@implementation TouchView

- (id)initWithFrame:(CGRect)frame {
    frame.origin.y = 0.0;
    self = [ super initWithFrame: frame ];
    if (self != nil) {
        self.multipleTouchEnabled = YES;
        for(int i=0; i<4; i++) {
            NSURL *url = [ NSURL URLWithString: [
```

```
                NSString stringWithFormat:
                    @"http://www.zdziarski.com/demo/%d.png", i+1 ]
            ];
            images[i] = [ [ UIImage alloc ]
                initWithData: [ NSData dataWithContentsOfURL: url ]
            ];
            offsets[i] = CGPointMake(0.0, 0.0);
        }

        offsets[0] = CGPointMake(0.0, 0.0);
        offsets[1] = CGPointMake(self.frame.size.width
            - images[1].size.width, 0.0);
        offsets[2] = CGPointMake(0.0, self.frame.size.height
            - images[2].size.height);
        offsets[3] = CGPointMake(self.frame.size.width
            - images[3].size.width, self.frame.size.height
            - images[3].size.height);
    }

    return self;
}

- (void)drawRect:(CGRect)rect {
    for(int i=0; i<4; i++ ) {
        [ images[i] drawInRect: CGRectMake(offsets[i].x, offsets[i].y,
            images[i].size.width, images[i].size.height)
        ];
    }
}

- (void)touchesBegan:(NSSet *)touches withEvent:(UIEvent *)event {
    UITouch *touch;
    int touchId = 0;

    NSEnumerator *enumerator = [ touches objectEnumerator ];
    while ((touch = (UITouch *) [ enumerator nextObject ])) {
        tracking[touchId] = -1;
        CGPoint location = [ touch locationInView: self ];
        for(int i=3;i>=0;i--) {
            CGRect rect = CGRectMake(offsets[i].x, offsets[i].y,
                images[i].size.width, images[i].size.height);
            if (CGRectContainsPoint(rect, location)) {
                NSLog(@"Begin Touch ID %d Tracking with image %d\n", touchId, i);
                tracking[touchId] = i;
                break;
            }
        }

        touchId++;
    }
}

- (void)touchesMoved:(NSSet *)touches withEvent:(UIEvent *)event {
    UITouch *touch;
    int touchId = 0;
```

```
        NSEnumerator *enumerator = [ touches objectEnumerator ];
        while ((touch = (UITouch *) [ enumerator nextObject ])) {
            if (tracking[touchId] != -1) {
                NSLog(@"Touch ID %d Tracking with image %d\n",
                    touchId, tracking[touchId]);

                CGPoint location = [ touch locationInView: self ];
                CGPoint oldLocation = [ touch previousLocationInView: self ];
                offsets[tracking[touchId]].x += (location.x - oldLocation.x);
                offsets[tracking[touchId]].y += (location.y - oldLocation.y);

                if (offsets[tracking[touchId]].x < 0.0)
                    offsets[tracking[touchId]].x = 0.0;
                if (offsets[tracking[touchId]].x
                    + images[tracking[touchId]].size.width > self.frame.size.width)
                {
                    offsets[tracking[touchId]].x = self.frame.size.width
                        - images[tracking[touchId]].size.width;
                }

                if (offsets[tracking[touchId]].y < 0.0)
                    offsets[tracking[touchId]].y = 0.0;
                if (offsets[tracking[touchId]].y
                    + images[tracking[touchId]].size.height > self.frame.size.height)
                {
                    offsets[tracking[touchId]].y = self.frame.size.height
                        - images[tracking[touchId]].size.height;
                }
            }
        }
        touchId++;
    }

    [ self setNeedsDisplay ];
}
@end

@implementation TouchDemoViewController

- (void)loadView {
    [ super loadView ];

    touchView = [ [ TouchView alloc ] initWithFrame: [
        [ UIScreen mainScreen ] applicationFrame ]
    ];
    self.view = touchView;
}

- (void)didReceiveMemoryWarning {
    [ super didReceiveMemoryWarning ];
}

- (void)dealloc {
    [ super dealloc ];
}
```

@end

Example 4-6. TouchDemo main (main.m)

```
#import <UIKit/UIKit.h>

int main(int argc, char *argv[]) {

    NSAutoreleasePool * pool = [ [ NSAutoreleasePool alloc ] init ];
    int retVal = UIApplicationMain(argc, argv, nil, @"TouchDemoAppDelegate");
    [ pool release ];
    return retVal;
}
```

What's Going On

The TouchDemo example works as follows:

1. When the application starts, it instantiates a new window and view controller. A subclass of UIView, named TouchView, is created and attached to the view controller.

2. When the user presses one or more fingers, the touchesBegan method is notified. It compares the location of each touch with the image's offsets and size to determine which images the user touched. It records the index in the tracking array.

3. When the user moves a finger, the touchesMoves method is notified. This determines which images the user originally touched and adjusts their offsets on the screen by the correct amount. It then calls the setNeedsDisplay method, which invokes the drawRect method for redrawing the view's contents.

Further Study

- Check out the following prototypes in your SDK's header files: *UITouch.h* and *UIEvent.h*. You'll find these deep within */Developer/Platforms/iPhoneOS.platform*, inside the UI Kit framework's *Headers* directory.

CHAPTER 5

Layer Programming with Quartz Core

The Quartz Core framework is referred to as Core Animation on the Leopard desktop. Quartz Core provides the underlying classes for managing the layers of UIView objects. It is also used to create 3D transformations of 2D objects for stunning animations and effects.

To use the Quartz Core framework, you'll need to add it to your Xcode project. Right-click on the *Frameworks* folder in your project, and then choose Add Framework. Navigate to the *QuartzCore.framework* folder, and then click Add.

 To find the Quartz Core framework, you may have to navigate manually into either */Developer/Platforms/iPhoneOS.platform* or */Developer/Platforms/iPhoneSimulator.platform* and locate the *Frameworks* folder in your SDK.

Understanding Layers

A layer is a low-level component found in displayable classes. Layers act like a sheet of poster board to which an object's contents are affixed. It acts as a flexible backing for the object's display contents and can bend or contort the content in many ways on the screen. Every object that is capable of rendering itself—namely, those derived from the UIView class—has a layer to which its contents are glued.

For example, the UIImageView class contains all the basic information about a two-dimensional image—its display region, resolution, and various methods for working with and rendering the image. The image itself is glued to the parent UIView class's layer, which is like the backing in a picture frame. The most basic layer behaves like a single piece of cardboard, and merely presents the image as-is. Layers can also contain multiple sublayers, which can be treated like transparencies; each with different content, stacked on top of each other to produce one composite image.

Since they are flexible, you can use layers to manipulate the contents affixed to them. The layer's class, CALayer, controls how this flexible backing is manipulated as it's displayed. If you bend the layer, the image will bend with it. If you rotate the layer, the image will come along for the ride. You can transform the layer, add an animation, or rotate, skew, or scale the image as if it were sitting on top of silly putty. The object sitting on top of the layer is completely oblivious to how it is being manipulated, allowing your application to continue working with the displayed object as if it were still a two-dimensional object. When the user sees the image, however, it's been transformed to whatever orientation the layer has been twisted to. Layers can transform more than just images. The display output for all of the other view classes covered in Chapters 3 and 10 also rest on top of a layer.

To access the layer, read the base `UIView` class's `layer` property:

```
CALayer *layer = myView.layer;
```

All objects derived from `UIView` will inherit this property, meaning you can transform, scale, rotate, and even animate navigation bars, tables, text boxes, and many other types of view classes.

The important thing to remember about layers is that all `UIView` objects have one and they control the way in which its contents are ultimately rendered on the screen.

Layer Hierarchies

Layers have a number of general-purpose methods and properties to work with sublayers and perform rendering. These methods allow you to "stack" a number of individual screen layers together to render a single composite screen image.

A single layer can have many sublayers. Sublayers can be arranged and are stitched together when the final screen is rendered. Consider a first-person shooter. Your game might consist of one layer to render the game characters, one to render the background, and one to render a head-up display (HUD). You might have a dedicated `UIView` class for each, and a fourth class representing the game screen:

```
UIView *gameView = [ [ UIView alloc ] initWithFrame:
    [ [ UIScreen mainScreen ] applicationFrame ]
];

UIView *backgroundView = [ [ UIView alloc ] initWithFrame...
UIView *characterView = [ [ UIView alloc ] initWithFrame...
UIView *HUDView = [ [ UIView alloc ] initWithFrame...
```

You can anchor each of the three `UIView` class's layers to the `gameView` object using the `CALayer` class's `addSublayer` method:

```
#import <QuartzCore/QuartzCore.h>

CALayer *gameLayer = gameView.layer;
[ gameLayer addSublayer: backgroundView.layer ];
[ gameLayer addSublayer: characterView.layer ];
[ gameLayer addSublayer: HUDView.layer ];
```

When the `gameView` object is displayed on the screen, all three sublayers will be merged and rendered. Each class renders its own layer individually, but when the game layer is drawn, all three will be merged together.

The `gameView` layer isn't the only layer that you can add to. Sublayers can have sublayers of their own, and an entire hierarchy of layers can be built. For example, your game might add a layer to the `HUDView` layer to display one component of the HUD, such as a team logo:

```
UIImageView *teamLogoView = [ [ UIImageView alloc ] initWithImage: myTeamLogo ];
[ HUDView.layer addSublayer: teamLogoView.layer ];
```

Whenever the `HUDView` layer is rendered, all of its sublayers will also be rendered.

Size and Offset

To change the size or offset at which a layer is rendered, set the layer's `frame` property. The layer's frame functions in the same way as a window or view class's frame does: by accepting an x/y origin as an offset and region size. The example below sets the `teamLogoView` layers offset to 150×100, and its size to 50×75:

```
CGRect teamLogoFrame = CGRectMake(150.0, 100.0, 50.0, 75.0);
teamLogoView.layer.frame = teamLogoFrame;
```

Alternatively, you can adjust the position of a layer without changing its size by setting the layer's `position` property. This property accepts a `CGPoint` structure to identify the offset to display the layer on the screen. Unlike the `frame` property, the `position` property specifies the midpoint of the layer, not the upper-left corner:

```
CGPoint logoPosition = CGPointMake(75.0, 50.0);
teamLogoView.layer.position = logoPosition;
```

Arrangement and Display

In addition to adding sublayers, the `CALayer` class provides a number of different methods to insert, arrange, and remove layers.

When you add a layer using `addSublayer`, it is added to the top of the layer hierarchy, so it will display in front of any existing sublayers. Using a set of alternative methods named `insertSublayer`, you can slip new layers in between existing layers.

To insert a layer at a specific index, use the `atIndex` argument:

```
[ gameLayer insertSublayer: HUDView.layer atIndex: 1 ];
```

To insert a layer above or below another layer, add the **above** or **below** argument:

```
[ gameLayer insertSublayer: HUDView.layer below: backgroundView.layer ];
[ gameLayer insertSublayer: HUDView.layer above: characterView.layer ];
```

To remove a layer from its parent (super) layer, call the child layer's `removeFromSuper` `layer` method:

```
[ HUDView.layer removeFromSuperlayer ];
```

To replace an existing sublayer with a different layer, use the `replaceSublayer` method:

```
[ gameLayer replaceSublayer: backgroundView.layer with: newBackgroundView.layer ];
```

To keep a sublayer on the stack but render it invisible, set the layer's `hidden` property. You can use the following code to toggle the HUD's display without actually removing the layer:

```
- (void) ToggleHUD {
    HUDView.layer.hidden = (HUDView.layer.hidden == NO) ? YES : NO;
}
```

Rendering

When updating a layer, the changes are not immediately rendered on the screen. This allows you to make a number of writes to layers privately, without showing the user until all operations have completed. When the layer is ready to be redrawn, invoke the layer's `setNeedsDisplay` method:

```
[ gameLayer setNeedsDisplay ];
```

Sometimes, it may be necessary only to redraw a part of the layer's contents. Redrawing the entire screen can slow down performance. To redraw only the portion of the screen that needs updating, use the **setNeedsDisplayInRect** method, passing in a `CGRect` structure of the region to update:

```
CGRect teamLogoFrame = CGRectMake(150.0, 100.0, 50.0, 75.0);
[ gameLayer setNeedsDisplayInRect: teamLogoFrame ];
```

If you're using the Core Graphics framework to perform rendering, you can render directly into a Core Graphics context. Use the `renderInContext` method to do this:

```
CGContextRef myCGContext = UIGraphicsGetCurrentContext();
[ gameLayer renderInContext: myCGContext ];
```

Transformations

To add a 3D or affine transformation to a layer, set the layer's `transform` or `affine` `Transform` properties, respectively. You'll learn more about transformations later in the chapter:

```
characterView.layer.transform = CATransform3DMakeScale(-1.0, -1.0, 1.0);

CGAffineTransform transform = CGAffineTransformMakeRotation(45.0);
backgroundView.layer.affineTransform = transform;
```

Layer Animations

Quartz Core's capabilities extend far beyond a mere sticky layer. It can be used to transform a 2D object into a stunning 3D texture that can be used to create beautiful transitions.

Chapter 3 introduced transitions as a means of transitioning between different UIView objects. You apply transitions and animations directly to layers or sublayers. As you recall from Chapter 3, animations are created as CATransition objects.

Layer transitions augment the existing CATransition class by providing a way to add animations using Quartz Core's animation engine. This allows the developer to take advantage of the 3D capabilities offered by Quartz Core without making significant changes to the code. When a layer is to be animated, a CATransition or CAAnimation object is attached to the layer. The layer then invokes Quartz Core to spawn a new thread that takes over all of the graphics processing for the animation. The developer needs only to add the desired animation to enhance an existing layer.

You can create a transition using the following code example:

```
CATransition *animation = [[CATransition alloc] init];
animation.duration = 1.0;
animation.timingFunction = [ CAMediaTimingFunction
    functionWithName: kCAMediaTimingFunctionEaseIn ];
animation.type = kCATransitionPush;
animation.subtype = kCATransitionFromRight;
```

 At the moment, the iPhone SDK is extremely limited in the types of transitions the user may create. About a dozen additional transitions, such as page curling and zooming transitions, are supported internally by the Quartz Core framework, but are restricted to use only in Apple's own applications.

You can create an animation by creating a CABasicAnimation object. The following example creates an animation that rotates the layer a full 360 degrees:

```
CABasicAnimation *animation = [ CABasicAnimation
    animationWithKeyPath: @"transform" ];
animation.toValue = [ NSValue valueWithCATransform3D: CATransform3D
MakeRotation(3.1415, 0, 0, 1.0) ];
animation.duration = 2;
animation.cumulative = YES;
animation.repeatCount = 2;
```

Once created, you can apply the animation or transition directly to a layer:

```
[ teamLogoView.layer addAnimation: animation forKey: @"animation" ];
```

Layer Transformations

Quartz Core's rendering capabilities allow a 2D image to be freely manipulated as if it were 3D. An image can be rotated on an x-y-z axis to any angle, scaled, and skewed. The CATransform3D suite of functions provides the magic behind Apple's Cover Flow technology (covered in Chapter 12) and other aesthetic effects used on the iPhone. The iPhone supports scale, rotation, affine, translation transformations, and others. An introduction to layer transformations is provided in this book, but Core Animation is a big animal, and there are many books on the subject.

For more information about creating animations, see *Core Animation for Mac OS X and the iPhone* by Bill Dudney (Pragmatic).

A transformation is executed on individual layers, allowing for multiple transformations to occur concurrently on a multilayer surface. The Quartz Core framework performs transformations using a CATransform3D object. This object is applied to a view's layer to bend or otherwise manipulate its layer into the desired 3D configuration. The application continues to treat the object as if it's a 2D object, but when it is presented to the user, the object conforms to whatever transformation has been applied to the layer. The following example creates a transformation for the purpose of rotating a layer:

```
CATransform3D myTransform;
myTransform = CATransform3DMakeRotation(angle, x, y, z);
```

The CATransform3DMakeRotation function creates a transformation that will rotate a layer by angle radians using an axis of x-y-z. The values for x-y-z define the axis and magnitude for each space (between -1 and +1). Assigning a value to an axis instructs the transformation to rotate using that axis. For example, if the x-axis is set to either -1 or +1, the object will be rotated on the x-axis in that direction, meaning it will be rotated vertically. Think of these values as inserting straws through the image for each axis. If a straw were inserted across the x-axis, the image would spin around the straw vertically. You can create more complex rotations using axis angle values. For most uses, however, values of -1 and +1 are sufficient.

To rotate a layer by 45 degrees on its horizontal axis (rotating vertically), you might use the following:

```
myTransform = CATransform3DMakeRotation(0.78, 1.0, 0.0, 0.0);
```

To rotate the same amount horizontally, specify a value for the y-axis instead:

```
myTransform = CATransform3DMakeRotation(0.78, 0.0, 1.0, 0.0);
```

The value 0.78, used in the previous example, is calculated as the radian value of the angle. To calculate radians from degrees, use the simple formula Mπ/180. For example,

$45π/180 = 45(3.1415) / 180 = 0.7853$. If you plan on working with the degrees measurement throughout your application, you can write a simple conversion function to help keep your code understandable:

```
double radians(float degrees) {
    return ( degrees * 3.14159265 ) / 180.0;
}
```

You'll then be able to call this function when creating transformations:

```
myTransform = CATransform3DMakeRotation(radians(45.0), 0.0, 1.0, 0.0);
```

Once the transformation has been created, apply it to the layer you're operating on. The CALayer object provides a transform property used to attach the transformation. The layer will execute whatever transformation is assigned to this property:

```
imageView.layer.transform = myTransform;
```

When the object is displayed, it will be displayed with the transformation applied to it. You will still refer to the object as a 2D object in your code, but it will be rendered according to the transformation.

BounceDemo: Layer Fun

This example creates two layers out of images downloaded from the Internet. It then attaches those layers to a view controller, where they can be easily manipulated later by means of a timer. The timer adjusts the on-screen position of each layer and adds an animation. This code should serve as a good, functional primer for building your own layering routines, as shown in Figure 5-1.

You can compile this application, shown in Examples 5-1 through 5-5, with the SDK by creating a *view-based application* project named *BounceDemo*. Be sure to pull out the Interface Builder code if you'd like to see how these objects are created from scratch.

Example 5-1. BouceDemo application delegate prototypes (BounceDemoAppDelegate.h)

```
#import <UIKit/UIKit.h>

@class BounceDemoViewController;

@interface BounceDemoAppDelegate : NSObject <UIApplicationDelegate> {
    UIWindow *window;
    BounceDemoViewController *viewController;
}

@property (nonatomic, retain) IBOutlet UIWindow *window;
@property (nonatomic, retain) IBOutlet BounceDemoViewController *viewController;

@end
```

Figure 5-1. BounceDemo example

Example 5-2. BouceDemo application delegate (BounceDemoAppDelegate.m)

```objc
#import "BounceDemoAppDelegate.h"
#import "BounceDemoViewController.h"

@implementation BounceDemoAppDelegate

@synthesize window;
@synthesize viewController;


- (void)applicationDidFinishLaunching:(UIApplication *)application {
    CGRect screenBounds = [ [ UIScreen mainScreen ] applicationFrame ];

    self.window = [ [ [ UIWindow alloc ] initWithFrame: screenBounds ]
        autorelease
    ];

    viewController = [ [ BounceDemoViewController alloc ] init ];

    [ window addSubview: viewController.view ];
    [ window makeKeyAndVisible ];
}
```

```
- (void)dealloc {
    [ viewController release ];
    [ window release ];
    [ super dealloc ];
}

@end
```

Example 5-3. BouceDemo view controller prototypes (BounceDemoViewController.h)

```
#import <UIKit/UIKit.h>

@interface BounceDemoViewController : UIViewController {
    UIImageView *image1, *image2;
    CGPoint directionImage1, directionImage2;
    NSTimer *timer;
}
- (void) handleTimer: (NSTimer *) timer;
@end
```

Example 5-4. BouceDemo view controller (BounceDemoViewController.m)

```
#import "BounceDemoViewController.h"
#import <QuartzCore/QuartzCore.h>

@implementation BounceDemoViewController

- (id)init {
    self = [ super init ];
    if (self != nil) {
        UIImage *image;
        NSURL *url;

        url = [ NSURL URLWithString:
                @"http://www.zdziarski.com/demo/1.png" ];
        image = [ UIImage imageWithData: [ NSData dataWithContentsOfURL: url ] ];
        image1 = [ [ UIImageView alloc ] initWithImage: image ];
        directionImage1 = CGPointMake(-1.0, -1.0);
        image1.layer.position = CGPointMake((image.size.width / 2)+1,
                                             (image.size.width / 2)+1);

        url = [ NSURL URLWithString: @"http://www.zdziarski.com/demo/2s.png" ];
        image = [ UIImage imageWithData: [ NSData dataWithContentsOfURL: url ] ];
        image2 = [ [ UIImageView alloc ] initWithImage: image ];
        directionImage2 = CGPointMake(1.0, 1.0);
        image2.layer.position = CGPointMake((image.size.width / 2)+1,
                                             (image.size.width / 2)+1);

        [ self.view.layer addSublayer: image2.layer ];
        [ self.view.layer addSublayer: image1.layer ];
    }
    return self;
}

- (void)loadView {
```

```
    [ super loadView ];
}

- (void)viewDidLoad {
    [ super viewDidLoad ];

    timer = [ NSTimer scheduledTimerWithTimeInterval: 0.01
                                             target: self
                                           selector: @selector(handleTimer:)
                                           userInfo: nil
                                            repeats: YES
             ];

    CABasicAnimation *anim1 =
        [ CABasicAnimation animationWithKeyPath: @"transform" ];
    anim1.toValue = [ NSValue valueWithCATransform3D:
        CATransform3DMakeRotation(3.1415, 1.0, 0, 0)
    ];

    anim1.duration = 2;
    anim1.cumulative = YES;
    anim1.repeatCount = 1000;
    [ image1.layer addAnimation: anim1 forKey: @"transformAnimation" ];
}

- (void)didReceiveMemoryWarning {
    [ super didReceiveMemoryWarning ];
}

- (void)dealloc {
    [ timer invalidate ];
    [ image1 release ];
    [ image2 release ];
    [ super dealloc ];
}

- (void) handleTimer: (NSTimer *) timer {
    CGSize size;
    CGPoint origin;

    /* Move the image1 */
    size = [ image1 image ].size;
    if (image1.layer.position.x <=
        ( (size.width / 2) + 1) - self.view.frame.origin.x)
        directionImage1.x = 1.0;
    if (image1.layer.position.x + (size.width / 2) + 1 >=
        (self.view.frame.size.width - self.view.frame.origin.x) - 1)
        directionImage1.x = -1.0;
    if (image1.layer.position.y <=
        ( (size.height / 2) + 1) - self.view.frame.origin.y)
        directionImage1.y = 1.0;
    if (image1.layer.position.y + (size.height / 2) + 1 >=
        (self.view.frame.size.height - self.view.frame.origin.y) - 1)
        directionImage1.y = -1.0;
    origin = image1.layer.position;
```

```
        origin.x += directionImage1.x;
        origin.y += directionImage1.y;
        image1.layer.position = origin;

        /* Move the image2 */
        size = [ image2 image ].size;
        if (image2.layer.position.x <=
            ( (size.width / 2) + 1) - self.view.frame.origin.x)
            directionImage2.x = 1.0;
        if (image2.layer.position.x + (size.width / 2) + 1
            >= (self.view.frame.size.width - self.view.frame.origin.x) - 1)
            directionImage2.x = -1.0;
        if (image2.layer.position.y <=
            ( (size.height / 2) + 1) - self.view.frame.origin.y)
            directionImage2.y = 1.0;
        if (image2.layer.position.y + (size.height / 2) + 1 >=
            (self.view.frame.size.height - self.view.frame.origin.y) - 1)
            directionImage2.y = -1.0;
        origin = image2.layer.position;
        origin.x += directionImage2.x;
        origin.y += directionImage2.y;
        image2.layer.position = origin;

        [ self.view setNeedsDisplayInRect: image1.layer.frame ];
        [ self.view setNeedsDisplayInRect: image2.layer.frame ];
}
@end
```

Example 5-5. BouceDemo main (main.m)

```
#import <UIKit/UIKit.h>

int main(int argc, char *argv[]) {

    NSAutoreleasePool * pool = [ [ NSAutoreleasePool alloc ] init ];
    int retVal = UIApplicationMain(argc, argv, nil, @"BounceDemoAppDelegate");
    [ pool release ];
    return retVal;
}
```

What's Going On

Here's how the bounce demo works:

1. When the application loads, its `BounceDemoAppDelegate` class is notified through its
   `applicationDidFinishLaunching` method. This method constructs the window and
   instantiates a view controller.

2. The view controller's `init` method creates two `UIImageView` objects by loading images from the Internet. The layers for these view objects are added as sublayers to
   the view controller's main view.

3. When the view loads, the `viewDidLoad` method is invoked, which creates a timer.
   The timer's target, `handleTimer`, adjusts the position of each layer by one pixel every

time it is called, to give the appearance that the images are bouncing around the screen. The `viewDidLoad` method also creates two animations: one to flip a layer vertically and another to flip it horizontally. The animations are added to the target objects and run automatically.

Further Study

Now that you have an understanding of layer manipulation and animations, try a couple of things before moving on.

- Read up on Core Animation on the Apple Developer Connection website. Change the animations in the project to apply fades, resizes, and other animations.
- Check out the following prototypes in your SDK's header files: *CALayer.h*, *CAAnimation.h*, and *CATransform3D.h*. You'll find these deep within */Developer/ Platforms/iPhoneOS.platform*, inside the Quartz Core framework's *Headers* directory.

CHAPTER 6

Making a Racket: Audio Toolbox and AVFoundation

The AVFoundation framework was introduced in version 2.2 of the iPhone SDK, and provides functionality for playing and mixing sound files, metering, and basic audio control. If you're adding simple sounds to your application, this framework can be implemented quickly and painlessly.

The Audio Toolbox framework is responsible for managing digital sound output on the iPhone. Unlike many of the frameworks covered in this book so far, the Audio Toolbox framework is predominantly C-oriented. This powerful framework allows you to generate and record digital sound. In addition to the examples provided in this chapter, many references have been written for Audio Toolbox, which are available on the Apple Developer Connection website. These include the following:

Core Audio Overview: AudioToolbox.framework
   http://developer.apple.com/documentation/MusicAudio/Conceptual/CoreAudioO verview/Introduction/chapter_1_section_1.html

Audio Toolbox Framework Reference
   http://developer.apple.com/DOCUMENTATION/MusicAudio/Reference/CAAudio ToolboxRef/index.html

Audio File Services Reference
   http://developer.apple.com/documentation/MusicAudio/Reference/AudioFileConver tRef/Reference/reference.html

Audio File Stream Services Reference
   http://developer.apple.com/documentation/MusicAudio/Reference/AudioStreamRe ference/AudioStreamReference.pdf

Audio Queue Services Reference
   http://developer.apple.com/documentation/MusicAudio/Reference/AudioQueueRe ference/AudioQueueReference.pdf

Because it exists on the desktop platform, the Audio Toolbox framework is documented fairly well. We won't cover it in its entirety here—just the pieces relevant to the iPhone SDK. Many pieces of the framework, such as MIDI controllers and Music Player APIs, aren't relevant or available on the iPhone.

In order to use the Audio Toolbox framework, you'll need to add it as a framework to your existing project. Right-click on the *Frameworks* folder in your Xcode project, and choose Add→Existing Frameworks. Navigate to the iPhone SDK's *Frameworks* directory and choose the *AudioToolbox.framework* folder.

AVFoundation Framework

Version 2.2 of the iPhone SDK introduced a new framework for playing and mixing audio: AVFoundation. The AVFoundation framework provides an easy-to-use interface for playing simple sound files. It may appear to be a simple class, but it does pack some punch. The framework not only plays individual sound files, but it can also play multiple sounds simultaneously. The `AVAudioPlayer` class provides per-sample volume control, allowing you to perform basic sound mixing, and can play a number of different file formats including *.mp3*, *m4a*, *.wav*, *.caf*, *.aif*, and others. In addition to this, it provides properties for reading power levels, allowing you to do something most geeks have loved to do since the Apple][days: build your own VU meters.

The AVFoundation framework is useful for adding sound support in applications such as instant messenger applications or simple games, which don't require sophisticated digital sound. To create digital sound streams, you'll still need to use the Audio Toolbox framework, covered later in this chapter.

In order to use the AVFoundation framework, you'll need to add it as a framework to your existing project. Right-click on the *Frameworks* folder in your Xcode project, and choose Add→Existing Frameworks. Navigate to your SDK's *Frameworks* directory and choose the *AVFoundation.framework* folder.

 You'll need to be using version 2.2 or later of the iPhone SDK in order to use the AVFoundation framework.

The Audio Player

The `AVAudioPlayer` class encapsulates a single sound to be played. The player is initialized with an `NSURL` object pointing to the resource to be played. To play multiple sounds concurrently, you can create a new `AVAudioPlayer` object for each sound. Think of the audio player, then, as a single track within a multitrack mixing board:

```
#import <AVFoundation/AVFoundation.h>

NSError *err;
AVAudioPlayer *player = [ [ AVAudioPlayer alloc ]
    initWithContentsOfURL: [ NSURL fileURLWithPath:
        [ [ NSBundle mainBundle ] pathForResource: @"sample"
```

```
        ofType:@"m4a" inDirectory:@"/" ] ]
    error: &err
];
```

You can also initialize a player with an NSData object pointing to raw data for your sound residing in memory:

```
#import <AVFoundation/AVFoundation.h>

NSError *err;
AVAudioPlayer *player = [ [ AVAudioPlayer alloc ]
    initWithData: myData
    error: &err
];
```

Player Properties

Once you have created and initialized an AVAudioPlayer object, you can set various properties for it.

You can mix the output from multiple players together using the player's volume property. The volume is represented as a value between 0.0 and 1.0:

```
player.volume = 0.5;
```

If the sound should repeat, set the numberOfLoops property to a nonzero value reflecting the number of iterations. The default is to play the sample only once:

```
player.numberOfLoops = 3;
```

If you'd like the sample to start playing at a particular time offset, you can place the "record needle" anywhere you like by setting the currentTime property. Later on, you'll be able to read this offset while the sample is playing. This property uses an NSTimeInterval, which is the equivalent of a double floating-point representing the number of seconds into the sample to play:

```
NSTimeInterval currentTime = player.currentTime;
player.currentTime = 5.0;
```

In addition to the properties you can manually adjust, some read-only properties also exist that can help identify the characteristics of the sound you've loaded.

You can read the number of channels present in the sample from the numberOfChannels property. This will return one channel for mono samples, or two channels for stereo samples:

```
NSUInteger channels = player.numberOfChannels
```

You can also read the duration of the sample (in seconds) through the duration property. This, too, is represented as an NSTimeInterval, which is typed to a double floating-point:

```
NSTimeInterval duration = player.duration
```

Playing Sounds

If you're queuing up a sound and want to be able to play it immediately on demand, use the prepareToPlay method to allocate all of the sound's resources and get the sound queued to play internally. It's OK if you don't call this yourself—it will be automatically invoked when the sound is actually played. If you don't call it, though, there may be a very slight delay while the sample queues up:

```
[ player prepareToPlay ];
```

When you're finally ready to play the sound, use the player's play method:

```
[ player play ];
```

You can also stop the sound at any time, using the stop method:

```
[ player stop ];
```

Delegate Methods

The AVAudioPlayerDelegate protocol defines methods that you can assign to a delegate to know when sounds have finished playing, intercept errors, and receive notification of interruptions.

When the play method is invoked, control is returned immediately to your program while the sound plays in the background. To receive a notification when the sound has finished playing, assign a delegate to the player's delegate property:

```
player.delegate = self;
```

When a sound has finished playing, the delegate's audioPlayerDidFinishPlaying method is invoked. Place this method in your delegate's code to receive the notification. A Boolean value is provided in the method parameters to specify whether the sound played successfully:

```
- (void)audioPlayerDidFinishPlaying:(AVAudioPlayer *)player
    successfully:(BOOL)flag
{
    /* Additional code to perform when player is finished */
}
```

If an error occurs while decoding the sound, the delegate's audioPlayer DecodeErrorDidOccur method is invoked. You can use this to gracefully handle errors that occurred while playing the sample:

```
- (void)audioPlayerDecodeErrorDidOccur:(AVAudioPlayer *)player
    error:(NSError *)error
{
    /* Code to handle decoder error */
}
```

If an incoming phone call, device lock, or some other activity interrupts the player, two delegate methods will be notified at the beginning and end of the interruption. They

---

can restart the player or perform some other action, like asking your user not to take phone calls while you're playing a sound (the nerve!):

```
- (void)audioPlayerBeginInterruption:(AVAudioPlayer *)player {
    /* Code to handle interruption */
}

- (void)audioPlayerEndInterruption:(AVAudioPlayer *)player {
    /* Code to handle end of interruption */
}
```

Metering

The `AVAudioPlayer` class can report meter values, which allows your application to read the output levels of the sound you are playing. The output levels can be used to render a visual indicator of the sound as it's playing. You can read both the average power level (in decibels) and the peak power level. To enable metering, set the `meteringEnabled` property:

```
player.meteringEnabled = YES;
```

As the sound is played, the `updateMeters` method can be invoked to update the meters values:

```
[ player updateMeters ];
```

The meter's average and peak power levels for each channel can then be read. Values are returned as floating-point, representing the number of decibels for each channel. These values typically range from `-100.0` to `0.0`:

```
for (int i=0; i<player.numberOfChannels; i++) {
    float power = [ player averagePowerForChannel: i ];
    float peak = [ player peakPowerForChannel: i ];
}
```

AVMeter: Build a VU Meter

This example takes advantage of the AVFoundation framework's metering functionality to render a pair of VU (volume unit) meters on the screen as it's playing audio content. The default project plays a file named *sample.mp3*, and also loads the images *avgMeterImage.png* and *peakMeterImage.png* to display the meters. These are all included with the online book examples, or you may provide your own. The example displays a navigation bar with a Play button. After pressing Play, the sample will be played and its meter levels read periodically. The meters on the screen, as shown in Figure 6-1, are updated with the meter readings from the `AVAudioPlayer`.

You can compile this application, shown in Examples 6-1 through 6-7, with the SDK by creating a *view-based application* project named *AVMeter*. In addition to this, you'll need to add two new files to your project: *AVMeterView.h* and *AVMeterView.m*. You

Figure 6-1. AVMeter example

can do this by selecting New File from Xcode's File menu, then selecting UIView Sub-class from the Cocoa Touch Classes template group underneath iPhone OS.

Be sure to pull out the Interface Builder code so you can see how these objects are created from scratch.

Example 6-1. AVMeter application delegate prototypes (AVMeterAppDelegate.h)

```
#import <UIKit/UIKit.h>

@class AVMeterViewController;

@interface AVMeterAppDelegate : NSObject <UIApplicationDelegate> {
    UIWindow *window;
    UINavigationController *navigationController;
    AVMeterViewController *viewController;
}

@property (nonatomic, retain) IBOutlet UIWindow *window;
@property (nonatomic, retain) IBOutlet AVMeterViewController *viewController;

@end
```

Example 6-2. AVMeter application delegate (AVMeterAppDelegate.m)

```
#import "AVMeterAppDelegate.h"
#import "AVMeterViewController.h"

@implementation AVMeterAppDelegate

@synthesize window;
@synthesize viewController;

- (void)applicationDidFinishLaunching:(UIApplication *)application {
    CGRect screenBounds = [ [ UIScreen mainScreen ] bounds ];

    self.window = [ [ [ UIWindow alloc ] initWithFrame: screenBounds ]
        autorelease
    ];

    viewController = [ [ AVMeterViewController alloc ] init ];
    navigationController = [ [ UINavigationController alloc ]
        initWithRootViewController: viewController
    ];

    [ window addSubview: [ navigationController view ] ];
    [ window makeKeyAndVisible ];
}


- (void)dealloc {
    [ navigationController release ];
    [ viewController release ];
    [ window release ];
    [ super dealloc ];
}
@end
```

Example 6-3. AVMeter view controller prototypes (AVMeterViewController.h)

```
#import <UIKit/UIKit.h>
#import <AVFoundation/AVFoundation.h>
#import "AVMeterView.h"

@interface AVMeterViewController : UIViewController {
    UIBarButtonItem *navButton;
    AVAudioPlayer *player;
    AVMeterView *meterView;
}
- (void)navButtonWasPressed;
- (void)setNavProperties;

@end
```

Example 6-4. AVMeter view controller (AVMeterViewController.m)

```
#import "AVMeterViewController.h"

@implementation AVMeterViewController
```

```objc
- (id)init {
    self = [ super init ];
    if (self != nil) {
        NSError *err;

        player = [ [ AVAudioPlayer alloc ]
            initWithContentsOfURL: [ NSURL fileURLWithPath: [
                [ NSBundle mainBundle ] pathForResource: @"sample" ofType:@"mp3"
            ] ] error: &err
        ];

        if (err)
            NSLog(@"Failed to initialize AVAudioPlayer: %@\n", err);

        [ self setNavProperties ];
        [ player prepareToPlay ];
    }
    return self;
}

- (void)loadView {
    [ super loadView ];

    CGRect frame = self.view.frame;
    meterView = [ [ AVMeterView alloc ] initWithFrame: frame ];
    meterView.player = player;


    UIImage *peak = [ [ UIImage alloc ] initWithContentsOfFile: [
        [ NSBundle mainBundle ] pathForResource: @"peakMeterImage" ofType:@"png"
    ] ];
    UIImage *avg = [ [ UIImage alloc ] initWithContentsOfFile: [
        [ NSBundle mainBundle ] pathForResource: @"avgMeterImage" ofType:@"png"
    ] ];

    meterView.meterPeakPowerImage = peak;
    meterView.meterAveragePowerImage = avg;

    self.view = meterView;
}

- (void)setNavProperties {
    navButton = [ [ [ UIBarButtonItem alloc ]
        initWithTitle: (player.playing == YES) ? @"Stop" : @"Play"
        style: UIBarButtonItemStylePlain
        target: self
        action:@selector(navButtonWasPressed)
    ] autorelease ];
    self.navigationItem.rightBarButtonItem = navButton;

    if (player.playing == YES)
        self.title = @"Playing";
    else
        self.title = @"Stopped";
```

```
    }

    - (void)navButtonWasPressed {
        if (player.playing == YES) {
            [ player stop ];
            [ meterView stopUpdating ];
        } else {
            [ player play ];
            [ meterView startUpdating ];
        }
        [ self setNavProperties ];
    }

    - (void)dealloc {
        [ super dealloc ];
    }
@end
```

Example 6-5. AVMeter view prototypes (AVMeterView.h)

```
#import <Foundation/Foundation.h>
#import <AVFoundation/AVFoundation.h>

@interface AVMeterView : UIView {
    AVAudioPlayer *player;
    float cachedAveragePowerForChannel[2], cachedPeakPowerForChannel[2];
    CGRect avgMeterFrame[2], peakMeterFrame[2];
    UIImage *meterAveragePowerImage, *meterPeakPowerImage;
    BOOL updating;

    float meterSpacing;
    float meterHorizontalBorder;
    float meterVerticalBorder;
}
- (id)initWithFrame:(CGRect)frame;
- (void)startUpdating;
- (void)stopUpdating;

@property(nonatomic,assign)    AVAudioPlayer *player;
@property(nonatomic,assign) UIImage *meterAveragePowerImage;
@property(nonatomic,assign) UIImage *meterPeakPowerImage;

@property(nonatomic,assign) float meterSpacing;
@property(nonatomic,assign) float meterHorizontalBorder;
@property(nonatomic,assign) float meterVerticalBorder;

@end
```

Example 6-6. AVMeter view (AVMeterView.m)

```
#import <CoreGraphics/CoreGraphics.h>
#import "AVMeterView.h"

@implementation AVMeterView
@synthesize player;
@synthesize meterAveragePowerImage;
```

```objc
@synthesize meterPeakPowerImage;
@synthesize meterSpacing;
@synthesize meterHorizontalBorder;
@synthesize meterVerticalBorder;

- (id)initWithFrame:(CGRect)frame {
    self = [ super initWithFrame: frame ];
    if (self != nil) {
        player = nil;
        updating = NO;

        meterAveragePowerImage = nil;
        meterPeakPowerImage = nil;

        meterSpacing = 40.0;
        meterHorizontalBorder = 20.0;
        meterVerticalBorder = 20.0;

        for(int i = 0; i < 2; i ++) {
            cachedPeakPowerForChannel[i] = 0.0;
            cachedAveragePowerForChannel[i] = 0.0;
        }

        /* Calculate meter positions */
        avgMeterFrame[0] = CGRectMake(meterHorizontalBorder,
            meterVerticalBorder,
            (frame.size.width / 2) - (meterSpacing/2)
                - meterHorizontalBorder,
            (frame.size.height) - meterVerticalBorder);
        avgMeterFrame[1] = CGRectMake(meterHorizontalBorder
                + (frame.size.width / 2),
            meterVerticalBorder,
            (frame.size.width / 2) - (meterSpacing/2) - meterHorizontalBorder,
            frame.size.height - meterVerticalBorder);

        peakMeterFrame[0] = CGRectMake(avgMeterFrame[0].origin.x,
            avgMeterFrame[0].origin.y,
            avgMeterFrame[0].size.width, meterPeakPowerImage.size.height);
        peakMeterFrame[1] = CGRectMake(avgMeterFrame[1].origin.x,
            avgMeterFrame[1].origin.y,
            avgMeterFrame[1].size.width, meterPeakPowerImage.size.height);
    }
    return self;
}

- (void)drawRect:(CGRect)rect {
    float averagePowerForChannel[2], peakPowerForChannel[2];
    BOOL renderedBottom;

    if (player.numberOfChannels < 1) {
        return;
    }

    /* Read meter values */
    if (!player || player.meteringEnabled == NO) {
```

```
        averagePowerForChannel[0] = averagePowerForChannel[1] = 0.0;
        peakPowerForChannel[0] = cachedPeakPowerForChannel[0];
        peakPowerForChannel[1] = cachedPeakPowerForChannel[1];
    } else {
        int channels = player.numberOfChannels;
        if (channels > 2)
            channels = 2;
        for(int i = 0; i < channels; i ++)
        {
            float db;
            [ player updateMeters ];
            db = [ player peakPowerForChannel: i ];
            peakPowerForChannel[i] = (50.0 + db) / 50.0;
            db = [ player averagePowerForChannel: i ];
            averagePowerForChannel[i] = (50.0 + db) / 50.0;
        }
        if (channels == 1) {
            peakPowerForChannel[1] = peakPowerForChannel[0];
            averagePowerForChannel[1] = averagePowerForChannel[0];
        }
    }

/* Either jump to accommodate new level or decrement meters */
renderedBottom = YES;
for(int i = 0; i < 2; i ++) {

    if (averagePowerForChannel[i] > cachedAveragePowerForChannel[i])
    {
        cachedAveragePowerForChannel[i] = averagePowerForChannel[i];
    }
    cachedAveragePowerForChannel[i] -= .02;
    if (cachedAveragePowerForChannel[i] < 0) {
        cachedAveragePowerForChannel[i] = 0;
    }

    if (peakPowerForChannel[i] > cachedPeakPowerForChannel[i]) {
        cachedPeakPowerForChannel[i] = peakPowerForChannel[i];
    }
    cachedPeakPowerForChannel[i] -= .01;
    if (cachedPeakPowerForChannel[i] < 0.0)
        cachedPeakPowerForChannel[i] = 0.0;

    if (   cachedPeakPowerForChannel[i] != 0.0
        || cachedAveragePowerForChannel[i] != 0.0)
    {
        renderedBottom = NO;
    }

    if (meterAveragePowerImage) {
      [ meterAveragePowerImage drawAsPatternInRect:
        CGRectMake(avgMeterFrame[i].origin.x,
            avgMeterFrame[i].origin.y + (avgMeterFrame[i].size.height
        -(avgMeterFrame[i].size.height * cachedAveragePowerForChannel[i])),
        avgMeterFrame[i].size.width,
        avgMeterFrame[i].size.height - (avgMeterFrame[i].size.height
```

```
              -(avgMeterFrame[i].size.height * cachedAveragePowerForChannel[i])))
            ];
        }

      if (meterPeakPowerImage) {
        [ meterPeakPowerImage drawAsPatternInRect:
          CGRectMake(peakMeterFrame[i].origin.x,
          peakMeterFrame[i].origin.y + (avgMeterFrame[i].size.height
          -(avgMeterFrame[i].size.height * cachedPeakPowerForChannel[i])),
          peakMeterFrame[i].size.width,
              meterPeakPowerImage.size.height)
        ];
      }
    }

  if (updating == YES || renderedBottom == NO) {
    [ NSTimer scheduledTimerWithTimeInterval: 0.01
                                      target: self
                                    selector: @selector(handleTimer:)
                                    userInfo: nil
                                     repeats: NO ];
    }
}

- (void)handleTimer:(NSTimer *)timer {
    [ self setNeedsDisplay ];
}

- (void)startUpdating {
    updating = YES;
    player.meteringEnabled = YES;
    [ self setNeedsDisplay ];
}

- (void)stopUpdating {
    updating = NO;
    player.meteringEnabled = NO;
    [ self setNeedsDisplay ];
}

- (void)dealloc {
    [ super dealloc ];
}
@end
```

Example 6-7. AVMeter main (AVMeterView.m)

```
#import <UIKit/UIKit.h>

int main(int argc, char *argv[]) {

    NSAutoreleasePool * pool = [ [ NSAutoreleasePool alloc ] init ];
    int retVal = UIApplicationMain(argc, argv, nil, @"AVMeterAppDelegate");
    [pool release];
    return retVal;
}
```

What's Going On

The AVMeter example introduces a reusable view class named `AVMeterView`. Here's how the example works:

1. When the application instantiates, the `AVMeterAppDelegate` class's `applicationDidFinishLaunching` method is notified. This creates the initial window, view controller, and a navigation controller.

2. The view controller, `AVMeterViewController`, creates its own `AVAudioPlayer` object and instantiates an instance of our custom class, `AVMeterView`, which is assigned as the controller's active view.

3. The controller initializes the audio player with a sample sound and attaches it to our custom `AVMeterView` object by setting its `player` property. It also loads and assigns images for the average and peak meter graphics.

4. When the user presses Play, the `navButtonWasPressed` method is invoked inside the view controller. This instructs the audio player to play, and also invokes the `AVMeterView` class's `startUpdating` method.

5. The `AVMeterView` class's `drawRect` method is overridden, and is invoked whenever the screen needs to be updated. The `drawRect` methods reads the player's meter values and calculates the position of the meter bars. It then calls a timer, which is designed to trigger a screen refresh.

Further Study

- The new AVFoundation class has some nice features. Be sure to check out its prototypes in your SDK's header files. You'll find these deep within */Developer/Platforms/iPhoneOS.platform*, inside the AVFoundation framework's *Headers* directory.

Audio Services

For simple, unmixed sounds, the Audio Toolbox framework provides a C-style audio service. You can play simple sounds using the `AudioServicesPlaySystemSound` function. A few rules apply to playing simple sounds. Sounds must be less than 30 seconds in length, and must be PCM or IMA4 formats. The file must also be stored in a *.caf*, *.aif*, or *.wav* file. Simple sounds cannot be played from memory, but only disk files. If you're developing on version 2.2 or greater of the SDK, you may want to use the AVFoundation framework in lieu of audio services.

In addition to the restrictions on simple sounds, you'll have very little control over the manner in which the sound is played. When played, the sound will be triggered immediately and at the current sound level set by the phone's user. You won't be able to loop sounds or manage stereo either. You can however, invoke a callback function when the sound is finished playing, so that you can clean up your sound objects and notify your application.

Example 6-8 illustrates the audio service calls to play a sound file named *sample.wav*.

Example 6-8. Audio services example (SoundExample.m)

```
#include <AudioToolbox/AudioToolbox.h>
#include <CoreFoundation/CoreFoundation.h>

// When the sound is finished playing, this function is called
static void SoundFinished (SystemSoundID soundID, void *sample)
{
    /* I'm all finished playing, so free up resources */

    AudioServicesDisposeSystemSoundID(sample);
    CFRelease(sample);
    CFRunLoopStop(CFRunLoopGetCurrent());
}

// Main loop
int main()
{
    /* System Sound ID, which we'll register to play our sound as */
    SystemSoundID soundID;
    NSURL *sample = [ [ NSURL alloc ] initWithString: @"sample.wav" ];

    OSStatus err = AudioServicesCreateSystemSoundID (sample, &soundID);
    if (err) {
        NSLog(@"Error occurred assigning system sound!");
        return(-1);
    }

    /* Add sound-completion callback */
    AudioServicesAddSystemSoundCompletion(soundID, NULL, NULL,
        SoundFinished, sample);

    /* Play it! */
    AudioServicesPlaySystemSound(soundID);
    CFRunLoopRun();
    return 0;
}
```

What's Going On

The audio services example works like this:

1. The application's `main` function is invoked when executed.
2. An `NSURL` object is created, pointing to the path of the sound file.
3. The `AudioServicesCreateSystemSoundID` function is called to create a system sound out of the sound file.

4. The sound completion callback function, SoundFinished, is registered as the callback.

5. The system sound identifier assigned to our sound is instructed to play by calling AudioervicesPlaySystemSound.

6. When the sound is finished playing, the SoundFinished function is called, which destroys the sound object.

Audio Queues

In addition to simple sounds, Audio Toolbox includes low-level functions for processing sound on a bit stream level. The framework includes many APIs that provide access to the raw data within audio files and many conversion tools. If you're writing games or other sound-intensive applications, you may need an audio queue to render a digital output stream or control stereo channel mixing. The queue, unlike audio service, works with streams of raw audio data rather than complete files.

Think of the audio queue as a conveyor belt full of boxes. On one end of the conveyor belt, boxes are filled with chunks of sound, and on the other end they are dumped into the iPhone's speakers. These boxes represent sound buffers that carry bits around, and the conveyor belt is the audio queue. The conveyor belt dumps your sound into the speakers and then circles back around to have the boxes refilled. It's your job as the programmer to define the size, type, and number of boxes, and write the software to fill the boxes with sound when needed.

The Audio Toolbox queue is strictly first-in-first-out; that is, the conveyor belt plays the samples in the order in which they are added.

Audio Toolbox's audio queue works like this:

1. An audio queue is created and assigned properties that identify the type of sound that will be played (format, sample rate, etc.).

2. Sound buffers are attached to the queue, which will contain the actual sound frames to be played. Think of a sound frame as a single box full of sound, whereas a sample is a single piece of digital sound within the frame.

3. The developer supplies a callback function, which the audio queue calls every time a sound buffer has been exhausted. This refills the buffer with the latest sound frames from your application.

Audio Queue Structure

Because the Audio Toolbox framework uses low-level C interfaces, it has no concept of a class. There are many moving parts involved in setting up an audio queue, and to make our examples more understandable, all of the different variables used will be encapsulated into a single user-defined structure we call AQCallbackStruct:

```
typedef struct AQCallbackStruct {
    AudioQueueRef queue;
    UInt32 frameCount;
    AudioQueueBufferRef mBuffers[AUDIO_BUFFERS];
    AudioStreamBasicDescription mDataFormat;
} AQCallbackStruct;
```

The following components are grouped into this structure to service the audio framework:

AudioQueueRef queue
> A pointer to the audio queue object your program will create.

Uint32 frameCount
> The total number of samples to be copied per audio sync. This is largely up to the implementer.

AudioQueueBufferRef mBuffers
> An array containing the total number of sound buffers that will be used. The proper number of elements will be discussed in the section "Sound Buffers" on page 160.

AudioStreamBasicDescription mDataFormat
> Information about the format of audio that will be played.

Before you can create the audio queue, you'll need to initialize a description of the audio stream:

```
AQCallbackStruct aqc;
aqc.mDataFormat.mSampleRate = 44100.0;
aqc.mDataFormat.mFormatID = kAudioFormatLinearPCM;
aqc.mDataFormat.mFormatFlags = kLinearPCMFormatFlagIsSignedInteger
    | kAudioFormatFlagIsPacked;
aqc.mDataFormat.mBytesPerPacket = 4;
aqc.mDataFormat.mFramesPerPacket = 1;
aqc.mDataFormat.mBytesPerFrame = 4;
aqc.mDataFormat.mChannelsPerFrame = 2;
aqc.mDataFormat.mBitsPerChannel = 16;
aqc.frameCount = 735;
```

In this example, we prepare a structure for 16-bit (two bytes per sample) stereo sound (two channels) with a sample rate of 44 Khz (44,100). Our output sample will be provided in the form of two 2-byte *short* integers, hence four total bytes per frame (two bytes each for the left and right channels).

The sample rate and frame size dictate how often the iPhone will ask for more sound. With a frequency of 44,100 samples per second, we can make our application sync the sound every 60th of a second by defining a frame size of 735 samples (44,100 / 60 = 735).

The format we'll be providing in this example is PCM (raw data), but the audio queue supports all of the audio formats supported by the iPhone. These include the following:

kAudioFormatLinearPCM
kAudioFormatAppleIMA4

---

kAudioFormatMPEG4AAC
kAudioFormatULaw
kAudioFormatALaw
kAudioFormatMPEGLayer3
kAudioFormatAppleLossless
kAudioFormatAMR

Provisioning Audio Output

Once you have defined the audio queue's properties, you can provision a new audio queue object. The `AudioQueueNewOutput` function is responsible for provisioning an output channel and attaching it to the audio queue. The prototype for this function follows:

```
AudioQueueNewOutput(
    const AudioStreamBasicDescription *inFormat,
    AudioQueueOutputCallback        inCallbackProc,
    void *                          inUserData,
    CFRunLoopRef                    inCallbackRunLoop,
    CFStringRef                     inCallbackRunLoopMode,
    UInt32                          inFlags,
    AudioQueueRef *                 outAQ);
```

inFormat
> The pointer to a structure describing the audio format that will be played. We defined this structure earlier as a member of data type `Audio StreamBasicDescription` within our `AQCallbackStruct` structure.

inCallbackProc
> The name of a callback function that will be called when the audio queue has an empty buffer that needs data.

inUserData
> A pointer to data that the developer can optionally pass to the callback function. It will contain a pointer to the instance of the user-defined `AQCallbackStruct` structure, which should contain information about the audio queue as well as any information relevant to the application about the samples being played.

inCallbackRunLoopMode
> Tells the audio queue how it should expect to loop the audio. `NULL` specifies that the callback function will be invoked whenever a sound buffer becomes exhausted. Additional modes are available to run the callback under other conditions.

inFlags
> Not used; reserved.

outAQ
> When the `AudioQueueNewOutput` function returns, this pointer will be set to the newly created audio queue. The presence of this argument allows an error code to be used as the return value of the function.

An actual call to this function, using the audio queue structure created earlier, looks like the following:

```
AudioQueueNewOutput(&aqc.mDataFormat,
    AQBufferCallback,
    &aqc,
    NULL,
    kCFRunLoopCommonModes,
    0,
    &aqc.queue);
```

In this example, the name of our callback function is specified as `AQBufferCallback`. We will create this function in the next few sections. It is the function that will be responsible for taking sound output from your application and copying it to a sound buffer.

Sound Buffers

A *sound buffer* contains sound data in transit to the output device. Going back to our box-on-a-conveyor-belt concept, the buffer is the box that carries your sound to the speakers. If you don't have enough sound to fill the box, it ends up going to the speakers incomplete, which could lead to gaps in the audio. The more boxes you have, the more sound you can queue up in advance to avoid running out (or running slow). The downside is that it also takes longer for the sound at the speaker end to catch up to the sound coming from the application. This could be problematic if the character in your game jumps, but the user doesn't hear it until after he's landed.

When the sound is ready to start, your code will create sound buffers and prime them with the first frames of the your application's sound output. The minimum number of buffers needed to start playback on an Apple desktop is only one, but on the iPhone it is three. In applications that might cause high CPU usage, it may be appropriate to use even more buffers to prevent underruns. To prepare the buffers with the first frames of sound data, each buffer is presented to your callback function once, which will fill them with sound. This means by the time you prime the buffers, you'd better have some sound to fill them with:

```
#define AUDIO_BUFFERS 3

unsigned long bufferSize;

bufferSize = aqc.frameCount * aqc.mDataFormat.mBytesPerFrame;
for (i=0; i<AUDIO_BUFFERS; i++) {
    AudioQueueAllocateBuffer(aqc.queue,
        bufferSize, &aqc.mBuffers[i]);
    AQBufferCallback (&aqc, aqc.queue, aqc.mBuffers[i]);
}
```

When this code executes, the audio buffers are filled with the first frames of sound data from your application. The queue is now ready to be activated, which turns on the conveyor belt sending the sound buffers to the speakers. As this occurs, the buffers are emptied of their contents (no, memory isn't zeroed) and the boxes come back around the conveyor belt for a refill:

```
AudioQueueStart(aqc.queue, NULL);
```

Later on, when you're ready to turn off the sound queue, just use the `AudioQueueDispose` function and everything stops:

```
AudioQueueDispose(aqc.queue, true);
```

Callback Function

The audio queue is now running and your application's callback function will be asked to fill a new sound buffer with data every 60th of a second. What hasn't been explained yet is how this happens. After a buffer is emptied and is ready to be refilled, the audio queue invokes the callback function you specified in your call to `AudioQueueNewOutput`. This callback function is where the application does its work; it fills the box with raw data that carries your output sound to the speakers. The audio queue invokes this function each time a buffer needs to be refilled. When called, you'll fill the audio queue buffer that is passed in by copying the latest sound frame from your application—in our example, 735 samples:

```
static void AQBufferCallback(
    void *aqc,
    AudioQueueRef inQ,
    AudioQueueBufferRef outQB)
{
```

The callback structure created at the beginning, `aqc`, is passed as a user-defined argument, followed by pointers to the audio queue and the audio queue buffer to be filled:

```
AQCallbackStruct *inData = (AQCallbackStruct *)aqc;
```

As the `AQCallbackStruct` structure is considered user data, it's supplied to the callback function as a void pointer, and needs to be cast back to an `AQCallbackStruct` structure (in this example, named `inData`) before it can be accessed. This code grabs a pointer to the raw audio data inside the buffer so the application can write its sound into it:

```
short *CoreAudioBuffer = (short *) outQB->mAudioData;
```

The `CoreAudioBuffer` variable represents the space inside the sound buffer where your application's raw samples will be copied at every sync. Your application will need to maintain a type of "record needle" to keep track of which sound bytes have already been sent to the audio queue:

```
if (inData->frameCount > 0) {
```

The `frameCount` variable specifies the number of frames that the buffer is expecting to see. This should be equivalent to the `frameCount` value that you supplied in the `AQCallbackStruct` structure—in our example, 735:

```
outQB->mAudioDataByteSize = 4 * inData->frameCount;
```

This is where you tell the buffer exactly how much data it's going to get: a packing list for the box. The total output buffer size should be equivalent to the size of both stereo channels (two bytes per channel = four bytes) multiplied by the number of frames sent (735):

```
for(i = 0 ; i < inData->frameCount * 2; i += 2) {
            CoreAudioBuffer[i]   = (  LEFT CHANNEL DATA );
            CoreAudioBuffer[i+1] = ( RIGHT CHANNEL DATA );
    }
```

Here, the callback function steps through each output frame in the buffer and copies the data from what will be your application's outputted sound into `CoreAudioBuffer`. Because the left and right channels are interleaved, the loop will have to account for this by skipping in increments of two:

```
AudioQueueEnqueueBuffer(inQ, outQB, 0, NULL);
    } /* if (inData->frameCount > 0) */
} /* AQBufferCallback */
```

Finally, once the frame has been copied into the sound buffer, it's placed back onto the play queue.

Volume Control

Samples played through the audio queue track with the system volume, but you might choose to fine-tune the magnitude of your sound output.

In the callback function used in the previous section, we copied sound frames from the application's sound output into sound buffers whenever a sync occurred. By adjusting these values with a volume multiplier, you can effectively raise and lower the output level of your samples:

```
for(i=0; i<aqc->frameCount*2; i+=2) {
            if (aqc->playPtr > aqc->sampleLen || aqc->playPtr < 0)
                sample = 0;
            else
                sample = (aqc->pcmBuffer[aqc->playPtr]);
            coreAudioBuffer[i]   =  sample * volumeMultiplier;
            coreAudioBuffer[i+1] = sample * volumeMultiplier;
            aqc->playPtr++;
    }
```

When the volume is factored in, the sample value is multiplied by the volume setting's value so that it is increased or decreased by the factor of the volume. If you wanted the maximum volume to be louder, set the volume multiplier to a value greater than 1.0. To decrease the volume, set the multiplier to a decimal number less than 1.0. Be careful not to overdrive your audio output, which could create distortion.

Example: PCM Player

This example uses good old-fashioned C and is run on the command line with a filename. It loads a raw PCM file and then plays it using the Audio Toolbox's audio queue. Because your application will likely be generating data internally rather than using a file, this example reads the file into a memory buffer first and then plays it from memory to illustrate the practical concept. Most applications can hook into this same architecture.

Because a raw PCM file doesn't contain any information about its frequency or frame size, this example will have to assume its own. We'll use a format for 16-bit 44Khz mono uncompressed PCM data. This is defined by the three definitions made at the top of the program:

```
#define BYTES_PER_SAMPLE 2
```

16-Bit = 2 Bytes:

```
#define SAMPLE_RATE 44100
```

44,100 samples per second = 44 Khz:

```
typedef unsigned short sampleFrame;
```

An unsigned short is equivalent to two bytes (per sample).

If you can't find a raw PCM file to run this example with, you can use a *.wav* file as long as it's encoded in 16-bit 44Khz raw PCM. Alternatively, you may adapt this example to use a different encoding by changing mFormatID within the audio queue structure. The example won't make any attempt to parse file headers of a *.wav*; it just assumes the data you're providing is raw, which is what a game or other type of application would provide. Wave file headers will be passed to the audio channel with the rest of the data, so you might hear a slight click or two of junk before the raw sound data inside the file is played.

Because Leopard also includes the Audio Toolbox framework, you can compile this example on the desktop as well as for iPhone:

```
$ gcc -o playpcm playpcm.c \
    -framework AudioToolbox -framework CoreAudio -framework CoreFoundation
```

Example 6-9 contains the code.

Example 6-9. Audio Toolbox example (playpcm.c)

```
#include <stdio.h>
#include <stdlib.h>
#include <errno.h>
#include <sys/stat.h>
#include <AudioToolbox/AudioQueue.h>

#define BYTES_PER_SAMPLE 2
#define SAMPLE_RATE 44100
typedef unsigned short sampleFrame;
```

```
#define FRAME_COUNT 735
#define AUDIO_BUFFERS 3

typedef struct AQCallbackStruct {
    AudioQueueRef queue;
    UInt32 frameCount;
    AudioQueueBufferRef mBuffers[AUDIO_BUFFERS];
    AudioStreamBasicDescription mDataFormat;
    UInt32 playPtr;
    UInt32 sampleLen;
    sampleFrame *pcmBuffer;
} AQCallbackStruct;

void *loadpcm(const char *filename, unsigned long *len);
int playbuffer(void *pcm, unsigned long len);
void AQBufferCallback(void *in, AudioQueueRef inQ, AudioQueueBufferRef outQB);

int main(int argc, char *argv[]) {
    char *filename;
    unsigned long len;
    void *pcmbuffer;
    int ret;

    if (argc < 2) {
        fprintf(stderr, "Syntax: %s [filename]\n", argv[0]);
        exit(EXIT_FAILURE);
    }

    filename = argv[1];
    pcmbuffer = loadpcm(filename, &len);
    if (!pcmbuffer) {
        fprintf(stderr, "%s: %s\n", filename, strerror(errno));
        exit(EXIT_FAILURE);
    }

    ret = playbuffer(pcmbuffer, len);
    free(pcmbuffer);
    return ret;
}

void *loadpcm(const char *filename, unsigned long *len) {
    FILE *file;
    struct stat s;
    void *pcm;

    if (stat(filename, &s))
        return NULL;
    *len = s.st_size;
    pcm = (void *) malloc(s.st_size);
    if (!pcm)
        return NULL;
    file = fopen(filename, "rb");
    if (!file) {
        free(pcm);
```

```
            return NULL;
        }
    fread(pcm, s.st_size, 1, file);
    fclose(file);
    return pcm;
}

int playbuffer(void *pcmbuffer, unsigned long len) {
    AQCallbackStruct aqc;
    UInt32 err, bufferSize;
    int i;

    aqc.mDataFormat.mSampleRate = SAMPLE_RATE;
    aqc.mDataFormat.mFormatID = kAudioFormatLinearPCM;
    aqc.mDataFormat.mFormatFlags =
        kLinearPCMFormatFlagIsSignedInteger
        | kAudioFormatFlagIsPacked;
    aqc.mDataFormat.mBytesPerPacket = 4;
    aqc.mDataFormat.mFramesPerPacket = 1;
    aqc.mDataFormat.mBytesPerFrame = 4;
    aqc.mDataFormat.mChannelsPerFrame = 2;
    aqc.mDataFormat.mBitsPerChannel = 16;
    aqc.frameCount = FRAME_COUNT;
    aqc.sampleLen = len / BYTES_PER_SAMPLE;
    aqc.playPtr = 0;
    aqc.pcmBuffer = pcmbuffer;

    err = AudioQueueNewOutput(&aqc.mDataFormat,
        AQBufferCallback,
        &aqc,
        NULL,
        kCFRunLoopCommonModes,
        0,
        &aqc.queue);
    if (err)
        return err;

    aqc.frameCount = FRAME_COUNT;
    bufferSize = aqc.frameCount * aqc.mDataFormat.mBytesPerFrame;

    for (i=0; i<AUDIO_BUFFERS; i++) {
        err = AudioQueueAllocateBuffer(aqc.queue, bufferSize,
            &aqc.mBuffers[i]);
        if (err)
            return err;
        AQBufferCallback(&aqc, aqc.queue, aqc.mBuffers[i]);
    }

    err = AudioQueueStart(aqc.queue, NULL);
    if (err)
        return err;

    while(aqc.playPtr < aqc.sampleLen) { select(NULL, NULL, NULL, NULL, 1.0); }
    sleep(1);
    return 0;
```

```
}

void AQBufferCallback(
    void *in,
    AudioQueueRef inQ,
    AudioQueueBufferRef outQB)
{

    AQCallbackStruct *aqc;
    short *coreAudioBuffer;
    short sample;
    int i;

    aqc = (AQCallbackStruct *) in;
    coreAudioBuffer = (short*) outQB->mAudioData;

    printf("Sync: %ld / %ld\n", aqc->playPtr, aqc->sampleLen);
    if (aqc->playPtr >= aqc->sampleLen) {
        AudioQueueDispose(aqc->queue, true);
        return;
    }

    if (aqc->frameCount > 0) {
        outQB->mAudioDataByteSize = 4 * aqc->frameCount;
        for(i=0; i<aqc->frameCount*2; i+=2) {
            if (aqc->playPtr > aqc->sampleLen || aqc->playPtr < 0)
                sample = 0;
            else
                sample = (aqc->pcmBuffer[aqc->playPtr]);
            coreAudioBuffer[i]   =   sample;
            coreAudioBuffer[i+1] = sample;
            aqc->playPtr++;
        }
        AudioQueueEnqueueBuffer(inQ, outQB, 0, NULL);
    }
}
```

What's Going On

Here's how the playpcm program works:

1. The application's main function is invoked when executed, which extracts the filename from the argument list (as supplied on the command line).

2. The main function calls loadpcm, which determines the length of the audio file and loads it into memory, returning this buffer to main.

3. The playbuffer function is called with the contents of this memory and its length. This function builds our user-defined AQCallbackStruct structure, whose construction is declared at the beginning of the program. This structure holds pointers to the audio queue, sound buffers, and the memory containing the contents of the file that was loaded. It also contains the sample's length and an integer called playPtr, which acts as record needle, identifying the last sample that was copied into the sound buffer.

4. A new sound queue is initialized and started. The callback function is called once for each sound buffer, and is used to sync the first samples into memory. The audio queue is then started. The program then sits and sleeps until the sample is finished playing.

5. As audio is played, the sound buffers become exhausted one by one. Whenever a buffer needs more sound data, the `AQBufferCallback` function is called.

6. The `AQBufferCallback` function increments `playPtr` and copies the next sound frames from memory to be played into the sound buffer. Because raw PCM samples are mono, the same data is copied into both left and right output channels.

7. When `playPtr` exceeds the length of the sound sample, this breaks the wait loop set up in `playpcm`, causing the function to return back to `main` for cleanup and exit.

Further Study

- Modify this example to play 8-bit PCM sound by changing the data type for `sampleFrame` and `BYTES_PER_SAMPLE`. You'll also need to amplify the volume, as the sound sample is now one byte in size, but the audio queue channel is two bytes in size.

- Check out *AudioQueue.h* in Mac OS X Leopard on the desktop. You can find these in */System/Library/Frameworks/AudioToolbox.framework/Headers/*.

Recording Sound

Recording sound operates in much the same way as an audio queue plays it, however, a queue is created and set up as a recording queue, providing an output to the application instead of accepting an input to the speakers. You can record sound into many different formats including Apple Lossless, PCM, and others. The example in this section will closely parallel our previous audio queue example, but with some changes. We'll document these throughout the example.

When recording sound, the audio queue's conveyor belt is spinning in reverse. The iPhone's microphone is doing all of the work of filling boxes with sound and sending them from the mic to your application. You're still responsible for telling the framework what kind of format and sample rate you'd like, but instead of filling boxes, you'll now be responsible for emptying them and writing them out to disk or some other storage mechanism. In the example to follow, you'll use Audio Toolbox's `AudioFile` functions to write directly out to a file instead of copying it to memory.

A recording queue is still strictly first-in-first-out; that is, the conveyor belt moves the samples in the order they are recorded.

Audio Toolbox's audio queue works like the following:

1. An audio queue is created and assigned properties that identify the type of sound that will be recorded (format, sample rate, etc.).
2. Sound buffers are attached to the queue, which will contain the actual sound frames as they are recorded. Think of a sound frame here as a single box full of sound that was recorded, whereas a sample is a single piece of digital sound within the box.
3. The developer supplies an "input" callback function, which the audio queue calls every time a sound buffer has been filled with recorded audio. This callback function is responsible for writing the recorded frames to disk (or some other destination) and sending the box around for another fill.

Audio Queue Structure

As you learned earlier, the Audio Toolbox framework uses low-level C function calls, and so it has no concept of a class. You must first create a callback structure to contain all of the variables that will be moving around in your recording application. Think of this as a context. The `AQCallbackStruct` structure below is similar to the playback version of this structure, but with a few added pieces:

```
typedef struct AQCallbackStruct {
    AudioStreamBasicDescription mDataFormat;
    AudioQueueRef queue;
    AudioQueueBufferRef mBuffers[AUDIO_BUFFERS];
    AudioFileID outputFile;
    unsigned long frameSize;
    long long recPtr;
    int run;
} AQCallbackStruct;
```

The following components are grouped into this structure to service the audio framework:

`AudioStreamBasicDescription mDataFormat`
    Information about the format of audio that will be recorded.

`AudioQueueRef queue`
    A pointer to the audio queue object your program will create.

`AudioQueueBufferRef mBuffers`
    An array containing the total number of sound buffers used.

`AudioFileID outputFile`
    Pointer to an output file, where the sound will be written as it is recorded.

`unsigned long frameSize`
    The total number of samples to be copied per audio sync. This is largely up to the implementer.

```
long long recPtr
```
A numeric pointer to the current position of the recording "needle" in terms of what raw sound data the application has already processed. This is incremented as more data is recorded.

```
int run
```
A value to key from in determining whether our audio queue should requeue the sound buffers; that is, whether or not to send the boxes back around for more sound. When it's time to stop recording, this should be set by your application to zero.

Before you can create the audio queue, you'll need to initialize a description of the audio input you'd like your application to receive:

```
AQCallbackStruct aqc;
aqc.mDataFormat.mFormatID = kAudioFormatLinearPCM;
    aqc.mDataFormat.mSampleRate = 44100.0;
    aqc.mDataFormat.mChannelsPerFrame = 2;
    aqc.mDataFormat.mBitsPerChannel = 16;
    aqc.mDataFormat.mBytesPerPacket =
    aqc.mDataFormat.mBytesPerFrame =
        aqc.mDataFormat.mChannelsPerFrame * sizeof (short int);
    aqc.mDataFormat.mFramesPerPacket = 1;
    aqc.mDataFormat.mFormatFlags =
            kLinearPCMFormatFlagIsBigEndian
          | kLinearPCMFormatFlagIsSignedInteger
          | kLinearPCMFormatFlagIsPacked;
    aqc.frameSize = 735;
```

In the preceding example, a structure is prepared to record 16-bit (two bytes per sample) stereo sound (two channels) with a sample rate of 44 Khz (44100). The output sample will be provided in the form of two 2-byte *short* integers, hence four total bytes per frame (two bytes for the left and right channel, each).

The sample rate and frame size dictate how often your application will receive more sound. With a frequency of 44100 samples per second, the application can be made to sync the sound every 60th of a second by defining a frame size of 735 samples (44100 / 60 = 735). This is very aggressive to accommodate real-time sound processing applications, so if you don't need to sync that often, you can choose a larger frame size, such as 22050, which will sync every ½ second.

The format used in the above example calls for PCM (raw data), but the audio queue supports many of the audio formats supported by the iPhone. These include the following:

kAudioFormatLinearPCM
kAudioFormatAppleIMA4
kAudioFormatMPEG4AAC
kAudioFormatULaw
kAudioFormatALaw

kAudioFormatMPEGLayer3
kAudioFormatAppleLossless
kAudioFormatAMR

Provisioning Audio Input

Once you have defined the audio queue's properties, you can provision a new audio queue object. The `AudioQueueNewInput` function is responsible for creating an input (recording) channel and attaching it to the queue. The prototype function follows:

```
AudioQueueNewInput(
    const AudioStreamBasicDescription *inFormat,
    AudioQueueInputCallback           inCallbackProc,
    void *                            inUserData,
    CFRunLoopRef                      inCallbackRunLoop,
    CFStringRef                       inCallbackRunLoopMode,
    UInt32                            inFlags,
    AudioQueueRef *                   outAQ);
```

inFormat

> Pointer to a structure describing the audio format to be recorded. You defined this structure earlier as a member of data type `AudioStreamBasicDescription` within the `AQCallbackStruct` structure.

inCallbackProc

> The name of a callback function to be called when the audio queue has a full buffer of recorded audio. The callback function is responsible for doing something with the sound buffer, such as writing it to disk, and then sending the buffer back around for more data.

inUserData

> A pointer to data that the developer can optionally pass to the callback function. Our example will contain a pointer to the instance of the user-defined `AQCallback Struct` structure, which will contain information about the audio queue as well as any information relevant to the application about the samples being recorded.

inCallbackRunLoopMode

> Tells the audio queue how it should expect to loop the audio. A `NULL` value indicates that the callback function should be invoked whenever a sound buffer is filled. Additional modes are available to run the callback under other conditions.

inFlags

> Not used; reserved.

outAQ

> When the `AudioQueueNewInput` function returns, this pointer will be set to the newly created audio queue. The presence of this argument allows an error code to be used as the return value of the function.

An actual call to this function, using the audio queue structure created earlier, follows. In this example, the name of our callback function is specified as `AQInputCallback`. It is this function that will be responsible for taking recorded sound delivered to your application and writing it to disk:

```
AudioQueueNewInput (
        &aqc.mDataFormat,
        AQInputCallback,
        &aqc,
        NULL,
        kCFRunLoopCommonModes,
        0,
        &aqc.queue
    );
```

Sound Buffers

A *sound buffer* contains sound data from the microphone while it is in transit to your application (the output device). Going back to our box-on-a-conveyor-belt concept, the buffer is the box that carries your sound between the microphone and your callback function. If the iPhone can't provide enough sound in the pipeline, you may end up with gaps or skipping in your recording. The more boxes you have, the more sound you can queue up in advance to avoid running out (or running slow). The downside is that it also takes longer for the sound at the microphone end to catch up to the sound going into the application. This could be problematic if you are writing a voice synthesizer or other type of application that requires close to real-time sound.

When recording is ready to start, sound buffers are created and placed on the audio queue. The minimum number of buffers needed to start a recording queue on an Apple desktop is only one, but on the iPhone it is three. In applications that might cause high CPU usage, it may be appropriate to use even more buffers to prevent recording underruns:

```
#define AUDIO_BUFFERS 3

for (i=0; i<AUDIO_BUFFERS; i++) {
        AudioQueueAllocateBuffer (aqc.queue, aqc.frameSize, &aqc.mBuffers[i]);
        AudioQueueEnqueueBuffer (aqc.queue, aqc.mBuffers[i], 0, NULL);
    }
```

In the playback example, the audio buffers were sent to the callback function to be primed with data. Since this example is recording sound instead of playing it, the buffer needs to be queued (sent around the conveyor belt) first so that the audio framework can fill it with recorded data. Once filled, the framework will automatically invoke your callback function.

The queue is now ready to be started, which turns on the conveyor belt sending the sound buffers your way from the microphone. As this occurs, the callback function will empty the buffers of their contents (no, it doesn't need to zero the data) and send the boxes back around the conveyor belt for a refill:

```
AudioQueueStart(aqc.queue, NULL);
```

Later on, when you're ready to turn off recording, deactivate the sound queue using the `AudioQueueStop` and `AudioQueueDispose` functions. The `AudioQueueStop` function only stops the queue, leaving it in a state where it can later be restarted. When the audio queue is disposed of, however, it is deallocated from memory, and cannot be restarted:

```
AudioQueueStop(aqc.queue, true);
AudioQueueDispose(aqc.queue, true);
```

Callback Function

Once the audio queue is running, your application will be periodically presented with a sound buffer containing data. What we haven't explained yet is how this happens. After a buffer is filled with recorded data, the audio queue calls the callback function you specified as the second argument to `AudioQueueNewInput`. This callback function is where the application does its work; it empties the box that carries the microphone's output, and places it back on the queue. When invoked, your callback function will empty the audio queue buffer by copying the latest sound frames to their destination; in the case of this example, into a file:

```
static void AQInputCallback (
    void                            *aqr,
    AudioQueueRef                   inQ,
    AudioQueueBufferRef             inQB,
    const AudioTimeStamp            *timestamp,
    unsigned long                   frameSize,
    const AudioStreamPacketDescription  *mDataFormat)
{
```

The callback structure you created at the very beginning, `aqc`, is passed into your callback function as a user-defined argument, followed by pointers to the audio queue itself and the audio queue buffer to be emptied:

```
AQCallbackStruct *aqc = (AQCallbackStruct *)aqr;
```

Because the `AQCallbackStruct` structure is considered user data, the audio queue presents it to the callback function as a void pointer. It will need to be cast back to an `AQCallbackStruct` structure pointer (here, named `aqc`) before it can be accessed.

Accessing Raw Data

In most cases, you'll be writing the audio directly to a file, but if you are going to access the raw audio data inside the buffer, you can tap into the raw input buffer:

```
short *CoreAudioBuffer = (short *) inQB->mAudioData;
```

The `CoreAudioBuffer` variable represents the space inside the sound buffer where the microphone's raw samples will be copied at each sync. Your application needs to maintain a type of "record needle" to keep track of what sound has already been sent to the audio queue. An example of copying data into allocated memory follows:

```
int recNeedle = 0;
myBuffer = malloc(aqc.frameSize * nSamples);
...
static void AQInputCallback (
    void                            *aqr,
    AudioQueueRef                   inQ,
    AudioQueueBufferRef             inQB,
    const AudioTimeStamp            *timestamp,
    unsigned long                   frameSize,
    const AudioStreamPacketDescription  *mDataFormat)
{
    AQCallbackStruct *aqc = (AQCallbackStruct *) aqr;

    short *CoreAudioBuffer = (short *) inQB->mAudioData;
    memcpy(myBuffer + recNeedle, CoreAudioBuffer,
        aqc.mDataFormat.mBytesPerFrame * aqc.frameSize);
    recNeedle += aqc.frameSize;
    if (!aqc->run)
      return;

    AudioQueueEnqueueBuffer (aqc->queue, inQB, 0, NULL);
}
```

Writing to a File

To write to a file, you'll use the Audio Toolbox's *AudioFile* set of functions. To prepare an audio file, you'll first need to define the file format. The code below configures the property needed for an AIFF audio file:

```
AudioFileTypeID fileFormat = kAudioFileAIFFType;
```

Use a `CFURL` structure to contain the actual file path to the audio file:

```
CFURLRef filename =
        CFURLCreateFromFileSystemRepresentation (
            NULL,
            (const unsigned char *) path_to_file,
            strlen (path_to_file),
            false
        );
```

 Make sure the path you choose for the file exists within your application's sandbox, using the `NSHomeDirectory` function, or similar functions. You will not be allowed to write a sound file anywhere outside of your sandbox.

Finally, you'll create the audio file itself with a call to `AudioFileCreateWithURL` containing the filename and format properties you just created. A pointer to the file is written into the `AQCallbackStruct` structure so that you'll know how to access the file whenever there is sound to write:

```
AudioFileCreateWithURL (
        filename,
        fileFormat,
        &aqc.mDataFormat,
        kAudioFileFlags_EraseFile,
        &aqc.mAudioFile
);
```

As new audio samples are recorded, you'll write to this file using the `AudioFileWrite Packets` function, which is another function built into Audio Toolbox specifically for writing audio packets into a file. You'll see how this works in the following example.

Example: Sound Recorder

Continuing in the spirit of good old-fashioned C hacking, this example can run on the command line with a filename and duration on either the iPhone or the desktop. It records data from the microphone for a preset duration provided and saves it to the filename provided.

Because Leopard also includes the Audio Toolbox framework, you can compile Example 6-10 for the desktop and iPhone:

```
$ gcc -o recorder recorder.c -framework AudioToolbox -framework CoreFoundation
```

Example 6-10. Sound recorder example (recorder.c)

```
#include <AudioToolbox/AudioQueue.h>
#include <AudioToolbox/AudioFile.h>
#include <AudioToolbox/AudioConverter.h>

#include <stdio.h>
#include <stdlib.h>
#include <errno.h>
#include <sys/stat.h>
#include <sys/select.h>

#define AUDIO_BUFFERS 3

typedef struct AQCallbackStruct {
    AudioStreamBasicDescription mDataFormat;
    AudioQueueRef queue;
    AudioQueueBufferRef mBuffers[AUDIO_BUFFERS];
    AudioFileID outputFile;
    unsigned long frameSize;
    long long recPtr;
    int run;
} AQCallbackStruct;
```

```
static void AQInputCallback (
    void                              *aqr,
    AudioQueueRef                     inQ,
    AudioQueueBufferRef               inQB,
    const AudioTimeStamp              *timestamp,
    unsigned long                     frameSize,
    const AudioStreamPacketDescription  *mDataFormat)
{
    AQCallbackStruct *aqc = (AQCallbackStruct *) aqr;

    /* Write data to file */
    if (AudioFileWritePackets (aqc->outputFile, false, inQB->mAudioDataByteSize,
        mDataFormat, aqc->recPtr, &frameSize, inQB->mAudioData) == noErr)
    {
        aqc->recPtr += frameSize;
    }

    /* Don't re-queue the sound buffers if we're supposed to stop recording */
    if (!aqc->run)
      return;

    AudioQueueEnqueueBuffer (aqc->queue, inQB, 0, NULL);
}

int main(int argc, char *argv[]) {
    AQCallbackStruct aqc;
    AudioFileTypeID fileFormat;
    CFURLRef filename;
    struct timeval tv;
    int i;

    if (argc < 3) {
        fprintf(stderr, "Syntax: %s [filename] [duration]", argv[0]);
        exit(EXIT_FAILURE);
    }

    aqc.mDataFormat.mFormatID = kAudioFormatLinearPCM;
    aqc.mDataFormat.mSampleRate = 44100.0;
    aqc.mDataFormat.mChannelsPerFrame = 2;
    aqc.mDataFormat.mBitsPerChannel = 16;
    aqc.mDataFormat.mBytesPerPacket =
    aqc.mDataFormat.mBytesPerFrame =
        aqc.mDataFormat.mChannelsPerFrame * sizeof (short int);
    aqc.mDataFormat.mFramesPerPacket = 1;
    aqc.mDataFormat.mFormatFlags =
            kLinearPCMFormatFlagIsBigEndian
          | kLinearPCMFormatFlagIsSignedInteger
          | kLinearPCMFormatFlagIsPacked;
    aqc.frameSize = 735;

    AudioQueueNewInput (&aqc.mDataFormat, AQInputCallback, &aqc, NULL,
        kCFRunLoopCommonModes, 0, &aqc.queue);

    /* Create output file */
```

```
fileFormat = kAudioFileAIFFType;
filename = CFURLCreateFromFileSystemRepresentation (NULL, argv[1],
    strlen (argv[1]), false);

AudioFileCreateWithURL (
    filename,
    fileFormat,
    &aqc.mDataFormat,
    kAudioFileFlags_EraseFile,
    &aqc.outputFile
);

/* Initialize the recording buffers */

for (i=0; i<AUDIO_BUFFERS; i++) {
    AudioQueueAllocateBuffer (aqc.queue, aqc.frameSize, &aqc.mBuffers[i]);
    AudioQueueEnqueueBuffer (aqc.queue, aqc.mBuffers[i], 0, NULL);
}

aqc.recPtr = 0;
aqc.run = 1;

AudioQueueStart (aqc.queue, NULL);

/* Hang around for a while while the recording takes place */

tv.tv_sec = atof(argv[2]);
tv.tv_usec = 0;
select(0, NULL, NULL, NULL, &tv);

/* Shut down recording */

AudioQueueStop (aqc.queue, true);
aqc.run = 0;

AudioQueueDispose (aqc.queue, true);
AudioFileClose (aqc.outputFile);

exit(EXIT_SUCCESS);
}
```

What's Going On

Here's how the record program works:

1. When the program starts, the application's main function extracts the filename and recording duration from the argument list (as supplied on the command line).

2. The main function builds our user-defined AQCallbackStruct structure, whose construction is declared at the beginning of the program. This structure holds pointers to the recording queue, sound buffers, and the output file that was created. It also contains the sample's length and an integer called recPtr, which acts as record needle, identifying the last sample that was written to disk.

3. A new recording queue is initialized and started. Each sound buffer is initialized and placed on the queue. The queue is then started. The program then sits and sleeps until the sample is finished recording.

4. As audio is recorded, the sound buffers are sent to the callback, where they become filled one by one. Whenever a buffer is ready to be emptied, the `AQInputCallback` function is called.

5. The `AQInputCallback` function increments `recPtr` and copies the sound frame to disk.

Further Study

- Modify this example to sync at one-second intervals.
- Check out *AudioFile.h* in Mac OS X Leopard on the desktop. This can be found in */System/Library/Frameworks/AudioToolbox.framework/Headers/*.

Vibrating

You may also be interested in how to make a racket without playing any sound; that is, how to cause the iPhone to vibrate. Depending on whether the iPhone's owner has his device placed on a conference room table, vibrating can create a variety of different nuisance sounds to get the user's attention. The audio service described at the beginning of this chapter has a nifty little constant sound identifier that you can use to accomplish this. Example 6-11 shows you how.

Example 6-11. Vibrating sample code

```
#import <AudioToolbox/AudioToolbox.h>
#import <UIKit/UIKit.h>

- (void)vibrate
{
    AudioServicesPlaySystemSound(kSystemSoundID_Vibrate);
}
```

CHAPTER 7

Network Programming with CFNetwork

One of the greatest strengths of the iPhone is its ability to deliver advanced functionality over an "always on" Internet connection. While the iPhone supports the usual set of standard C functions for network programming, Apple has also provided a framework, named CFNetwork, to provide name resolution, socket connectivity, and basic protocol communications.

You might consider using CFNetwork instead of standard BSD sockets if your application has a need for a run-loop; that is, you'll be able to use CFNetwork without spinning up threads or writing your own polling routines. The CFNetwork framework also adds an easy mechanism to handle reading and writing through socket streams, and supports common protocols such as HTTP and FTP out of the box. This allows you to focus on the more important aspects of your code, relieving you from the need to support individual protocols. CFNetwork is also supported in Leopard, meaning you can easily port your networking code to the desktop.

To use the CFNetwork framework, you'll need to add it to your Xcode project. Right-click on the *Frameworks* folder in your project, and then choose Add Framework. Navigate to the *CFNetwork.framework* folder, and then click Add.

Basic Sockets Programming

The most common use of the CFNetwork framework is to communicate across network sockets. A socket is a single channel of communication between two endpoints; think of it as the string connecting two tin cans. Sockets can be established between computers across a network (such as an HTTP connection between the iPhone and a web server), or locally between applications on the same device (such as two programs sharing data). The end responsible for initiating the connection is commonly referred to as the *client*, while the endpoint that receives and services the connection is considered the *server*. Another type of paradigm is peer-to-peer networking. Peer-to-peer networks employ ad-hoc connections between standalone client machines to share resources among each other, rather than connecting to a centralized server for the resources. In many situations, however, a central server is used to coordinate peers.

Socket Types

There are two primary types of sockets: UDP and TCP.

A *UDP* (User Datagram Protocol) socket is used for sending short messages called *datagrams* to the recipient. Datagrams are single packets of data that are sent and received without any "return postage." There is no guarantee that the recipient will receive a particular packet, and multiple packets may be received out of order. Datagrams are generally thought of as unreliable, in the same way that a carrier pigeon can be unreliable. This form of communication is used for sending short query/response-type messages that do not require authentication, such as DNS (name resolution) lookups, as well as by some protocols where lost packets are irrelevant; such as live video streams and online multiplayer games, where an interruption can be ignored.

The other type of socket, *TCP* (Transmission Control Protocol), is much more commonly used, as it provides the framework for a complete, structured "conversation" to occur between the two endpoints. TCP connections provide a means to ensure the message was received, and guarantees that packets are received in order. TCP is used by protocols including HTTP, FTP, and others where data must be reliably sent and received in order. In order to keep track of the ordering of packets, TCP employs a sequence number, which identifies the sequence of each packet. This not only keeps your conversation in order, but also adds a reasonable level of protection against some forms of spoofing (packet forgery by a malicious party).

CFSocket

The CFSocket object is the base structure used to create UDP and TCP sockets, and is used to set up, communicate over, and break down a connection. Because the CFNetwork framework is C-based, CFSocket is a structure, rather than a class, and all calls to its functions will include the socket as the first argument.

Creating new sockets

You can use the CFSocketCreate function to create both TCP and UDP sockets. This function is provided with the granular information needed to build a socket, including the type of memory allocator to use, protocol family (IPv4 or IPv6), and type of socket. A socket can perform its function in the background of an application by scheduling it on a run loop, so you'll also be able to supply a callback function to be invoked during certain socket events. This allows you to focus on your application, rather than writing your own run loop to wait for connections and data. The prototype for CFSocket Create follows:

```
CFSocketRef CFSocketCreate (
    CFAllocatorRef allocator,
    SInt32 protocolFamily,
    SInt32 socketType,
    SInt32 protocol,
    CFOptionFlags callBackTypes,
    CFSocketCallBack callout,
    const CFSocketContext *context
);
```

CFAllocatorRef allocator

Specifies the type of memory allocator to create the new socket. Use NULL or kCFAllocatorDefault to use the default. Other types of allocators include kCFAllocatorSystemDefault, the system's default allocator (which Apple strongly recommends against using), kCFAllocatorMalloc (which uses malloc(), realloc() and free()), kCFAllocatorMallocZone (which allocates space in unscanned memory), and kCFAllocatorNull (which does not allocate or deallocate memory; useful for cases when data should not be deallocated). You'll almost always want to use the default allocator unless your program calls for a very specific alternative.

SInt32 protocolFamily

The protocol family for the socket. The default is PF_INET (Internet Protocol also known as IPV4). For IPv6 sockets, use PF_INET6.

SInt32 socketType

Identifies the socket type. Use SOCK_STREAM for TCP sockets or SOCK_DGRAM for datagram (UDP) sockets.

SInt32 protocol

The protocol to be used for the socket. This can be one of IPPROTO_TCP or IPPROTO_UDP and should match the socket type specified.

CFOptionFlags callBackTypes

A CFSocket run loop can invoke callbacks for different types of socket events. For example, a callback can be issued when a socket connects, or when there is data available. You construct the callBackTypes argument using a bitmask, which you can set using a bitwise-OR operation. Apple's prototype defines the following enumeration of flags:

```
enum CFSocketCallBackType {
    kCFSocketNoCallBack = 0,
    kCFSocketReadCallBack = 1,
    kCFSocketAcceptCallBack = 2,
    kCFSocketDataCallBack = 3,
    kCFSocketConnectCallBack = 4,
    kCFSocketWriteCallBack = 8
};
typedef enum CFSocketCallBackType CFSocketCallBackType;
```

CFSocketCallBack callout

Specifies the function that should be called when one of the events identified in callBackTypes is triggered. Instead of writing your own run loop to wait for connections and send and receive data, using a run loop would instead call this function whenever one of the desired events occurs.

const CFSocketContext *context

A special structure containing a CFSocket's context, which can encapsulate a pointer to your own user-defined data for the socket. You'll learn about this in the next section.

CFTimeInterval timeout

Specifies the time to wait for a connection. If you supply a negative value, the connection will be established in the background, allowing your program to continue running. The callback will then be invoked when the connection is made.

Creating sockets from existing sockets

You can create a CFSocket object from an existing native socket by using the CFSocket CreateWithNative function. This function is very similar to the CFSocketCreate function, but accepts the existing socket as one of its arguments. This may be useful in cases where you have legacy code to build a socket, and want to plug it into the CFNetwork framework. The prototype follows:

```
CFSocketCreateWithNative (
    CFAllocatorRef allocator,
    CFSocketNativeHandle sock,
    CFOptionFlags callBackTypes,
    CFSocketCallBack callout,
    const CFSocketContext *context
);
```

In the example above, you'll immediately notice that the native socket argument isn't defined as an int, which is the standard on most systems, but rather a CFSocketNative Handle. The CFSocketNativeHandle data type is defined as the operating system's native data type for C-based sockets, so this will typically resolve to an int on most systems.

Socket functions

Once you have created the socket, you can perform a number of functions on it. You can use functions that are specific to the CFNetwork framework, and with a special function named CFSocketGetNative, you can also operate on the socket's lower-level native socket to perform native C-socket functions. The following relevant functions are available on CFSocket objects:

CFSocketGetNative

Returns the system's native socket, on which you can perform the native set of C-based socket operations. This is usually an int data type on most systems. In the example to follow, you'll see it call the native setsockopt() function. This allows you to plug in the CFNetwork framework without sacrificing any functionality, while maintaining compatibility with legacy code.

CFSocketConnectToAddress

Invokes a connect request on the local socket. This is used to connect the socket to a listening (server) socket, such as a web server.

CFSocketCopyAddress

Returns the local address of the CFSocket. This is useful in determining what IP address or addresses your socket is listening on.

CFSocketCopyPeerAddress

Returns the address of the remote socket that the CFSocket is connected to. This provides the IP address of the remote end of the connection, for events when your application is acting as the server.

CFSocketCreateRunLoopSource

Creates a run loop source object for a CFSocket object. You'll see how this works in the example to follow.

Enabling/disabling callbacks

Callbacks for CFSocket objects can be enabled or disabled at the programmer's discretion. This is useful in cases where the callback behavior for a socket changes depending on the socket's status. You can do this using the CFSocketDisableCallBacks and CFSocketEnableCallBacks functions.

Both functions accept a socket and a bitwise-OR'd set of callback flags as arguments, matching the callback flags you've already learned. To disable accept and read callbacks for a given socket, your code might look like the example below:

```
CFSocketDisableCallBacks(mySocket,
    kCFSocketAcceptCallBack | kCFSocketReadCallback);
```

To reenable them, simply swap the function name to CFSocketEnableCallBacks, as shown below:

```
CFSocketEnableCallBacks(mySocket,
    kCFSocketAcceptCallBack | kCFSocketReadCallback);
```

Sending data

The CFNetwork framework provides an abstracted routine for sending data, which helps simplify the process. To send data, use the CFSocketSendData command:

```
char joke[] = "Why did the chicken cross the road?";
kCFSocketError err = CFSocketSendData(mySocket, joke, (strlen(joke)+1), 10);
```

You can then check the error code to determine if data was sent successfully:

```
if (err == kCFSocketSuccess) {
    /* Success */
}
```

The CFNetwork framework uses the following error codes:

kCFSocketSuccess
> Operation succeeded

kCFSocketError
> Operation failed

kCFSocketTimeout
> Operation timed out

Callbacks

You can set certain events to trigger callbacks, such as incoming data or new connections. This allows you to write software that doesn't need to block or loop itself to check the status of the socket. CFNetwork uses a standard callback form factor for all callback functions, providing whatever data is relevant to the type of callback. The prototype for this function follows:

```
typedef void (*CFSocketCallBack) (
    CFSocketRef s,
    CFSocketCallBackType callbackType,
    CFDataRef address,
    const void *data,
    void *info
);
```

The following information is provided with each callback. Some information may differ, depending on the type of callback being sent.

CFSocketRef s
> The CFSocket corresponding to the event that occurred. This allows your callback function to support multiple sockets.

CFSocketCallBackType callbackType
> The enumerated value for the callback, identifying what kind of event has occurred. See the list of callback types from earlier.

CFDataRef address
> A CFData object containing the lower-level sockaddr information. You can use this to obtain the remote address to which the socket is connected. This is only provided during accept and data callbacks.

const void *data
> A pointer to special data that is relevant to the callback. For a data event, a CFData object is passed containing the received data. For an accept event, a pointer to a CFSocketNativeHandle is provided, pointing to the native socket object. For a connect event, a pointer to an SInt32 error code will be provided.

void *info
> The pointer supplied to the CFSocketContext structure associated with the socket. This will contain any user-defined data you've associated with the socket.

CFSocketContext

Because CFSockets can run in the background in a run loop, keeping track of the data that is associated with each connection can become tricky. For example, if you are writing a search engine, you might create hundreds of connections to various web servers, and will need to know which connection is associated with which callback events. The CFSocketContext object allows you to tie a pointer to any such proprietary information to a socket structure so that it is available whenever a callback is triggered.

The context structure prototype follows:

```
struct CFSocketContext {
    CFIndex version;
    void *info;
    CFAllocatorRetainCallBack retain;
    CFAllocatorReleaseCallBack release;
    CFAllocatorCopyDescriptionCallBack copyDescription;
};
typedef struct CFSocketContext CFSocketContext;
```

CFIndex version
> The version number of the structure. Apple insists this be set to 0.

void *info
> A pointer to your application's user-defined data, which will be associated with the CFSocket object when it is created. This pointer will be passed in the arguments list of all callbacks issued by the CFSocket object.

CFAllocatorRetainCallBack retain
> An optional callback used when the context is retained. Use NULL if no callback is necessary.

CFAllocatorReleaseCallBack release
> An optional callback used when the context is released. Use NULL if no callback is necessary.

CFAllocatorCopyDescriptionCallBack copyDescription
> An optional callback invoked when the object is copied into another context. Use NULL if no callback is necessary.

An example socket context follows:

```
char joke[] = "Why did the chicken cross the road?";
CFSocketContext CTX = { 0, joke, NULL, NULL, NULL };
```

When operating on a socket, you can obtain the socket's context by calling CFSocket GetContext. This function copies the contents of the socket's context into a local structure provided by the caller:

```
CFSocketContext localCTX;
CFSocketGetContext(mySocket, &localCTX);
```

Socket Streams

Socket streams provide an easy interface for reading and writing data to or from a socket. Each socket can be bound to a read and write stream, allowing for synchronous or asynchronous communication. Streams encapsulate most of the work needed for reading and writing byte streams, and replace the traditional error codes send() and recv() functions used in C. Two different stream objects are used with sockets: CFRead Stream and CFWriteStream.

Read streams

A special set of CFReadStream functions allow for simple read operations on a socket. A read buffer is used, much like in C, in which the read stream is looped until the desired number of bytes are read:

```
char buffer[1024];
CFIndex bytes_recvd;
int recv_len = 0;

memset(buffer, 0, sizeof(buffer));
while (!strchr(buffer, '\n') && recv_len < sizeof(buffer)) {
    bytes_recvd = CFReadStreamRead(readStream, buffer + recv_len,
        sizeof(buffer) -; recv_len);
    if (bytes_recvd < 0) {
        /* Error has occurred. Close the socket and return. */
    }
    recv_len += bytes_recvd;
}
```

A list of useful CFReadStream functions follows:

CFReadStreamOpen, CFReadStreamClose

Opens and closes a read stream. These functions allocate and release the resources needed to perform stream reads. A stream must first be opened before it can be attached to a socket.

CFReadStreamRead

The actual read function of the read stream. This function performs reading from the attached socket into the provided buffer, returning the number of bytes that have been read. Much like traditional sockets, the read can be looped until the desired number of bytes has been received.

CFReadStreamGetBuffer

Returns a pointer to the read stream's internal buffer of unread data, allowing the implementer to access the raw buffer directly.

CFReadStreamGetStatus

Returns the current status of the read stream. The status will be one of the following:

- `kCFStreamStatusNotOpen` (read stream is not open)

- `kCFStreamStatusOpening` (read stream is being opened for reading)

- `kCFStreamStatusOpen` (read stream is open and ready)

- `kCFStreamReading` (the stream is currently being read from)

- `kCFStreamStatusAtEnd` (no more data is available to read from the stream)

- `kCFStreamStatusClosed` (the readIin stream has been closed)

- `kFStreamStatusError` (an error has occurred on the read stream)

`CFReadStreamHasBytesAvailable`

Returns a Boolean value indicating whether incoming data is ready to be read without blocking. You can use this to periodically poll the socket about whether data is available, although this will be unnecessary if you are using a run loop.

`CFReadStreamScheduleWithRunLoop, CFReadStreamUnscheduleFromRunLoop`

Used to schedule or unschedule the stream into or from a run loop. Once scheduled, the loop client is called during certain events, such as opening, errors, and when data is available to be read. You can also schedule a single stream with multiple run loops and modes.

`CFReadStreamSetClient`

Assigns a client to receive callback for the stream while in the run loop.

If a socket already exists, the `CFStreamCreatePairWithSocket` function can automatically initialize a read and write stream:

```
/* The native socket, used for various operations */
CFReadStreamRef readStream;
CFWriteStreamRef writeStream;

CFSocketNativeHandle sock = *(CFSocketNativeHandle *) data;
CFStreamCreatePairWithSocket(kCFAllocatorDefault, sock,
&readStream, &writeStream);
```

To schedule a read stream onto the run loop, call its scheduler function. This will cause the actual operation of the read stream to be threaded into the background, and will activate its callback functions:

```
CFReadStreamScheduleWithRunLoop(readStream, CFRunLoopGetCurrent(),
        kCFRunLoopCommonModes);
```

When a read stream has been entered into a run loop, the client's callback functions are called whenever certain events occur:

```
typedef void (*CFReadStreamClientCallBack) (
    CFReadStreamRef stream,
    CFStreamEventType eventType,
    void *clientCallBackInfo
);
```

Similar to the CFSocket callback function, the stream callbacks provide information about the type of event and relevant data for the event. You can invoke a callback for the following events:

kCFStreamEventNone
: Undefined event.

kCFStreamEventOpenCompleted
: The stream has been successfully opened and is ready for further operations.

kCStreamEventHasBytesAvailable
: Data is available for the stream to read.

kCFStreamEventErrorOccurred
: An error has occurred on the read stream.

kCFStreamEventEndEncountered
: An EOF (end-of-file) has been reached, and there is no more data available on the stream.

Write streams

The complement to a read stream is a CFWriteStream. This stream is designated for writing, and manages the sending of data through a CFSocket. An example follows:

```
char data[] = "Beware the Jabberwocky.\n";
CFIndex bytes_sent = 0;
int send_len = 0;

if (CFWriteStreamCanAcceptBytes(writeStream)) {
    bytes_sent = CFWriteStreamWrite(writeStream, data + send_len,
        (strlen(data)+1) - send_len);
    if (bytes_sent < 0) {
        /* Send error occurred. Close the socket and return. */
    }
    send_len += bytes_sent;
}
```

A list of useful CFWriteStream functions follows:

CFWriteStreamOpen, CFWriteStreamClose
: Opens and closes a write stream. These functions allocate and release the resources needed to perform stream writes. A stream must first be opened before it can be attached to a socket.

CFWriteStreamWrite
: The actual write function for the write stream. This function performs the writing from a data source to the socket it is paired with, returning the number of bytes that have been sent. Much like traditional **send** functions performed on C sockets, the write can be looped until the desired number of bytes has been sent.

CFWriteStreamGetStatus

> Returns the current status of the write stream. The status will be one of the following:
>
> - kCFStreamStatusNotOpen (write stream is not open)
> - kCFStreamStatusOpening (write stream is being opened for writing)
> - kCFStreamStatusOpen (write stream is open and ready)
> - kCFStreamWriting (the stream is currently being written to)
> - kCFStreamStatusAtEnd (no more data can be written to the stream)
> - kCFStreamStatusClosed (the write stream has been closed)
> - kFStreamStatusError (an error has occurred on the write stream)

CFReadStreamCanAcceptBytes

> Returns a Boolean value indicating whether the stream can be written to.

CFWriteStreamScheduleWithRunLoop, CFWriteStreamUnscheduleFromRunLoop

> Used to schedule or unschedule the stream into or from a run loop. After scheduling, the loop client is called during certain events, such as opening, errors, and when data is written. You can also schedule a single stream with multiple run loops and modes.

CFWriteStreamSetClient

> Assigns a client to receive callback for the stream while in the run loop.

To schedule a write stream onto the run loop, call its scheduler function. This will cause the actual operation of the write stream to be threaded into the background, and will activate its callback functions:

```
CFWriteStreamScheduleWithRunLoop(writeStream, CFRunLoopGetCurrent(),
    kCFRunLoopCommonModes);
```

When a write stream has been entered into a run loop, the client's callback functions are called whenever certain events occur:

```
typedef void (*CFWriteStreamClientCallBack) (
   CFWriteStreamRef stream,
   CFStreamEventType eventType,
   void *clientCallBackInfo
);
```

Similar to the CFSocket callback function, the stream callbacks provide information about the type of event and relevant data for the event. A callback may be invoked for the following events:

kCFStreamEventNone

> Undefined event.

kCFStreamEventOpenCompleted

> The stream has been successfully opened and is ready for further operations.

`kCStreamEventCanAcceptBytes`

The stream is ready for writing.

`kCFStreamEventErrorOccurred`

An error has occurred on the read stream.

`kCFStreamEventEndEncountered`

An EOF (end-of-file) has been reached, and there is no more data available on the stream.

CFSocket Example: Joke Server

In this example, you'll put together your knowledge of the `CFSocket` and `CFSocket Context` structures, as well as streams to build a TCP server program that will tell the punch line to any joke asked of it. You'll store the joke's punch line in the `CFSocket Context` on the server side and provide the answer to the client. You'll notice an eerie similarity to standard C sockets programming, however the server example will show off the CFNetwork framework's run loop capabilities, which make socket management much easier.

The following code sets up the server socket. Comments have been provided inline:

```
/* The server socket */
CFSocketRef TCPServer;
#define PORT 2048

    /* The punchline to our joke */
char punchline[] = "To get to the other side!";

    /* Used by setsockopt */
int yes = 1;

    /* Build our socket context; this ties the punchline to the socket */
CFSocketContext CTX = {0, punchline, NULL, NULL, NULL};

    /* Create the server socket as a TCP IPv4 socket and set a callback */
    /* for calls to the socket's lower-level accept() function */
TCPServer = CFSocketCreate(kCFAllocatorDefault, PF_INET, SOCK_STREAM, IPPROTO_TCP,
    kCFSocketAcceptCallBack, (CFSocketCallBack)&AcceptCallback, &CTX);
if (TCPServer == NULL)
    return NULL;

    /* Re-use local addresses, if they're still in TIME_WAIT */
setsockopt(CFSocketGetNative(TCPSocket), SOL_SOCKET, SO_REUSEADDR,
    (void *)&yes, sizeof(yes));

/* Set the port and address we want to listen on */
struct sockaddr_in addr;
memset(&addr, 0, sizeof(addr));
addr.sin_len = sizeof(addr);
addr.sin_family = AF_INET;
addr.sin_port = htons(PORT);
addr.sin_addr.s_addr = htonl(INADDR_ANY);
```

```
NSData *address = [ NSData dataWithBytes: &addr, length:sizeof(addr) ];
if (CFSocketSetAddress(TCPServer, (CFDataRef)address) != kCFSocketSuccess) {
    fprintf(stderr, "CFSocketSetAddress() failed\n");
    CFRelease(TCPServer);
    return NULL;
}


CFRunLoopSourceRef sourceRef =
    CFSocketCreateRunLoopSource(kCFAllocatorDefault, TCPServer, 0);
CFRunLoopAddSource(CFRunLoopGetCurrent(), sourceRef, kCFRunLoopCommonModes);
CFRelease(sourceRef);

    /* Get on with our life, instead of waiting for incoming connections. */
```

Our listening socket is now set up, and a callback function will be invoked whenever a new connection is accepted. The callback function below is one example of how an incoming connection might be handled. In this example, the callback function creates and pairs a read and write stream to the socket. It then waits for the other end to tell a joke, then sends the punch line:

```
static void AcceptCallBack(CFSocketRef socket,
    CFSocketCallBackType type,
    CFDataRef address,
    const void *data,
    void *info)
{

    CFReadStreamRef readStream = NULL;
    CFWriteStreamRef writeStream = NULL;
    CFIndex bytes;
    UInt8 buffer[128];
    UInt8 recv_len = 0, send_len = 0;

    /* The native socket, used for various operations */
    CFSocketNativeHandle sock = *(CFSocketNativeHandle *) data;

    /* The punch line we stored in the socket context */
    char *punchline = info;

    /* Create the read and write streams for the socket */
    CFStreamCreatePairWithSocket(kCFAllocatorDefault, sock,
        &readStream, &writeStream);

    if (!readStream || !writeSream) {
        close(sock);
        fprintf(stderr, "CFStreamCreatePairWithSocket() failed\n");
        return;
    }

    /* Wait for the client to finish sending the joke; wait for newline */
    memset(buffer, 0, sizeof(buffer));
    while (!strchr(buffer, '\n') && recv_len < sizeof(buffer)) {
        bytes = CFReadStreamRead(readStream, buffer + recv_len,
            sizeof(buffer)-recv_len);
        if (bytes < 0) {
```

```
            fprintf(stderr, "CFReadStreamRead() failed\n");
            close(sock);
            return;
        }
        recv_len += bytes;
    }

    /* Send the punchline */
    while (send_len < (strlen(punchline+1))) {
    if (CFWriteStreamCanAcceptBytes(writeStream)) {
        bytes = CFWriteStreamWrite(writeStream,
            punchline + send_len,
            (strlen(punchline)+1) - send_len);
        if (bytes < 0) {
            fprintf(stderr, "CFWriteStreamWrite() failed\n");
            close(sock);
            return;
        }
        send_len += bytes;
    }
    }
    close(sock);
    return;
}
```

Further Study

- Have a look at *CFSocket.h*, *CFStream.h*, and *CFSocketContext.h*. You'll find these deep within your SDK's Core Foundation headers in */Developer/Platforms/ iPhoneOS.platform*.

CFHTTP and CFFTP

The CFNetwork framework provides easy APIs for making HTTP and FTP requests. You can make these requests through CFHTTP and CFFTP APIs. Rather than programming your application to speak a particular protocol, these APIs allow the framework to do all of the dirty work on your behalf, returning the raw protocol in a serialized form, which you can then send through a write stream connected to your desired host, or connect directly to a stream to open.

While many Cocoa classes, such as NSString and NSData, allow you to initialize objects with the contents of URLs, the CFHTTP and CFFTP APIs provide more granular control over the protocol layer, as you'll see in the examples to follow.

CFHTTP

You can use the CFHTTP API to create an HTTP request. This allows you to easily invoke HTTP GET, HEAD, PUT, POST, and most other standard requests. Creating a request involves the three-step process of creating the request object, defining the HTTP request message and headers, and serializing the message into raw protocol. Only HTTP POST requests generally contain a message body, which can contain POST form data to send. All other requests use an empty body while embedding the request parameters into the headers.

In the example below, an HTTP/1.1 GET request is created, specifying the URL *http://www.oreilly.com* and setting the Connection header to instruct the remote end to close the connection after sending data:

```
CFStringRef requestHeader = CFSTR("Connection");
CFStringRef requestHeaderValue = CFSTR("close");
CFStringRef requestBody = CFSTR("");

CFStringRef url = CFSTR("http://www.oreilly.com">http://www.oreilly.com");
CFStringRef requestMethod = CFSTR("GET");

CFURLRef requestURL = CFURLCreateWithString(kCFAllocatorDefault, url, NULL);
CFHTTPMessageRef request = CFHTTPMessageCreateRequest(kCFAllocatorDefault,
    requestMethod, requestURL, kCFHTTPVersion1_1);
CFHTTPMessageSetBody(request, requestBody);
CFHTTPMessageSetHeaderFieldValue(request, requestHeader, requestHeaderValue);

CFDataRef serializedRequest = CFHTTPMessageCopySerializedMessage(request);
```

The resulting pointer to a CFData structure provides the raw HTTP protocol output, which you would then send through a write stream to the destination server. In the example below, an HTTP GET request is created and opened through a read stream. As data flows in, the read stream's callbacks would normally be invoked to receive the new data:

```
int makeRequest(const char *requestURL)
{
    CFReadStream readStream;
    CFHTTPMessageRef request;
    CFStreamClientContext CTX = { 0, NULL, NULL, NULL, NULL };

    NSString* requestURLString = [ [ NSString alloc ] initWithCString:
        requestURL ];
    NSURL url = [ NSURL URLWithString: requestURLString ];

    CFStringRef requestMessage = CFSTR("");

    request = CFHTTPMessageCreateRequest(kCFAllocatorDefault, CFSTR("GET"),
        (CFURLRef) url, kCFHTTPVersion1_1);
    if (!request) {
        return -1;
    }
    CFHTTPMessageSetBody(request, (CFDataRef) requestMessage);
    readStream = CFReadStreamCreateForHTTPRequest(kCFAllocatorDefault, request);
    CFRelease(request);

    if (!readStream) {
        return -1;
    }
```

```
        if (!CFReadStreamSetClient(readStream, kCFStreamEventOpenCompleted |
                                               kCFStreamEventHasBytesAvailable |
                                               kCFStreamEventEndEncountered |
                                               kCFStreamEventErrorOccurred,
            ReadCallBack, &CTX))
        {
            CFRelease(readStream);
            return -1;    }

            /* Add to the run loop */
        CFReadStreamScheduleWithRunLoop(readStream, CFRunLoopGetCurrent(),
            kCFRunLoopCommonModes);

        if (!CFReadStreamOpen(readStream)) {
            CFReadStreamSetClient(readStream, 0, NULL, NULL);
            CFReadStreamUnscheduleFromRunLoop(readStream,
                CFRunLoopGetCurrent(),
                kCFRunLoopCommonModes);
            CFRelease(readStream);
            return -1;
        }

        return 0;
    }
```

CFFTP

The CFFTP API is similar to the CFHTTP API, and relies on read streams to transmit
FTP data. To create an FTP request, use the CFReadStreamCreateWithFTPURL function,
as shown below. This will create the initial read stream to the FTP server:

```
CFStringRef url = CFSTR("ftp://ftp.somedomain.com/file.txt");
CFURLRef requestURL = CFURLCreateWithString(kCFAllocatorDefault, url, NULL);

CFReadStreamRef readStream = CFReadStreamCreateWithFTPURL(
    kCFAllocatorDefault, requestURL);
```

Once you have created the read stream, you can tie a callback function to it so that a
read function will be called when data is ready:

```
CFReadStreamSetClient(
    readStream,
    kCFtreamEventHasBytesAvailable,
    readCallBack,
    NULL);
```

The callback function will be called whenever data is available, and will be able to read
the data off the stream:

```
void readCallBack(
    CFReadStreamRef stream,
    CFStreamEventType eventType,
    void *clientCallBackInfo)
{
    char buffer[1024];
```

```
        CFIndex bytes_recvd;
        int recv_len = 0;

        while(recv_len < total_size && recv_len < sizeof(buffer)) {
            bytes_recvd = CFReadStreamRead(stream, buffer + recv_len,
                sizeof(buffer) - recv_len);

            /* Write bytes to output or file here */
        }
        recv_len += bytes_recvd;
    }
```

You can now schedule the request in your main program's run loop, As the read stream is presented with data, your read callback will be invoked and will continue to perform on the data until the connection is closed or until the file has been completed:

```
CFReadStreamScheduleWithRunLoop(readStream,
    CFRunLoopGetCurrent(), kCFRunLoopCommonModes);
```

Further Study

- Have a look at *CFFTPStream.h*, *CFHTTPStream.h*, and *CFNetwork.h*. You'll find these deep within your SDK's Core Foundation headers in */Developer/Platforms/ iPhoneOS.platform*.

CHAPTER 8

Getting a Fix: Core Location

The Core Location framework provides access to the iPhone's geographical location systems. These include an integrated GPS, WiFi-based location positioning, and tower triangulation. The iPhone is a very location-aware device, and even stores the GPS coordinates to nearby towers in its cache. Using the Core Location framework, you're able to obtain the device's longitude and latitude coordinates, altitude, and other important data. Core Location uses a type of streaming notification so that your application receives updates as the GPS ascertains a more accurate fix.

Apple added a basic level of security to the Core Location interface, and when your application attempts to use it, the user will be prompted whether to allow it access to his current location. If the user restricts your application from using Core Location, you'll need to be prepared to deliver any remaining portions of your application's functionality without this information, or prompt the user for a zip code or other information. In addition to a user prompt, Apple has incorporated a Core Location blacklist into the iPhone's firmware. The iPhone will query this list on Apple's servers whenever it performs a lookup, and will kill any applications that have been blacklisted.

The process of performing a location lookup is relatively power-intensive, as it queries GPS satellites, local towers, and WiFi hotspots, so be conservative in your use of Core Location to avoid draining the user's battery.

To use the Core Location framework, you'll need to add it to your Xcode project. Right-click the *Frameworks* folder in your project, and then choose Add→Existing Framework. Navigate to the *CoreLocation.framework* folder, and then click Add.

 At the time of this writing, applications providing turn-by-turn directions or aviation-based navigation tools are restricted, by policy, from the AppStore. Be sure to check your agreements with Apple to ensure that its use of this information does not violate their terms.

The Core Location Manager

All Core Location functions are performed through a Core Location manager. The manager's function is to act as a query interface for your application. You'll instantiate a manager to set up and execute location-based queries, and again when you're finished, to turn the GPS off. The manager is instantiated as a CLLocationManager object. Queries for your location are not returned immediately. Instead, your application will be notified when information (or updates) to the user's whereabouts are ascertained. This information is periodically sent to the manager's delegate, which must implement the CLLocationManagerDelegate protocol. Subsequent updates to the device's location are sent as Core Location begins receiving more accurate information, or if the device is moved beyond a distance threshold set by the programmer.

In Example 8-1, you'll create your own class to act as a query class. The query class will act as delegate, invoke the Core Location manager class, receive notifications, and eventually release the manager when finished.

Example 8-1. MyCLQuery class definition

```
@interface MyCLQuery : NSObject
{
    CLLocationManager *manager;
}
- (void)startQuery;
- (void)stopQuery;
- (void)locationManager:(CLLocationManager *)locationManager
    didUpdateToLocation:(CLLocation *)newLocation
    fromLocation:(CLLocation *)oldLocation;
```

The MyCLQuery example class uses three methods. The startQuery method sets up the CLLocationManager object and begins the location query process. Once activated, the location manager runs in the background to determine your current position. As a fix is acquired, or the location changes, the didUpdateToLocation method is notified. This is the method responsible for reporting the new location to your application. Finally, when you're finished using Core Location, the stopQuery method must be called to turn off updates.

Query Parameters

You will need to supply some query parameters to tell Core Location what kind of information you need. These pertain to the level of accuracy needed, and when to send updates to your delegate. For example, an application designed to find the nearest restaurant might require less specific information than a geo-caching application, which would need very specific data about the user's position. If your application will be used at high velocities (such as while driving or on a bus), it might only require updates every few hundred feet; an application designed to be used on foot would call for more frequent updates.

You should configure at least three parameters before instructing the manager to begin a location lookup:

delegate

> This is the object that will receive location updates. The delegate object will need to have a proper implementation of the `CLLocationManagerDelegate` protocol. The delegate will be notified through its `didUpdateToLocation` method to receive these notifications from the Core Location manager, as shown in Example 8-1. In the examples throughout this chapter, `MyCLQuery` object will serve as the delegate.

desiredAccuracy

> Instructs the location manager as to what level of accuracy you need in your application. To conserve battery and to avoid unnecessary updates, use the least specific level of accuracy required for your particular purpose. Different levels of accuracy are returned by different facilities; for example, if only a single cell tower is within the signal's reach, Core Location might initially return a very large location breadth. As Core Location continues to receive more specific information back from WiFi lookups and the GPS, it will notify your application of the better fix. You may use the following settings, which instruct Core Location just how hard to work to acquire the user's position:

> kCLLocationAccuracyBest
> > Deliver the best possible accuracy

> kCLLocationAccuracyNearestTenMeters
> > Deliver accuracy within 10 meters (about 30 feet)

> kCLLocationAccuracyHundredMeters
> > Deliver accuracy within 100 meters (about 300 feet)

> kCLLocationAccuracyKilometer
> > Deliver accuracy within 1 kilometer (about 6/10 of a mile)

> kCLLocationAccuracyThreeKilometers
> > Deliver accuracy within 3 kilometers (about a mile and a half)

 One meter is equal to 1.09 yards. One kilometer is equal to 0.62 miles.

distanceFilter

> Sets the minimum amount of movement (in meters) before an update is sent to the delegate. Further updates will not be sent unless the device's position has moved by at least this value, or if the level of accuracy improves. To send updates for any movement, use the value `kCLDistanceFilterNone`.

Issuing a Query

Once you've determined what kind of Core Location query your application requires, you can instantiate a manager and assign it your query parameters. In the example below, a startQuery method is used to set up the query and invoke Core Location. The code below requests the best possible accuracy and asks for continual updates for any movement. Finally, it invokes the Core Location manager's startUpdatingLocation method, which initiates a location lookup and notifications to follow:

```
- (void) startQuery
{
    manager = [[ CLLocationManager alloc ] init ];

    manager.delegate = self;

    manager.desiredAccuracy = kCLLocationAccuracyBest;
    manager.distanceFilter = kCLDistanceFilterNone;

    NSLog(@"Core Location updates started");
    [ manager startUpdatingLocation ];
}
```

Receiving Updates

The MyCLQuery object in our example will serve as the delegate, so you'll need to implement the delegate's protocol methods. The Core Location manager provides two results pointing to both the new and old locations, making it easy to recognize movement. The following information is available from both of these CLLocation objects:

Longitude and latitude
> The longitude and latitude is read through the coordinate structure, accessible from the CLLocation object. This structure contains latitude and longitude members, both represented as double floating point; this is typed to a CLLocationDegrees data type.

Altitude
> The altitude property reads the altitude in meters. This value can be positive or negative, indicating the number of meters above or below sea level. This value is returned as a double floating point, and is typed to a CLLocationDistance.

Accuracy
> The horizontal and vertical accuracy is reported as a CLLocationAccuracy (double floating point) type. These values, accessible via the horizontalAccuracy and verticalAccuracy properties, will reflect the accuracy (in meters) of the coordinates and altitude provided. You're not always guaranteed to get the level of accuracy you requested, so it's important to check this to determine the overall radius of the position returned. As the accuracy continues to improve, these values will also be updated in subsequent notifications.

Timestamp

Updates are sent periodically as the accuracy of the GPS improves, or when the device is moved a given distance. If your application is time-critical, you can ensure that the data being reported back to it is recent by checking the `timestamp` property, which is an `NSDate` object containing the timestamp of the query.

Because Core Location uses many different facilities to acquire a location fix, it's possible that newer fixes might report back to the application with older timestamps than the previous location. For example, a global positioning query may take several seconds to return, whereas a WiFi location lookup may take less than a second. As a result, the more specific location returned with the satellite query will have an older query timestamp. The best way to handle this is to accept the newer information if it is more specific, and provide a visual indicator to the user that your application has narrowed down his location.

Description

Core Location also provides an `NSString` object describing the overall location. You can access this through the `description` property. Apple does not guarantee the formatting, so because this is subject to change, it is not a very good idea to parse data based on the description. It can be useful, however, to display to the user, or for debugging.

The example below receives notifications sent by the Core Location manager and logs the output to the console:

```
- (void)locationManager:(CLLocationManager *)locationManager
didUpdateToLocation:(CLLocation *)newLocation
fromLocation:(CLLocation *)oldLocation
{
    NSLog(@"Old Coordinates: %+.6f, %+.6f\n",
        oldLocation.coordinate.latitude,
        oldLocation.coordinate.longitude);
    NSLog(@"New Coordinates: %+.6f, %+.6f\n",
        newLocation.coordinate.latitude,
        newLocation.coordinate.longitude);
    NSLog(@"Altitude: %.6f\n", newLocation.altitude);
    NSLog(@"Description: %@\n", [ newLocation description ]);

    NSDate *timestamp = newLocation.timestamp;
    NSTimeInterval age = [ timestamp timeIntervalSinceNow ];
    NSLog(@"Notification age: %.4f\n", age);
}
```

Completing a Query

When your application is satisfied with the location information it has received, be sure to stop the manager to avoid draining the battery. This will also stop updates from being sent to your application. You can accomplish this through a simple call to the manager's `stopUpdatingLocation` method:

```
- (void) stopQuery
{
    [ manager stopUpdatingLocation ];
    [ manager release ];
}
```

Error Handling

An error can occur if the current position couldn't be ascertained or if the user denied the application from using his current location. When either of these occurs, a method named `didFailWithError` will notify the delegate of a failure:

```
- (void)locationManager:(CLLocationManager *)locationManager
      didFailWithError:(NSError *)error
{
    NSLog(@"Core Location failed with error: %@\n", [ error code ]);
}
```

The `didFailWithError` method supplies an `NSError` object, which is a standard Cocoa object used to report errors. The error code returned with the `NSError` object identifies the type of failure:

kCLErrorLocationUnknown

> Could not ascertain location. When this error is indicated, Core Location continues trying to get a fix in the background and will send an update if one becomes available. If your application decides to time out the query, ensure that it uses the manager's `stopUpdatingLocation` method to shut down Core Location.

> When this occurs, its best to notify the user that your application had trouble determining his location while still giving him the impression that it is continuing to scan. The easiest way to do this is with an activity indicator, which is explained in Chapter 10.

kCLErrorDenied

> The user denied your application access to Core Location. When this occurs, your application should be prepared to either continue on without the location or prompt the user for manual input, such as a zip code.

WhereYouAt: Redneck Core Location

If you've ever lived in the south, at some point someone has used the standard redneck vernacular, "where you at?" to acquire your position. This example demonstrates Core Location by querying a `CLLocationManager` object for the current location. When provided, this information will be presented in a text view to the user. Like most rednecks, it's nothing fancy—just a lot of fun.

This application, shown in Examples 8-2 through 8-6 can be compiled with the SDK by creating a *view-based application* project named *WhereYouAt*. Be sure to pull out the Interface Builder code if you'd like to see how these objects are created from scratch.

Example 8-2. WhereYouAt application delegate prototypes (WhereYouAtAppDelegate.h)

```
#import <UIKit/UIKit.h>

@class WhereYouAtViewController;

@interface WhereYouAtAppDelegate : NSObject <UIApplicationDelegate> {
    UIWindow *window;
    WhereYouAtViewController *viewController;
}

@property (nonatomic, retain) IBOutlet UIWindow *window;
@property (nonatomic, retain) IBOutlet WhereYouAtViewController *viewController;

@end
```

Example 8-3. WhereYouAt application delegate (WhereYouAtAppDelegate.m)

```
#import "WhereYouAtAppDelegate.h"
#import "WhereYouAtViewController.h"

@implementation WhereYouAtAppDelegate

@synthesize window;
@synthesize viewController;


- (void)applicationDidFinishLaunching:(UIApplication *)application {
    CGRect screenBounds = [ [ UIScreen mainScreen ] bounds ];

    self.window = [ [ [ UIWindow alloc ] initWithFrame: screenBounds ]
        autorelease
    ];

    viewController = [ [ WhereYouAtViewController alloc ] init ];

    [ window addSubview: viewController.view ];
    [ window makeKeyAndVisible ];
}

- (void)dealloc {
    [ viewController release ];
    [ window release ];
    [ super dealloc ];
}


@end
```

Example 8-4. WhereYouAt view controller prototypes (WhereYouAtViewController.h)

```
#import <UIKit/UIKit.h>
#import <CoreLocation/CoreLocation.h>

@interface WhereYouAtViewController : UIViewController <CLLocationManagerDelegate> {
    UITextView *textView;
```

```
    CLLocationManager *gps;
}

@end
```

Example 8-5. WhereYouAt view controller (WhereYouAtViewController.m)

```objc
#import "WhereYouAtViewController.h"

@implementation WhereYouAtViewController

- (void)loadView {
    [ super loadView ];
    textView = [ [ UITextView alloc ] initWithFrame: self.view.frame ];
    self.view = textView;
}

- (void)viewDidLoad {
    textView.text = @"Where you at? ...";
    gps = [ [ CLLocationManager alloc ] init ];
    gps.delegate = self;
    gps.desiredAccuracy = kCLLocationAccuracyBest;
    gps.distanceFilter = kCLDistanceFilterNone;
    [ gps startUpdatingLocation ];

}

- (void)locationManager:(CLLocationManager *)locationManager
    didUpdateToLocation:(CLLocation *)newLocation
           fromLocation:(CLLocation *)oldLocation;
{
    textView.text = [ NSString stringWithFormat: @"You now at...\n\n"
        "Description: %@\n"
        "Coordinates: %f, %f\n"
        "Altitude: %f\n"
        "Updated: %@\n",
        newLocation.description,
        newLocation.coordinate.latitude,
        newLocation.coordinate.longitude,
        newLocation.altitude,
        newLocation.timestamp ];
}

- (void)didReceiveMemoryWarning {
    [ super didReceiveMemoryWarning ];
}

- (void)dealloc {
    [ textView release ];
    [ super dealloc ];
}
@end
```

Example 8-6. WhereYouAt main (main.m)

```
#import <UIKit/UIKit.h>

int main(int argc, char *argv[]) {

    NSAutoreleasePool * pool = [ [ NSAutoreleasePool alloc ] init ];
    int retVal = UIApplicationMain(argc, argv, nil, @"WhereYouAtAppDelegate");
    [ pool release ];
    return retVal;
}
```

What's Going On

The *WhereYouAt* demo is a simple, yet useful example. Here's how it works:

1. When the application instantiates, it notifies the `WhereYouAtAppDelegate` class, which in turn builds the window and view controller.

2. When the view controller is loaded, it builds a `UITextView` object and sets it as the active view. This is where information is displayed to the user.

3. After the view is loaded, the `viewDidLoad` view controller method creates an instance of the `CLLocationManager` class and issues a query.

4. Whenever new location information is ascertained, the `didUpdateToLocation` delegate method is invoked with the latest location information. This is, in turn, displayed to the user.

Further Study

- You can find a great wealth of information about Core Location queries in *CLLocation.h* and *CLLocationManager.h*. You'll find these deep within your SDK's *CoreLocation.framework* headers in */Developer/Platforms/iPhoneOS.platform*.

CHAPTER 9

Address Book Frameworks

The iPhone SDK provides two frameworks for managing the address book: a low-level data access framework (*AddressBook.framework*) and a high-level user interface kit (*AddressBookUI.framework*). Because your application runs in a sandbox, it's not allowed to directly interface with the address book's underlying SQLite database. In this chapter, you'll learn how to query contact information using C-language function calls and how to use the UI for selecting contacts.

If your application is using the address book, you'll need to learn about the C-based data access functions, whether or not you choose to add an address book user interface. These functions allow you to read and write information about contacts. Since you're dealing with another individual's personal data, it's very important to ensure that your code is accurate and respectful of the user's wishes before changing anything. Unlike the Core Location framework, the user is never prompted to grant permission to your application before using the address book. This could change in future versions of iPhone firmware, due to the privacy risk it poses. Using the address book frameworks to harvest personal information about the user's contacts violates Apple's terms and conditions, and is possibly illegal in many countries.

To use the Address Book or Address Book UI frameworks, you'll need to add them to your Xcode project. Right-click on the *Frameworks* folder in your project, and then choose Add Framework. Navigate to the *AddressBook.framework* folder, and then click Add. Repeat this process to add the *AddressBookUI.framework* folder.

 To find the address book frameworks, you may have to navigate manually into either */Developer/Platforms/iPhoneOS.platform* or */Developer/Platforms/iPhoneSimulator.platform* and locate the *Frameworks* folder in your SDK.

Address Book Access

The interfaces for accessing the address book and individual contact data are C-based functions, which pass references around for various address book objects. The base object for managing address book entries is an `ABRecord`. An `ABRecord` can represent either a single person (`ABPerson`) or a group (`ABGroup`). Whenever a record is selected in the address book's UI or returned from a query using the framework, the system returns a pointer to an `ABRecord`, represented as `ABRecordRef`. A majority of your interaction with the address book API will involve working with `ABRecordRef` references.

An `ABRecordRef`, which represents a reference to exactly one contact, has many functions used to read or write information. You'll learn about many of these functions in this chapter. The most generic functions used to interact with records follow:

`ABRecordID ABRecordGetRecordID(ABRecordRef record);`
> Returns an `ABRecordID`; a 32-bit integer representing the ID of the record within the database. This can be useful when you need a primary key to keep track of multiple records. You can also query by record ID, as you'll learn in this chapter.

`ABRecordType ABRecordGetRecordType(ABRecordRef record);`
> Returns the type of entity that this record represents. Possible values for `ABRecordType` can correspond to either a person (`kABPersonType`) or a group (`kABGroupType`).

`CFStringRef ABRecordCopyCompositeName(ABRecordRef record);`
> Returns the full name of the person or group. All `CFStringRef` data types can be cast to an `NSString *`, giving you access to an `NSString` object containing the record name. For example, `NSString *name = (NSString *) ABRecordCopyComposite Name(record);`.

Top-Level Address Book Functions

You must initialize the address book before you can read from it or write to it. Use the `ABAddressBookCreate` function to obtain a handle to the address book:

```
#import <AddressBook/AddressBook.h>

ABAddressBookRef ab = ABAddressBookCreate();
```

You must explicitly save any changes that you make to the address book. When you're finished editing and want to commit changes, invoke the `ABAddressBookSave` function to do this:

```
CFErrorRef error;
BOOL success = ABAddressBookSave(ab, &error);
```

If you're not sure whether the address book needs to be saved, use the `ABAddress BookHasUnsavedChanges` function:

```
BOOL hasUnsavedChanges = ABAddressBookHasUnsavedChanges(ab);
```

To add or remove records, use the `ABAddressBookAddRecord` and `ABAddress BookRemoveRecord` functions:

```
CFErrorRef error;
BOOL success = ABAddressBookAddRecord(ab, myRecord, &error);
BOOL success = ABAddressBookRemoveRecord(ab, myRecord, &error);
```

Querying the Address Book

The Address Book framework provides only basic query functionality. Functions exist to query multiple records by name, or individual records by specific record IDs.

To obtain a count of the total number of records in the address book, use the `ABAddressBookGetPersonCount` function. This function returns a `CFIndex`, which is typed to a 32-bit integer:

```
CFIndex count = ABAddressBookGetPersonCount(ab);
NSLog(@"%ld total entries in the address book", count);
```

Two functions exist to query multiple address book records. Both return a `CFArrayRef`, which can be cast to an `NSArray *`; that is, a pointer to an `NSArray` object.

To obtain a list of all contacts in the database, use the `ABAddressBookCopyArrayOfAll People` function:

```
NSArray *array = (NSArray *)ABAddressBookCopyArrayOfAllPeople(ab);
NSLog(@"Retrieved %d contacts\n", [ array count ]);
```

To search the contact list for a specific name, use the `ABAddressBookCopyPeopleWith Name` function. You can search by first name, last name, or both. All matching records will be returned in the array:

```
NSArray *array = (NSArray *)ABAddressBookCopyPeopleWithName(ab,
    CFSTR("John Appleseed));
```

As the function names imply, the objects being returned are not the actual objects in the address book, but rather copies. To access the individual records within the array, use the `NSArray` class's `objectAtIndex` method:

```
ABRecordRef record = [ people objectAtIndex: 0 ];
```

In addition to querying multiple contacts, if you know the record ID of the contact you'd like to load, you can load it directly using the `ABAddressBookGetPerson WithRecordID` function:

```
ABRecordRef record = ABAddressBookGetPersonWithRecordID(ab, recordId);
```

Creating Records

To create a new contact, use the `ABPersonCreate` function. This will give you an empty record you can later add information to:

```
ABRecordRef record = ABPersonCreate();
```

Working with Records

Once you have an `ABRecordRef` in hand, you'll determine whether the record is that of a person or a group so you can access more specific information. First name, last name, and other pieces of information are all referred to as *properties*. An entity only has properties if it is an ABPerson record, and a varying amount of information will be available for each record.

To query information for a given record, use the ABRecordCopyValue function. The function prototype follows:

```
CFTypeRef ABRecordCopyValue(ABRecordRef record, ABPropertyID property);
```

When called, the ABRecordCopyValue function copies the property you specify and returns a reference:

```
CFStringRef firstName = ABRecordCopyValue(myRecord, kABPersonFirstNameProperty);
```

Because the kABPersonFirstNameProperty property is a CFStringRef, you may choose to cast it to an NSString *:

```
NSString *firstName = (NSString *) ABRecordCopyValue(myRecord,
    kABPersonFirstNameProperty);
```

Just as a CFStringRef can be cast to an NSString *, any property returning a CFDateRef can be cast to an NSDate *:

```
NSDate *birthday = (NSDate *) ABRecordCopyValue(myRecord,
    kABPersonBirthdayProperty);
```

The ABPropertyID you specified above is a value corresponding to the information you're looking up in the record. Properties for the ABPerson object follow. Because the data type returned by the ABRecordCopyValue function is a generic CFTypeRef, the resulting value can be cast to a more specific data type designed for that property.

Property	Description	Data type
kABPersonFirstNameProperty	First Name	CFStringRef
kABPersonLastNameProperty	Last name	CFStringRef
kABPersonMiddleNameProperty	Middle name	CFStringRef
kABPersonPrefixProperty	Surname; "Sir"	CFStringRef
kABPersonSuffixProperty	Suffix, "Jr." or "Sr."	CFStringRef
kABPersonNicknameProperty	Nickname	CFStringRef
kABPersonFirstNamePhoneticProperty	First name; phonetic	CFStringRef
kABPersonLastNamePhoneticProperty	Last name; phonetic	CFStringRef
kABPersonMiddleNamePhoneticProperty	Mid name; phonetic	CFStringRef
kABPersonOrganizationProperty	Company name	CFStringRef
kABPersonJobTitleProperty	Job title	CFStringRef
kABPersonDepartmentProperty	Department	CFStringRef
kABPersonBirthdayProperty	Birthday	CFDateRef
kABPersonNoteProperty	Notes	CFStringRef
kABPersonCreationDateProperty	Creation date	CFDateRef

Property	Description	Data type
kABPersonModificationDateProperty	Date last modified	CFDateRef
kABPersonKindProperty	Contact type	Enumeration

Writing properties

To write a property to an address book record, use the `ABRecordSetValue` function:

```
CFErrorRef error;
CFStringRef nickname = CFSTR("Sparky");
BOOL success = ABRecordSetValue(record, kABPersonNicknameProperty,
    nickname, &error);
```

To delete a property, use the `ABRecordRemoveValue` function:

```
CFErrorRef error;
BOOL success = ABRecordRemoveValue(myRecord, kABPersonNicknameProperty, &error);
```

When you have finished editing a record, don't forget to save the address book:

```
CFErrorRef error;
BOOL success = ABAddressBookSave(ab, &error);
```

Multivalue Properties

In addition to the properties listed previously, certain values for a record may contain multiple values. Multivalue properties are handled using an indexing mechanism, where the total number of values is first queried, followed by a call to retrieve an entry at a particular index. A pointer to the multivalue data is first obtained using the `ABRecordCopyValue` method previously described, and is cast to an `ABMultiValueRef`:

```
ABMultiValueRef phoneNumbers = ABRecordCopyValue(myRecord, kABPersonPhoneProperty);
```

You can then use the reference to determine the number of values and to retrieve individual values by index. The `ABMultiValueGetCount` function returns the number of items, and the `ABMultiValueCopyValueAtIndex` function copies the item at the index you specify:

```
NSMutableArray *phoneNumbersList = [ [ NSMutableArray alloc ] init ];

CFIndex nPhoneNumbers = ABMultiValueGetCount(phoneNumbers);
for(int i=0;i<nPhoneNumbers;i++) {
    NSString *phoneNumber = (NSString *)ABMultiValueCopyValueAtIndex(
        phoneNumbers, i);
    [ phoneNumbersList addObject: phoneNumber ];
    [ phoneNumber release ];
}
```

The following data types describe an individual entry within the multivalue properties listed.

Property	Description	Data type
kABPersonEmailProperty	Email addresses	CFStringRef
kABPersonAddressProperty	Address	CFDictionaryRef
kABPersonDateProperty	Associated dates	CFDateRef
kABPersonPhoneProperty	Phone numbers	CFStringRef
kABPersonInstantMessageProperty	IM IDs	CFDictionaryRef
kABPersonURLProperty	Website URLs	CFStringRef
kABPersonRelatedNamesProperty	Related names	CFStringRef

In addition to the actual entries within a multivalue property, entries are also given a label. The label describes the type of entry being returned. For example, labels for individual phone numbers might specify that the number is a home or mobile number. Labels for addresses might describe home or work addresses. To query the label for a given entry, use the ABMultiValueCopyLabelAtIndex function:

```
CFStringRef label = ABMultiValueCopyLabelAtIndex(phoneNumbers, i);
```

Certain properties have a defined set of labels. The following CFStringRef labels are specified in the *ABPerson.h* prototypes:

kABPersonDateProperty
      kABPersonAnniversaryLabel

kABPersonPhoneProperty
      kABPersonPhoneMobileLabel
      kABPersonPhoneMainLabel
      kABPersonPhoneHomeFAXLabel
      kABPersonPhoneWorkFAXLabel
      kABPersonPhonePagerLabel

kABPersonInstantMessageProperty
    Applies to the kABPersonInstantMessageServiceKey key within the dictionary:

      kABPersonInstantMessageServiceYahoo
      kABPersonInstantMessageServiceJabber
      kABPersonInstantMessageServiceMSN
      kABPersonInstantMessageServiceICQ
      kABPersonInstantMessageServiceAIM

kABPersonURLProperty
      kABPersonHomePageLabel

kABPersonRelatedNamesProperty
      kABPersonFatherLabel
      kABPersonMotherLabel
      kABPersonParentLabel

```
kABPersonBrotherLabel
kABPersonSisterLabel
kABPersonChildLabel
kABPersonFriendLabel
kABPersonSpouseLabel
kABPersonPartnerLabel
kABPersonAssistantLabel
kABPersonManagerLabel
```

Many properties use a generic set of labels for work, home, and other locations. These generic labels follow:

```
kABWorkLabel
kABHomeLabel
kABOtherLabel
```

Writing multivalue entries

In order to add a value to an existing multivalue property, you must first copy the multivalue dictionary from the record. You'll then operate on the new copy by adding a new value/label pair using the ABMultiValueAddValueAndLabel function. Finally, use the ABRecordSetValue function to write the entire dictionary back to the address book record, effectively replacing the entire multivalue property. In the example to follow, a new URL is added to the kABPersonURLProperty property:

```
CFErrorRef error;
ABMultiValueRef URLs = ABRecordCopyValue(myRecord, kABPersonURLProperty);
ABMutableMultiValueRef copyOfURLs = ABMultiValueCreateMutableCopy(URLs);
ABMultiValueAddValueAndLabel(copyOfURLs, "http://www.oreilly.com",
    kABPersonHomePageLabel, NULL);
ABRecordSetValue(myRecord, kABPersonURLProperty, copyOfURLs, &error);
```

To delete a value/label pair, use the ABMultiValueRemoveValueAndLabelAtIndex function:

```
CFErrorRef error;
ABMultiValueRef URLs = ABRecordCopyValue(myRecord, kABPersonURLProperty);
ABMutableMultiValueRef copyOfURLs = ABMultiValueCreateMutableCopy(URLs);
ABMultiValueRemoveValueAndLabelAtIndex(copyOfURLs, 0);
ABRecordSetValue(myRecord, kABPersonURLProperty, copyOfURLs, &error);
```

Be sure to save the record using the ABAddressBookSave function:

```
ABAddressBookSave(ab, &error);
```

Working with Dictionaries

Address book records use dictionaries to describe addresses and instant messenger accounts. These dictionaries are embedded within multivalue entries. To access these, copy the value and cast it to an NSDictionary *. From here, you'll be able to access the dictionary using a set of predefined keys:

```
ABMultiValueRef addresses = ABRecordCopyValue(record, kABPersonAddressProperty);

CFIndex nAddresses = ABMultiValueGetCount(addresses);
NSLog(@"%d addresses\n", nAddresses);

NSDictionary *address = ABMultiValueCopyValueAtIndex(addresses, 0);
for (id key in address)
{
    NSLog(@"key: %@, value: %@", key, [ address objectForKey: key ]);
}
```

The following keys are used for dictionary properties stored in the address book:

kABPersonAddressProperty
> kABPersonAddressStreetKey
> kABPersonAddressCityKey
> kABPersonAddressStateKey
> kABPersonAddressZIPKey
> kABPersonAddressCountryKey
> kABPersonAddressCountryCodeKey

kABPersonInstantMessengerProperty
> kABPersonInstantMessageServiceKey
> kABPersonInstantMessageUsernameKey

Image Data

Some contacts may have an image associated with them. Use the `ABPersonCopyImage Data` function to obtain the image data, returned as a `CFDataRef`. You can cast this to an `NSData *`, which can initialize a `UIImage` object. You learned about the `UIImage` class in previous chapters, and will read more about them in Chapter 10.

```
if (ABPersonHasImageData(myRecord)) {
    UIImage *addressBookImage = [ UIImage imageWithData:
        (NSData *) ABPersonCopyImageData(myRecord)
    ];
}
```

Further Study

- You can find a great wealth of information about address book properties and functions in the prototypes found inside the *AddressBook.framework* header directories. You'll find these deep within */Developer/Platforms/iPhoneOS.platform/* in your SDK headers.

Address Book UI

The Address Book UI framework provides two key user interfaces: a people "picker" navigation controller to choose contacts, and a view controller to display a single contact.

Person Views

The `ABPersonViewController` provides a simple interface to display a single contact to the user. The person view requires a `CFRecordRef`, which you learned about earlier in the chapter. This record is passed to the person view, which performs all the grunt work of loading and displaying the individual's contact information.

You create an `ABPersonViewController` in the same fashion as any other view controller:

```
ABPersonViewController *viewController = [ [ ABPersonViewController alloc ]
    init
];
```

Set the desired record to display to the `displayedPerson` property:

```
viewController.displayedPerson = myRecord;
```

Next, you'll create an array of properties you'd like to display to the user. Only the properties you specify will be displayed unless the contact is edited, in which case all will be displayed. The properties available are the same enumerated values you learned about earlier in this chapter. Each is added as an `NSNumber` object:

```
NSMutableArray *properties = [ [ NSMutableArray alloc ] init ];
[ properties addObject: [ NSNumber numberWithInt: kABPersonFirstNameProperty ]];
[ properties addObject: [ NSNumber numberWithInt: kABPersonLastNameProperty ]];
[ properties addObject: [ NSNumber numberWithInt: kABPersonOrganizationProperty ]];
viewController.displayedProperties = properties;
```

If you would like the user to be able to edit the contact, set the `allowsEditing` property to YES:

```
viewController.allowsEditing = YES;
```

People Pickers

If your application has a need to display a list of contacts to the user, the `ABPeoplePickerNavigationController` class was designed with you in mind. This navigation controller displays a list of contacts and allows the user to select one. Once selected, you can choose to display the contact to the user or use a delegate method to add your own behavior once the individual has been selected.

To create a people picker, instantiate an `ABPeoplePickerNavigationController` object:

```
ABPeoplePickerNavigationController *peoplePicker = [
    [ ABPeoplePickerNavigationController alloc ] init
];
```

If your picker will allow the user to view an individual contact, you'll assign a set of properties you wish the user to see. The default is to show the user all available fields. The properties available are the same enumerated values you learned about earlier in this chapter. Each is added as an NSNumber object:

```
NSMutableArray *properties = [ [ NSMutableArray alloc ] init ];
[ properties addObject: [ NSNumber numberWithInt: kABPersonFirstNameProperty ]];
[ properties addObject: [ NSNumber numberWithInt: kABPersonLastNameProperty ]];
[ properties addObject: [ NSNumber numberWithInt: kABPersonOrganizationProperty ]];
peoplePicker.displayedProperties = properties;
```

To assign a delegate to receive notifications when the user selects a person, assign your delegate to the peoplePickerDelegate property of the picker:

```
peoplePicker.peoplePickerDelegate = self;
```

You can then add the navigation controller to a window or existing view:

```
[ window addSubview: [ peoplePicker view ] ];
```

Delegate methods

Three delegate methods are invoked for different people picker actions. If the user decides to cancel his selection, the peoplePickerNavigationControllerDidCancel is notified. This method should gracefully handle a failure to select a contact:

```
- (void)peoplePickerNavigationControllerDidCancel:
    (ABPeoplePickerNavigationController *)peoplePicker
{
    /* Additional code to handle cancel */
}
```

When a person is selected, the delegate is notified with the ABRecordRef of the selected user and is consulted about whether it should continue. If the delegate returns YES, the contact is displayed to the user with an internal ABPersonViewController created by the people picker. If your application will perform some other action, return NO here and transition to a different screen:

```
- (BOOL)peoplePickerNavigationController:
    (ABPeoplePickerNavigationController *)peoplePicker
     shouldContinueAfterSelectingPerson:(ABRecordRef)person
{
    /* Additional code to handle contact selection */
}
```

If the user taps a property within the contact display, a third notification is sent to the delegate containing the selected property. This also asks the user if it should continue. If your application will perform some other action when the user selects a property, return NO here and transition to a different screen:

```
- (BOOL)peoplePickerNavigationController:
    (ABPeoplePickerNavigationController *)peoplePicker
     shouldContinueAfterSelectingPerson:(ABRecordRef)person
     property:(ABPropertyID)property
```

```
    identifier:(ABMultiValueIdentifier)identifier
{
    /* Additional code to handle property selection */
}
```

Further Study

- You can find additional information about the address book controller and properties inside the *AddressBookUI.framework* header directories. You'll find these
  deep within */Developer/Platforms/iPhoneOS.platform/* in your SDK headers.

CHAPTER 10

Advanced UI Kit Design

Chapter 3 introduced the UI Kit framework, which is at the heart of all GUI applications on the iPhone. This chapter covers the more complex and aesthetically rich components of the iPhone's user interface framework and shows you some advanced techniques to make your own software look as spectacular as Apple's own preloaded applications.

The following advanced components of UI Kit will be covered:

Common controls

UI Kit provides a set of controls that include switches, buttons, segmented controls, sliders, and more. Controls are used in navigation bars, table cells, and with other visual elements. The `UIControl` class is the base class for controls, providing standardized events notification, display properties, and values.

Preferences tables and section lists

The `UITableView` class you were introduced to in Chapter 3 supports alternative layouts to display preferences tables and section lists. Preferences tables are used for managing grouped program settings or displaying structured information. Section lists present a Rolodex-style fashion list of contacts, music, or other indexed data.

Progress and activity indicators

Progress indicators notify the user that an operation is in progress and convey status in the form of spinning icons and thermometers. The application can tell the indicator when to start and stop, and can control the progress bar's completion.

Activity indicators show the user that an activity is in progress. The application can indicate when it is using the network or provide general indicators instructing the user to wait.

Images

UI Kit provides classes for the manipulation and display of images. These classes can load most popular types of images and display, transform, layer, and clip them anywhere on the screen. Image classes can also be animated.

Text field keyboard properties

The iPhone supports several different keyboard styles, which are used widely by applications for various kinds of input. Apple's Mail application invokes a keyboard containing special characters for email address entry, whereas Safari invokes a different keyboard suitable for URL input, sporting a .COM button. Text fields contain special properties to define the style of keyboard that appears when typing.

Date pickers and picker views

Pickers provide a unified method of input for selecting options from a list. Pickers present lists in the form of spinning dials, which you can tailor to behave in different ways. Date and time pickers are more specialized controls, allowing the selection of custom dates, times, and time periods.

Tab bars

Tab bars provide a series of shortcut buttons across the bottom of the iPhone's screen, allowing the programmer to logically group the primary functions of an application. This is also a popular method to separate views of different data. The iPod application uses tab bars to separate playlists, artists, songs, and videos from each other, while the phone application uses a button bar to provide shortcuts to different functions of the phone, such as the keypad and contacts list.

Sensors and device information

The iPhone includes many sensors, such as the accelerometer and proximity sensor. Other sensors, such as the orientation sensor, are used internally to automatically manage screen rotation. The `UIDevice` class also allows you to read certain operating system-level information, such as the device's model, software version, and unique identifier. In this section, you'll learn how to read and make sense of the different indicators available on the iPhone.

Scroll views

Many objects with large content depend on scroll views to render them. Scroll views allow content to be scrolled into view and zoomed. You've been using them indirectly with tables and lists, and here you'll see just how they work.

Web views

A web view class is built into the UI Kit framework, allowing applications to display a web page. This is powerful for network-based tools that might choose to use web pages to refresh "latest news" windows or display other information. Web views can also display small PDFs and images.

Common Controls

Controls are diverse, multipurpose utility classes to augment a user interface. UI Kit supports many different types of controls, derived from a standard `UIControl` class. Controls provided in the SDK include switches, sliders, segmented controls, buttons, page controls, and text field controls. Controls are practical enhancements to classes derived from `UIView`, and can be attached directly to navigation bars, table cells, and even larger objects.

The controls implemented on the iPhone are noticeably different from those used in desktop applications. Desktop controls such as checkboxes and radio buttons won't cut it on a high-resolution device with limited touch screen precision (e.g., no stylus). For each desktop control in common use, a similar control has been designed specifically for the iPhone.

The UIControl Base Class

Controls are derived from a base class named `UIControl`, which provides a uniform interface for events notification, state changes, and display properties. The `UIControl` class is derived from the `UIView` class, so each control shares many properties of views, including the ability to attach to other views. Controls all share a common set of properties and methods.

Properties

`enabled`

> Controls are enabled by default. To disable a control, set its `enabled` property to `NO`, which will cause the control to ignore any touch events. When disabled, the control might also render itself differently so that it appears grayed out. While the actual rendering is left to the control's subclass, the property for this exists in `UIControl`.

`selected`

> When the user selects a control, the `UIControl` class sets its `selected` property to `YES`. Subclasses sometimes use this to cause a control to select itself or behave differently.

`contentVerticalAlignment`

> Specifies how the control's content should be positioned vertically. The default behavior is to top-align the content, so you may want to change this to `UIControl ContentVerticalAlignmentCenter` for text fields. Acceptable values for this field follow:
>
>   UIControlContentVerticalAlignmentCenter
>   UIControlContentVerticalAlignmentTop
>   UIControlContentVerticalAlignmentBottom
>   UIControlContentVerticalAlignmentFill

`contentHorizontalAlignment`

> Specifies how the text field's content should be positioned horizontally. Acceptable values for this field follow:
>
>   UIControlContentHorizontalAlignmentCenter
>   UIControlContentHorizontalAlignmentLeft

```
UIControlContentHorizontalAlignmentRight
UIControlContentHorizontalAlignmentFill
```

Event notifications

The `UIControl` class provides a standard mechanism to register and receive events. This lets you instruct your control to notify a method in your delegate class whenever a certain event occurs. To register an event, use the `addTarget` method:

```
[ myControl addTarget: myDelegate action: @selector(myActionMethod:)
    forControlEvents: UIControlEventValueChanged
];
```

Events can be logically OR'd together, allowing you to specify multiple events with a single call to `addTarget`. The events to follow are supported by the base `UIControl` class, and therefore apply to all controls unless otherwise specified:

UIControlEventTouchDown
> Notify all individual touch *down* events. These occur whenever the user taps down on the screen, or when additional fingers are placed down.

UIControlEventTouchDownRepeat
> Notify all multi-touch tap down events whenever the tap count is greater than 1. These occur whenever a user taps down a second, third, or fourth finger.

UIControlEventTouchDragInside
> Notify when a touch is dragged inside the control's window.

UIControlEventTouchDragOutside
> Notify when a touch is dragged outside the control's window.

UIControlEventTouchDragEnter
> Notify when a touch is dragged from the outside to the inside of a control's window.

UIControlEventTouchDragExit
> Notify when a touch is dragged from the inside to the outside of a control's window.

UIControlEventTouchUpInside
> Notify all touch *up* events occurring inside the control.

UIControlEventTouchUpOutside
> Notify all touch up events originating outside the control. Notifications will not be sent unless the tap originated from inside the control.

UIControlEventTouchCancel
> Notify all touch *cancel* events, where a touch was canceled by adding too many fingers or being interrupted by a lock or phone call.

UIControlEventValueChanged
> Notify when the value of the control has changed. Used in sliders, segmented controls, and other value-based controls. You can configure slider controls to notify when the slider is dropped, or as it is being dragged.

`UIControlEventEditingDidBegin`

> Notify when editing begins inside a text-based control.

`UIControlEventEditingChanged`

> Notify when text is being changed inside a text-based control.

`UIControlEventEditingDidEnd`

> Notify when editing ends inside a text-based control.

`UIControlEventEditingDidEndOnExit`

> Notify when editing ends inside a text-based control by pressing the return key (or equivalent).

`UIControlEventAllTouchEvents`

> Notify all touch events.

`UIControlEventAllEditingEvents`

> Notify all text-based editing events.

`UIControlEventAllEvents`

> Notify all events.

In addition to the default events, custom control classes may use the value range `0x0F000000` through `0x0FFFFFFF` to define their own events.

To remove an action for one or more events, use the `UIControl` class's `removeTarget` method. Using the `nil` value will remove all actions for the given event target:

```
[ myControl removeTarget: myDelegate action: nil
    forControlEvents: UIControlEventAllEvents
];
```

To obtain a list about all actions specified for a control, use the `allTargets` method. This returns an `NSSet` containing the complete list of events:

```
NSSet *myActions = [ myControl allTargets ];
```

Alternatively, you can obtain a list of all actions for a given event target using the `actionsForTarget` method:

```
NSArray *myActions = [ myControl actionsForTarget: UIControlEventValueChanged ];
```

If you're designing a custom control class, you can end notifications for the base `UIControl` events or your own custom events using the `sendActionsForControlEvents` method. For example, if the value of your control is being changed, you can send the appropriate event notification, which will be propagated to the event targets specified by the code using your control. An example of this follows:

```
[ self sendActionsForControlEvents: UIControlEventValueChanged ];
```

When the delegate class is notified of the event, it will receive a pointer to the sender of the event. Your action method should follow the construction of the example below, which handles an event for a segmented control:

```
-(void) myAction: (id)sender
{
```

```
    UISegmentedControl *control = (UISegmentedControl *) sender;
    if (control == myControl1) {
        /* Query the control for a value */

        /* Respond to action for myControl1 */
    }
}
```

Segmented Controls

The segmented control replaces the radio button used on desktop operating systems with an interface similar to the front of a modern kitchen appliance, such as a dishwasher or microwave oven. The user sees a pushbutton bar; pressing one button causes all others to pop out. Segmented controls are useful where a limited number of related selections are available for one option.

Creating the control

As is the case with other view classes, you'll initialize a segmented control with a frame. The frame's coordinates are offset to the view hosting the control, which is usually the cell of a preferences table or a navigation bar:

```
UISegmentedControl *segmentedControl = [ [ UISegmentedControl alloc ]
    initWithItems: nil
];

segmentedControl.segmentedControlStyle = UISegmentedControlStyleBar;
```

You can choose one of three different styles for segmented controls, depending on where the control is being used.

Style	Description
UISegmentedControlStylePlain	Large white buttons with gray border, appropriate for preference cells
UISegmentedControlStyleBordered	Large white buttons with black border, appropriate for table cells
UISegmentedControlStyleBar	Small buttons ideal for a navigation bar

If you are using the UISegmentedControlStyleBar style, you can also set a tint for the entire control by using the control's tintColor property:

```
UIColor *myTint = [ [ UIColor alloc ] initWithRed: 0.75
    green: 1.0
    blue: 0.75
    alpha: 1.0
];

segmentedControl.tintColor = myTint;
```

Adding segments

Each segment within a segmented control is represented by a button containing a label or image. You'll need to create a segment for each selectable item in your control. You can have as many segments as will fit on the screen, but the user can select only one segment at a time. The *PageDemo* example from Chapter 3 illustrated buttons for bunnies and ponies:

```
[ segmentedControl insertSegmentWithTitle: @"Bunnies"
    atIndex: 0 animated: NO
];

[ segmentedControl insertSegmentWithTitle: @"Ponies"
    atIndex: 1 animated: NO
];
```

Each button is assigned an index number (0, 1, 2, and so on). This numeric value serves for ordering and as a button identifier for your application.

To add a segment containing an image, use the `insertSegmentWithImage` method:

```
UIImage *myBunnies = [ UIImage applicationImageNamed: @"bunnies.png" ];

[ segmentedControl insertSegmentWithImage: myBunnies
    atIndex: 0 animated: NO
];
```

You can also remove a segment. To remove an individual segment, use the `remove Segment` method:

```
[ segmentedControl removeSegmentAtIndex: 1 animated: YES ];
```

To remove all segments at once, invoke `removeAllSegments`. This causes the control to visibly shed its buttons:

```
[ segmentedControl removeAllSegments ];
```

Segment titles

If, at any time, it's necessary to change the title of a button, use the `setTitle` method:

```
[ segmentedControl setTitle:@"Unicorms" forSegment: 0 ];
```

You can also read the titles using the `titleForSegmentAtIndex` method:

```
NSString *myTitle = [ segmentedControl titleForSegmentAtIndex: 0 ];
```

Images

In addition to text, segmented controls can display images inside their buttons. Any images used should be included in the application's program folder by dragging the image into the Xcode project's *Resources* folder. You can add an image to an existing segment using the `setImage` method. This is similar to the `insertSegmentWithImage` method you've already learned about, but operates on an existing segment:

```
[ segmentedControl setImage: [ UIImage applicationImageNamed:@"unicorns.png" ]
    forSegmentAtIndex: 0
];
```

You can also read a segment's image using the `imageForSegmentAtIndex` method:

```
UIImage *myImage = [ segmentedControl imageForSegmentAtIndex: 0 ];
```

The control itself will not perform any image scaling, so it will try to display your image on the button even if the image is too large. This requires care in designing button images to ensure they fit into the button space. You can manually set the segment's width using the control's `setWidth` method:

```
[ segmentedControl setWidth: 64.0 forSegmentAtIndex: 0 ];
```

Momentary clicks

The default behavior of the segmented control is to retain the selected button until another is selected. You can change this behavior to automatically release the button shortly after it is pressed. Set the control's `momentary` property to YES to enable this functionality:

```
segmentedControl.momentary = YES;
```

Initializing default segment

By default, no segment will be selected unless you specify one. To set the default segment, set the `selectedSegmentIndex` property:

```
segmentedControl.selectedSegmentIndex = 0;
```

Displaying the control

Once you have configured the control, display it by adding it as a subview to any type of object that can host it or by specifying it as the view to a navigation title or other object. Examples follow.

Adding to parent view:

```
[ parentView addSubview: segmentedControl ];
```

Adding to navigation bar (via view controller):

```
self.navigationItem.titleView = segmentedControl;
```

Reading the control

To read the current value of a segmented control, read the `selectedSegmentIndex` property. This provides a value corresponding to the segment number that is currently selected. The value is set based on the number assigned to it when it was first inserted into the control:

```
int x = segmentedControl.selectedSegmentIndex;
```

To receive a notification when a button is pressed, use the UIControl class's addTarget method to add an action for the UIControlEventValueChanged event. Your target class can then read the control's selected index:

```
[ segmentedControl addTarget: self action:
    @selector(controlPressed:)
    forControlEvents: UIControlEventValueChanged
];
```

Your action class will be called whenever a new segment is selected:

```
-(void) controlPressed: (id)sender
{
    UISegmentedControl *control = (UISegmentedControl *) sender;
    if (control == mySegmentedControl) {

        int x = control.selectedSegmentIndex;

      /* Additional code to respond to segment change */
    }
}
```

Switches

In the same way that the segmented control replaced the radio button, the switch replaced the checkbox. Switch controls are used to turn features on and off. The switch control is by far the simplest control to use, but can still be customized to a degree.

Creating the control

A switch is initialized using the standard initWithFrame method, but the size of the frame is ignored. Instead, the switch determines its own best size. This method allows you to define only the offset relative to the class it will be anchored to, such as a table cell or parent view. You can set the size as 0×0, acknowledging that it will be automatically set:

```
UISwitch *switch = [ [ UISwitch alloc ]
    initWithFrame: CGRectMake(170.0, 5.0, 0.0, 0.0)
];
```

Alternate colors

While not supported by the SDK, you can set a destructive switch to use a bright orange warning color when activated, rather than the standard blue. Features that could result in a performance impact or have other consequences can display these warning colors by using the hidden setAlternateColors method. This is particularly useful when distributing applications internally for debugging or review, identifying controls that will be removed when the application is released:

```
[ switch setAlternateColors: YES ];
```

This undocumented API is subject to change at any time. Your application could also potentially be rejected from listing in the iTunes store if you use undocumented APIs, so be sure to remove this feature before going into production.

Displaying the control

Once you have initialized the switch, you can display it by adding it as a subview to any type of object that can host it or by specifying it as the view to a navigation title or other object. Examples follow.

Adding to parent view:

```
[ parentView addSubview: switch ];
```

Adding to navigation bar (via view controller):

```
self.navigationItem.titleView = switch;
```

Switch position

The switch control can be read through its on property. This provides a Boolean value identifying whether the switch has been activated:

```
BOOL switchPosition = switch.on;
```

You can also activate the switch in your code using the setOn method. An example follows:

```
[ switch setOn: YES animated: YES ];
```

To receive a notification when the switch is toggled, use the UIControl class's addTarget method to add an action for the UIControlEventValueChanged event. Your action class then reads the switch's value:

```
[ switch addTarget: self action: @selector(switchStatusChanged:)
    forControlEvents:UIControlEventValueChanged
];
```

Your action class will be called whenever the switch is toggled:

```
-(void) switchStatusChanged: (id)sender
{
    UISwitch *control = (UISwitch *) sender;
    if (control == mySwitch) {

        BOOL on = control.on;

      /* Additional code to respond to switch state */
    }
}
```

Sliders

Sliders provide a visual range that the user can change by using a slide bar, and are configurable to accommodate a range of values. You can set ranges for the slider values, add images at the ends, and make various other aesthetic tweaks. The slider is ideal for presenting options with large (yet imprecise) ranges of numeric values, such as a volume setting, sensitivity controls, and the like. Commonly seen on the desktop, sliders must have been determined good enough for Apple to port them to the iPhone, too. The iPhone's version of a slider is more finger-friendly.

Creating the control

The slider control is a standard `UIControl` object and you can initialize it by invoking the control's `initWithFrame` method to specify its offset and width. The height of the frame is ignored, and can be set to 0×0:

```
UISlider *slider = [ [ UISlider alloc ] initWithFrame:
    CGRectMake(0.0, 0.0, 200.0, 0.0)
];
```

You should set the value range for the control on creation so you know what data to expect in return. If you provide no default range, values between `0.0` and `1.0` are used. The `UISlider` class provides two properties to set these—`minimumValue` and `maximumValue`:

```
slider minimumValue: 0.0;
slider maximumValue: 100.0;
```

You can also set a default value for the slider at this time by setting the slider's `value` property:

```
slider.value = 50.0;
```

The slider can display images at either end of the control. You can set these in a similar fashion to images in a segmented control. Copy the images into the *Resources* folder in Xcode. This will cause then to be copied into the application's program directory when installed on the iPhone. Adding images will cause a reduction in the control's slider bar, so be sure to increase the width of the control to accommodate the images:

```
[ slider setMinimumTrackImage:
    [ UIImage applicationImageNamed:@"min.png" ]
    forState: UIControlStateNormal
];

[ slider setMaximumTrackImage:
    [ UIImage applicationImageNamed:@"max.png" ]
    forState: UIControlStateNormal
];
```

You can display different images for each state of the slider. The following states are available:

```
UIControlStateNormal
UIControlStateHighlighted
UIControlStateDisabled
UIControlStateSelected
```

For debugging, an undocumented API exists to display the value of the slider within the control. Invoke the setShowValue method to display this next to the slider:

```
[ slider setShowValue: YES ];
```

 This undocumented API is subject to change at any time. Your application could also potentially be rejected from listing in the iTunes store if you use undocumented APIs, so be sure to remove this feature before going into production.

Displaying the control

Once you have initialized the slider, display it by adding it as a subview to any type of object that can host it or by specifying it as the view to a navigation title or other object. Examples follow.

Adding to parent view:

```
[ parentView addSubview: slider ];
```

Adding to navigation bar (via view controller):

```
self.navigationItem.titleView = slider;
```

Reading the control

The slider control reads as a floating-point value within the range you specified at the control's creation. You can query the value using its value property:

```
float value = slider.value;
```

To receive a notification whenever the slider value is changed, use the UIControl class's addTarget method to add an action for the UIControlEventValueChanged event. Your action class then reads the slider's value:

```
[ slider addTarget: self action: @selector(sliderValueChanged:)
     forControlEvents:UIControlEventValueChanged
];
```

Your action class will be called whenever the slider is dropped in a new position:

```
-(void) sliderValueChanged: (id)sender
{
    UISlider *control = (UISlider *) sender;
    if (control == mySlider) {

        float value = control.value;

      /* Additional code to respond to slider value */
```

```
        }
    }
```

To have this event trigger as the slider is being dragged, set the slider's `continuous` property:

```
slider.continuous = YES;
```

Text Field Controls

In Chapter 3, you were introduced to the `UITextField` class, which can be used to add text cells to tables and other objects. The `UITextField` class inherits from `UIControl`, and you can use so many of the properties of the `UIControl` class to further tailor the behavior of a `UITextField` object.

Style options

In addition to the text styling options discussed in Chapter 3, the `UITextField` control allows you to set alignment, border style, and a number of different aesthetic options. These include the properties to follow:

`textAlignment`
> Specifies how the text within the control should be positioned. The default behavior is to left-align its content:
> ```
> UITextAlignmentLeft
> UITextAlignmentRight
> UITextAlignmentCenter
> ```

`borderStyle`
> Specifies the style of the border surrounding the text control. The default behavior is to use no border. You may use the following values. The style will be ignored if a custom background image is being used:
> ```
> UITextBorderStyleNone
> UITextBorderStyleLine
> UITextBorderStyleBezel
> UITextBorderStyleRoundedRect
> ```

`placeholder`
> Draws a string as a gray placeholder for empty text fields. This value is displayed when a text field has not yet been edited and is without a value. Accepts an `NSString` object.

`clearsOnBeginEditing`
> If the text field should be cleared when the user taps on it, set this Boolean value to `YES`. By default, the text field moves the cursor to the position tapped within the text field, and does not delete text.

adjustsFontSizeToFitWidth
> When set to YES, this property causes the text to automatically shrink to fit the size of the text window. The default behavior is to retain the original font size, allowing long text to scroll out of view.

background
> Accepts a UIImage object and sets it as the text field's background. This causes the border style property to be ignored.

clearButtonMode
> Defines the behavior of the clear button. A clear button is a small "X" button appearing to the right of the text field, allowing the user to clear all text by tapping. The default behavior is set to UITextFieldViewNever, which hides the clear button. You can set the following modes:
>
>> UITextFieldViewModeNever
>> UITextFieldViewModeWhileEditing
>> UITextFieldViewModeUnlessEditing
>> UITextFieldViewModeAlways

LeftView, leftViewMode, rightView, rightViewMode
> These properties allow you to attach derivatives of the UIView class to the right and left of the text field. UIButton objects such a magnifying glasses or bookmarks buttons are commonly attached to text fields. Each view has an accompanying mode, which you can set using the same values as the clearButtonmode property.

Rendering overrides

In addition to the styling options for a UITextField object, you can add many different overrides to custom UITextField objects, which affect how the text field is rendered.

These methods return a CGRect structure, specifying the boundaries for each component of a text field. If you are creating a custom UITextField class, you can override these methods to change one or more boundaries. Never call these methods directly; they are callbacks for the iPhone runtime to invoke. An example follows:

```
- (CGRect)clearButtonRectForBounds: (CGRect) bounds {
    return CGRectMake(bounds.origin.x + bounds.size.x - 50,
        bounds.origin.y + bounds.size.y - 20,
        16, 16);
}
```

The following overrides are available when creating a subclass of UITextField:

borderRectForBounds
> Specifies the border rectangle.

textRectForBounds
> Specifies the boundaries of the displayed text.

`placeholderRectForBounds`
  Specifies the boundaries of the placeholder text.

`editingRectForBounds`
  Specifies the boundaries of the text when edited.

`clearButtonRectForBounds`
  Specifies the boundaries in which to render the clear button.

`leftViewRectForBounds`
  Specifies the boundaries in which to render the left view.

`rightViewRectForBounds`
  Specifies the boundaries in which to render the right view.

Delegate methods

You can assign a delegate to a `UITextField` using the class's `delegate` property. This delegate receives a number of different events that can be overridden to receive notification of certain events occurring in the text field.

Each method is provided a pointer to the text field in which the action occurred, allowing you to handle multiple text fields within one delegate. The following delegate methods are available:

`-(BOOL)textFieldShouldBeginEditing:(UITextField *)textField;`
  Returns a Boolean value specifying whether the text field should be permitted to begin editing. To disable editing for the text field entirely, this method should always return `NO` (although it's easier to just disable the control). This is useful when a custom text field requires other actions to be taken prior to making it read-write.

`-(void)textFieldDidBeginEditing:(UITextField *)textField;`
  Invoked whenever the user taps inside of the text field to enable editing. The text field becomes the first responder when it begins editing.

`-(BOOL)textFieldShouldEndEditing:(UITextField *)textField;`
  Returns a Boolean value specifying whether the text field should be permitted to end editing. When editing is ended, the text field resigns as first responder. To prevent a field from disappearing when the user finishes editing it, return `NO`. This can be useful in messaging applications, where the text field should always remain active.

`-(void)textFieldDidEndEditing:(UITextField *)textField;`
  Invoked whenever editing has been completed within the given text field, and the text field has resigned as first responder.

`-(BOOL)textField:(UITextField    *)textField,    shouldChangeCharactersInRange:`
`(NSRange)range, replacementString:(NSString *)string;`
  Invoked when the user invokes autocorrect to change the given text to the suggested text. This is useful if you're adding an undo option to your application and want to keep track of the last change made within the field, or to record a log of

all edits for auditing purposes. To prevent the text from being changed, return NO. The method's parameters provide an NSRange object identifying the position of the text to be changed. The suggested replacement text is also provided.

-(BOOL)textFieldShouldClear:(UITextField *)textField;
> Returns a Boolean value specifying whether the text field should be allowed to clear at the user's request. This is useful if certain events must occur before the text field can clear, or if the text field should not be permitted to clear unless certain other conditions are met.

-(BOOL)textFieldShouldReturn:(UITextField *)textField;
> Returns a Boolean value specifying whether pressing the return key should allow editing to end. If you want to end editing when the user presses the return key, invoke the resignFirstResponder method here. This will cause the text field to end editing and the keyboard will be dismissed:

```
- (BOOL) textFieldShouldReturn:(UITextField *)textField {

    [ textField resignFirstResponder ];
    return YES;
}
```

The application may take other actions when the user presses the return key. For example, you may choose to begin a search or verify the information entered into the text field.

Notifications

Since the UITextField class derives from the UIControl class, the notification system used in the UIControl class is also available to text fields. In addition to the UIControl class's standard events, you may also use the following custom events, specific to the UITextField class:

UITextFieldTextDidBeginEditingNotification
> Triggered when a text field enters editing mode. The object property of the notification provides the text being edited.

UITextFieldTextDidChangeNotification
> Triggered when text within the field has been changed. The object property of the notification stores the changed text.

UITextFieldTextDidEndEditingNotification
> Triggered when a text field exits edit mode. The object property of the notification stores the final text.

Because a text field uses the keyboard for text entry, action notifications may also be sent when one or more of the following events occur:

UIKeyboardWillShowNotification
> Sent before the keyboard is displayed.

`UIKeyboardDidShowNotification`
  Sent after the keyboard is displayed.

`UIKeyboardWillHideNotification`
  Sent before the keyboard is hidden.

`UIKeyboardDidHideNotification`
  Sent after the keyboard is hidden.

Scrolling text fields

When editing a text field near the bottom of the screen, the action of the keyboard popping up can sometimes hide the field. As of iPhoneOS version 2.2, scrolling has been automated. To add the same level of functionality to earlier versions of firmware, the view containing the control can be scrolled up to bring the text field into view. This relies on two text field delegate methods, `textFieldDidBeginEditing` and `textFieldShouldReturn`.

For a given text field, set its delegate to the containing view class:

```
textControl.delegate = self;
```

When the user taps on the text field, the `textFieldDidBeginEditing` delegate method will be notified. Use this to change the view class's origin and size by a fixed amount. You can animate this to give the appearance of scrolling; Core Animation handles all of the frames in between (the "tweening"), so you just tell it where you want the view to end up, and Core Animation fills in the blanks for you.

The following code will scroll the view up by 240 pixels when the user taps the text field:

```
- (void)textFieldDidBeginEditing:(UITextView *)textview {

    [ UIView beginAnimations: nil context: NULL ];
    [ UIView setAnimationDuration: 0.3 ];

    CGRect frame = self.view.frame;
    frame.origin.y -= 240.0;
    frame.size.height += 240.0;
    self.view.frame = frame;

    [ UIView commitAnimations ];
}
```

When the user presses the return key, the frame can be scrolled back to the way it was. You can also dismiss the keyboard by resigning first responder. The same type of transaction is created to animate this change and give the appearance of scrolling:

```
- (BOOL)textFieldShouldReturn:(UITextView *) textView {

    [ UIView beginAnimations: nil context: NULL ];
    [ UIView setAnimationDuration: 0.3 ];

    CGRect frame = self.view.frame;
    frame.origin.y += 240.0;
```

```
        frame.size.height -= 240.0;
        self.view.frame = frame;

        [ UIView commitAnimations ];
        [ textView resignFirstResponder ];
        return YES;
    }
```

If you are using multiple text fields in the same view, it may be necessary to compare the UITextView pointer passed into the method, so that you can make different scroll adjustments depending on the position of the text field and based on the position of the scroll bars. The example you've just read used a scrolling value of 240.0, however you will need different values here depending on where your particular text fields are located on the screen. See the section on Scroll Views for more information about scrolling.

Buttons

Buttons are simple controls capable of displaying text or an image, which notify an application when pressed. You can attach button controls to UIView objects, table cells, and a number of other objects. Because they derive from the UIControl class, they share the same notification structure as the base class. In addition to this, the UIButton class provides a number of additional features.

Creating the control

The button control is a standard UIControl object and you can initialize it by invoking the control's initWithFrame method to specify its offset and width. Additionally, the UIButton class provides a static buttonWithType method for creating a number of pre-defined styles on the fly:

```
    UIButton *myButton = [ UIButton buttonWithType: UIButtonTypeRoundedRect ];
```

You can supply the following button styles as the type argument with the buttonWith Type method.

Style	Description
UIButtonTypeCustom	Custom button; no styling is provided
UIButtonTypeRoundedRect	White button with rounded edges, like a preferences table cell or address book card
UIButtonTypeDetailDisclosure	Blue disclosure next to any text
UIButtonTypeInfoLight	Info circle next to any text, for widgets
UIButtonTypeInfoDark	Dark info circle for white backgrounds
UIButtonTypeContactAdd	Blue plus button (+) next to any text

After creating a button, you can set its offset and size by assigning a CGRect structure to the button's frame property:

```
CGRect *myButtonFrame = CGRectMake(25.0, 25.0, 100.0, 100.0);
myButton.frame = myButtonFrame;
```

Button titles can be set for any given button state. Use the setTitle method to set this:

```
[ myButton setTitle: @"Click Here" forState: UIControlStateNormal ];
```

You can also set button images for a given button state. Use the setImage method to assign these:

```
[ myButton setImage:
    [ UIImage applicationImageNamed: @"button.png" ]
    forState: UIControlStateNormal
];
```

Additionally, you can set title color and shadow for each button state, as well as the background for the button. The setTitleColor and setTitleShadowColor methods both require a UIColor object as an argument. The setBackgroundImage method requires a UIImage object:

```
[ myButton setTitleColor:
    [ UIColor redColor ] forState: UIControlStateNormal
];

[ myButton setTitleShadowColor:
    [ UIColor grayColor ] forState: UIControlStateNormal
];

[ myButton setBackgroundImage:
    [ UIImage applicationImageNamed: @"background.png" ]
    forState: UIControlStateNormal
];
```

Each of the five methods you've just read about contains an argument named forState. This determines in which state the button's title, image, or other properties will appear. You can program the button to change its appearance when the state changes. These states are the same you've already learned about for the UIControl class:

```
UIControlStateNormal
UIControlStateHighlighted
UIControlStateDisabled
UIControlStateSelected
```

When a button is highlighted or disabled, the UIButton class can tweak its appearance. The following properties allow you to fine tune how you'd like the button to appear:

adjustsImageWhenHighlighted
> By default, an image is drawn lighter when the button is pressed (highlighted). To disable this functionality, set this property to NO.

adjustImageWhenDisabled
> By default, an image is drawn darker when the button is disabled. To disable this functionality, set this property to NO.

`showsTouchWhenHighlighted`
> To cause the button to glow when pressed, set this property to YES. This is useful for info buttons or buttons that are somehow important.

Displaying the control

Once you have initialized the button, display it by adding it as a subview to any type of object that can host it. An example follows:

```
[ myView addSubview: button ];
```

Rendering overrides

In addition to the numerous styling options for a `UIButton` object, you can add different overrides to custom `UIButton` objects, which affect how a button is rendered.

These methods return a `CGRect` structure, specifying the boundaries for each component of a button. If you are creating a custom `UIButton` class, you can override these methods to change one or more boundaries. Never call these methods directly. An example follows:

```
- (CGRect) imageRectForContentRect: (CGRect) bounds {
    return myButtonImageBounds;
}
```

The following overrides are available when subclassing `UIButton`:

`backgroundRectForBounds`
> Specifies the boundaries in which to render the background image.

`contentRectForBounds`
> Specifies the boundaries in which to render the button's content.

`titleRectForContentRect`
> Specifies the boundaries in which to render the button's title text.

`imageRectForContentRect`
> Specifies the boundaries in which to render the button's image.

Page Controls

Page controls provide a visual indicator for applications that "flick" between pages using the thumb, rather than navigation buttons, or need to otherwise display a page indicator. You'll learn about page flicking in Chapter 13, which incorporates this control. A page control is rendered as a series of dots across the top or bottom of the screen, and is updated by your application as the user flips between pages. They are most commonly found at the bottom of the iPhone's home screen (springboard) when adding more icons than fit on a single screen, and in Safari, when the page selection window is opened. Page controls are ideal for custom view classes in which the developer seeks to display information across multiple pages.

Creating the control

To create a page control, use the standard `initWithFrame` method to specify the offset and size of the page control. Specifying a size of 0 will automatically set the horizontal size, vertical size, or both, based on the number of pages. Specifying a width of the screen's width will center the control horizontally within its display region:

```
UIPageControl *pageControl = [ [ UIPageControl alloc ]
    initWithFrame: CGRectMake(0.0, 400.0, 320.0, 0.0)
];
```

To set the number of pages the control will infer, set the `numberOfPages` property:

```
pageControl.numberOfPages = 5;
```

By default, the first page is selected. To select a different page, set the `currentPage` property. Pages are zero-indexed, so the first page is specified as page 0:

```
pageControl.currentPage = 0;
```

By default, the indicator will be displayed even if there is only one page. To hide the indicator when only one page is configured, set the `hidesForSinglePage` value to `NO`:

```
pageControl.hidesForSinglePage = NO;
```

Finally, if you'd like the indicator to avoid updating the current page until after you've had time to perform your own operations, set the `defersCurrentPageDisplay` to `YES`. This will require that you call the control's `updateCurrentPageDisplay` in order to update the current page:

```
pageControl.defersCurrentPageDisplay = YES;
[ pageControl updateCurrentPageDisplay ];
```

Displaying the control

Once you have initialized the page control, display it by adding it as a subview to any type of object that can host it. An example follows:

```
[ myView addSubview: pageControl ];
```

The page control is configured to use a transparent background, so if you want the control to respond to taps like it does on the Springboard, you'll need to ensure it has another view object behind it.

Notifications

When the user taps the page control, an event is created for `UIControlEventValueChanged`. You can specify an action using the `UIControl` class's `addTarget` method:

```
[ myView addTarget: self action:@selector(pageChanged:)
    forControlEvents: UIControlEventValueChanged
];
```

The action method is then notified, which can read the new page value and take the appropriate action:

```
- (void) pageChanged: (id) selector {
    UIPageControl *control = (UIPageControl *) selector;
    NSInteger page = control.currentPage;

    /* Additional code to handle page change */
}
```

Further Study

Now that you've had a full introduction to controls, try your hand at adding some to your code:

- Create an application using various controls. Attach controls to `UIView` classes, navigation bars, and other objects. Which objects can you attach controls to?
- Check out the following prototypes in your SDK's header files: *UIControl.h*, *UISwitch.h*, *UISlider.h*, *UIButton.h*, *UITextField.h*, and *UISegmentedControl.h*. You'll find these deep within */Developer/Platforms/iPhoneOS.platform*, inside the UI Kit framework's *Headers* directory.

Preferences Tables

Preferences tables provide an aesthetically rich interface for displaying and changing program settings or displaying structured information, such as a contact or network info. When possible, an application should use a *preference bundle* (discussed in Chapter 11) to add a settings tab to the iPhone's Settings application, but the downfall to this is that it requires quitting your application to change settings. Apple has provided sanctioned APIs for creating preferences tables in your application too, which is useful for changing runtime settings. In addition to settings, if your application displays a grouped table of information, such as a proprietary display of contacts or network information, this type of table may also be useful to organize your data. Preferences tables provide resizable cells capable of hosting controls, text boxes, and informational text. They also provide a mechanism for logically grouping similar preferences together.

The SDK has conveniently wrapped the preferences table class into the existing `UITableView` class you learned about in Chapter 3. As a result, you can create a preferences table in much the same way as a standard table, with only minor tweaks to adjust its style and logical groupings.

 Deep down, the interfacing with the `UITableView` class instantiates a lower-level UI Kit object named `UIPreferencesTable`. This object is hidden from the SDK, but used widely by open source developers writing code with the third-party tool chain. The SDK has made it more convenient to work with all major table structures by consolidating the interfaces for them into the `UITableView` class, which is all you'll need to learn.

Creating a Preferences Table

You must put some forethought into implementing a preferences table, as a *data source* delegate is used to query for the information used to fill the table. You do this in a similar fashion to the generic list-like implementation of the UITableView class you learned about in Chapter 3, but with a higher level of complexity. The runtime class invokes a set of protocol methods in the data source to return information about the preferences table, just like a standard table. Much to the discouragement of the iPhone developer community, this is quite distant from an object-oriented model. Instead, the construction for the entire preferences table is bulky and complex, in contrast with Apple's traditionally elegant design style.

Just to recap, the preferences table refers to a complete settings page or an information page. A table can have many logical groupings of like settings. Within each group, a single table cell displays each individual setting to the user. The content for the cell includes optional title, text, and controls, if any.

The conversation between a preferences table and its data source looks (something) like Figure 10-1.

Because a preferences table is assembled in two pieces (the table and the data source), the cleanest way to put one together is to create a subclass of UITableViewController as you did in Chapter 3, and have it act as the table's data source. This allows your application to create an instance of the controller class (which includes its own table object) and display it on the screen.

Subclassing the table view controller

To create a self-contained preferences table, create a subclass of UITableViewController and include all of the protocol methods needed to bind it as a data source delegate. The following example creates a subclass named MyPreferencesViewController:

```
@interface MyPreferencesViewController : UITableViewController
{

}

/* Preferences table methods */

- (id)init;
- (void)loadView;
- (void)dealloc;

/* Data source methods */

- (NSInteger)numberOfSectionsInTableView:(UITableView *)tableView;
- (NSInteger)tableView:(UITableView *)tableView
    numberOfRowsInSection:(NSInteger)section;
- (UITableViewCell *)tableView:(UITableView *)tableView
    cellForRowAtIndexPath:(NSIndexPath *)indexPath;
- (CGFloat)tableView:(UITableView *)tableView
```

```
    heightForRowAtIndexPath:(NSIndexPath *)indexPath;
 - (NSString *)tableView:(UITableView *)tableView
    titleForHeaderInSection:(NSInteger)section;
```

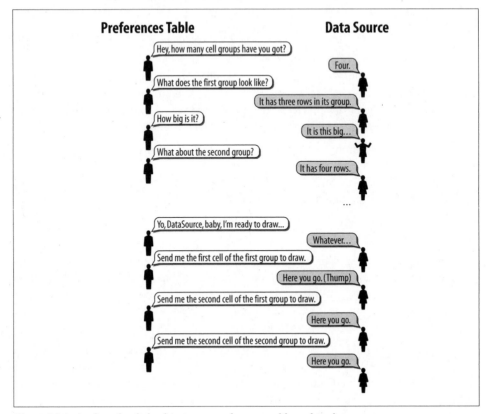

Figure 10-1. Analogy for dialog between a preferences table and its data source

The methods used for the data source break down as follows:

numberOfSectionsInTableView

>   Returns the number of logical groups in the preferences table. The group count should not include group labels. Each logical group will appear as a separate "balloon" on the screen.

numberOfRowsInSection

>   Returns the number of rows in the given preferences group. The row count should not include group labels. Your data source will treat each row as a UITableView Cell object, returned by the cellForRowAtIndexPath method, explained next.

cellForRowAtIndexPath

>   Returns a UITableViewCell object corresponding to the group and row specified. This method should check for an existing cell on the queue in the same way as the *TableDemo* table example from Chapter 3.

`titleForHeaderInSection`

Returns an `NSString` object containing the group label for the given preferences group.

`heightForRowAtIndexPath`

Returns a custom height for the group and row specified. This allows you to customize certain cells to be a specific height.

Initializing the table

When you initialize a table view controller, an internal `UITableView` object is created within the class to represent the table view belonging to the controller. Because you're creating a special type of table (a preferences table), you'll need to create a table view controller with a different underlying table style. Override your `MyPreferencesView Controller` class's `init` method and manually create the table view using the `UITable ViewController` superclass's alternative `initWithStyle` method:

```
(id)init {
    self = [ super initWithStyle: UITableViewStyleGrouped ];

    if (self != nil) {

        /* Additional initialization code */
    }

    return self;
}
```

If you are working with a `UITableView` by itself (that is, without a table view controller), you can use the table view class's alternative `initWithFrame` method, which includes a style argument. An example follows:

```
UITableView *myTableView = [ [ UITableView alloc ]
    initWithFrame: myRect
    style: UITableViewStyleGrouped
];
```

After creating the object, call its `reloadData` method to load all the elements in the preference table. This causes the table to invoke its data source and begin loading information about cell groupings and geometry. You can manually reload the table at any time by calling the table class's `reloadData` method:

```
[ self.tableView reloadData ];
```

Preferences table cells

Each cell in a preferences table is created as a `UITableViewCell` object, or a subclass of it. Cells are returned through the `cellForRowAtIndexPath` callback method, which you must write and which is called by the preferences table class automatically as new rows are being drawn on the screen. For example, if your table invokes the `cellForRowAtIndex Path` method, specifying index path [0 1], the method is expected to return the cell corresponding to the first group (group 0) and the second row (row 1). The method should check the queue to ensure the cell has not already been created, and then create and return it:

```
- (UITableViewCell *)tableView:(UITableView *)tableView
    cellForRowAtIndexPath:(NSIndexPath *)indexPath
{

    NSString *CellIdentifier = [ fileList objectAtIndex:
        [ indexPath indexAtPosition: 1 ]
    ];

    UITableViewCell *cell = [ tableView
        dequeueReusableCellWithIdentifier: CellIdentifier
    ];

    /* Create cell from scratch */
    if (cell == nil) {
        cell = [ [ [ UITableViewCell alloc ]
            initWithFrame: CGRectZero
            reuseIdentifier: CellIdentifier
          ] autorelease ];

        /* Example cell contents */
        cell.text = @"Debugging";
    }

    /* Return either the new cell or the queued cell */
    return cell;
}
```

Controls

The UITableViewCell class can accommodate a number of different controls, allowing you to add a switch, slider, or other type of control to an individual preferences table cell. Add controls to the UITableViewCell object as a subview.

When creating a new preferences table cell, add the control using the cell's addSubview method:

```
cell = [ [ [ UITableViewCell alloc ] initWithFrame: CGRectZero
            reuseIdentifier: CellIdentifier
          ] autorelease ];

cell.text = @"Advanced Mode";

/* Add a switch to the example cell */
UISwitch *debugSwitch = [ [ UISwitch alloc ]
    initWithFrame: CGRectMake(200.0, 10.0, 0.0, 0.0)
];

/* Attach the switch to the cell */
[ cell addSubview: debugSwitch ];
```

The preceding example creates a switch control with a frame offset to the right of the cell. The example also creates a cell with the title "Advanced Mode" and attaches the switch control to it. All of this takes place within the `cellForRowAtIndexPath` method, before returning the newly created cell.

Text fields

You can add text fields in the same way as other controls. By using the `UIControl` class's notification framework, edits and other relevant events can be relayed to your delegate class.

Text fields include an offset and a display region specifying the size of the text field. This allows you to create either a dedicated text cell (displaying only text across the entire cell), or a cell with both a boldface title (set with the `title` property) and a text field:

```
UITextField *textField = [ [ UITextField alloc ]
    initWithFrame: CGRectMake(20.0, 10.0, 280.0, 50.0)
];

[ cell addSubview: textField ];
```

You can also display text and make it uneditable using the `setEnabled` method:

```
textField.text = @"Some text";
[ cell setEnabled: NO ];
```

You can read the value using the same property:

```
NSString *text = textField.text;
```

Displaying the Preferences Table

A preferences table is displayed in the same way as a view controller—by attaching its underlying view to a window or by pushing it onto a navigation controller.

Use the following to set the active view for the window:

```
[ window addSubview: myTableViewController.view ];
```

Use the following to push it onto a navigation controller:

```
[ navigationController pushViewController: myTableViewController.view
    animated: YES
];
```

ShootStuffUp: Preferences Table Example

You are writing a spaceship shoot-'em-up game, which needs a set of preferences to control everything from sound volume to debugging messages. In this example, the `UITableViewController` class is subclassed to create a custom `ShootStuffUpTableViewController` object (Figure 10-2). This object contains its own data source for the

Figure 10-2. ShootStuffUp example

underlying table structure. It creates each cell and assigns some of the controls you learned about in the previous section.

You can compile this application, shown in Examples 10-1 through 10-5, with the SDK by creating a *view-based application* project named *ShootStuffUp*. Be sure to pull out the Interface Builder code if you'd like to see how these objects are created from scratch.

Example 10-1. ShootStuffUp application delegate prototypes (ShootStuffUpAppDelegate.h)

```
#import <UIKit/UIKit.h>

@class ShootStuffUpViewController;

@interface ShootStuffUpAppDelegate : NSObject <UIApplicationDelegate> {
    UIWindow *window;
    ShootStuffUpViewController *viewController;
    UINavigationController *navigationController;
}

@property (nonatomic, retain) IBOutlet UIWindow *window;
@property (nonatomic, retain) IBOutlet ShootStuffUpViewController *viewController;
```

```
@end
```

Example 10-2. ShootStuffUp application delegate (ShootStuffUpAppDelegate.m)

```objc
#import "ShootStuffUpAppDelegate.h"
#import "ShootStuffUpViewController.h"

@implementation ShootStuffUpAppDelegate

@synthesize window;
@synthesize viewController;


- (void)applicationDidFinishLaunching:(UIApplication *)application {
    CGRect screenBounds = [ [ UIScreen mainScreen ] bounds ];

    self.window = [ [ [ UIWindow alloc ] initWithFrame: screenBounds ] autorelease ];
    viewController = [ [ ShootStuffUpViewController alloc ] init ];
    navigationController = [ [ UINavigationController alloc ]
 initWithRootViewController: viewController ];

    [ window addSubview: [ navigationController view ] ];
    [ window makeKeyAndVisible ];
}


- (void)dealloc {
    [ viewController release ];
    [ window release ];
    [ super dealloc ];
}


@end
```

Example 10-3. ShootStuffUp table view controller prototypes (ShootStuffUpViewController.h)

```objc
#import <UIKit/UIKit.h>

@interface ShootStuffUpViewController : UITableViewController {

    UISlider *musicVolumeControl;
    UISlider *gameVolumeControl;
    UISegmentedControl *difficultyControl;

    UISlider *shipStabilityControl;
    UISwitch *badGuyControl;
    UISwitch *debugControl;

    UITextField *versionControl;
}

- (id) init;
- (void) dealloc;
- (NSInteger)numberOfSectionsInTableView:(UITableView *)tableView;
```

```
- (NSInteger)tableView:(UITableView *)tableView numberOfRowsIn
Section:(NSInteger)section;
- (NSString *)tableView:(UITableView *)tableView titleForHeader
InSection:(NSInteger)section;
- (UITableViewCell *)tableView:(UITableView *)tableView cellForRow
AtIndexPath:(NSIndexPath *)indexPath;

@end
```

Example 10-4. ShootStuffUp table view controller (ShootStuffUpViewController.m)

```
#import "ShootStuffUpViewController.h"

@implementation ShootStuffUpViewController

- (id) init {
    self = [ super initWithStyle: UITableViewStyleGrouped ];

    if (self != nil) {
        self.title = @"Game Settings";
    }
    return self;
}

- (void) loadView {
    [ super loadView ];
}

- (BOOL)shouldAutorotateToInterfaceOrientation:
    (UIInterfaceOrientation)interfaceOrientation
{
    return (interfaceOrientation == UIInterfaceOrientationPortrait);
}

- (void)didReceiveMemoryWarning {

    [ super didReceiveMemoryWarning ];
}

- (void)dealloc {
    [ musicVolumeControl release ];
    [ gameVolumeControl release ];
    [ difficultyControl release ];
    [ shipStabilityControl release ];
    [ badGuyControl release ];
    [ debugControl release ];
    [ versionControl release ];
    [ super dealloc ];
}

- (NSInteger)numberOfSectionsInTableView:(UITableView *)tableView {
    return 3;
}

- (NSInteger)tableView:(UITableView *)tableView
    numberOfRowsInSection:(NSInteger)section
```

```
{
    switch (section) {
        case(0):
            return 3;
            break;
        case(1):
            return 3;
            break;
        case(2):
            return 1;
            break;
    }

    return 0;
}

- (NSString *)tableView:(UITableView *)tableView
    titleForHeaderInSection:(NSInteger)section
{
    switch (section) {
        case(0):
            return @"Game Settings";
            break;
        case(1):
            return @"Advanced Settings";
            break;
        case(2):
            return @"About";
            break;
    }
    return nil;
}

- (UITableViewCell *)tableView:(UITableView *)tableView
    cellForRowAtIndexPath:(NSIndexPath *)indexPath
{
    NSString *CellIdentifier = [ NSString stringWithFormat: @"%d:%d",
        [ indexPath indexAtPosition: 0 ], [ indexPath indexAtPosition:1 ]
    ];

    UITableViewCell *cell = [ tableView
        dequeueReusableCellWithIdentifier: CellIdentifier
    ];

    if (cell == nil) {
        cell = [ [ [ UITableViewCell alloc ]
            initWithFrame: CGRectZero reuseIdentifier: CellIdentifier
        ] autorelease ];

        cell.selectionStyle = UITableViewCellSelectionStyleNone;

        switch ([ indexPath indexAtPosition: 0]) {
            case(0):
                switch([ indexPath indexAtPosition: 1]) {
                    case(0):
```

```objc
            musicVolumeControl = [ [ UISlider alloc ]
                    initWithFrame: CGRectMake(170, 0, 125, 50) ];
            musicVolumeControl.minimumValue = 0.0;
            musicVolumeControl.maximumValue = 10.0;
            musicVolumeControl.value = 3.5;
            [ cell addSubview: musicVolumeControl ];
            cell.text = @"Music Volume";
            break;
        case(1):
            gameVolumeControl = [ [ UISlider alloc ]
                    initWithFrame: CGRectMake(170, 0, 125, 50) ];
            gameVolumeControl.minimumValue = 0.0;
            gameVolumeControl.maximumValue = 10.0;
            gameVolumeControl.value = 3.5;
            [ cell addSubview: gameVolumeControl ];
            cell.text = @"Game Volume";
            break;
        case(2):
            difficultyControl = [ [ UISegmentedControl alloc ]
                    initWithFrame: CGRectMake(170, 5, 125, 35) ];
            [ difficultyControl insertSegmentWithTitle: @"Easy"
                    atIndex: 0 animated: NO ];
            [ difficultyControl insertSegmentWithTitle: @"Hard"
                    atIndex: 1 animated: NO ];
             difficultyControl.selectedSegmentIndex = 0;
            [ cell addSubview: difficultyControl ];
            cell.text = @"Difficulty";
            break;
    }
    break;
case(1):
    switch ([ indexPath indexAtPosition: 1 ]) {
        case(0):
            shipStabilityControl = [ [ UISlider alloc ]
                    initWithFrame: CGRectMake(170, 0, 125, 50) ];
            shipStabilityControl.minimumValue = 0.0;
            shipStabilityControl.maximumValue = 10.0;
            shipStabilityControl.value = 3.5;
            [ cell addSubview: shipStabilityControl ];
            cell.text = @"Ship Stability";
            break;
        case(1):
            badGuyControl = [ [ UISwitch alloc ]
                    initWithFrame: CGRectMake(200, 10, 0, 0) ];
            badGuyControl.on = YES;
            [ cell addSubview: badGuyControl ];
            cell.text = @"Bad Guys";
            break;
        case(2):
            debugControl = [ [ UISwitch alloc ]
                    initWithFrame: CGRectMake(200, 10, 0, 0) ];
            debugControl.on = NO;
            [ cell addSubview: debugControl ];
            cell.text = @"Debug";
            break;
```

```
            }
            break;
        case(2):
            versionControl = [ [ UITextField alloc ]
                    initWithFrame: CGRectMake(170, 10, 125, 38) ];
            versionControl.text = @"1.0.0 Rev. B";
            [ cell addSubview: versionControl ];
            [ versionControl setEnabled: NO ];
            cell.text = @"Version";
            break;
        }
    }

    return cell;
}

@end
```

Example 10-5. ShootStuffUp main (main.m)

```
#import <UIKit/UIKit.h>

int main(int argc, char *argv[]) {

    NSAutoreleasePool * pool = [ [ NSAutoreleasePool alloc ] init ];
    int retVal = UIApplicationMain(argc, argv, nil, @"ShootStuffUpAppDelegate");
    [ pool release ];
    return retVal;
}
```

What's Going On

You've just read through a full-blown application that displays a preferences table. Here's how it works:

1. When you run the application, the delegate class creates a subclass of the UITable ViewController. This class incorporates the data source for the preferences table and underlying variable storage for controls.

2. The table view controller's init method is overridden and instructs its superclass to create it having a preferences table style, UITableViewStyleGrouped.

3. The table view controller is added to the navigation controller's stack, and when it is displayed, its reloadData method is invoked. Because we haven't overridden reloadData, the parent UITableView class's version of the method is invoked. This begins the communication to the data source by calling the various data source methods. The preferences table talks to the data source to establish the basic construction and geometry of the table and its controls.

4. The cellForRowAtIndex method first checks to see whether the cell already exists in the table's memory queue. If not, a new UITableViewCell object is created. The cell's title and controls are set based on the row and group number, and any controls are created and added as subviews of the preference cell.

Further Study

Now that you've had a taste of how preferences tables work, try some exercises to better acquaint yourself:

- Incorporate your knowledge of the UIControl class's notification framework to intercept value changes as they occur in real time.
- Use examples from Chapter 3 to create a main view for this application that displays all of the preference's values. Use a navigation control to allow the user to navigate between the preferences table and your display view.

Section Lists

The UITableView class is very versatile. It not only accommodates standard list-like tables and preferences tables, but also another type of table commonly used in iPhone software: section lists. When a table gets long enough, finding an item can be like finding a needle in a haystack. A section list provides a visual structure similar to a standard table, but expands it to include individual row groupings and a Rolodex-like index to quickly flip to a section heading. You can assign each grouping a section title, such as genres in a book or the first letter of a contact. You'll find section lists in use in the iPhone's own contact and song lists.

Like other tables, the section list uses a data source. A data source is a protocol interface to query an object for the contents and construction of the table. The data source for a section list provides the protocol methods needed to build the section list's groupings, section titles, index, and individual row cells. As with other table classes covered in this book, the examples provided here create a subclass of the UITableViewController object that can both contain a section table and the accompanying data source. This architecture is the easiest to illustrate and is ideal for creating specialized reusable classes.

 In a lower level of the framework, UI Kit instantiates a class named UISectionList, which encapsulates a UISectionTable, comprising the table portion of the list. As is the case with preferences tables, these lower-level objects are hidden from the developer, so you'll once again be working with the UITableView class's standard interfaces to build this object.

Creating the Section List

You create section lists in much the same way as a preferences table, and use the same overrides to base their construction on. The two differences between the construction of a section list and a preferences table are the underlying table structure and extra delegate methods to add index sidebar.

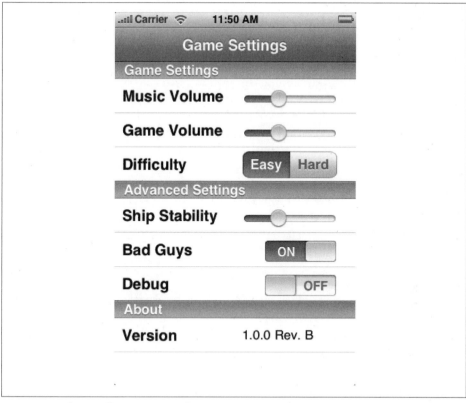

Figure 10-3. ShootStuffUp as a section list

The two table formats are so similar, in fact, that simply replacing the following line from the *ShootStuffUp* example in the last section will render your preferences table as a section list.

Replace the following code:

```
self = [ super initWithStyle: UITableViewStyleGrouped ];
```

With this code:

```
self = [ super init ];
```

When you create the underlying table, its default style now allows for sections and indexing (Figure 10-3). By replacing the preceding line of code with a call to `init`, you're returning the table style to its default, which is created internally when not done manually:

Your table view controller will use some of the same delegate methods as a preferences table. An example follows:

```
#import <UIKit/UIKit.h>

@interface MySectionListViewController : UITableViewController {
```

```
}
    - (id) init;
    - (void) dealloc;
    - (NSInteger)numberOfSectionsInTableView:(UITableView *)tableView;
    - (NSInteger)tableView:(UITableView *)tableView
        numberOfRowsInSection:(NSInteger)section;
    - (NSString *)tableView:(UITableView *)tableView
        titleForHeaderInSection:(NSInteger)section;
    - (UITableViewCell *)tableView:(UITableView *)tableView
        cellForRowAtIndexPath:(NSIndexPath *)indexPath;

    @end
```

If you will be adding an index bar (the Rolodex-style bar that appears in your iPhone's contacts list), you'll add one additional override to obtain the index names:

```
    - (NSArray *)sectionIndexTitlesForTableView:(UITableView *)tableView;
```

The methods used for the data source break down as follows:

numberOfSectionsInTableView
> Returns the number of individual sections to be displayed in the preferences table. Only include empty sections if you want them displayed as empty.

numberOfRowsInSection
> Returns the number of rows in a given section.

cellForRowAtIndexPath
> Returns a UITableViewCell object corresponding to the section and row specified. This method should check for an existing cell on the queue in the same way as the *TableDemo* table example from Chapter 3.

titleForHeaderInSection
> Returns an NSString object containing the section label for the given section. This can be a single character (such as in contact lists) or full strings (such as genres of books).

heightForRowAtIndexPath
> Returns a custom height for the group and row specified. This allows you to customize certain cells to be a specific height.

sectionIndexTitlesForTableView
> Returns an NSArray object containing an array of NSString objects to use to build an index bar.

sectionForSectionIndexTitle
> Associates a given index title with a section number so that tapping on the index will position the section on-screen. This is especially useful when creating nonalphabetic indexes, such as book genres, etc.

Adding an Index Bar

When you add an index bar to a section list, a Rolodex-style bar appears to the right, allowing the user to quickly select the desired section by clicking on an index tab. Index titles are traditionally alphabetic, but you may configure an index bar to have any given set of titles.

To add an index bar, add a data source method named `sectionindexTitlesForTable View`. An example follows:

```
- (NSArray *)sectionIndexTitlesForTableView:(UITableView *)tableView {

    return [ NSMutableArray arrayWithObjects:
        @"A", @"B", @"C", @"D", @"E", @"F",
        @"G", @"H", @"I", @"J", @"K", @"L",
        @"M", @"N", @"O", @"P", @"Q", @"R",
        @"S", @"T", @"U", @"V", @"W", @"X",
        @"Y", @"Z", @"#", nil
    ];
}
```

Displaying the Section List

A section list is displayed in the same way as a standard table view controller—by attaching its underlying view to a window or by pushing it onto a navigation controller.

Use the following to set the active view for the window:

```
[ window addSubview: myTableViewController.view ];
```

Use the following to push it onto a navigation controller:

```
[ navigationController pushViewController: myTableViewController.view
        animated: YES ]
    ];
```

TableDemo: A Better File Browser

The *TableDemo* example from Chapter 3 displays a simple table containing a list of files and directories present in your application's home directory on the iPhone. This version of the table demo creates a separate alphabetical section for files and places each file in the section corresponding to its first letter (Figure 10-4). The example continues to makes use of a table view controller, and attaches this to a navigation bar controller to present user editing buttons and a Reload button. The user will be able to press Edit to delete items from the list (don't worry, it won't actually delete any files). Swipe functionality is also active, allowing the user to swipe to delete a cell.

You can compile this application, shown in Examples 10-6 through 10-10, with the SDK by creating a *view-based application* project named *TableDemo*. Be sure to pull out the Interface Builder code if you'd like to see how these objects are created from scratch.

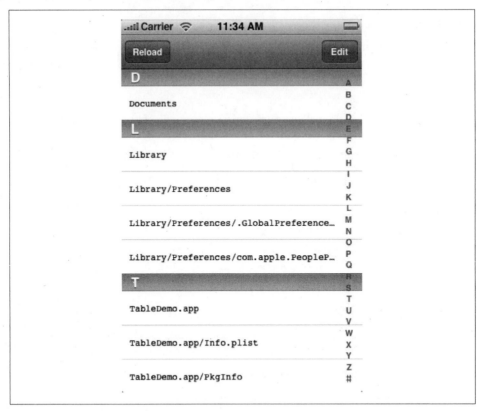

Figure 10-4. TableDemo example

Example 10-6. TableDemo application delegate prototypes (TableDemoAppDelegate.h)

```
#import <UIKit/UIKit.h>

@class TableDemoViewController;

@interface TableDemoAppDelegate : NSObject <UIApplicationDelegate> {
    UIWindow *window;
    TableDemoViewController *viewController;
    UINavigationController *navigationController;
}

@property (nonatomic, retain) IBOutlet UIWindow *window;
@property (nonatomic, retain) IBOutlet TableDemoViewController *viewController;

@end
```

Example 10-7. TableDemo application delegate (TableDemoAppDelegate.m)

```
#import "TableDemoAppDelegate.h"
#import "TableDemoViewController.h"

@implementation TableDemoAppDelegate
```

```
@synthesize window;
@synthesize viewController;


- (void)applicationDidFinishLaunching:(UIApplication *)application {
    CGRect screenBounds = [ [ UIScreen mainScreen ] bounds ];

    self.window = [ [ [ UIWindow alloc ] initWithFrame: screenBounds ] autorelease ];
    viewController = [ [ TableDemoViewController alloc ] init ];
    navigationController = [ [ UINavigationController alloc ]
        initWithRootViewController: viewController ];

    [ window addSubview: [ navigationController view ] ];
    [ window makeKeyAndVisible ];
}

- (void)dealloc {
    [ viewController release ];
    [ navigationController release ];
    [ window release ];
    [ super dealloc ];
}

@end
```

Example 10-8. TableDemo view controller prototype (TableDemoViewController.h)

```
#import <UIKit/UIKit.h>

@interface TableDemoViewController : UITableViewController {

    int nActiveSections;
    NSMutableArray *fileList[27];
    NSMutableArray *activeSections;
    NSMutableArray *sectionTitles;
}

- (void) startEditing;
- (void) stopEditing;
- (void) reload;

@end
```

Example 10-9. TableDemo view controller (TableDemoViewController.m)

```
#import "TableDemoViewController.h"

@implementation TableDemoViewController

- (id)init {
    self = [ super init ];

    if (self != nil) {

        /* Build a list of files */
```

```
        [ self reload ];

        /* Initialize navigation bar buttons */

        self.navigationItem.rightBarButtonItem
        = [ [ [ UIBarButtonItem alloc ]
            initWithBarButtonSystemItem: UIBarButtonSystemItemEdit
            target: self
            action: @selector(startEditing) ] autorelease ];

        self.navigationItem.leftBarButtonItem
        = [ [ [ UIBarButtonItem alloc ]
            initWithTitle:@"Reload"
            style: UIBarButtonItemStylePlain
            target: self
            action:@selector(reload) ]
          autorelease ];
    }

    return self;
}

- (NSArray *)sectionIndexTitlesForTableView:(UITableView *)tableView {

    return [ NSMutableArray arrayWithObjects:
        @"A", @"B", @"C", @"D", @"E", @"F",
        @"G", @"H", @"I", @"J", @"K", @"L",
        @"M", @"N", @"O", @"P", @"Q", @"R",
        @"S", @"T", @"U", @"V", @"W", @"X",
        @"Y", @"Z", @"#", nil
    ];
}

- (void) startEditing {
    [ self.tableView setEditing: YES animated: YES ];

    self.navigationItem.rightBarButtonItem
    = [ [ [ UIBarButtonItem alloc ]
        initWithBarButtonSystemItem: UIBarButtonSystemItemDone
        target: self
        action: @selector(stopEditing) ] autorelease ];
}

- (void) stopEditing {
    [ self.tableView setEditing: NO animated: YES ];

    self.navigationItem.rightBarButtonItem
    = [ [ [ UIBarButtonItem alloc ]
        initWithBarButtonSystemItem: UIBarButtonSystemItemEdit
        target: self
        action: @selector(startEditing) ] autorelease ];
}

- (void) reload {
    NSDirectoryEnumerator *dirEnum;
```

```
    NSString *file;

    for(int i=0;i<27;i++) {
        fileList[i] = [ [ NSMutableArray alloc ] init ];
    }
    dirEnum = [ [ NSFileManager defaultManager ] enumeratorAtPath:
        NSHomeDirectory()
    ];

    while ((file = [ dirEnum nextObject ])) {
        char index = ( [ file cStringUsingEncoding: NSASCIIStringEncoding ] )[0];

        if (index >= 'a' && index <= 'z') {
            index -= 32;
        }
        if (index >= 'A' && index <= 'Z') {
            index -= 65;
            [ fileList[(int) index] addObject: file ];
        } else {
            [ fileList[26] addObject: file ];
        }
    }

    nActiveSections = 0;
    activeSections = [ [ NSMutableArray alloc ] init ];
    sectionTitles = [ [ NSMutableArray alloc ] init ];
    for(int i=0;i<27;i++) {
        if ( [fileList[i] count ]>0) {
            nActiveSections++;
            [ activeSections addObject: fileList[i] ];
            if (i < 26)
                [ sectionTitles addObject: [ NSString stringWithFormat:
                        @"%c", i + 65 ] ];
            else
                [ sectionTitles addObject: @"0-9" ];
        }
    }

    [ self.tableView reloadData ];
}

- (NSString *)tableView:(UITableView *)tableView
    titleForHeaderInSection:(NSInteger)section
{
    return [ sectionTitles objectAtIndex: section ];
}

- (NSInteger)numberOfSectionsInTableView:(UITableView *)tableView {
    return nActiveSections;
}


- (NSInteger)tableView:(UITableView *)tableView
    numberOfRowsInSection:(NSInteger)section
{
```

```
        return [ [ activeSections objectAtIndex: section] count ];
}

- (NSInteger)tableView:(UITableView *)tableView sectionForSection
IndexTitle:(NSString *)title atIndex:(NSInteger) index {
    int i = 0;
    for (NSString * sectionTitle in sectionTitles) {
        if ([ sectionTitle isEqualToString: title ]) {
            [ tableView scrollToRowAtIndexPath:
                [ NSIndexPath indexPathForRow: 0 inSection: i ]
                    atScrollPosition: UITableViewScrollPositionTop animated: YES ];
            return i;
        }
        i++;
    }
    return -1;
}

- (UITableViewCell *)tableView:(UITableView *)tableView
    cellForRowAtIndexPath:(NSIndexPath *)indexPath
{

    NSString *CellIdentifier = [[ activeSections objectAtIndex:
        [ indexPath indexAtPosition: 0 ]] objectAtIndex:
            [ indexPath indexAtPosition: 1 ] ];

    UITableViewCell *cell = [ tableView
        dequeueReusableCellWithIdentifier: CellIdentifier ];
    if (cell == nil) {
        cell = [ [ [ UITableViewCell alloc ]
            initWithFrame: CGRectZero reuseIdentifier: CellIdentifier
        ] autorelease ];

        cell.text = CellIdentifier;

        UIFont *font = [ UIFont fontWithName: @"Courier" size: 12.0 ];
        cell.font = font;
    }

    return cell;
}

- (void)tableView:(UITableView *)tableView
    commitEditingStyle:(UITableViewCellEditingStyle) editingStyle
    forRowAtIndexPath:(NSIndexPath *) indexPath
{
    if (editingStyle == UITableViewCellEditingStyleDelete) {

        /* Delete cell from data source */

        UITableViewCell *cell = [ self.tableView cellForRowAtIndexPath: indexPath ];
        for(int i = 0; i < [ [ activeSections objectAtIndex:
            [ indexPath indexAtPosition: 0 ] ] count ]; i++)
        {
            if ([ cell.text isEqualToString: [
```

```
                [ activeSections objectAtIndex: [ indexPath indexAtPosition: 0 ] ]
                    objectAtIndex: i ] ])
            {
                [ [ activeSections objectAtIndex:
                    [ indexPath indexAtPosition: 0 ] ] removeObjectAtIndex: i ];
            }
        }

        /* Delete cell from table */

        NSMutableArray *array = [ [ NSMutableArray alloc ] init ];
        [ array addObject: indexPath ];
        [ self.tableView deleteRowsAtIndexPaths: array
            withRowAnimation: UITableViewRowAnimationTop ];
    }
}

- (void)tableView:(UITableView *)tableView
    didSelectRowAtIndexPath:(NSIndexPath *)indexPath
{

    UITableViewCell *cell = [ self.tableView cellForRowAtIndexPath: indexPath ];

    UIAlertView *alert = [ [ UIAlertView alloc ]
        initWithTitle: @"File Selected"
        message:
            [ NSString stringWithFormat: @"You selected the file '%@'", cell.text ]
        delegate: nil
        cancelButtonTitle: nil
        otherButtonTitles: @"OK", nil
    ];

    [ alert show ];
}


- (void)loadView {
    [ super loadView ];
}


- (BOOL)shouldAutorotateToInterfaceOrientation:
    (UIInterfaceOrientation)interfaceOrientation
{
    return YES;
}


- (void)didReceiveMemoryWarning {
    [ super didReceiveMemoryWarning ];
}


- (void)dealloc {
    for(int i=0;i<27;i++) {
```

```
            [ fileList[i] release ];
    }
    [ super dealloc ];
}

@end
```

Example 10-10. TableDemo main (main.m)

```
#import <UIKit/UIKit.h>

int main(int argc, char *argv[]) {

    NSAutoreleasePool * pool = [[NSAutoreleasePool alloc] init];
    int retVal = UIApplicationMain(argc, argv, nil, @"TableDemoAppDelegate");
    [pool release];
    return retVal;
}
```

What's Going On

The *TableDemo* example works as follows:

1. The application instantiates as all other examples thus far have; by calling the program's `main` function, which invokes the `TableDemoAppDelegate` class's `applicationDidFinishLaunching` method, and builds the appropriate window, view controller, and navigation controller classes.

2. The view controller is created as an instance of `UITableViewController`. The controller's `init` method is overridden to load a list of files into an array of `NSMutableArray` objects named `fileList` based on its first character. If the first character is alphabetical, it's added in `fileList` arrays 0-25, otherwise it's added to `fileList` array 26.

3. All 27 `fileList` arrays are checked for contents. Nonempty arrays are added as sections to the section table by adding them to an array named `activeSections`. Array titles are also stored separately so we can keep track of which sections are being displayed.

4. When the table is rendered, the controller's data source methods are automatically called. The `numberOfRowsInSection` method returns the number of rows for the section, whose contents are stored in `activeSections`. The `cellForRowAtIndex Path` creates a new cell using the filename as the cell title.

5. If the user taps the Edit button, the button's designated selector, `startEditing`, is notified. This replaces the button with a Done button and enables editing of the table. The table automatically indents each cell and adds a delete icon.

6. If the user deletes a row either by editing or swiping, he will be asked for confirmation. Once he confirms, this delete request will trigger the `commitEditingStyle` method to be notified of the request. The method checks to ensure that the request is a delete request and then deletes the object from both the file list and the table.

7. If the user presses the Reload button, the file list is reread and the table is refreshed.

Further Study

See if you can take what you've previously learned and apply it to this example:

- Use `NSDirectoryEnumerator` class's `fileAttributes` method to identify which files are directories. Create a new section for each directory and add the contents of each directory to the section. Use the directory name for the section name.

- Add a new view controller that displays the contents of a file in a `UITextView`. If the file is binary, display a hexadecimal readout. When the user taps on a file, a new view controller should be pushed on the navigation controller's stack that displays the contents of the file. The new view controller should have a Back button.

- If you haven't already done so, check out the following prototypes in your SDK's header files: *UITableView.h*, *UITableViewCell.h*, and *UITableViewController.h*. You'll find these deep within */Developer/Platforms/iPhoneOS.platform*, inside the UI Kit framework's *Headers* directory.

Progress and Activity Indicators

Activity indicators notify the user that an operation is in progress. Progress indicators do the same, and give the user a general idea of how far along the process is toward completion. The SDK supports two types of indicators:

`UIActivityIndicatorView`
> This class presents a spinning clock-like animation—the kind seen when turning on the iPhone's WiFi or Bluetooth support, or when your Mac desktop boots up.

`UIProgressView`
> This class provides a thermometer-like readout, allowing the application to express how far along an operation is until completion.

Both types of indicators derive from the `UIView` base class; meaning you can layer them on top of text views, alert sheets, table cells, and any other object that derives from `UIView`.

UIActivityIndicatorView: Things That Spin

The `UIActivityIndicatorView` class is a simple animation class small enough to attach to nearly any `UIView` object, including table cells and action sheets. The indicator displays a clock-like animation of tick marks making revolutions around a circle.

You create the indicator with a frame identifying the indicator's size and the coordinates relative to the view to which it is attached:

```
UIActivityIndicatorView *activityIndicator = [ [ UIActivityIndicatorView alloc ]
    initWithFrame: CGRectMake(260.0, 12.0, 25.0, 25.0)
];
```

The indicator supports three styles, which you can assign by setting the indicator's activityIndicatorViewStyle property:

```
activityIndicator.activityIndicatorViewStyle = UIActivityIndicatorViewStyleGray;
```

You may use the following styles.

Style	Description
UIActivityIndicatorViewStyleWhiteLarge	Large white indicator
UIActivityIndicatorViewStyleWhite	Standard-sized white indicator
UIActivityIndicatorViewStyleGray	Gray indicator, for white backgrounds

To automatically hide the view when the indicator is stopped, use the hidesWhen Stopped property. The default is to hide the indicator, so set this property to NO if you want to display the indicator when it's frozen:

```
activityIndicator.hidesWhenStopped = NO;
```

You can add the progress indicator object to any existing view object, such as a table cell or view:

```
[ tableCell addSubview: activityIndicator ];
```

Finally, to start and stop the animation, use the startAnimating and stopAnimating methods:

```
[ activityIndicator startAnimating ];

[ activityIndicator stopAnimating ];
```

UIProgressView: When Spinny Things Are Tacky

The UIProgressView object is a close cousin to UIActivityIndicatorView. Instead of displaying a drool-inciting animation, the progress view class draws a thermometer-like indicator and provides an interface to set its fill level as your application crunches on its operation. The advantage of using a progress bar is that it can reflect more or less accurately how much work the application has actually done.

To create a progress view, the class's initialization method includes a frame identifying the bar's size and display origin:

```
UIProgressView *progressView = [ [ UIProgressView alloc ]
    initWithFrame: CGRectMake(175.0, 20.0, 125.0, 25.0)
];
```

The indicator supports two different styles, which you can assign by setting the progress view's `progressViewStyle` property:

```
progressView.progressViewStyle = UIProgressViewStyleBar;
```

You may use the following styles.

Style	Description
UIProgressViewStyleDefault	Standard progress bar
UIProgressViewStyleBar	Dark gray bar, for use in toolbars

To display the progress view, add it to an existing `UIView` object. You can add progress views to table cells, toolbars, and other view classes:

```
[ myToolbar addSubview: progressView ];
```

When the progress bar is displayed, the application can update its progress to indicate how far along it is in its operation. The progress value is a floating-point value between `0.0` and `1.0`:

```
progressView.progress = 0.5;
```

Network Activity Indicators

When your application is using the network, it should alert the user by placing a network indicator on the iPhone's status bar. To do this, use a `UIApplication` property named `networkActivityIndicatorVisible`. Set this Boolean value to enable or disable the network indicator:

```
UIApplication *myApp = [ UIApplication sharedApplication ];
myApp.networkActivityIndicatorVisible = YES;
```

Further Study

- Use your knowledge of navigation controllers from Chapter 3 to create a `UIProgressView` object in the toolbar. Use an `NSTimer` object or a separate thread to fill the bar. When it has reached its full capacity, drain the progress view back to zero. This is an ideal use when your application needs to check online for updates or product announcements.

- Check out *UIProgressView.h* and *UIActivityIndicatorView.h* prototypes. You'll find these deep within */Developer/Platforms/iPhoneOS.platform*, inside the UI Kit framework's *Headers* directory.

Images

The UI Kit framework provides classes to work with individual images and an image view class that can display them. Apple has also provided a special type of navigation controller for selecting images from a library.

The Image Object

The `UIImage` class encapsulates an image and its underlying data. It can draw directly inside a view or act as an image container in more powerful image view classes. The class provides methods to load an image from various sources, set the image's orientation on the screen, and provide information about the image. For simple graphics, you can use `UIImage` objects in a view class's `drawRect` method to render both images and patterns.

You can initialize a `UIImage` object with the contents of a file, website URL, raw data, or the contents of a Core Graphics image. Both static and instance methods exist; these can either reference and cache images or instantiate new image objects, depending on the needs of your application.

The easiest way to reference an image is through the `UIImage` class's static methods. Rather than managing instances of images, the static methods provide a direct interface to shared objects residing in the framework's internal memory cache. This helps declutter your application and eliminates the need to clean up. Both static and instance methods exist to create the same objects.

Working with files (static methods)

The `imageNamed` and `imageWithContentsOfFile` methods allow you to access image files by either the name of the file within your bundle or the full path to the file, respectively.

To access a file within your application's program folder, use the `imageNamed` method:

```
UIImage *image = [ UIImage imageNamed: @"image.png" ];
```

To access a file anywhere else within your sandbox, use the `imageWithContentsOfFile` method:

```
NSString *path = [ NSString stringWithFormat: @"%@/Documents/
image.png", NSHomeDirectory() ];
UIImage *image = [ UIImage imageWithContentsOfFile: path ];
```

Working with URLs and raw data (static methods)

If the image is resident in memory, you can initialize a `UIImage` object by creating an `NSData` object and providing it as raw input to the `imageWithData` method. You've already learned about the `NSData` class in previous chapters. You can initialize `NSData` structures in a number of ways, including the results of an HTTP fetch.

In the example to follow, the variable `imagePtr` is assumed to be a pointer to the raw image data in your application, and `imageSize` is assumed to be the image's size in memory:

```
NSData *imageData = [ NSData initWithBytes: imagePtr length: imageSize ];
UIImage *image = [ UIImage imageWthData: imageData ];
```

To create a `UIImage` containing the contents of a web object, use the `NSData` class to download it, and then initialize your image object:

```
NSURL *url = [ NSURL URLWithString:
    @" http://oreilly.com/catalog/covers/9781934356258_cat.gif"
];

NSData *imageData = [ NSData dataWithContentsOfUrl: url ];
UIImage *image = [ UIImage imageWithData: imageData ];
```

Working with Core Graphics (static methods)

If you're programming games or other graphics applications using the Core Graphics framework, you can initialize a `UIImage` object with the contents of an existing `CGImage` object:

```
UIImage *image = [ UIImage imageWithCGImage: myCGImageRef ];
```

Working with files (instance methods)

The `initWithContentsOfFile` methods allow you to access image files by a pathname. An example follows:

```
NSString *path = [ NSString stringWithFormat: @"%@/Documents/image.png",
    NSHomeDirectory()
];

UIImage *image = [ [ UIImage alloc ] initWithContentsOfFile: path ];
```

Working with URLs and raw data (instance methods)

If the image is resident in memory, you can initialize a `UIImage` object by creating an `NSData` object and providing it as raw input to the `initWithData` method.

In the example to follow, the variable `imagePtr` is assumed to be a pointer to the raw image data in your application, and `imageSize` is assumed to be the image's size in memory:

```
NSData *imageData = [ NSData initWithBytes: imagePtr length: imageSize ];
UIImage *image = [ [ UIImage alloc ] initWithData: imageData ];
```

To instantiate a `UIImage` containing the contents of a web object, use the `NSData` class to download it, and then initialize your image object:

```
NSURL *url = [ NSURL URLWithString:
    @" http://oreilly.com/catalog/covers/9781934356258_cat.gif"
];
```

```
NSData *imageData = [ NSData dataWithContentsOfUrl: url ];
UIImage *image = [ [ UIImage alloc ] initWithData: imageData ];
```

Working with Core Graphics (instance methods)

If you're programming games or other graphics applications using the Core Graphics
framework, an instance method also exists to initialize a UIImage object with the contents of an existing CGImage object:

```
UIImage *image = [ [ UIImage alloc ] initWithCGImage: myCGImageRef ];
```

Displaying an image

View classes use internal drawing routines called when their drawRect methods are
invoked. Unlike other image classes, a UIImage object cannot be attached directly to a
view object as a subview, because it isn't a view class. Instead, a UIView class calls an
image's drawInRect method from within the view's drawRect routine. This instructs the
image to render within the UIView class's display region.

A view object's drawRect method is called whenever a portion of its window needs to
be rendered. To render the contents of a UIImage inside the window, invoke the object's drawInRect method:

```
- (void)drawRect:(CGRect)rect {
    CGRect myRect;

    myRect.origin.x = 0;
    myRect.origin.y = 0;
    myRect.size = myImage.size;

    [ myImage drawInRect: myRect ];
}
```

Be careful not to allocate any new objects inside the drawRect method, because it's called
every time the window needs to be redrawn.

The drawRect method is called only when the view is initially drawn. To force an update,
use the view class's setNeedsDisplay or setNeedsDisplayInRect method:

```
[ myView setNeedsDisplay ];
[ myVIew setNeedsDisplayInRect: redrawThisRect ];
```

Drawing patterns

If the image is a pattern, you can use another method provided in the UIImage class,
drawAsPatternInRect, to repeat the image throughout the entire view region:

```
[ myImage drawAsPatternInRect: rect ];
```

This method will tile the image within the frame being drawn.

Orientation

An image's orientation determines how it's rotated in the display. Because the iPhone can be held one of six different ways, it may be necessary to rotate all of your images if the orientation changes. Use the image's `imageOrientation` property to set its orientation:

```
myImage.imageOrientation = UIImageOrientationUp;
```

You can set the following orientations.

Orientation	Description
UIImageOrientationUp	Default orientation
UIImageOrientationDown	Image rotated 180 degrees
UIImageOrientationLeft	Image rotated 90 degrees counter-clockwise
UIImageOrientationRight	Image rotates 90 degrees clockwise
UIImageOrientationUpMirrored	Up, horizontally flipped
UIImageOrientationDownMirrored	Down, horizontally flipped
UIImageOrientationLeftMirrored	Rotated 90 degrees counter-clockwise, vertically flipped
UIImageOrientationRightMirrored	Rotated 90 degrees clockwise, vertically flipped

Image size

You can read an image's size by reading the `size` property. This provides a `CGSize` structure containing `width` and `height` variables:

```
CGSize imageSize = myImage.size;
NSLog(@"Image size: %dx%d", imageSize.width, imageSize.height);
```

ImageFun: Fun with Images and Patterns

This example illustrates the rendering of images and patterns within a view class's `drawRect` method. You'll create an empty subclass of `UIVIew` and then override the `drawRect` method to include rendering routines, drawing up a pattern and an icon in the main window. It will download two image files, which it will use to draw a pattern and image on the screen (Figure 10-5). The image will fade in on a timer.

You can compile this application, shown in Examples 10-11 through 10-13, with the SDK by creating a *window-based application* project named *ImageFun*. Be sure to pull out the Interface Builder code if you'd like to see how all objects are created from scratch.

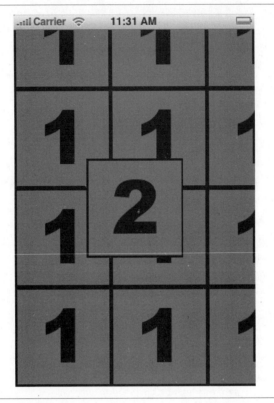

Figure 10-5. ImageFun example

Example 10-11. ImageFun application delegate prototypes (ImageFunAppDelegate.h)

```
#import <UIKit/UIKit.h>

@interface ImageFunView : UIView
{
    UIImage *pattern;
    UIImage *image;
    float alpha;
}
- (void)drawRect:(CGRect)rect;
@end

@interface ImageFunAppDelegate : NSObject <UIApplicationDelegate> {
    UIWindow *window;
    ImageFunView *mainView;
}

@property (nonatomic, retain) IBOutlet UIWindow *window;

@end
```

Example 10-12. ImageFun application delegate (ImageFunAppDelegate.m)

```objc
#import "ImageFunAppDelegate.h"

@implementation ImageFunView

- (id)initWithFrame:(CGRect) rect {
    self = [ super initWithFrame: rect ];
    if (self != nil) {
        NSLog(@"Loading pattern");
        NSURL *url = [ NSURL URLWithString:
            @"http://www.zdziarski.com/demo/1.png" ];
        pattern = [ [ UIImage alloc ] initWithData:
            [ NSData dataWithContentsOfURL: url ]
         ];

        NSLog(@"Loading image");
        NSURL *url2 = [ NSURL URLWithString:
            @"http://www.zdziarski.com/demo/2.png" ];
        image = [ [ UIImage alloc ] initWithData:
            [ NSData dataWithContentsOfURL: url2 ]
         ];

        alpha = 0.0;
    }

    return self;
}

- (void)drawRect:(CGRect)rect {
    CGRect myRect;

    myRect.size = image.size;
    myRect.origin.x = (320.0 - image.size.width) / 2;
    myRect.origin.y = (460.0 - image.size.height) / 2;

    [ pattern drawAsPatternInRect: rect ];

    [ image drawInRect: myRect blendMode: kCGBlendModeNormal alpha: alpha ];

    NSTimer *timer = [ NSTimer scheduledTimerWithTimeInterval: 0.01
        target: self
            selector: @selector(handleTimer:)
        userInfo: nil
        repeats: NO
    ];
}

- (void) handleTimer: (NSTimer *) timer {
    if (alpha < 1.0) {
        alpha += 0.01;
        [ self setNeedsDisplay ];
    }
}

- (void)dealloc {
```

```
    [ super dealloc ];
}
@end

@implementation ImageFunAppDelegate

@synthesize window;

- (void)applicationDidFinishLaunching:(UIApplication *)application {
    CGRect screenBounds = [ [ UIScreen mainScreen ] applicationFrame ];
    CGRect viewRect = screenBounds;
    viewRect.origin.x = viewRect.origin.y = 0;

    self.window = [ [ [ UIWindow alloc ] initWithFrame: screenBounds ]
        autorelease
    ];

    mainView = [ [ ImageFunView alloc ] initWithFrame: viewRect ];

    [ window addSubview: mainView ];
    [ window makeKeyAndVisible ];
}

- (void)dealloc {
    [ mainView release ];
    [ window release ];
    [ super dealloc ];
}

@end
```

Example 10-13. ImageFun main (main.m)

```
#import <UIKit/UIKit.h>

int main(int argc, char *argv[]) {

    NSAutoreleasePool * pool = [[NSAutoreleasePool alloc] init];
    int retVal = UIApplicationMain(argc, argv, nil, @"ImageFunAppDelegate");
    [pool release];
    return retVal;
}
```

UIImageView: An Image with a View

The UIImageView class provides a way to encapsulate an image within a view class or to provide an animation within a view. This is useful when an image needs to be anchored to other view objects, or for applications such as slideshows, where an entire view region might contain an image.

A UIImageView object acts as a view class wrapper for UIImage; that is, you first create the UIImage object, and then you use it to initialize a UIImageView object using the UIImageView class's initWithImage or setImage methods:

```
UIImage *image = [ UIImage imageNamed: @"image.png" ];
UIImageView *imageView = [ [ UIImageView alloc ]
    initWithImage: image
];
```

You can assign an array of images to an image view in order to build an animation:

```
NSMutableArray *myImages = [ [ NSMutableArray alloc ] init ];
[ myImages addItem: myImage1 ];
[ myImages addItem: myImage2 ];
[ myImages addItem: myImage3 ];
imageView.animationImages = myImages;
```

Once you have defined an animation, set its duration and repeat count properties:

```
imageView.animationDuration = 5.0; /* Five seconds */
imageView.repeatCount = 3;
```

Once the new `UIImageView` object has been configured, you can attach it to any type of view object, table cell, or other similar object:

```
[ myOtherView addSubview: imageView ];
```

To scale the image, create a new frame reflecting the adjusted size. You can then apply the new image size by assigning the frame to the object's `frame` property:

```
CGRect rect = imageView.frame;
CGSize size = CGSizeMake(160.0, 240.0);
rect.size = size;
imageView.frame = rect;
```

To enable or disable the view's animation, use the `startAnimating` and `stopAnimating` methods:

```
[ imageView startAnimating ];
if ([ imageView isAnimating ] == YES) {
    [ imageView stopAnimating ];
}
```

You'll use the `UIImageView` class extensively in Chapters 12 and 13.

Image Pickers

An image picker is a type of navigation controller class that allows you to add a simple image selector or camera interface to your application. The user is presented with an image selection screen and can choose a photo from his photo library, saved photo album, or the camera. When the user selects a photo, the picker's delegate is notified using methods from the `UIImagePickerDelegate` protocol.

You create the image picker as a `UIImagePickerController` object, and you can add it to the window as a standalone navigation controller:

```
UIImagePickerController *picker = [ [ UIImagePickerController alloc ] init ];
[ window addSubview: [ picker view ] ];
```

Image sources

You can define various sources to present to the user using the `sourceType` property:

```
picker.sourceType = UIImagePickerControllerSourceTypePhotoLibrary;
```

You may use the following sources.

Style	Description
UIImagePickerControllerSourceTypePhotoLibrary	Photo library
UIImagePickerControllerSourceTypeCamera	Camera
UIImagePickerControllerSourceTypeSavedPhotosAlbum	Saved photos

Image editing

To allow the user to move and scale the image to his liking, enable image editing by setting the `allowsImageEditing` property to `YES`:

```
picker.allowsImageEditing = YES;
```

Image selection

When the user has selected a picture, the picker's delegate is notified through its `didFinishPickingImage` method. The delegate is supplied with a `UIImage` object containing the image and an `NSDictionary` containing any editing properties, if editing was enabled.

To assign a delegate to the picker, set the picker's delegate property:

```
picker.delegate = self;
```

Add the following method to your delegate class to be notified when the user picks an image:

```
- (void)imagePickerController:(UIImagePickerController *)picker
    didFinishPickingImage:(UIImage *)image
    editingInfo:(NSDictionary *)editingInfo
{
    /* Code to handle image selection */
}
```

The parameters provide you with a pointer to the image picker controller reporting the action, so you can handle multiple pickers in one delegate. You're also provided with a pointer to the `UIImage` object itself and a dictionary object containing information about how the image was scaled and moved on the screen.

You'll also want to be notified if the user cancels image selection. Add a method named `imagePickerControllerDidCancel` to your delegate. It will be invoked with a pointer to the image picker that was canceled:

```
- (void)imagePickerControllerDidCancel:(UIImagePickerController *)picker {
    /* Additional code to handle image selection canceled */
}
```

Keyboard Properties

When Steve Jobs introduced the iPhone in one of his most intently anticipated keynote speeches, he expressed a vision for a device that could successfully redefine the user's experience as it saw fit—not just the buttons on an application, but the ability to create an entirely new user interface based on the specific needs of an application. Jobs's hatred for physical buttons clearly included physical keyboards, because Apple has found a use for nearly a dozen different "virtual" keyboard styles on the iPhone, and has provided an elegant interface to define them based on what kind of input is needed.

When a user taps a text field, the runtime automatically raises the keyboard for the user to type. This allows the developer to worry only about displaying text fields instead of managing the keyboard. Apple has elegantly designed its framework so that the text field has all authority over the keyboard's behavior, instead of the keyboard object itself. When a keyboard appears, it automatically adapts itself to match the behavior defined in the text field.

Think of this approach as the driver settings in a car. Each driver has a special way she likes her vehicle configured: seat height, mirrors, and pedal positions. If someone else wanted to drive, you wouldn't think about installing a new driver's seat just to switch drivers. Instead, the car automatically reconfigures the seat for the new driver. Think of the text field as the driver, and the keyboard as the car seat that gets reconfigured.

For preferences tables and other such views consisting of many different text fields, you can define various keyboard behaviors so that each cell will have its own style. All of the properties described in this section are available within most text objects—namely, those that import `UITextInputTraits`. You can find these traits in UI Kit's *UITextInput Traits.h* prototype.

Keyboard Style

The UI Kit framework supports eight different keyboard styles. You can assign a different style for each text field.

Set the style using the text object's `keyboardType` method:

```
textView.keyboardType = UIKeyboardTypePhonePad;
```

The following keyboard styles are supported.

Style	Description
UIKeyboardTypeDefault	Default keyboard: all characters available
UIKeyboardTypeASCIICapable	Default keyboard with ASCII support
UIKeyboardTypeNumbersAndPunctuation	Standard phone pad, supporting + * # symbols
UIKeyboardTypeURL	URL keyboard with .COM button; supports only URI characters
UIKeyboardTypeNumberPad	Number pad for numeric entry

Style	Description
UIKeyboardTypePhonePad	Phone pad for phone number entry
UIKeyboardTypeNamePhonePad	Phone pad also supporting entering name
UIKeyboardTypeEmailAddress	Keyboard for email address entry

Both the keyboard and phone pad layouts are the same size, so no additional window changes are needed to switch between the two.

Keyboard Appearance

In addition to the keyboard type, you can also adjust the keyboard's appearance by setting the keyboardAppearance property:

```
textView.keyboardAppearance = UIKeyboardAppearanceDefault;
```

The following keyboard appearances are available.

Style	Description
UIKeyboardAppearanceDefault	Default appearance; light gray
UIKeyboardAppearanceAlert	Dark gray/graphite

Return Key

For keyboards with a return key, you can assign the key various styles using the text object's returnKeyType property:

```
textView.returnKeyType = UIReturnKeyGo;
```

The following styles are supported.

Style	Description
UIReturnKeyDefault	Default: gray button labeled Return
UIReturnKeyGo	Blue button labeled Go
UIReturnKeyGoogle	Blue button labeled Google, used for searches
UIReturnKeyJoin	Blue button labeled Join
UIReturnKeyNext	Gray button labeled Next
UIReturnKeyRoute	Blue button labeled Route
UIReturnKeySearch	Blue button labeled Search
UIReturnKeySend	Blue button labeled Send
UIReturnKeyYahoo	Blue button labeled Yahoo!, used for searches
UIReturnKeyDone	Blue button labeled Done
UIReturnKeyEmergencyCall	Emergency call button

Autocapitalization

Keyboards can automatically capitalize the first letter of a new line or sentence. To toggle this, set the text object's `autocapitalizationType` property:

```
textView.autocapitalizationType = UITextAutocapitalizationTypeNone;
```

The following autocapitalization types are supported:

- `UITextAutocapitalizationTypeNone`
- `UITextAutocapitalizationTypeWords`
- `UITextAutocapitalizationTypeSentences`
- `UITextAutocapitalizationTypeAllCharacters`

Autocorrection

When entering text, the text view and keyboard objects work together to present possible corrections to typing mistakes. This is based on an internal dictionary of commonly mistyped words, combined with a typing cache that keeps track of your own typing. The iPhone generates the dictionary in */private/var/mobile/Library/Keyboard/dynamic-text.dat*.

Autocorrection is enabled by default, but you can toggle it using the text view's `autocorrectionType` property:

```
textView.autocorrectionType = UITextAutocorrectionTypeDefault ;
```

The following autocorrection types are available:

```
UITextAutocorrectionTypeDefault
UITextAutocorrectionTypeNo
UITextAutocorrectionTypeYes
```

Secure Text Entry

When typing passwords or other private data into a text window, the information shouldn't be cached in the iPhone. Turning on secure text entry disables autocorrection and word caching features for the text field. To activate secure text mode, set the `secureTextEntry` property:

```
textView.secureTextEntry = YES;
```

Pickers

Pickers are click wheels for the iPhone: large, spinning dials that can host any number of different options. Pickers are used in place of drop-down menus to provide a graphically rich selection interface for the user. The `UIPickerView` class was designed as a full-blown view class rather than a control, due to its sheer complexity and screen real estate. This allows you to attach pickers to other views or windows.

Creating a Picker

A `UIPickerView` class consumes a whopping 320×216 pixels on the screen, but can be vertically offset anywhere in the window. Like tables, the `UIPickerView` class uses a data source. Unlike tables, pickers do not make use of index paths, but reference each row by an `NSInteger` value. Pickers can have multiple dials, each referred to as a *component*.

A picker view uses a delegate as a data source, allowing the data source to exist in a separate class or view controller, as in the case of the tables in Chapter 3 and the preferences tables and section lists described earlier in this chapter.

The display region of a picker view is automatically set at a default 320×216 frame. If you try to initialize the picker with a customized frame size, it will be ignored. You can place the picker anywhere on the screen, but they are generally located at either the top or bottom:

```
UIPickerView *pickerView = [ [ UIPickerView alloc ]
    initWithFrame: CGRectMake(0.0, 280.0, 0.0, 0.0)];
pickerView.delegate = self;
pickerView.dataSource = self;
```

Picking picker properties

Many of the picker view's properties have been privatized in the SDK, giving the developer less control over it than internal classes make available. Pickers have variable options to toggle sounds, make multiple selections, and make aesthetic tweaks, but these interfaces are not available to an SDK developer. The only aesthetic option available is the selection window.

To show a translucent window across the current selection, set the picker's `showsSelectionIndicator` property to `YES`:

```
pickerView.showsSelectionIndicator = YES;
```

Picker data source

After creating the picker view, you must code the data source to provide information about the construction of the picker. The following methods are required to build a data source. They are required components of the `UIPickerViewDataSource` protocol:

`numberOfComponentsInPickerView`
Defines the number of individual click wheels (columns) to be displayed with the picker view.

`numberOfRowsInComponent`
You may assign each dial in the picker a different number of possible values (rows). This method should return the total number of rows for the dial number specified.

In addition to this, the `UIPickerViewDelegate` protocol implements the following methods to obtain specific information about the picker's components.

titleForRow

Returns the actual dial value for a given row of a given dial (component). These are returned as `NSString` objects.

viewForRow

This method can override the default behavior of the picker to display any `UIView` class in a component dial.

widthForComponent

Returns the width for a given component (dial). If this method is not implemented, the picker will size-to-fit.

rowHeightForComponent

Returns the height for a given component (dial). If this method is not implemented, the picker will size-to-fit.

The prototypes and function for these methods will be illustrated in the example later in this section.

Displaying the Picker

Once you have created and configured the picker view and coded your data source methods, you're ready to attach the picker to your view controller:

```
[ self.view addSubview: pickerView ];
```

Reading the Picker

The most direct way to obtain the index of the selected column in the picker view is to use the view's `selectedRowInComponent` method:

```
int selectedRow = [ pickerView selectedRowInComponent: 0 ];
```

A delegate method also exists and is notified whenever the user selects a row in the picker view. Use this to alert an object so it can respond to a new row selection:

```
pickerView.delegate = myObject;
```

To receive a notification when a dial's value is changed, add the following delegate method, named `didSelectRow`, to your class:

```
- (void)pickerView:(UIPickerView *)pickerView
  didSelectRow:(NSInteger)row inComponent:(NSInteger)component
{
    NSLog(@"Selected row %d from dial %d", row, component);

    /* Additional code to handle row selection */
}
```

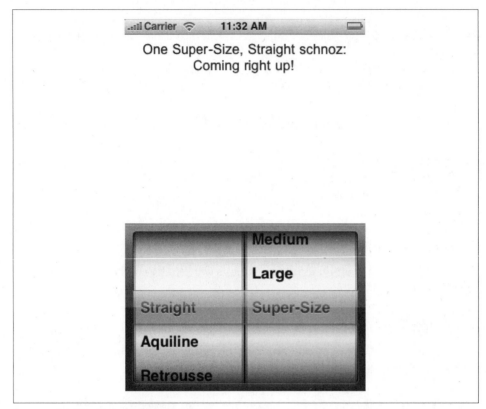

Figure 10-6. NosePicker example

NosePicker: Picking Your Nose

In this example, a `UIPickerView` containing different nose styles and sizes is presented to the user (Figure 10-6). You will first create a view controller, which then hosts the picker view as a subview. You'll be able to scroll a list of noses and choose one.

You can compile this application, shown in Examples 10-14 through 10-18, with the SDK by creating a *view-based application* project named *NosePicker*. Be sure to pull out the Interface Builder code if you'd like to see how all objects are created from scratch.

Example 10-14. NosePicker application delegate prototypes (NosePickerAppDelegate.h)

```
#import <UIKit/UIKit.h>

@class NosePickerViewController;

@interface NosePickerAppDelegate : NSObject <UIApplicationDelegate> {
    UIWindow *window;
    NosePickerViewController *viewController;
}
```

```
@property (nonatomic, retain) IBOutlet UIWindow *window;
@property (nonatomic, retain) IBOutlet NosePickerViewController *viewController;

@end
```

Example 10-15. NosePicker application delegate (NosePickerAppDelegate.m)

```
#import "NosePickerAppDelegate.h"
#import "NosePickerViewController.h"

@implementation NosePickerAppDelegate

@synthesize window;
@synthesize viewController;


- (void)applicationDidFinishLaunching:(UIApplication *)application {
    CGRect screenBounds = [ [ UIScreen mainScreen ] bounds ];

    self.window = [ [ [ UIWindow alloc ] initWithFrame: screenBounds ] autorelease ];
    viewController = [ [ NosePickerViewController alloc ] init ];

    [ window addSubview: viewController.view ];
    [ window makeKeyAndVisible ];
}


- (void)dealloc {
    [ viewController release ];
    [ window release ];
    [ super dealloc ];
}


@end
```

Example 10-16. NosePicker view controller prototypes (NosePickerViewController.h)

```
#import <UIKit/UIKit.h>

@protocol UIPickerViewDataSource, UIPickerViewDelegate;

@interface NosePickerViewController : UIViewController <UIPickerViewDelegate,
 UIPickerViewDataSource> {
    UIPickerView *pickerView;
    UITextView *textView;
    NSMutableArray *noses;
    NSMutableArray *sizes;
    int selection[2];
}
- (void)updateText;
- (NSInteger)numberOfComponentsInPickerView:(UIPickerView *)pickerView;
- (NSInteger)pickerView:(UIPickerView *)pickerView
    numberOfRowsInComponent:(NSInteger)component;
- (NSString *)pickerView:(UIPickerView *)pickerView
    titleForRow:(NSInteger)row forComponent:(NSInteger)component;
```

```
- (void)pickerView:(UIPickerView *)pickerView
    didSelectRow:(NSInteger)row inComponent:(NSInteger)component;

@end
```

Example 10-17. NosePicker view controller (NosePickerViewController.m)

```
#import "NosePickerViewController.h"

@implementation NosePickerViewController

- (id)init {
    self = [ super init ];
    if (self != nil) {
        noses = [ [ NSMutableArray alloc ] init ];
        [ noses addObject: @"Straight" ];
        [ noses addObject: @"Aquiline" ];
        [ noses addObject: @"Retrousse" ];
        [ noses addObject: @"Busque" ];
        [ noses addObject: @"Sinuous" ];
        [ noses addObject: @"Melanesian" ];
        [ noses addObject: @"African" ];

        sizes = [ [ NSMutableArray alloc ] init ];
        [ sizes addObject: @"Small" ];
        [ sizes addObject: @"Medium" ];
        [ sizes addObject: @"Large" ];
        [ sizes addObject: @"Super-Size" ];

        selection[0] = selection[1] = 0;
    }
    return self;
}

- (void)loadView {
    CGRect bounds = [ [ UIScreen mainScreen ] applicationFrame ];

    [ super loadView ];

    pickerView = [ [ UIPickerView alloc ]
        initWithFrame: CGRectMake(0.0, bounds.size.height - 216.0, 0.0, 0.0)
    ];

    pickerView.delegate = self;
    pickerView.dataSource = self;
    pickerView.showsSelectionIndicator = YES;
    [ self.view addSubview: pickerView ];

    textView = [ [ UITextView alloc ] initWithFrame:
        CGRectMake(0.0, 0.0, bounds.size.width, bounds.size.height - 216.0)
    ];

    textView.font = [ UIFont fontWithName: @"Arial" size: 18.0 ];
    textView.textAlignment = UITextAlignmentCenter;
    textView.editable = NO;
```

```
    [ self updateText ];
    [ self.view addSubview: textView ];
}

- (void)updateText {
    textView.text = [ NSString stringWithFormat:
        @"One %@, %@ schnoz:\nComing right up!\n",
        [ sizes objectAtIndex: selection[1] ],
        [ noses objectAtIndex: selection[0] ]
    ];
}

- (NSInteger)numberOfComponentsInPickerView:(UIPickerView *)pickerView {
    return 2;
}

- (NSInteger)pickerView:(UIPickerView *)pickerView
    numberOfRowsInComponent:(NSInteger)component
{
    switch(component) {
        case(0):
            return [ noses count ];
            break;
        case(1):
            return [ sizes count ];
            break;
    }
    return 0;
}

- (NSString *)pickerView:(UIPickerView *)pickerView
    titleForRow:(NSInteger)row forComponent:(NSInteger)component
{
    switch (component) {
        case(0):
            return [ noses objectAtIndex: row ];
            break;
        case(1):
            return [ sizes objectAtIndex: row ];
    }
    return nil;
}

- (void)pickerView:(UIPickerView *)pickerView
    didSelectRow:(NSInteger)row inComponent:(NSInteger)component
{
    selection[component] = row;
    [ self updateText ];
}

- (BOOL)shouldAutorotateToInterfaceOrientation:
    (UIInterfaceOrientation)interfaceOrientation
{
    return (interfaceOrientation == UIInterfaceOrientationPortrait);
}
```

```
- (void)didReceiveMemoryWarning {
    [ super didReceiveMemoryWarning ];
}

- (void)dealloc {
    [ pickerView release ];
    [ noses release ];
    [ sizes release ];
    [ super dealloc ];
}

@end
```

Example 10-18. NosePicker main (main.m)

```
#import <UIKit/UIKit.h>

int main(int argc, char *argv[]) {

    NSAutoreleasePool * pool = [[NSAutoreleasePool alloc] init];
    int retVal = UIApplicationMain(argc, argv, nil, @"NosePickerAppDelegate");
    [pool release];
    return retVal;
}
```

What's Going On

1. When the application instantiates, a new view controller is created which, in turn, initializes an array of noses and nose sizes. Variable storage is also initialized for the currently selected dials, stored in `selection`.

2. When the view controller's `loadView` method is invoked, `UIPickerView` and `UITextView` objects are created and added as subviews to the view controller. The delegate and data source for the picker view are set to the view controller. The controller's `updateText` method is invoked once to set the text within the text view.

3. The `UIPickerView` class's internal plumbing calls its data source, which returns the number of components, rows, and titles for each row in the picker view.

4. When the user selects a new item from either dial on the picker view, the view's delegate (the view controller) is notified through the picker view `didSelectRow` method. This updates the last row selected for a given dial and refreshes the text display to reflect the currently selected nose and size combination.

Further Study

When you've finished picking your nose, give some of these other exercises a try:

- Check out the *UIPickerView.h* prototypes. You'll find these deep within */Developer/Platforms/iPhoneOS.platform*, in the UI Kit framework's *Headers* directory.
- Inside the prototypes, you'll find an alternative set of data source methods, which return `UIView` objects instead of `NSString` objects. Use these to create a set of custom `UIImageView` objects for the picker.

Date/Time Pickers

The `UIDatePicker` class is a control that encapsulates and customizes a `UIPickerView` class specifically to accept date, time, and duration input. The date picker automatically configures its columns to conform to the specified style, so there's no low-level work involved in configuring dials. You can also customize it for any range of dates.

The `UIDatePicker` relies heavily on the `NSDate` class, which is part of the foundation class set used in Cocoa on the desktop. More information about this class can be found in online Cocoa references from the Apple Developer Connection website. For the purpose of the examples used here, we'll create an `NSDate` using its simplest method, `initWithString`:

```
NSDate *myDate = [ [ NSDate alloc ]
    initWithString: @"1963-11-22 12:30:00 -0500" ];
```

Creating the Date/Time Picker

The `UIDatePicker` is much more straightforward than the standard `UIPickerView`. It builds its own data source based on the date ranges you specify. To use it, just create the object:

```
UIDatePicker *datePicker = [ [ UIDatePicker alloc ]
    initWithFrame: CGRectMake(0.0, 0.0, 0.0, 0.0)];
```

By default, the picker presents the current date and time, and presents dials for day of week with month and day, hour, minute, and AM/PM. The user can select any date or time combination by default. The following subsections explain further customizations to the picker's operation.

Date picker mode

The date/time picker supports four different selection modes. Define this mode by setting the `datePickerMode` property as follows:

```
datePicker datePickerMode = UIDatePickerModeTime;
```

The following modes are supported.

Mode	Description
UIDatePickerModeTime	Hour, minute, and AM/PM selection

Mode	Description
UIDatePickerModeDate	Month, day, and year
UIDatePickerModeDateAndTime	Default; day of week + month + day, hour, minute, and AM/PM selection
UIDatePickerModeCountDownTimer	Hour and minute display for timers

Time intervals

You can set the minute dial to display minutes in various intervals, as long as the interval divides evenly into 60. The default is to display the minute dial with one-minute intervals. To use a different interval, set the `minuteInterval` property to the desired interval:

```
datePicker.minuteInterval = 10;
```

Date ranges

You can specify a range of allowable dates by setting the `minimumDate` and `maximumDate` properties. If the user attempts to scroll to a date beyond this range, the dial will scroll back to the closest valid date. Both methods expect an `NSDate` object:

```
NSDate *minDate = [ [ NSDate alloc ]
    initWithString: @"1773-12-16 12:00:00 -0500" ];
NSDate *maxDate = [ [ NSDate alloc ]
    initWithString: @"1776-07-04 12:00:00 -0500" ];

datePicker.minimumDate = minDate;
datePicker.maximumDate = maxDate;
```

If one or both of these date range properties isn't set, the default behavior will allow the user to select any past or future date. This can be useful, for example, when selecting a birthday, which could be any date in the past, but capped at the current day.

To set the date you would like to be displayed by default, set the `date` property:

```
datePicker.date = minDate;
```

Alternatively, you may use the `setDate` method. If you choose to animate, the dials will scroll to the date you specify:

```
[ datePicker setDate: maxDate animated: YES ];
```

Displaying the Date Picker

Once you have created the date picker, attach it to a view object using the same method as that of the `UIPickerView`:

```
[ self addSubview: datePicker ];
```

The picker is always 216 pixels high, regardless of the frame size passed to it. You'll need to make sure you've allocated enough screen space to host it.

Reading the Date

The date is generally read from the date picker when the user transitions to a different view, such as leaving a preferences table. The `date` property provides an `NSDate` object when read:

```
NSDate *selectedDate = datePicker.date;
```

Because the date picker is a subclass of the `UIControl` class (unlike `UIPickerView`), you can also hook a delegate into the `UIControl` class's notification structure:

```
[ datePicker addTarget: self action:
    @selector(dateChanged:)
    forControlEvents:UIControlEventValueChanged
];
```

Your action class will be called whenever the user selects a new date:

```
-(void) dateChanged: (id)sender
{
    UIDatePicker *control = (UIDatePicker *) sender;
    NSDate *selectedDate = control.date;

  /* Additional code to respond to date change */
}
```

DatePicker: Independence Day Picker

This simple example illustrates the use of a basic date picker object to select a date between the Boston Tea Party (December 16, 1773) and American Independence Day (July 4, 1776). The example simply creates a `UIDatePicker` object and displays it to the user (Figure 10-7). When the user selects a new date, this information is updated in the text view above the picker.

You can compile this application, shown in Examples 10-19 through 10-23, with the SDK by creating a *view-based application* project named *DatePicker*. Be sure to pull out the Interface Builder code if you'd like to see how all objects are created from scratch.

Example 10-19. DatePicker application delegate prototypes (DatePickerAppDelegate.h)

```
#import <UIKit/UIKit.h>

@class DatePickerViewController;

@interface DatePickerAppDelegate : NSObject <UIApplicationDelegate> {
    UIWindow *window;
    DatePickerViewController *viewController;
}

@property (nonatomic, retain) IBOutlet UIWindow *window;
@property (nonatomic, retain) IBOutlet DatePickerViewController *viewController;

@end
```

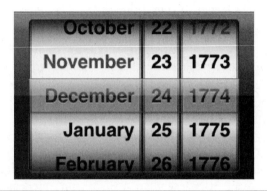

Figure 10-7. DatePicker example

Example 10-20. DatePicker application delegate (DatePickerAppDelegate.m)

```objc
#import "DatePickerAppDelegate.h"
#import "DatePickerViewController.h"

@implementation DatePickerAppDelegate

@synthesize window;
@synthesize viewController;


- (void)applicationDidFinishLaunching:(UIApplication *)application {
    CGRect screenBounds = [ [ UIScreen mainScreen ] bounds ];

    self.window = [ [ [ UIWindow alloc ] initWithFrame: screenBounds ] autorelease ];
    viewController = [ [ DatePickerViewController alloc ] init ];

    [ window addSubview: viewController.view ];
    [ window makeKeyAndVisible ];
}


- (void)dealloc {
```

```
    [ viewController release ];
    [ window release ];
    [ super dealloc ];
}


@end
```

Example 10-21. DatePicker view controller prototypes (DatePickerViewController.h)

```
#import <UIKit/UIKit.h>

@protocol UIPickerViewDataSource, UIPickerViewDelegate;

@interface DatePickerViewController : UIViewController {
    UIDatePicker *pickerView;
    UITextView *textView;
    NSDate *minDate, *maxDate;
}
-(void) dateChanged: (id)sender;

@end
```

Example 10-22. DatePicker view controller (DatePickerViewController.m)

```
#import "DatePickerViewController.h"

@implementation DatePickerViewController

- (id)init {
    self = [ super init ];
    if (self != nil) {
        minDate = [ [ NSDate alloc ]
            initWithString: @"1773-12-16 12:00:00 -0500" ];
        maxDate = [ [ NSDate alloc ]
            initWithString: @"1776-07-04 12:00:00 -0500" ];
    }
    return self;
}

- (void)loadView {
    CGRect bounds = [ [ UIScreen mainScreen ] applicationFrame ];

    [ super loadView ];

    pickerView = [ [ UIDatePicker alloc ] initWithFrame:
        CGRectMake(0.0, bounds.size.height - 216.0, 0.0, 0.0) ];

    pickerView.minimumDate = minDate;
    pickerView.maximumDate = maxDate;
    pickerView.datePickerMode = UIDatePickerModeDate;
    pickerView.date = minDate;

    [ pickerView addTarget: self action:
     @selector(dateChanged:)
        forControlEvents:UIControlEventValueChanged
```

```
        ];

    [ self.view addSubview: pickerView ];

    textView = [ [ UITextView alloc ] initWithFrame:
        CGRectMake(0.0, 0.0, bounds.size.width, bounds.size.height - 216.0) ];
    textView.font = [ UIFont fontWithName: @"Arial" size: 22.0 ];
    textView.textColor = [ UIColor redColor ];
    textView.textAlignment = UITextAlignmentCenter;
    textView.text = [ pickerView.date description ];
    textView.editable = NO;

    [ self.view addSubview: textView ];
}

-(void) dateChanged: (id)sender
{
    UIDatePicker *control = (UIDatePicker *) sender;
    NSDate *selectedDate = control.date;
    textView.text = [ selectedDate description ];
}

- (BOOL)shouldAutorotateToInterfaceOrientation:
(UIInterfaceOrientation)interfaceOrientation
{
    return (interfaceOrientation == UIInterfaceOrientationPortrait);
}


- (void)didReceiveMemoryWarning {
    [ super didReceiveMemoryWarning ];
}

- (void)dealloc {
    [ pickerView release ];
    [ super dealloc ];
}

@end
```

Example 10-23. DatePicker main (main.m)

```
#import <UIKit/UIKit.h>

int main(int argc, char *argv[]) {

    NSAutoreleasePool * pool = [[NSAutoreleasePool alloc] init];
    int retVal = UIApplicationMain(argc, argv, nil, @"DatePickerAppDelegate");
    [pool release];
    return retVal;
}
```

What's Going On

1. When the application is run, its application delegate creates a new view controller, which, in turn, initializes a set of NSDate objects containing the minimum and maximum dates.

2. When the view controller's loadView method is invoked, UIDatePicker and UIText View objects are created and added as subviews to the view controller. The date picker is initialized with minimum and maximum dates, and the current value is set to the minimum date. An observer is added to invoke the dateChanged method whenever the user selects a new date.

3. The UIDatePicker class's internal plumbing builds the picker based on the dates and style specified.

4. When the user selects a new item from any dial on the picker, the UIControl notification framework invokes the target's dateChanged method. This reads the new date and displays it in the text view above the date picker.

Further Study

When you've finished spinning dials, consider some additional reading:

- Check out the *UIDatePicker.h* prototypes. You'll find these deep within */Devel oper/Platforms/iPhoneOS.platform*, inside the UI Kit framework's *Headers* directory.

Tab Bars

Tab bars are one of Apple's solutions for a universal device with no physical buttons. With iPhone applications so rich in features, many have four or five important functions that the user may need to get to quickly. Located at the bottom of the screen, tab bars provide what would traditionally be looked at as shortcut buttons on other mobile devices. Going back to Apple's book metaphor, tab bars are the bookmarks to different chapters of an application. They also help the developer to logically group functions within an application, to present the primary functions the application will provide.

Many of the preloaded iPhone applications use tab bars, including the Mobile Phone application, YouTube, and the iTunes WiFi Music Store. The tabs separate related pages of data (e.g., Featured Music, Purchased Songs, etc.) or provide shortcuts to different functions within a single application (e.g., Contacts, Recent Calls, Voicemail, etc.).

Tab Bar Controllers

In UI Kit, the UITabBar class represents tab bars and the UITabBarController class encapsulates them, which makes it easy to manage a number of different views and transitions. Like other view controllers, tab bars are designed to be autonomous in their presentation. Internally, they handle all of the mess of button selection and view transition—they "just work."

Tab bar controllers work in a similar fashion to navigation controllers: navigation controllers read the navigation bar properties of each view controller class pushed on its stack. The view controller itself defines the properties of its bar, and those are displayed when the view is displayed. Similarly, a tab bar controller allows you to add a series of view controllers to it, and each view controller identifies its own button properties, which are then displayed by the tab bar controller.

Think of this approach as mass production for a box of crayons. Each crayon you place in the box has its own pigment and label. If you printed a list of available colors on the side of the box, you'd have to change the box every time you manufactured a different set of colors. A more cost-effective way to design the box would be to place a clear plastic window on the front so the customer can see the individual colors inside the box. This lets you swap out crayons without changing the box.

Each view you want to display is like a single crayon, and the tab bar controller is the box. Rather than hardcoding the button titles and images into the tab bar controller, the tab bar controller simply arranges each view so that its own "label" (tab bar button) shows through the box. This way, the labels belong to the views instead of the controller. The tab bar controller then handles the work of transitioning to the selected view when the user presses its button.

Building a Tab Bar Controller

To build a tab bar controller, you'll first need the individual pages you'll want to provide buttons for. Create each page as a UIViewController object, like you've been doing since Chapter 3.

Build a collection

You may have several different types of view controllers within your application to handle various functions. If you are writing a game application, you may have controllers such as GameViewController, SettingsViewController, HighScoreViewController, and AboutViewController. Before you create the tab bar, you'll first create an array of the view controller objects you want to display in the tab bar. An example of this follows:

```
NSMutableArray *viewControllers = [ [ NSMutableArray alloc ] init ];
[ viewControllers addObject: myGameViewController ];
[ viewControllers addObject: mySettingsViewController ];
[ viewControllers addObject: myHighScoreViewController ];
[ viewControllers addObject: myAboutViewController ];
```

Configure button properties

As you learned from the crayon box illustration, each view controller comes with its own "label" defining what its tab bar button should look like. The tab bar then displays the tab bar button according to the view controller's properties. Configure the tab bar button within the view controller's `init` method to define its title and/or `tabBarItem` property:

```
- (id) init {
    self = [ super init ];
    if (self != nil) {
        self.tabBarItem = [ [ UITabBarItem alloc ]
            initWithTitle: @"High Scores"
            image: [ UIImage imageNamed: @"high_scores.png"
            tag: 4
        ];
    }
    return self;
}
```

Set the `tabBarItem` property to a `UITabBarItem` object. You can initialize tab bar items in one of two ways. The `initWithTitle` method, as shown in the previous example, allows you to use a title and image to render the button with user-defined data. A method also exists to create a number of system buttons—standard buttons used widely throughout many iPhone applications. To create these system buttons, use the `initWithTabBarSystemItem` method:

```
self.tabBarItem = [ [ UITabBarItem alloc ]
    initWithTabBarSystemItem: UITabBarSystemItemFavorites tag: 4
];
```

You may use the following system buttons identifiers:

```
UITabBarSystemItemMore
UITabBarSystemItemFavorites
UITabBarSystemItemFeatured
UITabBarSystemItemTopRated
UITabBarSystemItemRecents
UITabBarSystemItemContacts
UITabBarSystemItemHistory
UITabBarSystemItemBookmarks
UITabBarSystemItemSearch
UITabBarSystemItemDownloads
UITabBarSystemItemMostRecent
UITabBarSystemItemMostViewed
```

Creating the tab bar controller

Once each view has assigned itself a tab bar button, you can create a tab bar controller object and add the array of view controllers to it:

```
UITabBarController *tabBarController = [ [ UITabBarController alloc ] init ];
tabBarController.viewControllers = viewControllers;
```

Displaying the tab bar controller

After you have created the tab bar controller, display it by adding it as a subview to a window or another view:

```
[ window addSubview: tabBarController.view ];
[ window makeKeyAndVisible ];
```

Customizable Buttons

By default, a tab bar controller allows the user to customize the layout of buttons when more than five exist. This can be done by clicking the More tab, followed by an Edit button on the navigation bar. You may choose to only allow certain tabs to be customized, or you may disable all customizations. To do this, set the tab bar controller's customizableViewControllers to an array of view controllers you want to allow the user to customize:

```
NSMutableArray *customizableControllers = [ [ NSMutableArray alloc ] init ];
[ customizableControllers addObject: myGameViewController ];
[ customizableControllers addObject: mySettingsViewController ];
tabBarController.customizableViewControllers = customizableControllers;
```

Use nil to disable all customization:

```
tabBarController.customizableViewControllers = nil;
```

Navigation

When you display the tab bar controller, the controller handles its own navigation so that the selected tab's view is automatically transitioned to the front of the screen. If more than five view controllers are attached to a tab bar controller, the tab bar controller will automatically display a tab labeled More. When the user taps on this button, the view controllers that could not fit on the screen will be displayed in a table list form.

To read or change the currently active view controller, use the selectedViewController property:

```
tabBarController.selectedViewController = myGameViewController;
UIViewController *activeController = tabBarController.selectedViewController;
if (activeController == myGameViewController) {
    /* myGameViewController is currently active */
}
```

You can also refer to buttons by index:

```
tabBarController.selectedIndex = 3;
```

If you specified more than five view controllers, the "More" view controller will be assigned its own index.

Delegate Actions

To be notified when a view is selected on the tab bar, assign a tab bar controller delegate:

```
tabBarController.delegate = self;
```

The delegate will be notified whenever a view controller is selected, through a call to a delegate method named `didSelectViewController`:

```
- (void)tabBarController:(UITabBarController *)tabBarController
    didSelectViewController:(UIViewController *)viewController
{
    /* Additional special code to handle selection */
}
```

The delegate will also be notified whenever the user has finished customizing the tab bar layout. You can receive this notification by adding a delegate method named `didEndCustomizingViewControllers`:

```
- (void)tabBarController:(UITabBarController *)tabBarController
    didEndCustomizingViewControllers:(NSArray *)viewControllers
    changed:(BOOL)changed
{
    /* Additional special code to handle end of customizing tab bar */
}
```

TabDemo: Another Textbook Approach

In Chapter 3, you were introduced to transitions by means of a page-flipping example. This example is similar, except you'll use eight pages representing eight different view controllers in an application. Each page will be controlled by a button on the tab bar which, when pressed, will flip to the corresponding page. The tab bar automatically handles the transition to the selected view controller.

You can compile this application, shown in Examples 10-24 through 10-28, with the SDK by creating a *view-based application* project named *TabDemo*. Be sure to pull out the Interface Builder code if you'd like to see how all objects are created from scratch.

Example 10-24. TabDemo application delegate prototypes (TabDemoAppDelegate.h)

```
#import <UIKit/UIKit.h>

@class TabDemoViewController;

@interface TabDemoAppDelegate : NSObject <UIApplicationDelegate> {
    UIWindow *window;
    UITabBarController *tabBarController;
```

```
        NSMutableArray *viewControllers;
}

@property (nonatomic, retain) IBOutlet UIWindow *window;

@end
```

Example 10-25. TabDemo application delegate (TabDemoAppDelegate.m)

```
#import "TabDemoAppDelegate.h"
#import "TabDemoViewController.h"

@implementation TabDemoAppDelegate

@synthesize window;

- (void)applicationDidFinishLaunching:(UIApplication *)application {
    CGRect screenBounds = [ [ UIScreen mainScreen ] bounds ];

    self.window = [ [ [ UIWindow alloc ] initWithFrame: screenBounds ]
        autorelease
    ];

    viewControllers = [ [ NSMutableArray alloc ] init ];
    for(int i = 0; i < 8; i ++) {
        [ viewControllers addObject: [
            [ TabDemoViewController alloc ] initWithPageNumber: i ]
        ];
    }

    tabBarController = [ [ UITabBarController alloc ] init ];
    tabBarController.viewControllers = viewControllers;

    [ window addSubview: tabBarController.view ];
    [ window makeKeyAndVisible ];
}

- (void)dealloc {
    [ window release ];
    [ super dealloc ];
}

@end
```

Example 10-26. TabDemo view controller prototypes (TabDemoViewController.h)

```
#import <UIKit/UIKit.h>

@interface TabDemoViewController : UIViewController {
    UITextView *textView;
    int page;
}
- (id) initWithPageNumber:(int)pageNumber;

@end
```

Example 10-27. TabDemo view controller (TabDemoViewController.m)

```objc
#import "TabDemoViewController.h"

@implementation TabDemoViewController

- (id) initWithPageNumber:(int)pageNumber {
    self = [ super init ];
    if (self != nil) {
        page = pageNumber;
        self.title = [ NSString stringWithFormat: @"Page %d", page ];
        self.tabBarItem = [ [ UITabBarItem alloc ] initWithTitle:
            [ NSString stringWithFormat: @"Page %d", page ] image: nil tag: page ];
    }
    return self;
}

- (void) loadView {
    [ super loadView ];

    CGRect bounds = [ [ UIScreen mainScreen ] applicationFrame ];
    textView = [ [ UITextView alloc ] initWithFrame: bounds ];
    textView.text = [ [ NSString alloc ]
        initWithFormat: @"Text for page %d", page
    ];

    self.view = textView;
}

- (BOOL)shouldAutorotateToInterfaceOrientation:
    (UIInterfaceOrientation)interfaceOrientation
{
    return (interfaceOrientation == UIInterfaceOrientationPortrait);
}

- (void)didReceiveMemoryWarning {
    [ super didReceiveMemoryWarning ];
}

- (void)dealloc {
    [ textView release ];
    [ super dealloc ];
}

@end
```

Example 10-28. TabDemo main (main.m)

```objc
#import <UIKit/UIKit.h>

int main(int argc, char *argv[]) {

    NSAutoreleasePool * pool = [[NSAutoreleasePool alloc] init];
    int retVal = UIApplicationMain(argc, argv, nil, @"TabDemoAppDelegate");
    [pool release];
```

```
        return retVal;
    }
```

What's Going On

1. When the application is run, its application delegate creates a series of eight different view controllers and adds them to an array named viewControllers. The TabDemoViewController class uses its own initWithPageNumber method, which customizes its title, button, and display text according to the page number passed to it.

2. A UITabBarController is created and assigned the array of eight view controllers. The tab bar controller is then added to the main window.

3. Whenever a new tab is pressed, the tab bar controller automatically handles the transition to the new view. It also displays the More button on its own, and allows the user to customize button positions. That's it! It's that simple.

Further Study

Now that you've learned how to get people to press your buttons, have a little more fun with tab bars:

- Try your hand at creating system buttons and your own custom button images.
- Modify this demo so that when the user selects page 3, it automatically reselects page 4, just to mess with their head.
- Check out the *UITabBar.h*, *UITabBarController.h*, and *UITabBarItem.h* prototypes. You'll find these deep within */Developer/Platforms/iPhoneOS.platform*, inside the UI Kit framework's *Headers* directory.

Sensors and Device Information

The iPhone includes many sensors, such as the accelerometer and proximity sensor. Other sensors, such as the orientation sensor, are used internally to automatically manage screen rotation, but may be of value for custom applications. In addition to sensors, the UIDevice class also allows you to read certain operating system-level information, such as the device's model, software version, and unique identifier.

Reading the Orientation

While most view controller classes do the work of changing the device's user interface, custom applications might choose to handle their own orientation changes. The orientation sensor can be read through the UIDevice class, and provides a set of simple enumerated values to identify the orientation.

To read the orientation, obtain an instance of the current `UIDevice` object:

```
UIDevice *device = [ UIDevice currentDevice ];
```

Access the orientation from the object's orientation property:

```
UIDeviceOrientation = device.orientation;
```

You may set the following values as the orientation.

`UIDeviceOrientationUnknown`
Catchall for errors or hardware failures.

`UIDeviceOrientationPortrait`
Oriented upright vertically in portrait mode.

`UIDeviceOrientationPortraitUpsideDown`
Oriented upside-down vertically in portrait mode.

`UIDeviceOrientationLandscapeLeft`
Device is rotated counter-clockwise in landscape mode.

`UIDeviceOrientationLandscapeRight`
Device is rotated clockwise in landscape mode.

`UIDeviceOrientationFaceUp`
Device is lying flat, face up; such as on a table.

`UIDeviceOrientationFaceDown`
Device is lying flat, face down; such as on a table.

Reading Device Information

In addition to the device's orientation, you can read other information from the `UIDevice` instance. To read these, first obtain an instance of the current device:

```
UIDevice *device = [ UIDevice currentDevice ];
```

You can subsequently read the following properties. Each provides an `NSString` object to describe the device.

Property	Description
name	Name assigned to the iPhone by its owner
model	Device model; "iPhone," "iPod Touch," etc.
localizationModel	The localized version of the model
systemName	OS name; "iPhone OS"
systemVersion	The operating system version
uniqueIdentifier	Unique identifier of the device

Reading the Accelerometer

The orientation API gets its information from a small accelerometer built into the iPhone. This tiny piece of hardware reports the raw x-y-z position of the device. While reading the orientation can give you a general idea of how the device is being held, reading the accelerometer allows you to sense the slightest movement of the device. This is frequently used in games, where the user can move the device to steer a character or shake it to roll dice or erase a drawing pad.

Because the iPhone's accelerometer doesn't include a gyroscope, it can't provide information about speed, or as much detail about the state of the device as, say, a Nintendo Wii controller. It has proven useful, however, for simple applications such as simple games, bobble heads, and drawing programs.

 Remember, not all of your customers will appreciate the iPhone's accelerometer. Adding an option to enable multi-touch controls can help to increase your potential audience.

To read the accelerometer, obtain the shared instance of the UIAccelerometer object, which is available to your application:

```
UIAccelerometer *accelerometer = [ UIAccelerometer sharedInstance ];
```

You can now access the x-y-z position of the accelerometer by accessing their respective properties, as shown below:

```
UIAccelerationValue x = accelerometer.x;
UIAccelerationValue y = accelerometer.y;
UIAccelerationValue z = accelerometer.z;
```

The UIAccelerationValue data type is defined as a double floating point.

Tracking movement

To track movement of the accelerometer, you'll want your application to be notified whenever the device accelerates. To do this, assign an object as the accelerometer's delegate:

```
accelerometer.delegate = self;
```

Your delegate class will then be notified whenever the device accelerates:

```
- (void)accelerometer:(UIAccelerometer *)accelerometer
 didAccelerate:(UIAcceleration *)acceleration {
    /* Additional code to handle acceleration */
}
```

Finally, you can set the accelerometer's updateInterval property with an NSTimeInterval to set the time interval at which you'd like to receive updates from the accelerometer:

```
NSTimeInterval timeInterval = 0.5;
accelerometer.updateInterval = timeInterval;
```

 Don't set the update interval too low or your application might get bog-
ged down with delegate calls. Apple internally specifies a minimum
value, but this minimum does not appear to be published.

Proximity Sensor

If an application is performing a task that would normally require the user to hold the
device to his face, the proximity sensor should be activated to cause the iPhone to shut
its display off.

To activate the proximity sensor, obtain a shared instance of your `UIApplication` object
and access its `proximitySensingEnabled` property:

```
UIApplication *myApp = [ UIApplication sharedApplication ];
myApp.proximitySensingEnabled = YES;
```

When active, the proximity sensor will automatically shut down the screen when it
senses a face nearby. There is presently no sanctioned delegate method or other SDK-
friendly means of notifying the application when this occurs. Apple must have thought
some of their developers would do creepy things with it.

 Be sure to disable the proximity sensor when the device should no longer
be held to the user's face.

Further Study

- Check out the *UIDevice.h* and *UIAccelerometer.h* prototypes. You'll find these
  deep within */Developer/Platforms/iPhoneOS.platform*, inside the UI Kit framework's *Headers* directory.

Scroll Views

Think of scroll views as one of those red secret decoder slides you find in cereal boxes.
Placing this small red flap of plastic over part of a secret codebook reveals a small
portion of the page. The rest of the page is still there, but you can't see it until you slide
the lens over it. The red lens represents the iPhone's screen, and reveals only the content
the user has scrolled over. The rest of the content is hidden from view, falling off the
screen, until the user scrolls the window to the part he wants to see. Scroll views not
only allow you to scroll content, but to zoom in and out, and even page flip.

Creating the Scroll View

The `UIScrollView` class is responsible for all UI Kit-based scrolling. Creating a scroll view is the equivalent of creating both a red lens and blank pages in a secret codebook:

```
CGRect bounds = [ [ UIScreen mainScreen ] applicationFrame ];
UIScrollView *scrollView = [ [ UIScrollView alloc ] initWithFrame: bounds ];
```

Once you have created the scroll view, you'll glue the content of another view onto the scroll view's blank pages. This creates a scrolling content window:

```
[ scrollView addSubview: myBiggerView ];
```

You must provide the content's actual size to the scroll view so that it knows how much to scroll:

```
scrollView.contentSize = myBiggerView.frame.size;
```

To enable zooming in or out, adjust the scroll view's `maximumZoomScale` and `minimum ZoomScale` properties. This will allow the user to pinch and resize the content:

```
scrollView.maximumZoomScale = 3.00; /* Allow zooming in to 3x original size */
scrollView.minimumZoomScale = 0.25; /* Allow zooming out to 25% of original size */
```

To enable zooming, you'll also need to add a `UIScrollViewDelegate` delegate that responds to a method named `viewForZoomingInScrollView`. This method returns the `UIView` object to use when zooming content:

```
scrollView.delegate = self;
- (UIView *)viewForZoomingInScrollView:(UIScrollView *)scrollView {
    return myBiggerView;
}
```

 For large data sizes, you'll want to start off with a zoom scale below actual size (`1.0`) to allow the user to zoom in smoothly.

Properties

In addition to the basic properties just outlined, scroll views have many other properties, which can fine-tune the behavior of your content. You can customize the `UIScroll View` class in many ways. The following properties are the most commonly used:

indicatorStyle
> Specifies the type of scrollbar indicators you'd like to use. The default behavior is to draw black scroll bars with a white border, which works against most backgrounds. The following styles are available:
>
> ```
> UIScrollViewIndicatorStyleDefault
> UIScrollViewIndicatorStyleBlack
> UIScrollViewIndicatorStyleWhite
> ```

---

contentOffset
> A CGPoint structure containing the offset of the content to display in the upper-left corner of the window. The default is to begin at 0×0, but you may position your content differently.

directionalLockEnabled
> The default behavior is to allow the user to scroll both horizontally and vertically simultaneously. Set this property to YES to cause the behavior to lock the user into either horizontal or vertical scrolling, depending on the initial gesture.

bounces
> When the user reaches the edge of the scrollable region, this feature allows the user to drag slightly beyond the boundaries. When user lifts his finger, the region will bounce back into place like a rubber band, giving the user a visual cue that he's reached the beginning or end of the document. If you don't want the user to be able to scroll past the viewable content, set this property to NO.

bouncesZoom
> Like the bounces option, this method allows the user to zoom beyond the minimum or maximum zoom levels, then bounces the user back to within range. If you don't want the user to be able to zoom past the ranges you've specified, set this property to NO.

pagingEnabled
> When paging is enabled, the scroll view is split up into separate segments and the user's scrolling experience will be that of flipping pages. You can use this to perform page *flicking*, explained in Chapter 13.

Delegate Methods

When a delegate is assigned to the scroll view, the following delegate methods are notified during special events:

-(void)scrollViewDidScroll:(UIScrollView *)scrollView;
> Notified when the view is scrolled. Includes a pointer to the scroll view that was scrolled, at which point its contentOffset property can be read to determine where it is scrolled to.

-(void)scrollViewWillBeginDragging:(UIScrollView *)scrollView;
> Notified when the user first begins dragging in any direction. This, too, can be used to read the contentOffset property of the scroll view, whose pointer is passed in as an argument.

-(void)scrollViewDidEndDragging:(UIScrollView   *)scrollView   willDecelerate:
(BOOL)decelerate;
> Notified when the user lifts a dragging finger. A Boolean value is also provided indicating whether the scroll view will need to decelerate before reporting a final resting position.

```
-(void)scrollViewWillBeginDecelerating:(UIScrollView *)scrollView;
```
Notified when the user lifts his finger up as the scroll view continues to move. This can be used to read the contentOffset property to identify specifically where the user last scrolled to before lifting his finger, even though this will not be the final resting position of the scroll bars.

```
-(void)scrollViewDidEndDecelerating:(UIScrollView *)scrollView;
```
Notified when the above deceleration completes and the scroll view ceases scrolling. By the time this notification is received, the scroll view's contentOffset property will reflect the final resting position of the scroll bar.

```
-(void)scrollViewDidEndZooming:(UIScrollView    *)scrollView    withView:(UIView
*)view atScale:(float)scale;
```
Notified when the user has zoomed to a given magnification. The scale, represented in a floating-point value, will be passed as an argument.

```
-(BOOL)scrollViewShouldScrollToTop:(UIScrollView  *)scrollView;, -(void)scroll
ViewDidScrollToTop:(UIScrollView *)scrollView;
```
When the user taps on the iPhone's status bar, the scroll view delegate can determine if the view should scroll back to the top.

BigImage: Scrolling a Weather Map

This example uses the NSData object you've learned about to download a large weather map and display it to the user in a scroll view. You'll see how another UIView class (UIImageView) is attached to scroll view, and how its delegate works.

You can compile this application, shown in Examples 10-29 through 10-33, with the SDK by creating a *view-based application* project named *BigImage*. Be sure to pull out the Interface Builder code if you'd like to see how all objects are created from scratch.

Example 10-29. BigImage application delegate prototypes (BigImageAppDelegate.h)

```objc
#import <UIKit/UIKit.h>

@class BigImageViewController;

@interface BigImageAppDelegate : NSObject <UIApplicationDelegate> {
    UIWindow *window;
    BigImageViewController *viewController;
}

@property (nonatomic, retain) IBOutlet UIWindow *window;
@property (nonatomic, retain) IBOutlet BigImageViewController *viewController;

@end
```

Example 10-30. BigImage application delegate (BigImageAppDelegate.m)

```objc
#import "BigImageAppDelegate.h"
#import "BigImageViewController.h"
```

```
@implementation BigImageAppDelegate

@synthesize window;
@synthesize viewController;


- (void)applicationDidFinishLaunching:(UIApplication *)application {
    CGRect screenBounds = [ [ UIScreen mainScreen ] bounds ];

    self.window = [ [ [ UIWindow alloc ] initWithFrame: screenBounds ] autorelease ];
    viewController = [ [ BigImageViewController alloc ] init ];

    [ window addSubview: viewController.view ];
    [ window makeKeyAndVisible ];
}


- (void)dealloc {
    [viewController release];
    [window release];
    [super dealloc];
}


@end
```

Example 10-31. BigImage view controller prototypes (BigImageViewController.h)

```
#import <UIKit/UIKit.h>

@interface BigImageViewController : UIViewController <UIScrollViewDelegate> {
    UIScrollView *scrollView;
    UIImageView *imageView;
}

@end
```

Example 10-32. BigImage view controller (BigImageViewController.m)

```
#import "BigImageViewController.h"

@implementation BigImageViewController

- (id)init {
    self = [ super init ];
    if (self != nil) {
        imageView = [ [ UIImageView alloc ] initWithImage:
            [ UIImage imageWithData:
            [ NSData dataWithContentsOfURL:
              [ NSURL URLWithString:
                @"http://forecast.weather.gov/wwamap/png/US.png" ]
            ]
        ] ];
    }
    return self;
```

```
}

- (void)loadView {
    [ super loadView ];
    CGRect bounds = [ [ UIScreen mainScreen ] applicationFrame ];

    scrollView = [ [ UIScrollView alloc ] initWithFrame: bounds ];
    scrollView.contentSize = imageView.frame.size;
    scrollView.maximumZoomScale = 3.0;
    scrollView.minimumZoomScale = 0.25;
    scrollView.delegate = self;
    scrollView.bounces = NO;
    [ scrollView addSubview: imageView ];

    self.view = scrollView;
}

- (UIView *)viewForZoomingInScrollView:(UIScrollView *)scrollView {
    return imageView;
}

- (BOOL)shouldAutorotateToInterfaceOrientation:
    (UIInterfaceOrientation)interfaceOrientation
{
    return (interfaceOrientation == UIInterfaceOrientationPortrait);
}

- (void)didReceiveMemoryWarning {
    [ super didReceiveMemoryWarning ];
}

- (void)dealloc {
    [ UIScrollView release ];
    [ UIImageView release ];
    [ super dealloc ];
}

@end
```

Example 10-33. BigImage main (main.m)

```
#import <UIKit/UIKit.h>

int main(int argc, char *argv[]) {

    NSAutoreleasePool * pool = [[NSAutoreleasePool alloc] init];
    int retVal = UIApplicationMain(argc, argv, nil, @"BigImageAppDelegate");
    [pool release];
    return retVal;
}
```

What's Going On

1. When the application is run, its application delegate builds a view controller and attaches it to a window, as usual. The view controller is initialized, which causes a `UIImageView` object to be created. The contents of the image view are downloaded from the national weather service.

2. When the view controller is loaded, a `UIScrollView` object is created. The image view is anchored to the scroll view and the scroll view's zooming and aesthetic properties are set.

3. The scroll view's internal plumbing handles the entire scrolling process, scroll bar display, and other related functions.

4. When the user zooms, the scroll view's delegate method `viewForZoomingInScroll View` is called. This returns the same `UIImageView` object, since we don't have a higher resolution copy to work with.

Further Study

Scroll views are an easy way to scale down large data presented to the user:

- Try your hand at creating scroll views for some of your own content.
- Check out the *UIScrollView.h* prototypes. You'll find these deep within */Developer/Platforms/iPhoneOS.platform*, inside the UI Kit framework's *Headers* directory.

Web Views

Chapter 3 introduced the `UITextView` object and its hidden `setHTML` method for the creation of HTML-formatted windows. You can use the `UIWebView` class to build a browser-like page, providing many of the basic routines you'd find in a web browser: fetching pages remotely, navigating forward and back, and perform zooming and scaling. It is also useful for displaying rich text, using varying fonts and sizes. A web view can even detect phone numbers in web pages, allowing the user to tap them to initiate a phone call. Web views are one of the core components that make Safari tick. Web views can handle more than web pages, too; they can display images and PDFs. Web views can display any of these locally or remotely, based on the content you feed them.

Creating the Web View

The web view is created as any other `UIView` class is, using an `initWithFrame` method:

```
CGRect bounds = [ [ UIScreen mainScreen ] applicationFrame ];
UIWebView *webView = [ [ UIWebView alloc ] initWithFrame: bounds ];
```

Once you have created it, you can set a few properties. To automatically scale the page to fit the screen, set the scalesPageToFit property to YES:

```
webView.scalesPageToFit = YES;
```

If you would like the web view to automatically detect phone numbers and allow the user to tap on them to dial, set the detectsPhoneNumbers property to YES:

```
webView.detectsPhoneNumbers = YES;
```

Displaying the Web View

To display the web view, anchor it to an existing window or view class:

```
[ self.view addSubview: webView ];
```

Loading Content

Once you have created the web view, you can load content a number of different ways. The most common way to load content is by using the loadRequest method to load a local or remote resource. The loadRequest method accepts an NSURLRequest object, which can be created from an existing NSURL object, which you've already learned about. An example to create and load a remote web page follows:

```
NSURL *url = [ NSURL URLWithString: @"http://www.oreilly.com" ];
NSURLRequest *request = [ NSURLRequest requestWithURL: url ];
[ webView loadRequest: request ];
```

To load a local file resource, use the NSURL class's fileURLWithPath initializer:

```
NSURL *url = [ NSURL fileURLWithPath: filePath ];
NSURLRequest *request = [ NSURLRequest requestWithURL: url ];
[ webView loadRequest: request ];
```

The UIWebView class also supports loading an NSString object as source. You may optionally provide a base URL to instruct the UIWebView object how to follow links and load remote resources:

```
[ webView loadHTMLString: myHTML
    baseURL: [ NSURL URLWithString: @"http://www.mywebsite.com" ]
];
```

Navigation

The UIWebView class manages browser navigation internally. You can control forward and back actions using the goForward and goBack methods, as shown below:

```
[ webView goBack ];
[ webView goForward ];
```

To reload existing content, use the web view's reload method:

```
[ webView reload ];
```

To cancel the loading of content, use the `stopLoading` method:

```
[ webView stopLoading ];
```

Delegate Methods

The web view class supports a set of `UIWebViewDelegate` delegate methods. These methods will be notified when certain events occur. To use these, assign a delegate to your web view:

```
webView.delegate = self;
```

The following delegate methods are notified by the web view. Each delegate method provides a pointer to the web view as its first parameter, allowing you to service multiple web views with a single delegate:

`-(BOOL)webView:(UIWebView *)webView, shouldStartLoadWithRequest:(NSURLRequest *)request, navigationType:(UIWebViewNavigationType)navigationType;`

> Notified when the web view is instructed to load content. Should return `YES` to commence loading. The navigation type parameter provided refers to the origin of the request, and can be any one of the following:
>
> ```
> UIWebViewNavigationTypeLinkClicked
> UIWebViewNavigationTypeFormSubmitted
> UIWebViewNavigationTypeBackForward
> UIWebViewNavigationTypeReload
> UIWebViewNavigationTypeFormResubmitted
> UIWebViewNavigationTypeOther
> ```

`-(void)webViewDidStartLoad:(UIWebView *)webView;`

> Notified when the web view begins loading a request.

`-(void)webViewDidFinishLoad:(UIWebView *)webView;`

> Notified when the web view finishes loading a request.

`-(void)webView:(UIWebView *)webView, didFailLoadWithError:(NSError *)error;`

> Notified if an error occurs in the loading of a request. An `NSError` object is provided to identify the type of error that has occurred.

WebDemo: Google Search Utility

This example uses a `UIWebView` to display the results of a Google search. Enter the search terms into a `UIView` class named `UISearchBar`, which is a simple view class for accepting search input. Unfortunately, Apple has privatized the search bar's underlying `UISearchField`, which Safari uses to display both an address field and a search field within the same navigation bar. In this example, the user will enter search criteria and press the Search button. This will invoke a query to Google based on the input provided and will display the output in the web view (Figure 10-8).

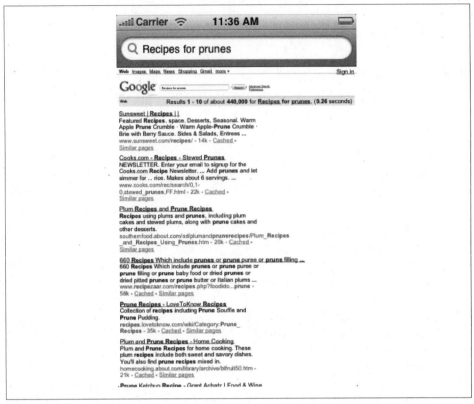

Figure 10-8. WebDemo example

You can compile this application, shown in Examples 10-34 through 10-38, with the SDK by creating a *view-based application* project named *WebDemo*. Be sure to pull out the Interface Builder code if you'd like to see how all objects are created from scratch.

Example 10-34. WebDemo application delegate prototypes (WebDemoAppDelegate.h)

```
#import <UIKit/UIKit.h>

@class WebDemoViewController;

@interface WebDemoAppDelegate : NSObject <UIApplicationDelegate> {
    UIWindow *window;
    WebDemoViewController *viewController;
}

@property (nonatomic, retain) IBOutlet UIWindow *window;
@property (nonatomic, retain) IBOutlet WebDemoViewController *viewController;

@end
```

Example 10-35. WebDemo application delegate (WebDemoAppDelegate.m)

```
#import "WebDemoAppDelegate.h"
#import "WebDemoViewController.h"

@implementation WebDemoAppDelegate

@synthesize window;
@synthesize viewController;

- (void)applicationDidFinishLaunching:(UIApplication *)application {
    CGRect screenBounds = [ [ UIScreen mainScreen ] bounds ];

    self.window = [ [ [ UIWindow alloc ] initWithFrame: screenBounds ] autorelease ];
    viewController = [ [ WebDemoViewController alloc ] init ];

    [ window addSubview: viewController.view ];
    [ window makeKeyAndVisible ];
}


- (void)dealloc {
    [ viewController release ];
    [ window release ];
    [ super dealloc ];
}


@end
```

Example 10-36. WebDemo view controller prototypes (WebDemoViewController.h)

```
#import <UIKit/UIKit.h>

@interface WebDemoViewController : UIViewController <UISearchBarDelegate> {
    UISearchBar *searchBar;
    UIWebView *webView;
}

@end
```

Example 10-37. WebDemo view controller (WebDemoViewController.m)

```
#import "WebDemoViewController.h"

@implementation WebDemoViewController

- (id)init {
    self = [ super init ];
    if (self != nil) {

    }
    return self;
}

- (void)loadView {
```

```
    [ super loadView ];
    CGRect bounds = [ [ UIScreen mainScreen ] applicationFrame ];

    searchBar = [ [ UISearchBar alloc ] initWithFrame:
        CGRectMake(0.0, 0.0, bounds.size.width, 48.0) ];
    searchBar.delegate = self;
    searchBar.placeholder = @"Google";
    [ self.view addSubview: searchBar ];

    webView = [ [ UIWebView alloc ] initWithFrame:
        CGRectMake(0.0, 48.0, bounds.size.width, bounds.size.height - 48.0) ];
    webView.scalesPageToFit = YES;
    [ self.view addSubview: webView ];
}

- (void)searchBarSearchButtonClicked:(UISearchBar *)activeSearchBar {
    NSString *query = [ searchBar.text
        stringByReplacingOccurrencesOfString: @" " withString: @"+" ];
    NSURL *url = [ NSURL URLWithString:
        [ NSString stringWithFormat: @"http://www.google.com/search?q=%@", query ] ];
    NSURLRequest *request = [ NSURLRequest requestWithURL: url ];
    [ webView loadRequest: request ];
}

- (BOOL)shouldAutorotateToInterfaceOrientation:(UIInterfaceOrientation)
interfaceOrientation {

    return (interfaceOrientation == UIInterfaceOrientationPortrait);
}

- (void)didReceiveMemoryWarning {
    [ super didReceiveMemoryWarning ];
}

-   (void)dealloc {
    [ searchBar release ];
    [ webView release ];
    [ super dealloc ];
}

@end
```

Example 10-38. WebDemo main (main.m)

```
#import <UIKit/UIKit.h>

int main(int argc, char *argv[]) {

    NSAutoreleasePool * pool = [[NSAutoreleasePool alloc] init];
    int retVal = UIApplicationMain(argc, argv, nil, @"WebDemoAppDelegate");
    [pool release];
    return retVal;
}
```

What's Going On

1. When the application instantiates, its application delegate builds a view controller and attaches it to a window, as usual. The view controller is initialized, which causes UISearchBar and UIWebView objects to be created. The view controller is assigned as the delegate for the search bar.

2. When the user submits a set of search terms, the search bar notifies its delegate's searchBarSearchButtonClicked method. The method formats a Google URL based on the terms provided and builds an NSURLRequest object. The object is then handed to the web view when its loadRequest method is invoked.

3. The web view's internal plumbing handles the entire process of fetching and displaying the web page, scrolling, and clicking on links.

Further Study

Web views are very easy to implement and look great. Try a few other activities before moving on:

- Try loading your own web content into a web view using the loadHTMLString method.

- Add a navigation controller with a toolbar. Add functional forward, back, stop, and reload buttons to the toolbar.

- Replace the UISearchBar with a UINavigationBar. Add a UITextField object as a subview and change the code to act like the address bar of a browser.

- Check out the *UIWebView.h* and *UISearchBar.h* prototypes. You'll find these deep within */Developer/Platforms/iPhoneOS.platform*, inside the UI Kit framework's *Headers* directory.

CHAPTER 11

Application Settings

A setting, or preference, for an application contains two pieces: a *key* and a *value*. The key refers to a unique value identifying the setting, for example `musicVolume`. The value refers to the value stored for the given key. Working with settings involves creating and modifying key/value pairs within property lists.

Property lists are XML-formatted files that store the key and value pairs that make up an application's settings. They are nothing new to Apple developers, as they are supported by most recent versions of Mac OS X, and can be read and written to directly from dictionary classes without actually having to parse a file.

Dictionaries and Property Lists

Property lists are flat files on disk, but are represented in your application as a dictionary with keys and values. The `NSDictionary` class provides the methods needed to read and write property lists to and from disk, and can realize key and value pairs without implementing any complex parsing functions by the developer. The `NSMutableDictionary` class builds on top of this to provide a mechanism to add and remove individual key/value pairs.

Creating a Dictionary

Dictionaries can be created in a number of ways. The simplest way is to use the `NSMutableDictionary` class:

```
NSMutableDictionary *dict = [ [ NSMutableDictionary alloc ] init ];
```

Managing Keys

Once you have created the dictionary, you can add individual key/value pairs to it using the `setValue` method:

```
[ dict setValue: @"myValue" forKey: @"myKey" ];
```

You can also set any object as the value of a key using the **setObject** method:

```
[ dict setObject: myObject forKey: @"myKey" ];
```

To remove a key/value pair, use the **removeObjectForKey** method:

```
[ dict removeObjectForKey: @"myKey" ];
```

Use the **removeAllObjects** method to remove all key/value pairs:

```
[ dict removeAllObjects ];
```

Writing Property Lists

Property lists are written to disk when you invoke the dictionary's **writeToFile** method. The dictionary class automatically converts its data into an XML format and writes it to the path specified:

```
[ dict writeToFile: path atomically: YES ];
```

If the file is written *atomically*, the property list is written to a temporary file first, then renamed to the path specified. This is useful if other parts of your application might be reading the property list, and can help prevent crashing should another thread load a partially written property list.

Reading Property Lists

To read back a property list that you've previously stored, the **NSDictionary** class provides a **dictionaryWithContentsOfFile** method. This allows you to load the property list directly into a dictionary class without any knowledge of the property file's format, and without any parsing.

To read a property list file into a dictionary object, create the dictionary object using the **initWithContentsOfFile** method:

```
NSString path = [ NSString stringWithFormat:
    @"%@/Library/Preferences/bookmarks.plist", NSHomeDirectory()
];
NSMutableDictionary *dict = [ [ NSMutableDictionary alloc ]
    initWithContentsOfFile: path
];
```

If the dictionary object already exists in memory, use the **setDictionary** method to replace the contents of the dictionary with that of the file:

```
[ dict setDictionary: [ NSDictionary dictionaryWithContentsOfFile: path ] ];
```

From here, you can work on the dictionary using the methods you've already learned.

Further Study

- Have a look at *NSDictionary.h* prototypes. You'll find these in */System/Library/ Frameworks/Foundation.framework/Headers*.

- Take the *ShootStuffUp* example from Chapter 10 and write code to read and write the example's settings on disk. Use this to automatically adjust the controls when the example loads.

Preference Bundles

In Chapter 10, you learned how to build a preferences table to allow users to change settings in real time. This is ideal for applications where exiting the application to change a setting can be problematic. For most applications, however, the global settings for an application can (and should) be changed from within the Settings application included with the iPhone. When you create a preference bundle, your application's icon will appear at the bottom of the Settings application, giving your users a centralized and standardized place to edit application settings.

Xcode provides a template for creating preferences bundles, and gives you enough content to get you started. To add a preferences bundle to your application, open your project in Xcode and select New File from the File menu. You'll be prompted to select a file type. Select the Settings category from the iPhone OS group, and select the Settings Bundle file. When prompted, name the file *Settings.bundle* and add it to your project. A sample bundle will be added to your application with an example text field, switch, and slider setting.

To edit the settings in your bundle, open the file named *Root.plist*. This will appear underneath the *Settings.bundle* folder that now exists on the sidebar of your project.

By default, the property list will be displayed in a property list editor, making it easy to add new key/value pairs with a few clicks. If you wish to work on the file's raw contents, right-click the file and select Plain Text File from the Open As menu. This will open the file in a text editor, where you can edit the raw XML. Since editing a property list in Xcode's property editor is effortless, we'll show you how it's done under the hood.

Adding Keys

Each entry in the preferences bundle is represented by a dictionary underneath the `PreferenceSpecifiers` section of the property list. Whichever items are defined in this array will be displayed to the user when editing your application's preferences. Each row in the array can define a new field or group separator for the preferences table that is displayed.

To add a new row, right-click the `PreferenceSpecifiers` array and select Add Row. A new row will be added to the top of the array. Right-click the new item and select

Dictionary from the Value Type menu. This will change the item from a string entry field into a dictionary that you can use to define a new cell. Alternatively, you may select an existing item and copy it. Select the PreferenceSpecifiers array again, then paste. This will duplicate the row, giving you a template to work from.

Group separators

Group separators allow you to break your preferences table up into logical groups. To add a group separator, add a key to the dictionary named Type. Set the value for this key to PSGroupSpecifier. Create a second key named Title, whose value represents the name to display as the group label. Both rows should be of type String:

```
<array>
    <dict>
        <key>Type</key>
        <string>PSGroupSpecifier</string>
        <key>Title</key>
        <string>Main Settings</string>
    </dict>
</array>
```

Text fields

Text fields allow you to accept direct input from the user, such as a username or password. To add a text field, add the following keys to a new dictionary item within the PreferenceSpecifiers array. All key values are represented as strings unless otherwise specified:

Type
: The type for a text field is PSTextFieldSpecifier.

Title
: The title to display to the left of the field, for example, "Username."

Key
: The name of the key to represent the actual value. This will be addressed in your code.

DefaultValue
: The default value for the field. An empty value is acceptable here to indicate no value.

IsSecure
: This is a Boolean field that you should set to true if the field is accepting secure text, such as a password. The correct syntax for declaring a Boolean field follows:

```
<key>IsSecure</key>
<true/>
```

KeyboardType
: Defines the type of keyboard that should be raised when the user enters this field. Supported values include:

- Alphabet
- NumbersAndPunctuation
- NumberPad
- URL
- EmailAddress

AutocapitalizationType

Allows you to define if and how the Settings application should autocapitalize the user's input into this field. Possible values include:

- None
- Word
- Sentences
- AllCharacters

AutoCorrectionType

Allows you to define if and how the Settings application should autocorrect text entered into this field. Possible values are Default, Yes, and No.

A complete text field might look like the following example:

```
<dict>
    <key>Type</key>
    <string>PSTextFieldSpecifier</string>
    <key>Title</key>
    <string>Username</string>
    <key>Key</key>
    <string>username_preference</string>
    <key>DefaultValue</key>
    <string></string>
    <key>IsSecure</key>
    <false/>
    <key>KeyboardType</key>
    <string>Alphabet</string>
    <key>AutocapitalizationType</key>
    <string>None</string>
    <key>AutocorrectionType</key>
    <string>No</string>
</dict>
```

Toggle switches

Toggle switch entries will render a UISwitch in the preferences pane, which the user can set On or Off. This is useful for adding Boolean preferences to activate or deactivate a given feature. To add a toggle switch field, add the following keys to a new dictionary item within the PreferenceSpecifiers array. All key values are represented as strings unless otherwise specified:

Type

The type for a switch field is PSToggleSwitchSpecifier.

Title

The title to display to the left of the field, for example, "Extra Lives."

Key

The name of the key to represent the actual value. This will be addressed in your code.

TrueValue

The value to set the `Key` field to when the switch is turned to the `On` position.

FalseValue

The value to set the `Key` field to when the switch is turned to the `Off` position.

DefaultValue

This Boolean value specifies the default position for the switch. This should be set to **true** to place the switch in the `On` position by default, or set to **false** to place the switch in the `Off` position by default. An example follows:

```
<key>DefaultValue</key>
<false/>
```

A complete switch entry might look like the example below:

```
<dict>
    <key>Type</key>
    <string>PSToggleSwitchSpecifier</string>
    <key>Title</key>
    <string>Extra Points</string>
    <key>Key</key>
    <string>extrapoints_preference</string>
    <key>DefaultValue</key>
    <false/>
    <key>TrueValue</key>
    <string>YES</string>
    <key>FalseValue</key>
    <string>NO</string>
</dict>
```

Sliders

Entries for sliders will draw a `UISlider` in the preferences table. Sliders allow the user to loosely specify a range of values, and are useful for visually accommodating difficulty in a game, sound volume, or other such value ranges. To add a slider field, add the following keys to a new dictionary item within the `PreferenceSpecifiers` array. All key values are represented as strings unless otherwise specified.

Sliders do not accommodate titles, so it's generally best to keep sliders in a separate group, using the group label as the title:

Type

The type for a multivalue field is `PSMultiValueSpecifier`.

Key

> The name of the key to represent the actual value. This will be addressed in your code.

MinimumValue

> A numeric field identifying the minimum value for the slider. You can define this as either an `integer` type field or a `real` type field, depending on whether you want values represented as integers or floating-point numbers. An example follows:

```
<key>MinimumValue</key>
<real>10.0</real>
```

MaximumValue

> A numeric field identifying the minimum value for the slider. You can define this as either an `integer` type field or a `real` type field, depending on whether you want values represented as integers or floating-point numbers, and it should match the type used to set the `MinimumValue` field.

DefaultValue

> A numeric field identifying the default value for the slider. You can define this as either an `integer` type field or a `real` type field, and does not need to match the value fields' types.

MinimumValueImage, MaximumValueImage

> To display an image next to the minimum and/or maximum value ends of the slider, specify the filename of the image relative to the program folder.

A complete slider might look like the example below:

```
<dict>
    <key>Type</key>
    <string>PSSliderSpecifier</string>
    <key>Key</key>
    <string>musicvolume_preference</string>
    <key>DefaultValue</key>
    <real>5.0</real>
    <key>MinimumValue</key>
    <real>0.0</real>
    <key>MaximumValue</key>
    <real>10.0</real>
    <key>MinimumValueImage</key>
    <string>minvalue.png</string>
    <key>MaximumValueImage</key>
    <string>maxvalue.png</string>
</dict>
```

Multivalue fields

The equivalent to a drop-down menu in the Settings application is a multivalue field. Multivalue fields allow you to specify a number of different options, giving the user the option to choose one from the list. To add a multivalue field, add the following keys to a new dictionary item within the `PreferenceSpecifiers` array. All key values are represented as strings unless otherwise specified.

Sliders do not accommodate titles, so it's generally best to keep sliders in a separate group, using the group label as the title.

Type
> The type for a slider field is `PSSliderSpecifier`.

Key
> The name of the key to represent the actual value. This will be addressed in your code.

Title
> The title to display to the left of the field, for example, "Difficulty."

Titles
> An array of possible selections, as displayed to the user. An example follows:

```
<key>Titles</key>
        <array>
            <string>Easy</string>
             <string>Medium</string>
            <string>Hard</string>
        </array>
```

Values
> An array containing the actual values mapped to each title. These will be the values your application sees. An example follows. Each value is mapped to the titles displayed in the `Titles` array:

```
<key>Values</key>
        <array>
            <string>1</string>
             <string>2</string>
            <string>3</string>
        </array>
```

DefaultValue
> The value of the default selection. This should map to an element in the `Values` array.

A complete multivalue field might look like the example below:

```
<dict>
    <key>Type</key>
    <string>PSMultiValueSpecifier</string>
    <key>Title</key>
    <string>Difficulty</string>
    <key>Key</key>
    <string>difficulty_preference</string>
    <key>Values</key>
    <array>
        <string>1</string>
        <string>2</string>
```

```
        <string>3</string>
    </array>
    <key>Titles</key>
    <array>
        <string>Easy</string>
        <string>Medium</string>
        <string>Hard</string>
    </array>
    <key>DefaultValue</key>
    <string>2</string>
</dict>
```

Child panes

In addition to groups, preferences bundles allow you to specify additional child panes. When the user taps on the child pane, the Settings application will scroll to the new pane and present that pane's options. A Back button will be automatically presented to the user, allowing him to navigate back to your root pane.

To add a child pane, specify the following string fields:

Type
> The type for a child pane is PSChildPaneSpecifier.

Key
> A unique key for the child pane.

Title
> The title of the child pane to display to the user. The child pane is presented as a button with a disclosure arrow.

File
> The name of another property list within *Settings.bundle* containing the child pane you'd like to display. Leave off the *.plist* extension from the filename.

A complete child pane entry might look like the example below:

```
<dict>
    <key>Type</key>
    <string>PSChildPaneSpecifier</string>
    <key>Title</key>
    <string>Extended Preferences</string>
    <key>Key</key>
    <string>extended_preferences</string>
    <key>File</key>
    <string>Extended</string>
</dict>
```

Reading Preference Bundle Values

The preferences set from within your bundle are stored in a standard property list in your application sandbox's *Library/Preferences* folder. To load values individually, use the NSUserDefaults class to access property list settings:

```
NSString *difficulty = [ [ NSUserDefaults standardUserDefaults ]
    stringForKey:@"difficulty_preference" ];
```

Alternatively, you can load the property list containing all preferences directly into an NSDictionary object and work with it as you learned earlier in this chapter:

```
NSDictionary *settings = [ NSUserDefaults standardUserDefaults
    dictionaryRepresentation ];
NSLog(@"Difficulty: %@\n", [ settings valueForKey: @"difficulty_preference" ]);
```

Further Study

Now that you've learned about preference bundles, try these exercises:

- Take the *ShootStuffUp* demo from Chapter 10 and convert it into a preferences bundle.
- Check out the *NSUserDefaults.h* prototypes. You'll find these in */System/Library/Frameworks/Foundation.framework/Headers*.

CHAPTER 12

Cover Flow

Chapter 5 introduced you to the Quartz Core framework and how to work with Core Animation to create stunning 3D transformations. It is the basis for Apple's Cover Flow technology, which you'll find in the iPhone's iPod application when flipping through albums in landscape mode. Apple privatized its Cover Flow class so that it cannot be used with the SDK. This chapter will provide you with an SDK-compliant recipe to render a cover flow, but Apple could still reject your application if they believe it too closely copies the functionality of one of its own preloaded apps.

Layton Duncan of Polar Bear Farm, author of Search, Record, Telegram, and other popular AppStore applications, originally wrote code to illustrate an iPhone version of Apple's *CovertFlow* example from the desktop Xcode examples. We've taken Layton's original example, cleaned it up, and rewritten it to be compliant with the SDK's sanctioned interfaces, so you can create stunning Cover Flow effects without using any private APIs.

Apple's own Cover Flow class uses a private UI Kit object named `UICoverFlowLayer` to render its content. This class is privatized, so we couldn't use it to create an SDK-compliant example (otherwise your application would break the rules). As a result, the behavior of our example will be very close to Apple's own Cover Flow views, but may not be identical. A little fine-tuning should get this example just where you like it for your application.

CovertFlow: SDK Cover Flow Programming

In this example, you'll create a subclass of the `UIScrollView` class named `CFView` class. The `CFView` class is initialized with a set of images representing your album covers (or whatever content you want to present). The class uses Core Animation to create a Cover Flow-style layout on the iPhone's screen. As you scroll with your finger, the underlying `UIScrollView` class invokes its delegate's `scrollViewDidScroll` method. This method calculates which album cover is at the center position of the screen and rotates it into view. See Figure 12-1.

Figure 12-1. CovertFlow example

The `CFView` class was designed with reusability in mind. To implement this into your own code, look at how the view controller class initializes it and reads its `selectedCover` property.

You can compile this application, shown in Examples 12-1 through 12-5, with the SDK by creating a *view-based application* project named *CovertFlow* (note the name "Covert" with a "t"). You'll need to add the *Quartz Core framework* to your project in order to compile it. Be sure to pull out the Interface Builder code so you can see how these objects are created from scratch.

Example 12-1. CovertFlow application delegate prototypes (CovertFlowAppDelegate.h)

```
#import <UIKit/UIKit.h>

@class CovertFlowViewController;

@interface CovertFlowAppDelegate : NSObject <UIApplicationDelegate> {
    UIWindow *window;
    CovertFlowViewController *viewController;
}
```

```objective-c
@property (nonatomic, retain) IBOutlet UIWindow *window;
@property (nonatomic, retain) IBOutlet CovertFlowViewController *viewController;

@end
```

Example 12-2. CovertFlow application delegate (CovertFlowAppDelegate.m)

```objective-c
#import "CovertFlowAppDelegate.h"
#import "CovertFlowViewController.h"

@implementation CovertFlowAppDelegate

@synthesize window;
@synthesize viewController;


- (void)applicationDidFinishLaunching:(UIApplication *)application {
    CGRect screenBounds = [ [ UIScreen mainScreen ] bounds ];

    self.window = [ [ [ UIWindow alloc ] initWithFrame: screenBounds ] autorelease ];
    viewController = [ [ CovertFlowViewController alloc ] init ];

    [ window addSubview: viewController.view ];
    [ window makeKeyAndVisible ];
}


- (void)dealloc {
    [ viewController release ];
    [ window release ];
    [ super dealloc ];
}


@end
```

Example 12-3. CovertFlow view controller prototypes (CovertFlowViewController.h)

```objective-c
#import <UIKit/UIKit.h>
#import <QuartzCore/QuartzCore.h>

/* Number of pixels scrolled before next cover comes front */
#define SCROLL_PIXELS 60.0

/* Size of each cover */
#define COVER_WIDTH_HEIGHT 128.0

@interface CFView : UIScrollView <UIScrollViewDelegate>
{
    CAScrollLayer *cfIntLayer;
    NSMutableArray *_covers;
    NSTimer *timer;
    int selectedCover;
}
- (id) initWithFrame:(struct CGRect)frame covers:(NSMutableArray *)covers;
- (void)layoutLayer:(CAScrollLayer *)layer;
```

```
@property(nonatomic,getter=getSelectedCover) int selectedCover;

@end

@interface CovertFlowViewController : UIViewController {
    NSMutableArray *covers;
    CFView *covertFlowView;
}


@end
```

Example 12-4. CovertFlow view controller (CovertFlowViewController.m)

```
#import "CovertFlowViewController.h"

@implementation CFView

- (id) initWithFrame:(struct CGRect)frame covers:(NSMutableArray *)covers {
    self = [ super initWithFrame: frame ];

    if (self != nil) {
        _covers = covers;
        selectedCover = 0;

        self.showsVerticalScrollIndicator = YES;
        self.showsHorizontalScrollIndicator = NO;
        self.delegate = self;
        self.scrollsToTop = NO;
        self.bouncesZoom = NO;

        cfIntLayer = [ [ CAScrollLayer alloc ] init ];
        cfIntLayer.bounds = CGRectMake(0.0, 0.0, frame.size.width,
            frame.size.height + COVER_WIDTH_HEIGHT);
        cfIntLayer.position = CGPointMake(160.0, 304.0);
        cfIntLayer.frame = frame;

        for(int i = 0; i < [ _covers count ]; i++) {
            NSLog(@"Initializing cfIntLayer layer %d\n", i);
            UIImageView *background = [ [ [ UIImageView alloc ] initWithImage:
                [ _covers objectAtIndex: i ] ] autorelease ];
            background.frame = CGRectMake(0.0, 0.0, COVER_WIDTH_HEIGHT,
                COVER_WIDTH_HEIGHT);
            [ cfIntLayer addSublayer: background.layer ];
        }

        self.contentSize = CGSizeMake(320.0, ( ( frame.size.height) +
            (SCROLL_PIXELS * ([ _covers count ] -1)) ) );

        [ self.layer addSublayer: cfIntLayer ];
        [ self layoutLayer: cfIntLayer ];
    }

    return self;
}
```

```
- (void)scrollViewDidScroll:(UIScrollView *)scrollView {

    selectedCover = (int) roundf((self.contentOffset.y/SCROLL_PIXELS));
    if (selectedCover > [ _covers count ] -1) {
        selectedCover = [ _covers count ] - 1;
    }
    [ self layoutLayer: cfIntLayer ];
}

- (void)setSelectedCover:(int)index {

    if (index != selectedCover) {
        selectedCover  = index;
        [ self layoutLayer: cfIntLayer ];
        self.contentOffset = CGPointMake(self.contentOffset.x, selectedCover *
            SCROLL_PIXELS);
    }
}

- (int) getSelectedCover {
    return selectedCover;
}

-(void) layoutLayer:(CAScrollLayer *)layer
{
    CALayer *sublayer;
    NSArray *array;
    size_t i, count;
    CGRect rect, cfImageRect;
    CGSize cellSize, spacing, margin, size;
    CATransform3D leftTransform, rightTransform, sublayerTransform;
    float zCenterPosition, zSidePosition;
    float sideSpacingFactor, rowScaleFactor;
    float angle = 1.39;
    int x;

    size = [ layer bounds ].size;

    zCenterPosition = 60;      /* Z-Position of selected cover */
    zSidePosition = 0;         /* Default Z-Position for other covers */
    sideSpacingFactor = .85;   /* How close should slide covers be */
    rowScaleFactor = .55;      /* Distance between main cover and side covers */

    leftTransform = CATransform3DMakeRotation(angle, -1, 0, 0);
    rightTransform = CATransform3DMakeRotation(-angle, -1, 0, 0);

    margin   = CGSizeMake(5.0, 5.0);
    spacing  = CGSizeMake(5.0, 5.0);
    cellSize = CGSizeMake (COVER_WIDTH_HEIGHT, COVER_WIDTH_HEIGHT);

    margin.width += (size.width - cellSize.width * [ _covers count ]
                    - spacing.width * ([ _covers count ] - 1)) * .5;
    margin.width = floor (margin.width);
```

```
/* Build an array of covers */
array = [ layer sublayers ];
count = [ array count ];
sublayerTransform = CATransform3DIdentity;

/* Set perspective */
sublayerTransform.m34 = -0.006;

/* Begin a CATransaction so that all animations happen simultaneously */
[ CATransaction begin ];
[ CATransaction setValue: [ NSNumber numberWithFloat: 0.3f ]
                forKey:@"animationDuration" ];

for (i = 0; i < count; i++)
{
    sublayer = [ array objectAtIndex:i ];
    x = i;

    rect.size = *(CGSize *)&cellSize;
    rect.origin = CGPointZero;
    cfImageRect = rect;

    /* Base position */
    rect.origin.x = size.width / 2 - cellSize.width / 2;
    rect.origin.y = margin.height + x * (cellSize.height + spacing.height);

    [ [ sublayer superlayer ] setSublayerTransform: sublayerTransform ];

    if (x < selectedCover)         /* Left side */
    {
        rect.origin.y += cellSize.height * sideSpacingFactor
            * (float) (selectedCover - x - rowScaleFactor);
        sublayer.zPosition = zSidePosition - 2.0 * (selectedCover - x);
        sublayer.transform = leftTransform;
    }
    else if (x > selectedCover)    /* Right side */
    {
        rect.origin.y -= cellSize.height * sideSpacingFactor
            * (float) (x - selectedCover - rowScaleFactor);
        sublayer.zPosition = zSidePosition - 2.0 * (x - selectedCover);
        sublayer.transform = rightTransform;
    }
    else                           /* Selected cover */
    {
        sublayer.transform = CATransform3DIdentity;
        sublayer.zPosition = zCenterPosition;

        /* Position in the middle of the scroll layer */
        [ layer scrollToPoint: CGPointMake(0, rect.origin.y
            - (([ layer bounds ].size.height - cellSize.width)/2.0))
        ];

        /* Position the scroll layer in the center of the view */
        layer.position =
        CGPointMake(160.0f, 240.0f + (selectedCover * SCROLL_PIXELS));
```

```
        }
        [ sublayer setFrame: rect ];

    }
    [ CATransaction commit ];
}

@end

@implementation CovertFlowViewController

- (id)init {
    self = [ super init ];
    if (self != nil) {
        covers = [ [ NSMutableArray alloc ] init ];

        for(int i = 1; i < 6; i++) {
            NSLog(@"Loading demo image %d\n", i);
            UIImage *image = [ [ UIImage alloc ] initWithData:
                [ NSData dataWithContentsOfURL:
                    [ NSURL URLWithString: [ NSString stringWithFormat:
                        @"http://www.zdziarski.com/demo/%d.png", i ] ] ]
                ];

            [ covers addObject: image ];
        }
    }
    return self;
}

- (void)loadView {
    [ super loadView ];

    covertFlowView = [ [ CFView alloc ] initWithFrame:
        self.view.frame
        covers: covers
    ];

    covertFlowView.selectedCover = 2;
    self.view = covertFlowView;
}


- (BOOL)shouldAutorotateToInterfaceOrientation:
    (UIInterfaceOrientation)interfaceOrientation
{
    return (interfaceOrientation == UIInterfaceOrientationPortrait);
}


- (void)didReceiveMemoryWarning {
    [ super didReceiveMemoryWarning ];
}
```

```
- (void)dealloc {
    [ covertFlowView release ];
    [ super dealloc ];
}

@end
```

Example 12-5. CovertFlow main (main.m)

```
#import <UIKit/UIKit.h>

int main(int argc, char *argv[]) {

    NSAutoreleasePool * pool = [[NSAutoreleasePool alloc] init];
    int retVal = UIApplicationMain(argc, argv, nil, @"CovertFlowAppDelegate");
    [pool release];
    return retVal;
}
```

What's Going On?

Here's how the *CovertFlow* example works:

1. When the application instantiates, a window and view controller are created, just as in any other view-based application.

2. The view controller creates an instance of the CFView class, included in the example. It then downloads five demo images from a website and builds an array of UIImage objects. This array is passed to the CFView class's custom initialization method.

3. The CFView class initializes its own properties as a UIScrollView class. It then creates a sublayer for each image it was configured with. The sublayers are transformed to either a side view or a front view.

4. When you set the selectedCover property, the cover is transformed to a front view and the scroll view's position is set to center the selected cover.

5. When the user scrolls with his finger, the scrollViewDidScroll method is invoked. This calculates the position of the scroll window and sets the active cover based on where the user has scrolled. The layers are then animated to flip to the correct album cover.

Further Study

Now that you have an understanding of layer manipulation and animations, try a few things before moving on:

- Change this example up to automatically scroll through each cover using an NSTimer object.

- We've intentionally left this example's skeleton using the portrait orientation. Apply what you've learned in this book to display a table of covers when the iPhone is in portrait mode, and switch to the Cover Flow view when rotated to landscape mode.

- Check out the following prototypes in your SDK's header files: *CAScrollLayer.h*, *CAAnimation.h*, and *CATransform3D.h*. You'll find these deep within */Developer/ Platforms/iPhoneOS.platform*, inside the Quartz Core framework's *Headers* directory.

CHAPTER 13

Page Flicking

One of the more aesthetically pleasing UI features of the iPhone is the ability to thumb through a series of pages, flicking the previous page to the left or right to bring up the next page. In Chapter 10, you learned about page controls and scroll views. Put together, these classes can provide the same style page flipping as seen on the iPhone's home screen, or when flipping through photos.

This chapter provides a recipe for a fully functional class named PageScrollView, which does the heavy lifting involved in setting up such a display. At the heart of its plumbing, the PageScrollView class creates a scrolling content area having a width of all the pages you'd like to display put together. For example, the iPhone's screen is 320 pixels wide. To display 10 pages, you'd create a UIScrollView with a content size of 3,200 pixels. Each page is then "glued" onto a different portion of the scroll view. Using the UIScrollView class's pagingEnabled property, each section of the UIScrollView is split up evenly to create screen-sized "pages" that snap to a single position, just like the springboard. As the user scrolls, the scroll view automatically snaps to the closest page, depending on where he scrolled. The user can also tap anywhere on the page control at the bottom of the screen to flip pages. The page number being displayed is easily calculated by taking the width of the entire scrolling content size and dividing by the width of a single page.

For applications using potentially hundreds of pages, you won't have the memory to accommodate a scroll region to fit them all. The second example in this chapter shows you a second recipe for a PageScrollView class that uses a scroll region the size of only three pages: left, right, and center. As the user scrolls, the nonvisible portions of the scroll view (usually the left and right pages) are dynamically swapped out to contain the contents of adjacent pages. This conserves memory and gives the illusion of a seamless scroll containing all views.

PageControl: Page Flicking Example

This example (shown in Figure 13-1) implements a custom class named PageScroll View to display five pages of content that you can thumb through by scrolling left or

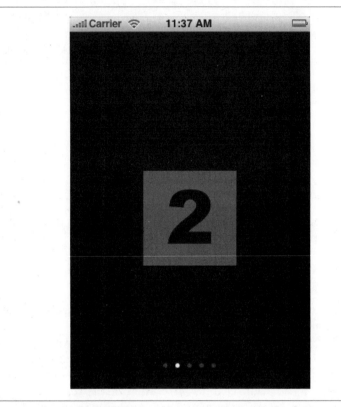

Figure 13-1. PageControl example

right. The `PageScrollView` class provided in this example is entirely self-contained. It accepts an `NSMutableArray` containing a `UIView` class-derived object for each page. The class then makes room for a `UIPageControl` and automatically updates it as the user flicks with his thumb. The user can also tap the page control on either the left or right to change pages. As is the case with all examples in this book, the `PageScrollView` class doesn't break any SDK rules and uses only the sanctioned interfaces available. It also illustrates how a protocol implementation works, by means of the `PageScrollViewDelegate` protocol, which notifies its delegate of page changes. Because the `UIScrollView` class handles all of the animation work of scrolling, you won't need to use Core Animation here at all.

You can compile this application, shown in Examples 13-1 through 13-7, with the SDK by creating a *view-based application* project named *PageControl*. In addition to this, you'll need to add two new files to your project: *PageScrollView.h* and *PageScrollView.m*. You can do this by selecting New File from Xcode's File menu, then selecting Objective-C class from the Cocoa template group underneath Mac OS X.

Be sure to pull out the Interface Builder code so you can see how these objects are created from scratch.

Example 13-1. PageControl application delegate prototypes (PageControlAppDelegate.h)

```objc
#import <UIKit/UIKit.h>

@class PageControlViewController;

@interface PageControlAppDelegate : NSObject <UIApplicationDelegate> {
    UIWindow *window;
    PageControlViewController *viewController;
}

@property (nonatomic, retain) IBOutlet UIWindow *window;
@property (nonatomic, retain) IBOutlet PageControlViewController *viewController;

@end
```

Example 13-2. PageControl application delegate (PageControlAppDelegate.m)

```objc
#import "PageControlAppDelegate.h"
#import "PageControlViewController.h"

@implementation PageControlAppDelegate

@synthesize window;
@synthesize viewController;


- (void)applicationDidFinishLaunching:(UIApplication *)application {
    CGRect screenBounds = [ [ UIScreen mainScreen ] bounds ];

    self.window = [ [ [ UIWindow alloc ] initWithFrame: screenBounds ]
        autorelease
    ];

    viewController = [ [ PageControlViewController alloc ] init ];

    [ window addSubview: viewController.view ];
    [ window makeKeyAndVisible ];
}

- (void)dealloc {
    [ viewController release ];
    [ window release ];
    [ super dealloc ];
}
@end
```

Example 13-3. PageControl PageScrollView class prototypes (PageScrollView.h)

```objc
#import <UIKit/UIKit.h>

@interface PageScrollView : UIView <UIScrollViewDelegate> {
    UIScrollView *scrollView;
    UIPageControl *pageControl;

    CGRect _pageRegion, _controlRegion;
```

```
        NSMutableArray *_pages;
        id _delegate;
}
-(void)layoutViews;
-(void) notifyPageChange;

@property(nonatomic,assign,getter=getPages)         NSMutableArray * pages;
@property(nonatomic,assign,getter=getCurrentPage) int              currentPage;
@property(nonatomic,assign,getter=getDelegate)     id               delegate;
@end

@protocol PageScrollViewDelegate<NSObject>

@optional

-(void) pageScrollViewDidChangeCurrentPage:
    (PageScrollView *)pageScrollView currentPage:(int)currentPage;
@end
```

Example 13-4. PageControl PageScrollView class (PageScrollView.m)

```
#import "PageScrollView.h"

@implementation PageScrollView

-(id)initWithFrame:(CGRect)frame {
    self = [ super initWithFrame: frame ];
    if (self != nil) {
        _pages = nil;
        _pageRegion = CGRectMake(frame.origin.x, frame.origin.y,
            frame.size.width, frame.size.height - 60.0);
        _controlRegion = CGRectMake(frame.origin.x, frame.size.height - 60.0,
            frame.size.width, 60.0);
        self.delegate = nil;

        scrollView = [ [ UIScrollView alloc ] initWithFrame: _pageRegion ];
        scrollView.pagingEnabled = YES;
        scrollView.delegate = self;
        [ self addSubview: scrollView ];

        pageControl = [ [ UIPageControl alloc ] initWithFrame: _controlRegion ];
        [ pageControl addTarget: self action: @selector(pageControlDidChange:)
            forControlEvents: UIControlEventValueChanged ];
        [ self addSubview: pageControl ];
    }
    return self;
}

-(void)setPages:(NSMutableArray *)pages {
    if (_pages != nil) {
        for(int i=0;i<[_pages count];i++) {
            [ [ _pages objectAtIndex: i ] removeFromSuperview ];
        }
    }
    _pages = pages;
    scrollView.contentOffset = CGPointMake(0.0, 0.0);
```

```
        scrollView.contentSize = CGSizeMake(_pageRegion.size.width * [ _pages count ],
            _pageRegion.size.height);
        pageControl.numberOfPages = [ _pages count ];
        pageControl.currentPage = 0;
        [ self layoutViews ];
}

- (void)layoutViews {
    for(int i=0;i<[ _pages count];i++) {
        UIView *page = [ _pages objectAtIndex: i ];
        CGRect bounds = page.bounds;
        CGRect frame = CGRectMake(_pageRegion.size.width * i, 0.0,
            _pageRegion.size.width, _pageRegion.size.height);
        page.frame = frame;
        page.bounds = bounds;
        [ scrollView addSubview: page ];
    }
}

-(id)getDelegate {
    return _delegate;
}

- (void)setDelegate:(id)delegate {
    _delegate = delegate;
}

-(NSMutableArray *)getPages {
    return _pages;
}

-(void)setCurrentPage:(int)page {
    [ scrollView setContentOffset:
        CGPointMake(_pageRegion.size.width * page, scrollView.contentOffset.y)
        animated: YES
    ];
    pageControl.currentPage = page;
}

-(int)getCurrentPage {
    return (int) (scrollView.contentOffset.x / _pageRegion.size.width);
}

- (void)scrollViewDidEndDecelerating:(UIScrollView *)scrollView {
    pageControl.currentPage = self.currentPage;
    [ self notifyPageChange ];
}

-(void) pageControlDidChange: (id)sender
{
    UIPageControl *control = (UIPageControl *) sender;
    if (control == pageControl) {
        self.currentPage = control.currentPage;
    }
    [ self notifyPageChange ];
```

```
}

-(void) notifyPageChange {
    if (self.delegate != nil) {
        if ([ _delegate conformsToProtocol:@protocol(PageScrollViewDelegate) ]) {
            if ([ _delegate respondsToSelector:
                @selector(pageScrollViewDidChangeCurrentPage:currentPage:) ])
            {
                [ self.delegate pageScrollViewDidChangeCurrentPage:
                    (PageScrollView *)self currentPage: self.currentPage
                ];
            }
        }
    }
}

@end
```

Example 13-5. PageControl view controller prototypes (PageControlViewController.h)

```
#import <UIKit/UIKit.h>
#import "PageScrollView.h"

@interface PageControlViewController : UIViewController <PageScrollViewDelegate> {
    NSMutableArray *pages;
    PageScrollView *scrollView;
}
-(void) pageScrollViewDidChangeCurrentPage:(PageScrollView *)pageScrollView
 currentPage:(int)currentPage;

@end
```

Example 13-6. PageControl view controller (PageControlViewController.m)

```
#import "PageControlViewController.h"

@implementation PageControlViewController

- (void)loadView {
    [ super loadView ];

    /* Load demo images for pages */
    pages = [ [ NSMutableArray alloc ] init ];
    for(int i = 0; i < 5; i++) {
        NSLog(@"Loading demo image %d\n", i);

        UIImage *background = [ [ UIImage alloc ] initWithData:
            [ NSData dataWithContentsOfURL: [ NSURL URLWithString:
              @"http://www.zdziarski.com/demo/black.png" ] ]
        ];

        UIImage *image = [ [ UIImage alloc ] initWithData:
            [ NSData dataWithContentsOfURL: [ NSURL URLWithString:
            [ NSString stringWithFormat:
              @"http://www.zdziarski.com/demo/%d.png", i+1 ] ] ]
        ];
```

```
        UIImageView *page = [ [ UIImageView alloc ] initWithFrame: [
            [ UIScreen mainScreen ] applicationFrame ]
        ];
        page.image = background;

        UIImageView *subview = [ [ UIImageView alloc ] initWithFrame: [
            [ UIScreen mainScreen ] applicationFrame ]
        ];
        subview.image = image;
        subview.bounds = CGRectMake(0.0, 0.0, image.size.width, image.size.height);

        [ page addSubview: subview ];
        [ pages addObject: page ];
    }

    scrollView = [ [ PageScrollView alloc ] initWithFrame: self.view.frame ];
    scrollView.pages = pages;
    scrollView.delegate = self;
    self.view = scrollView;
}

- (void)didReceiveMemoryWarning {
    [ super didReceiveMemoryWarning ];
}

- (void)dealloc {
    [ scrollView release ];
    [ super dealloc ];
}

-(void) pageScrollViewDidChangeCurrentPage:
    (PageScrollView *)pageScrollView currentPage:(int)currentPage
{
    NSLog(@"I'm now on page %d\n", currentPage);
}
@end
```

Example 13-7. PageControl main (main.m)

```
#import <UIKit/UIKit.h>

int main(int argc, char *argv[]) {
    NSAutoreleasePool * pool = [ [ NSAutoreleasePool alloc ] init ];
    int retVal = UIApplicationMain(argc, argv, nil, @"PageControlAppDelegate");
    [ pool release ];
    return retVal;
}
```

What's Going On?

Here's how the *PageControl* example works:

1. When the application instantiates, a window and view controller are created, just as in any other view-based application.

2. The view controller creates an instance of the PageScrollView class, included in the example. It then downloads five demo images from a website and builds an array of UIImageView objects. The PageScrollView class will accept any derivative of the UIView class. This array is assigned to the PageScrollView class's pages property.

3. The PageScrollView class initializes a UIScrollView that is 1,600 pixels wide (320 × 5 pages). Each page is added with an x-origin having a multiple of 320 pixels (the width of the screen). The scroller's paging is enabled to automatically snap to a single page. A UIPageControl is added to the bottom of the screen, and the first page in the scroll view is displayed.

4. When the user scrolls or taps the page control, the new page scrolls into view and the delegate is notified of the page change.

5. If the pages property is set again, the scroll view reconfigures itself to the new set of pages.

Further Study

Scroll views are very versatile tools, and provide some great advanced functionality, as you've just learned. Try these exercises while you're in the code.

- Reconfigure the scroll view so that it scrolls pages vertically rather than horizontally.

- If you haven't already done so, check out the following prototypes in your SDK's header files: *UIScrollView.h*, *UIView.h*, and *UIPageControl.h*. You'll find these deep within */Developer/Platforms/iPhoneOS.platform*, inside the UI Kit framework's *Headers* directory.

A PageScrollView for Many Views

In the previous example, you learned how to roll a custom UIScrollView class whose content area accommodated all of the views it displayed. This works well when dealing with only a small number of views, but if you are flipping through hundreds of photos, this will consume too much memory. The advantage to using the former approach with a small number of views is that you can display the horizontal scroll indicator, which will give the user an idea of how many objects he is scrolling through. The advantage to using the class example here is that you can display many more views.

The example below revises the PageScrollView class to use a content area the size of only three pages. As the user scrolls left or right, the pages in view are quietly swapped out with new pages. The result is a thumb scroller that looks and feels exactly like the *PageControl* demo, but can handle hundreds of pages. A property has also been added to hide the UIPageControl object at the bottom of the page. To do this, set the showsPageControl property to NO.

The class is defined in Examples 13-8 and 13-9. To use this class with the PageControl demo, simply replace the class files with these.

Example 13-8. PageScrollView prototypes (PageScrollView.h)

```objc
#import <UIKit/UIKit.h>

@interface PageScrollView : UIView <UIScrollViewDelegate> {
    UIScrollView *scrollView;
    UIPageControl *pageControl;

    CGRect _pageRegion, _controlRegion;
    NSMutableArray *_pages;
    id _delegate;
    BOOL _showsPageControl;
    int _zeroPage;
}
-(void)layoutViews;
-(void)layoutScroller;
-(void)notifyPageChange;

@property(nonatomic,assign,getter=getPages) NSMutableArray *pages;
@property(nonatomic,assign,getter=getCurrentPage)       int   currentPage;
@property(nonatomic,assign,getter=getDelegate)          id    delegate;
@property(nonatomic,assign,getter=getShowsPageControl) BOOL showsPageControl;
@end

@protocol PageScrollViewDelegate<NSObject>

@optional

-(void) pageScrollViewDidChangeCurrentPage:(PageScrollView *)
pageScrollView currentPage:(int)currentPage;

@end
```

Example 13-9. PageScrollView (PageScrollView.m)

```objc
#import "PageScrollView.h"

@implementation PageScrollView

-(id)initWithFrame:(CGRect)frame {
    self = [ super initWithFrame: frame ];
    if (self != nil) {
        _pages = nil;
        _zeroPage = 0;
        _pageRegion = CGRectMake(frame.origin.x, frame.origin.y,
            frame.size.width, frame.size.height - 60.0);
        _controlRegion = CGRectMake(frame.origin.x, frame.size.height - 60.0,
            frame.size.width, 60.0);
        self.delegate = nil;
```

```
        scrollView = [ [ UIScrollView alloc ] initWithFrame: _pageRegion ];
        scrollView.pagingEnabled = YES;
        scrollView.delegate = self;
        [ self addSubview: scrollView ];

        pageControl = [ [ UIPageControl alloc ] initWithFrame: _controlRegion ];
        [ pageControl addTarget: self action: @selector(pageControlDidChange:)
            forControlEvents: UIControlEventValueChanged
        ];
        [ self addSubview: pageControl ];
    }
    return self;
}

-(void)setPages:(NSMutableArray *)pages {
    if (pages != nil) {
        for(int i=0;i<[_pages count];i++) {
            [ [ _pages objectAtIndex: i ] removeFromSuperview ];
        }
    }
    _pages = pages;
    scrollView.contentOffset = CGPointMake(0.0, 0.0);
    if ([ _pages count] < 3) {
        scrollView.contentSize = CGSizeMake(_pageRegion.size.width *
            [ _pages count ], _pageRegion.size.height);
    } else {
        scrollView.contentSize = CGSizeMake(_pageRegion.size.width * 3,
            _pageRegion.size.height);
        scrollView.showsHorizontalScrollIndicator = NO;
    }
    pageControl.numberOfPages = [ _pages count ];
    pageControl.currentPage = 0;
    [ self layoutViews ];
}

- (void)layoutViews {
    if ([ _pages count ] <= 3) {
        for(int i=0;i<[ _pages count];i++) {
            UIView *page = [ _pages objectAtIndex: i ];
            CGRect bounds = page.bounds;
            CGRect frame = CGRectMake(_pageRegion.size.width * i, 0.0,
                _pageRegion.size.width, _pageRegion.size.height);
            page.frame = frame;
            page.bounds = bounds;
            [ scrollView addSubview: page ];
        }
        return;
    }

    /* For more than 3 views, add them all hidden, layout according to page */
    for(int i=0;i<[ _pages count];i++) {
        UIView *page = [ _pages objectAtIndex: i ];
        CGRect bounds = page.bounds;
        CGRect frame = CGRectMake(0.0, 0.0, _pageRegion.size.width,
```

```
                _pageRegion.size.height);
            page.frame = frame;
            page.bounds = bounds;
            page.hidden = YES;
            [ scrollView addSubview: page ];
        }
        [ self layoutScroller ];
}

- (void)layoutScroller {
    UIView *page;
    CGRect bounds, frame;
    int pageNum = [ self getCurrentPage ];

    if ([ _pages count ] <= 3)
        return;

    NSLog(@"Laying out scroller for page %d\n", pageNum);

    /* Left boundary */
    if (pageNum == 0) {
        for(int i=0;i<3;i++) {
            page = [ _pages objectAtIndex: i ];
            bounds = page.bounds;
            frame = CGRectMake(_pageRegion.size.width * i, 0.0,
                _pageRegion.size.width, _pageRegion.size.height);
            NSLog(@"\tOffset for Page %d = %f\n", i, frame.origin.x);
            page.frame = frame;
            page.bounds = bounds;
            page.hidden = NO;
        }
        page = [ _pages objectAtIndex: 3 ];
        page.hidden = YES;
        _zeroPage = 0;
    }

    /* Right boundary */
    else if (pageNum == [ _pages count ] -1) {
        for(int i=pageNum-2;i<=pageNum;i++) {
            page = [ _pages objectAtIndex: i ];
            bounds = page.bounds;
            frame = CGRectMake(_pageRegion.size.width * (2-(pageNum-i)), 0.0,
                _pageRegion.size.width, _pageRegion.size.height);
            NSLog(@"\tOffset for Page %d = %f\n", i, frame.origin.x);
            page.frame = frame;
            page.bounds = bounds;
            page.hidden = NO;
        }
        page = [ _pages objectAtIndex: [ _pages count ]-3 ];
        page.hidden = YES;
        _zeroPage = pageNum - 2;
    }

    /* All middle pages */
    else {
```

```objectivec
        for(int i=pageNum-1; i<=pageNum+1; i++) {
            page = [ _pages objectAtIndex: i ];
            bounds = page.bounds;
            frame = CGRectMake(_pageRegion.size.width * (i-(pageNum-1)), 0.0,
                _pageRegion.size.width, _pageRegion.size.height);
            NSLog(@"\tOffset for Page %d = %f\n", i, frame.origin.x);
            page.frame = frame;
            page.bounds = bounds;
            page.hidden = NO;
        }
        for(int i=0; i< [ _pages count ]; i++) {
            if (i < pageNum-1 || i > pageNum + 1) {
                page = [ _pages objectAtIndex: i ];
                page.hidden = YES;
            }
        }
        scrollView.contentOffset = CGPointMake(_pageRegion.size.width, 0.0);
        _zeroPage = pageNum-1;
    }
}

-(id)getDelegate {
    return _delegate;
}

- (void)setDelegate:(id)delegate {
    _delegate = delegate;
}

-(BOOL)getShowsPageControl {
    return _showsPageControl;
}

-(void)setShowsPageControl:(BOOL)showsPageControl {
    _showsPageControl = showsPageControl;
    if (_showsPageControl == NO) {
        _pageRegion = CGRectMake(self.frame.origin.x, self.frame.origin.y,
            self.frame.size.width, self.frame.size.height);
        pageControl.hidden = YES;
        scrollView.frame = _pageRegion;
    } else {
        _pageRegion = CGRectMake(self.frame.origin.x, self.frame.origin.y,
            self.frame.size.width, self.frame.size.height - 60.0);
        pageControl.hidden = NO;
        scrollView.frame = _pageRegion;
    }
}

-(NSMutableArray *)getPages {
    return _pages;
}

-(void)setCurrentPage:(int)page {
    [ scrollView setContentOffset: CGPointMake(0.0, 0.0) ];
    _zeroPage = page;
```

```
    [ self layoutScroller ];
    pageControl.currentPage = page;
}

-(int)getCurrentPage {
    return (int) (scrollView.contentOffset.x / _pageRegion.size.width) + _zeroPage;
}

- (void)scrollViewDidEndDecelerating:(UIScrollView *)scrollView {
    pageControl.currentPage = self.currentPage;
    [ self layoutScroller ];
    [ self notifyPageChange ];
}

-(void) pageControlDidChange: (id)sender
{
    UIPageControl *control = (UIPageControl *) sender;
    if (control == pageControl) {
        [ scrollView setContentOffset: CGPointMake
            (pageRegion.size.width * (control.currentPage - _zeroPage), 0.0)
          animated: YES
        ];
    }
}

- (void)scrollViewDidEndScrollingAnimation:(UIScrollView *)scrollView {
        [ self layoutScroller ];
        [ self notifyPageChange ];
}

-(void) notifyPageChange {
    if (self.delegate != nil) {
        if ([ _delegate conformsToProtocol:@protocol(PageScrollViewDelegate) ]) {
            if ([ _delegate respondsToSelector:
                @selector(pageScrollViewDidChangeCurrentPage:currentPage:) ])
            {
                [ self.delegate pageScrollViewDidChangeCurrentPage:
                    (PageScrollView *)self currentPage: self.currentPage
                ];
            }
        }
    }
}
@end
```

What's Going On?

Here's how this new and improved PageScrollView class works:

1. When the class is instantiated, a UIScrollView class is created. If three or fewer pages are attached, the scroll view behaves like the previous example: it allocates content space in the scroll view for all pages. If more than three pages are attached, the scroll view's content space is set to the width of three pages. This allows the

user to scroll left or right from a center position. All views are then added, but hidden.

2. After the user scrolls, the layoutScroller method is called. This determines which page the user has selected based on the position of the scroll view and the page number of the leftmost page (_zeroPage). The method then resets the origin of the current page and its two nearest pages so that they are oriented correctly on the scroll view. Since the user can only see the current page, he will not see adjacent pages being swapped out.

3. If the user is on the leftmost (first) or rightmost (last) page, the page will be oriented on one end of the scroll view so that the user can't scroll beyond it. If the user is on any other page, the page is oriented in the center of the scroll view, and the page's left and right neighbors are swapped in on either side. The zero page is then set to the page number of the leftmost page so the class can track which page the user is on.

4. If the user taps on the page control, the page control scrolls to the position of the previous or next page. When the scrolling animation has completed, the UIScroll View class invokes the scrollViewDidEndScrollingAnimation delegate method. This calls layoutScroller, which goes through the same layout process again.

CHAPTER 14

Media Player Framework

The Media Player framework makes it ridiculously easy to add video and audio playing capabilities to your application. The movie player controller automatically handles the orientation changes and window transitions to play many different video formats on the iPhone's screen. A single call to the movie controller to play the movie will automatically display the player and its controls. The application can choose which controls to display, adjust the playback position, and control the video's play and stop functions. The movie player supports MOV, MP4, M4V, and 3GP formats, as well as many audio formats.

To use the Media Player framework, you'll need to add it to your Xcode project. Right-click on the *Frameworks* folder in your project, and then choose Add Framework. Navigate to the *MediaPlayer.framework* folder, and then click Add.

Movie Player Controllers

The `MPMoviePlayerController` class is initialized with an `NSURL` object, which you've already learned about. You can instantiate the `NSURL` class to refer to a local file or a remote website URL. To initialize the movie player controller, use the class's `initWith ContentURL` method and provide an `NSURL` object. An example follows:

```
MPMoviePlayerController *moviePlayer = [ [ MPMoviePlayerController alloc ]
    initWithContentURL: [ NSURL URLWithString: @"http:// ..." ] ];
```

To initialize a movie player to play a local file, use the `NSURL` class's `fileURLWithPath` method:

```
NSString *path = [ NSString stringWithFormat: @"%@/Documents/movie.m4a",
    NSHomeDirectory()
];

MPMoviePlayerController *moviePlayer = [ [ MPMoviePlayerController alloc ]
    initWithContentURL: [ NSURL fileURLWithPath: path ] ];
```

Properties

Once you have created the movie player controller, you can set a few properties.

Controls

You can specify the configuration of the movie's controls by setting the `movieControl Mode` property:

```
moviePlayer.movieControlMode = MPMovieControlModeDefault;
```

You may use the following values to define this property.

Mode	Description
MPMovieControlModeDefault	Displays play/pause, volume, and timeline
MPMovieControlModeVolumeOnly	Displays only the volume control
MPMovieControlModeHidden	No controls

Aspect ratio

You may also adjust the movie's aspect ratio by setting the `scalingMode` property:

```
moviePlayer.scalingMode = MPMovieScalingModeAspectFit;
```

You may use the following aspect ratio values.

Value	Description
MPMovieScalingModeNone	No scaling applied
MPMovieScalingModeAspectFit	Fit to screen uniformly
MPMovieScalingModeAspectFill	Fill entire screen uniformly; may clip
MPMovieScalingModeFill	Fill entire screen; do not maintain aspect

Background color

The background color is used when the movie player is transitioning to and from playback, and is also used to fill the empty space when the movie does not fill the entire screen. The default background color is black, but you may change this by setting the `backgroundColor` property to a `UIColor` object:

```
moviePlayer.backgroundColor = [ UIColor whiteColor ];
```

Starting and Stopping the Movie

To play the movie, invoke the movie player's `play` method:

```
[ moviePlayer play ];
```

The movie player controller will automatically transition your current view to the movie player and begin playing the movie.

The movie will stop when the user taps the Done button or when the controller's
stop method is invoked:

```
[ moviePlayer stop ];
```

When the movie stops, the player automatically transitions back to the previous view
your application was displaying.

Notifications

Your application can configure notifications to be sent when the movie player finishes
loading content, finishes playing, or when the user changes its aspect ratio. The movie
player posts events to Cocoa's notification center, which you can configure to relay
those events to an object in your application. To receive a notification, use the
NSNotificationCenter class to add an observer to the movie player:

```
NSNotificationCenter *notificationCenter = [ NSNotificationCenter defaultCenter ];
[ notificationCenter addObserver: self
    selector:@selector(moviePlayerPreloadDidFinish:)
    name: MPMoviePlayerContentPreloadDidFinishNotification
    object: moviePlayer
];
```

Notifications are sent to your delegate class and the target method you specify. The
notification parameter lets you know which event triggered the invocation of the delegate method:

```
-(void)moviePlayerPreloadDidFinish:(NSNotification*)notification
{
    NSLog(@"All my content are belong to me!\n");
}
```

You may observe the following notifications:

MPMoviePlayerContentPreloadDidFinishNotification
    Posted when the movie player has finished preloading its content. Because content
    can be played while only partially loaded, this notification may be posted after the
    content has already begun playing.

MPMoviePlayerScalingModeDidChangeNotification
    Posted when the user changes the scaling mode of the movie. The user can tap a
    scaling icon to switch between full screen and windowed modes.

MPMoviePlayerPlaybackDidFinishNotification
    Posted when the movie has finished playing or when the user presses the Done
    button.

Further Study

Movie players are simple objects, so we'll let you try your hand at them without too
much hand-holding.

- Take any existing example from this book and add an `MPMoviePlayerController`. You won't need to add any transitions or special code, as the controller will automatically take over the screen when you begin playing.
- Check out the *MPMoviePlayerController.h* prototypes in your SDK's header files. You'll find them deep within */Developer/Platforms/iPhoneOS.platform*, inside the MediaPlayer framework's *Headers* directory.
- Check out the *NSNotification.h* prototypes in Mac OS X's header files. You'll find them in */System/Library/Frameworks/Foundation.framework/Headers*.

Index

Symbols and Numbers

+ (plus sign), identifying static methods, 20
2D objects, 135
3D objects, 135
3G/EDGE, 110
[ ] (brackets), using in Objective-C, 17
– (minus sign), declaring instance methods, 20

A

ABAddressBookAddRecord function, 208
ABAddressBookCopyArrayOfAllPeople
    function, 209
ABAddressBookCopyPeopleWithName
    function, 209
ABAddressBookCreate function, 208
ABAddressBookGetPersonCount function,
    209
ABAddressBookGetPersonWithRecordID
    function, 209
ABAddressBookHasUnsavedChanges
    function, 208
ABAddressBookRemoveRecord function, 208
ABAddressBookSave function, 208, 213
ABMultiValueCopyLabelAtIndex function,
    212
ABMultiValueCopyValueAtIndex function,
    211
ABMultiValueGetCount function, 211
ABMultiValueRemoveValueAndLabelAtIndex
    function, 213
ABPersonCopyImageData function, 214
ABPersonCreate function, 209
ABRecord object, 208
ABRecordCopyValue function, 210

ABRecordCopyValue method, 211
ABRecordRef pointer, 208, 209
ABRecordRemoveValue function, 211
ABRecordSetValue function, 211, 213
accessories, 100
accessoryType property, 100, 101
accuracy, receiving updates, 200
action property (buttons), 70
action sheets, 40, 87–94
    dismissing, 90
actionsForTarget method, 223
actionSheetStyle property, 89
Active SDK, 16
activity indicators, 219, 263–266
Address Book framework
    multivalue properties, 211–213
    records, creating/working with, 209–211
    top-level functions, 208
Address Book frameworks, 207–217
    access, 207
Address Book UI frameworks, 207–217
AddressBook.framework, 207
AddressBook.framework folder, 207
AddressBookUI.framework interface kit, 207
addSublayer method, 133
addTarget method, 71
    notifications and, 239
adjustsFontSizeToFitWidth property
    (UITextField), 232
affineTransform property, 134
.aif files, 144, 155
alert views, 40
alerts, 87–94
alloc method, 19, 20, 46
allTargets method, 223

We'd like to hear your suggestions for improving our indexes. Send email to *index@oreilly.com*.

allTouches method (UIEvent), 120
altitude property, 200
animations
    layer, 135
    transition, 80–87
.app extension, 1
Apple Developer Connection, 6
Apple developer keys, 6
Apple Lossless, 167
application badges, 41, 110
application services, 41, 112
application templates, 11, 29
applicationDidBecomeActive method, 112
applicationDidFinishLaunching method, 66
applicationFrame method, 42, 66
applicationIconBadgeNumber property, 111
applications, 1
    building/installing, 9–17
    preference bundles, 317–324
    settings, 315–324
applicationWillResignActive method, 112
applicationWillTerminate method, 111, 112
AppStore, 6
ARM architecture, 6
arrays (character), 61
aspect radio, 350
assign keyword, 22
atIndex argument, 133
audio queues, 157–167
    buffers and, 160
    callback functions, 161
    output, 159
    structure, 157
    structures, 168–170
    volume controls, 162
Audio Toolbox framework, 143–177
    queues, 157
    services, 155
audioPlayerDecodeErrorDidOccur method, 146
audioPlayerDidFinishPlaying method, 146
AudioQueueDispose function, 161, 172
AudioQueueNewInput function, 170
    callback functions, 172
AudioQueueNewOutput function, 159
AudioQueueStop function, 172
AudioServicesPlaySystemSound function, 155
autocapitalizationType property, 277
autocorrectionType property, 277

AVAudioPlayer class, 144
    metering, 147
    properties, 145
AVAudioPlayerDelegate protocol, 146
AVFoundation framework, 143–177

B

backBarButtonItem property, 70
background property (UITextField), 232
bars, 32
barStyle property, 70
    toolbar styles and, 74
BaseWidgetDelegate protocol, 23
Bluetooth, 110
borderRectForBounds override (UITextField), 232
borderStyleproperty (UITextField), 231
bounces property (UIScrollView), 303
bouncesZoom property (UIScrollView), 303
bounds method, 42
brackets ([ ]), using in Objective-C, 17
buffers (sound), 160–161
    callback functions and, 161
Build and Go, 3
build directory, 4
bundles (application), 1
buttons, 69, 236–238
    customizable, 294
    image/text, 72
buttonWithType method, 236

C

C programming language, 1, 13, 17
C++ programming language, 1, 13, 17
CAAnimation.h header file, 87
.caf files, 144, 155
CALayer class, 131, 133
CALayer.h header file, 87
callback functions
    audio queues and, 161
    recording sound, 172
CAMediaTimingFunction.h header file, 87
categories, 23–25
CATransform3D class, 136
CATransform3DMakeRotation function, 136
CATransition objects, 81, 135
cellForRowAtIndexPath method, 242
CFBundleDisplayName property, 5

CFFTP API and, 194

G

geometry, 115–130
    structures, 115–118
GET requests, 192
graphics, 61
group separators, 318
gyroscope, 300

H

HEAD requests, 192
head-up display (HUD), 132
header files, 14–15
Headers folder, 14
heightForRowAtIndexPath method, 99
hierarchies (layer), 132
home screen (Springboard), 5
horizontal (x) values, 115
HTML
    displaying, 62
    web views and, 307
HTTP requests, 62, 180, 192–195
    CFHTTP API and, 192
HUD (head-up display), 132

I

icon.png file, 3
    Xcode and, 5
icons (multi-touch), tracking, 125
id data type, 19
imageForSegmentAtIndex method, 226
imageNamed method, 98, 266
images, 219, 225, 266–275
    pickers, 273
    table cells, adding to, 99
imageWithContentsOfFile method, 266
@implementation code blocks, 19
#import preprocessor directive, 19
#include processor directive, 19
indicatorStyle property (UIScrollView), 302
Info.plist file, 3, 29
inheritance, using categories and, 24
init method, 46, 54
    images, adding to table cells and, 99
    navigation controller properties and, 68
    UIImageView objects and, 141
    view controllers, creating, 50

initWithBarButtonSystemItem method, 72
initWithContentsOfFile method, 267, 316
initWithData method, 267
initWithFrame method, 42, 46, 50, 307
    slide controls, initializing, 229
    switches, 227
initWithImage method, 272
initWithNibName method
    Interface Builder, loading from, 52
initWithRootViewController method, 67
initWithTitle method
    image/text buttons and, 72
initWithTitle property, 69
input objects, 32
insertSegmentWithImage method, 225
insertSublayer method, 133
inspector tool, 32
install build option, 17
instance methods, 20
instance variables, 22
Interface Builder, 27–37
    removing from projects, 36
    templates, 28
    UI Kit components and, 39
        loading from, 52
    User Interface
        designing, 32
        elements, 30–32
@interface code blocks, 18
@interface statements, 20
interfaces, 20
iPhone Developer Program portal, 8
iPhone SDK
    downloading/installing, 7
    installing, 5–8
iPhone simulators, testing applications on, 7
iPhoneOS.platform, 14
iPhoneSimulator.platform, 14
iPod, 12

J

Jobs, Steve, 275

K

kABPersonAddressProperty, 211
kABPersonBirthdayProperty, 210
kABPersonCreationDateProperty, 210
kABPersonDateProperty, 211

Quartz Core, programming for, 131
Library folder, 2
linking to frameworks, 15
loadRequest method, 308
loadView method, 51, 54
local variable names, 20
locationInView method, 119
longitude, receiving updates, 200

M

.m4a files, 144
macro flags (C), 19
main function, 13
    UI Kit, 39
MainWindow template, 29
    views, connecting, 34
manager (Core Location), 198–205
maximumDate property, 286
Media Player framework, 349–352
messages, sending from methods, 17
meteringEnabled property, 147
methods, 17, 18–20
minimumDate property, 286
minus sign (–), declaring instance methods, 20
minuteInterval property, 286
Mobile Phone applications, 12
model-view-controller (MVC), 10
movies, starting and stopping, 350
.mp3 files, 144
MPMovieControlModeDefault property, 350
MPMovieControlModeHidden property, 350
MPMovieControlModeVolumeOnly property, 350
MPMoviePlayerContentPreloadDidFinishNotification notification, 351
MPMoviePlayerController class, 349
MPMoviePlayerPlaybackDidFinishNotification notification, 351
MPMoviePlayerScalingModeDidChangeNotification notification, 351
MPMovieScalingModeAspectFill aspect ratio values, 350
MPMovieScalingModeAspectFit aspect ratio values, 350
MPMovieScalingModeFill aspect ratio values, 350
MPMovieScalingModeNone aspect ratio values, 350
MSMutableArray class (Cocoa), 72

multi-touch events, 115–130
    handling, 118–130
    processing, 123
multipleTouchEnabled method, 123
MVC (model-view-controller), 10
MyApp executable, 3
MyApp.app application folder, 2

N

navigation bars, 40, 66–80
    sliders, 230
    styles, 70
navigation controllers, 40, 66–80
    creating, 67
    properties, 68
navigation-based applications, 39
    templates, 12
network programming, 179–195
NeXT, 1
notifications, 239
    movie players, 351
notifier methods, 20
NSBundle class, 2
NSDate class, 285
NSDictionary class, 315
NSHomeDirectory function, 2, 62
NSInteger object, 111
NSMutableDictionary class, 315
NSNotificationCenter class, 351
NSString class, 61, 62
    titleForRow method, 279
NSTimeInterval datatype, 145
NSURL object, 62, 113
    Audio Players and, 144
    MPMoviePlayerController class and, 349
NSURLRequest object, 308
numberOfChannels property, 145
numberOfComponentsInPickerView method, 278
numberOfLoops property, 145
numberOfPage property, 239
numberOfRowsInComponent method, 278
numberOfRowsInSection method, 242
numberOfSectionsInTableView method, 242

O

objectAtIndex method, 209
Objective-C, 1, 13

categories, 23–25
messaging, 17
properties, 21
protocols, 22
transitioning to, 17–26
OpenGL ES application templates, 12
OpenGLES framework, 13
openURL method, 113
orientation changes, 52
orientations, 300
origin (windows), 42

P

page controls, 238–240
page flicking, 335–348
PageScrollView class, 335
pagingEnabled property (UIScrollView), 303
PCM files, 163
    recording sounds and, 167
phase property (UITouch class), 118
phone calls, initiating, 113
picker views, 220, 277–285
    reading, 279
pie.png file, 3
PkgInfo file, 3
placeholderproperty (UITextField), 231
placeholderRectForBounds override
        (UITextField), 233
PLATFORM variable, 14
play method, 146, 350
plus sign (+), identifying static methods, 20
PNG (portable network graphics), 3
Polar Bear Farm, 325
pop up windows, 87
portable network graphics (PNG), 3
posing, 25
position property (layers), 133
POST requests, 192
preference bundle, 240
preference bundle values, 323
preference bundles, 317–324
preferences tables, 219, 240–252
    displaying, 245
PreferenceSpecifiers section of property lists,
        317
prepareToPlay method, 146
previousLocationInView method, 119
program directory, 1
    Xcode and, 5

program termination, 112
progress indicators, 219, 263–266
properties, 209
property lists, 315–317
protocol statement, 23
protocols, 22
prototypes, 14–15
proximity sensor, 301
proximitySensingEnabled property, 301
public (external) variable names, 20
pushViewController method, 67
PUT requests, 192

Q

Quartz Core framework, 80, 131–142, 325
queries
    Address Book, 209
    Core Location
        completing, 201
        issuing, 200
        parameters, 198

R

"record needle" offsets, 145
recv( ) function (C), 186
reloadData method, 102
removeAllObjects method, 316
removeAllSegments method, 225
removeFromSuperlayer method, 134
removeObjectForKey method, 316
removeSegment method, 225
removeTarget method, 223
renderInContext method, 134
required statement, 23
Resources folder, 29
    Interface Builder, loading from, 52
retain keyword, 22
return key, 276
returnKeyType property, 276
reuse identifiers, 97
rightView property (UITextField), 232
rightViewMode property (UITextField), 232
rightViewRectForBounds override
        (UITextField), 233
root view controllers, 67
row numbers of table cells, 96
rowHeight property, 99
rowHeightForComponent method, 279

S

Safari web browser, 113
sandboxes, 2
scalingMode property, 350
scroll views, 220, 301–307
scrolling text, 235
SDK environment variable, 14
.sdk extension, 14
section lists, 219
section numbers of table cells, 96
segmented controls, 224–227
  adding, 71
selected property, 221
selectedRowInComponent method, 279
selectedSegmentIndex property, 226
selectedTextColor property, 98
selectionStyle property, 99
send( ) function (C), 186
sendActionsForControlEvents method, 223
sendEvent method, 120
sensors, 220, 298–301
servers, 179
setBackgroundImage method, 237
setDate method, 286
setDictionary method, 316
setHTML method, 307
setImage method, 225, 272
setNeedsDisplay method, 134, 268
setNeedsDisplayInRect method, 134, 268
setObject methods, 316
setShowValue method, 230
setStatusBarHidden method, 109
setStatusBarOrientation method, 110
Settings Bundle file, 317
Settings.bundle folder, 317
setTitle method, 225, 237
setTitleColor method, 237
setTitleShadowColor method, 237
setValue method, 315
setWidth method, 226
shadowOffset property, 100
sharedApplication method, 109
showFromTabBar method, 89
showFromToolBar method, 89
showInView method, 89
simulators (iPhone), testing applications on, 7
size (windows), 42
sizeToFit method, 74
skeleton directories, 4

"slide-up" pages, 88
sliders, 229–231, 320
Smalltalk programming language, 17
sockets, 179–192
  creating from existing sockets, 182
  functions, 182
  streams, 186–190
sound buffers, 160–161
  callback functions and, 161
  recording, 171
sound files, 143–177
sounds, 146
  recording, 167–177
sourceType property, 274
Springboard home screen, 5
SQLite databases, 207
startQuery method, 198, 200
startUpdatingLocation method, 200
static methods, 20
status bars, 41, 109
stop method, 146
stopUpdatingLocation method, 201, 202
streams (socket), 186–190
  read, 186
  write, 188
stringWithContentsOfURL method, 62
structures (C/C++), 18
style property (buttons), 69
switches, 227
@synthesize directive, 22
synthesizing, 28
system buttons, 72

T

Tab Bar controller, 33
tab bars, 220, 291–298
  application templates, 12
table views, 41, 94–109
  cells, 97–101
  labels, 99
tapCount property (UITouch class), 119
taps, counting/dragging, 121
target property (buttons), 69
TCP (Transmission Control Protocol) sockets, 180
templates, 11
  Interface Builder and, 28
text fields, 318
text fonts, 59

W

.wav files, 144, 155
web views, 220, 307–313
widgets, 12
widthForComponent method, 279
WiFi, 110
window object, 33
window property (UITouch class), 119
window templates, 29
window-based applications
    templates, 12, 29
    UI Kit, 39
windows, 28
    UI elements and, 32
    UI Kit and, 40–50
        creating, 42
write streams, 188
writeToFile method, 316
WWDR Intermediate Certificate, 9

X

x (horizontal) values, 115
Xcode, 1, 4–5
    building/installing applications, 10
    frameworks, adding, 15
    project layout, 12
    Quartz Core framework, add to projects,
        131
    templates and, 29
xcodebuild command, 17
.xib extension, 29, 52
XML, 315

Y

y (vertical) values, 115

About the Author

Jonathan Zdziarski is better known as the hacker "NerveGas" in the iPhone development community. His work in cracking the iPhone helped lead the effort to port the first open source applications. His initial book on the iPhone, O'Reilly's *iPhone Open Application Development*, gained an immediate cult following and taught developers how to write applications for the popular device before the SDK was ever conceived. Prior to the release of *iPhone Forensics* (O'Reilly), Jonathan wrote and supported an iPhone forensics manual distributed exclusively to law enforcement; additionally, he has assisted many forensic examiners in their investigations. Jonathan frequently consults to law enforcement agencies and teaches an iPhone forensics workshop in his spare time to train forensic examiners and corporate security personnel.

Jonathan is also a full-time research scientist specializing in machine-learning technology to combat online fraud and spam; furthermore, he is involved in the development of networking products capable of learning how to better protect customers. He is founder of the DSPAM project, a high-profile, next-generation spam filter that was acquired in 2006 by Sensory Networks, Inc. He lectures widely on the topic of spam and is a foremost researcher in the fields of machine-learning and algorithmic theory.

Jonathan's website is *http://www.zdziarski.com*.

Colophon

The image on the cover of *iPhone SDK Application Development* is a red-billed streamertail hummingbird (*Trochilus polytmus*). The hummingbird, a native of Jamaica, is affectionately nicknamed the "doctor bird" because its long tail feathers cross like the coattails that once were a part of doctors' uniforms.

The country of Jamaica houses more than 200 species of birds, but the popular red-billed streamertail, common throughout Jamaica and featured on the country's currency, is the national bird. Bird watchers from around the world often travel to Jamaica to view the red-billed streamertail and its cousin, the black-billed streamertail. Bird enthusiasts will find that the best time to spot streamertails is during the seasons of winter and spring, as that is when hummingbirds from Mississippi and the Atlantic flyway migrate to Jamaica.

Female hummingbirds build nests out of moss and plants and will bind their nests with threads from spiders' webs. After an incubation period of two to three weeks, the female hummingbird will give birth to featherless babies, whom she will feed regurgitated insects until they can fly some distance on their own.

The small size of the red-billed streamertail and other hummingbirds renders them vulnerable to predators. In spite of this vulnerability, the agile hummingbird often taunts predators such as hawks in an effort to seize more territory when migrating. However, this bold behavior can backfire against other predators. Larger species of the praying mantis will entice the hummingbird by remaining motionless until the bird ventures close. Once the bird does so, the praying mantis will suddenly pierce the hummingbird's chest with one of its spiny forelegs and then consume the bird's flesh.

The cover image is from *Dover's Animals*. The cover font is Adobe ITC Garamond. The text font is Linotype Birka; the heading font is Adobe Myriad Condensed; and the code font is LucasFont's TheSansMonoCondensed.

Related Titles from O'Reilly

Macintosh

AppleScript: The Definitive
Guide, *2nd Edition*

AppleScript: The Missing Manual

Appleworks 6: The Missing
Manual

The Best of the Joy of Tech

FileMaker Pro 8: The Missing
Manual

FileMaker Pro 9: The Missing
Manual

GarageBand 2:
The Missing Manual

iBook Fan Book

iLife '05: The Missing Manual

iMovie 6 & iDVD:
The Missing Manual

iPhoto 6: The Missing Manual

iPhoto '08: The Missing Manual

iPod: The Missing Manual,
6th Edition

iWork '05: The Missing Manual

Mac Annoyances

Mac OS X Tiger Pocket Guide

Mac OS X Leopard Pocket Guide

Mac OS X: The Missing Manual,
Tiger Edition

Mac OS X: The Missing Manual,
Leopard Edition

Mac OS X Power Hound,
2nd Edition

Mac OS X Unwired

Modding Mac OS X

Office 2004 for the Macintosh:
The Missing Manual

Office 2008 for the Macintosh:
The Missing Manual

Revolution in The Valley

Switching to the Mac:
The Missing Manual,
Leopard Edition

Mac Developers

Building Cocoa Applications:
A Step-By-Step Guide

Cocoa in a Nutshell

Essential Mac OS X Panther
Server Administration

Learning Carbon

Learning Cocoa with
Objective-C, *2nd Edition*

Learning Unix for
Mac OS X Tiger

Mac OS X for Java Geeks

Mac OS X Panther Hacks

Mac OS X Tiger in a Nutshell

Mac OS X Tiger for Unix Geeks,
4th Edition

Objective-C Pocket Reference

Running Mac OS X Tiger

The O'Reilly Advantage

Stay Current and Save Money

Did you know that if you register your O'Reilly books, you'll get automatic notification and upgrade discounts on new editions?

And that's not all! Once you've registered your books you can:

» Win free books, T-shirts and O'Reilly Gear

» Get special offers available only to registered O'Reilly customers

» Get free catalogs announcing all our new titles (US and UK Only)

Registering is easy! Just go to www.oreilly.com/go/register

O'REILLY®

Try the online edition
free for 45 days

Building Applications for the AppStore

iPhone SDK
Application Development

O'REILLY®   Jonathan Zdziarski

Get the information you need when you need it, with Safari Books Online. Safari Books Online contains the complete version of the print book in your hands plus thousands of titles from the best technical publishers, with sample code ready to cut and paste into your applications.

Safari is designed for people in a hurry to get the answers they need so they can get the job done. You can find what you need in the morning, and put it to work in the afternoon. As simple as cut, paste, and program.

To try out Safari and the online edition of the above title FREE for 45 days, go to www.oreilly.com/go/safarienabled and enter the coupon code ENKBAAA.

To see the complete Safari Library visit:
safari.oreilly.com